THE CAMBRIDGE TRANSLATIONS OF MEDIEVAL PHILOSOPHICAL TEXTS

The third volume of *The Cambridge Translations of Medieval Philosophical Texts* will allow scholars and students access, for the first time in English, to major texts that form the debate over mind and knowledge at the center of medieval philosophy.

Beginning with thirteenth-century attempts to classify the soul's powers and to explain the mind's place within the soul, the volume proceeds systematically to consider the scope of human knowledge and the role of divine illumination, intentionality and mental representation, and attempts to identify the object of human knowledge in terms of concepts and propositions. The authors included are Henry of Ghent, Peter John Olivi, William Alnwick, Peter Aureol, William Ockham, William Crathorn, Robert Holcot, Adam Wodeham, as well as two anonymous Parisian masters of arts.

This volume will be an important resource for scholars and students of medieval philosophy, history, theology, and literature.

Robert Pasnau is Assistant Professor of Philosophy at the University of Colorado at Boulder. He is the author of *Theories of Cognition in the Later Middle Ages* (1997) and *Thomas Aquinas on Human Nature* (2002), both published by Cambridge University Press.

D0707445

THE CAMBRIDGE TRANSLATIONS OF
MEDIEVAL PHILOSOPHICAL TEXTS

GENERAL EDITOR: ELEONORE STUMP, ST. LOUIS UNIVERSITY

FOUNDING EDITOR: NORMAN KRETZMANN

Also in the series:

Volume 1: *Logic and the Philosophy of Language*
EDITED BY NORMAN KRETZMANN AND ELEONORE STUMP

Volume 2: *Ethics and Political Philosophy*
EDITED BY A. S. MCGRADE, JOHN KILCULLEN,
AND MATTHEW KEMPSHALL

Forthcoming volumes:

Volume 4: *Metaphysics*
EDITED BY SCOTT MACDONALD

Volume 5: *Philosophical Theology*
EDITED BY THOMAS WILLIAMS

The Cambridge Translations of Medieval Philosophical Texts

VOLUME THREE
MIND AND KNOWLEDGE

EDITOR

ROBERT PASNAU
UNIVERSITY OF COLORADO AT BOULDER

PUBLISHED BY THE PRESS SYNDICATE OF THE UNIVERSITY OF CAMBRIDGE
The Pitt Building, Trumpington Street, Cambridge, United Kingdom

CAMBRIDGE UNIVERSITY PRESS
The Edinburgh Building, Cambridge CB2 2RU, UK
40 West 20th Street, New York, NY 10011-4211, USA
477 Williamstown Road, Port Melbourne, VIC 3207, Australia
Ruiz de Alarcón 13, 28014 Madrid, Spain
Dock House, The Waterfront, Cape Town 8001, South Africa

http://www.cambridge.org

First published 2002

Printed in the United States of America

Typeface Bembo 11/13 pt.   *System* DeskTopPro$_{/UX}$ [BV]

A catalog record for this book is available from the British Library.

Library of Congress Cataloging in Publication Data
Mind and knowledge / edited by Robert Pasnau.
p. cm. – (The Cambridge translations of medieval philosophical texts ; v. 3)
Includes bibliographical references and index.
ISBN 0-521-79356-4 – ISBN 0-521-79795-0 (pbk.)
1. Knowledge, Theory of.   2. Philosophy, Medieval.   I. Pasnau, Robert.   II. Series.
B738.K56 M56 2002
121–dc21   2001037821

ISBN 0 521 79356 4 hardback
ISBN 0 521 79795 0 paperback

CONTENTS

ACKNOWLEDGMENTS

I would like to thank

- Rega Wood, for letting me use her Wodeham translation as the basis for my own;
- Susan Brower–Toland, for extremely helpful suggestions regarding my Wodeham translation;
- Charles Bolyard, for agreeing to collaborate with me on the translation of Aureol;
- Eleonore Stump, for carefully reading over the final typescript;
- Russell Friedman, for confirming my suspicions regarding the Aureol text, and for providing a copy of the Vatican manuscript;
- Raymond Macken, for supplying me with a copy of the definitive Henry of Ghent manuscript, which proved mostly unneeded thanks to
- Gordon Wilson, who shared with me his preliminary work on Ghent's text;
- Scott MacDonald, Timothy Noone, and John Wippel, for advice on various matters.

This is the third of three book-length translations I've taken on over the last seven years, and the last I plan to take on for the foreseeable future. It is possible to be a translator and a philosopher at the same time, but not to be a translator, a philosopher, and a father. I choose b and c.

GENERAL INTRODUCTION

When the first volume of this series appeared thirteen years ago, the editors ruefully remarked on the scarcity of reliable editions and translations of medieval philosophical texts. Since then the situation has improved incrementally, but remains far from satisfactory. Without reliable texts, it is hard even for specialists to learn what medieval authors actually thought. Without translations, it is yet harder for nonspecialists to see why medieval scholarship is an enterprise worth supporting.

This volume attempts to convey some sense of later medieval work on the nature of mind and knowledge. In keeping with the principles of the series, the volume contains complete treatises or questions, except in two cases where the length was prohibitive. The selections are drawn entirely from Latin (hence Christian) works, and consequently the volume captures only at secondhand the fascinating intercontinental and interdenominational dimensions of medieval philosophy. But even given this constraint, the authors included here display an extremely wide range of styles and viewpoints. Moreover, the selections represent the full range of literary genres, from Aristotelian commentaries to Biblical commentaries, and from sermons to academic disputations. The selections focus on authors not widely available in translation. Indeed, for most of the authors included here, this marks the first time that *any* of their works have been published in English.

Not every medieval theologian and philosopher deserves to be translated. The twelve selections were chosen both for their significance within the medieval context, and for their relevance to contemporary philosophy. Often, the connections to modern discussions will be immediate and striking. But it would of course be foolish to force the medieval debate onto any kind of contemporary Procrustean bed: Very often these selections are interesting because of their differences from the terms of today's debate. Instead of the relationship between mind and body, for instance, the medievals focused on the relationship between soul and body. They debated whether the mind (or intellect) is a part of the soul, and if so whether sensory input to the mind is sufficient for knowledge without any kind of further illumination. And rather than attempting to analyze what distinguishes knowledge from true belief, the medievals were more interested in the mechanisms of cognition, and in the way the senses and intellect represent the external world.

The difficulty of these texts varies widely. Some are suitable for absolute beginners; others are as difficult as anything the scholastics ever wrote, which is to say they are very hard indeed. A rough ordering from easiest to hardest might go as follows: 3, 1, 6, 2, 11, 4, 5, 10, 9, 8, 7, 12.

The selections are arranged in rough chronological order, with a few adjustments for the sake of topical continuity. The first two selections are studies of the soul composed by unknown members of the Faculty of Arts at the University of Paris. The first, composed around 1225, is an attempt to synthesize earlier work on the soul and its powers. On its own terms, this is a rather mundane and unoriginal work, but it is nevertheless extremely interesting as a benchmark from which to assess the originality of later scholastic developments. The second of these treatises, a question-commentary on the *De anima*, is based on lectures from around 1270. Whereas Translation 1 signals the beginning of Averroes's influence on medieval philosophy, this second anonymous author is a devoted follower of Averroistic psychology, willing to follow the Commentator on even the most radical claims, regardless of their compatibility with Christianity.

The remaining ten selections are authored entirely by theologians, and this often makes for a difference, at least in the broader context of the views being presented. This is especially so in Translation 3, which shows Bonaventure delivering a sermon at the University of Paris, and arguing on Biblical and theological grounds for an Augustinian theory of divine illumination. Bonaventure is struggling against the rising Aristotelian tide that would completely dominate the universities well before the end of the thirteenth century. Translations 4 and 5, in turn, show divine illumination taking its last stand, in the work of Henry of Ghent, who attempts to find a place for the theory within a broadly Aristotelian theory of cognition. These two selections are notable not just for their defense of divine illumination, but for their serious and extended discussion of skepticism, an issue that would become more important in the fourteenth century.

The next four selections present theologians from the Franciscan order debating the nature of mental representation. Translation 6 shows the iconoclastic Peter John Olivi introducing a long philosophical excursion into the beginning of his commentary on the Gospel of John. Olivi was a critic of conventional Aristotelian accounts that postulated intervening representations in the processes of sensation and thought – so-called sensible and intelligible species. Olivi proposed in general that these species simply be eliminated, and here he extends this claim to the level of mental concepts, arguing that the so-called mental word is nothing over and above the act of thinking conceptually.

Another aspect of the medieval debate over cognition concerned the sense in which external things could be said to exist within the mind. It was common among later scholastics to speak of external objects having intentional existence or intelligible being within the mind. In Translation 7, William Alnwick exposes this view to a searching analysis, and concludes that such being within intellect is nothing other than the intelligible species or (if species do not exist) the act of thought.

Despite Alnwick's deflationary claims, others thought this sort of mental existence could do important work in explaining knowledge and cognition. Most influential in this regard was Peter Aureol, who placed such *apparent being* (as he called it) at the center of his philosophical psychology, even analyzing consciousness in its terms. In Translation 8, Aureol implicitly relies on this theory to explain the much discussed distinction between intuitive and abstractive cognition, arguing that intuitive cognition concerns an object that has a certain sort of presence – direct and actual – within the mind or senses. An important part of Aureol's argument concerns perceptual illusions, which Aureol argued should count as intuitive despite being nonveridical. In Translation 9, William Ockham attacks Aureol's arguments, after quoting from Aureol's own writings at length. Like Olivi before him, Ockham denies that cognition requires any kind of internal object, whether that object has real or merely apparent, intentional being. Meeting Aureol's challenge head on, Ockham takes up the hardest sorts of cases for his view, cases of sensory illusion, and argues for a direct realist theory of perception.

William Crathorn defends a more traditional theory of cognition in Translation 10, complete with sensible and intelligible species that are literally likenesses of external things. Crathorn's indirect realism leads him to a series of skeptical arguments showing that the senses alone are inadequate for certain knowledge unless supplemented by premises showing that God would not allow human beings to be systematically deceived about the external world. This discussion is one of the most vivid examples of the increasing later medieval interest in the problem of skepticism.

The final two selections concern a question debated extensively in the fourteenth century, regarding the objects of intellectual knowledge. The two standard views were that we have knowledge of things, and that we have knowledge of propositions, where propositions were taken to be particular linguistic tokens, either mental, spoken, or written. In Translation 11, Robert Holcot defends a version of the second view, and argues that the former is unworkable. Writing at roughly the same time, Adam Wodeham proposes a novel third approach in Translation 12. Wodeham agrees with Holcot that knowledge concerns propositions rather than things, but he denies that propositions should be understood as particular linguistic tokens. Instead, Wodeham attempts to articulate the idea of a proposition-type, an abstract state of affairs signified by phrases such as *man's being an animal*. It is entities of this sort, Wodeham argues, that are true and false, believed and known.

All together, these translations display the tremendous growth of philosophy during the thirteenth and fourteenth centuries. In 1225, it was considered progress for the anonymous author of Translation 1 to piece together from the work of others a flimsy outline of the soul and its powers. Only 100 years later, Latin philosophy had matured to an astonishing degree: Regardless of what the art historians may tell us, *this* was the true renaissance of Western thought. Whereas our anonymous arts master from circa 1225 is largely content to synthesize the work of Averroes and others, carefully attempting to reconcile all sides, our arts master from circa 1270 pushes hard on central philosophical questions, often proposing novel and controversial solutions. By the 1330s, theologians were expected to know not only the full Aristotelian corpus and the commentary tradition, but also the Church Fathers and the work of modern theologians like Aquinas, Scotus, Henry of Ghent, and Ockham. Attitudes toward authority changed dramatically over this time. In Translation 1, the work of many different authors is embraced gratefully, without any embarrassment or scruples about just how trustworthy these sources might be. By the 1330s, even the most venerable philosophical authorities were open to question. William Crathorn quotes Averroes at length, but then adds that "I invoke the Commentator not because his words move me very much, but because some take his words as the truth" (p. 257). Aristotle doesn't fare much better. Though again Crathorn invokes his authority repeatedly, he does so with a critical eye, remarking once that "because the Philosopher in this passage assumes many things that are neither known per se, nor demonstrated, nor appear true, there is no need to adhere to what he says there" (p. 272).

Translation is sometimes tedious, but that is as nothing compared to its worst feature, the inevitable frustration of encountering words and phrases for which there is simply no satisfactory translation. A few remarks on this score may prove helpful, or at least therapeutic.

The first and most obvious such problem is *anima*. There is no real frustration here, because there is no choice. The Latin *anima*, from the Greek ψυχή (*psuche*), must be translated into English as soul. The problem is that *anima* has very different connotations from the English term. For us, the soul is a spiritual, ghostlike entity; even philosophers find it hard to escape this sense of the term. But for these Latin authors, *anima* suggests something much more concrete, even scientific: It suggests the principle that animates all living things. Hence there was no real question among medieval authors over the existence of the soul, but there were serious questions over whether the soul could in fact be spiritual and immortal.

Another term for which there is no real choice is *scientia*. In most contexts, it would be profoundly misleading to translate this as anything other than *knowledge*. This is problematic, however, because medieval authors often give *scientia* a technical sense that barely overlaps with our modern notion of knowledge. Taking Aristotle's *Posterior Analytics* as their guide, they thought of knowledge in the strict sense as the product of a demonstrative syllogism ultimately grounded in propositions that are self-evident (*nota per se*). But very often the term *scientia* is not used in this strict sense. Henry of Ghent begins both of the replies translated here (Translation 4, p. 97; Translation 5, p. 114) by setting out a broad sense of *scientia* that clearly does correspond to our term 'knowledge.' Other authors implicitly use the term in this broad sense. So there is no basis for departing from the conventional translation of *scientia* as *knowledge*, although in some contexts (especially Translation 7) it is useful to resort to the more specific phrase 'demonstrative knowledge,' even when the underlying Latin is simply *scientia*.

Cognitio is a term that proves frustrating only to translators that are overly concerned to avoid technical vocabulary. I myself have grown so accustomed to 'cognition' in English that it seems entirely unobjectionable, but I sense that others find it imposing and perhaps even obscure. Still, it is unquestionably the correct term for translating the ubiquitous *cognitio.* This is the most general Latin term for all kinds of sensory and intellectual states; it extends to any sort of belief or sensation about the world, true or false.

A word that is more seriously frustrating is the verb *intelligere.* Again, it is fairly clear what this word means: It refers to the activity of intellectual cognition. In other words, *intelligere* picks out whatever it is that the intellect does. Unfortunately, English has no such verb, and so a translator is left with two choices: either render the word awkwardly but literally, using some version of the phrase 'cognize intellectively' or render it gracefully but perhaps misleadingly, as *understand* or *think.* In most of these translations, I've decided that the literal but awkward option is unnecessary, and so I generally resort to the term 'understand.'

What about 'think'? The trouble here is that Latin has another term, *cogitare,* for which *think* is just the right translation. (Think of *Cogito ergo sum.*) Just as with the English 'think,' the Latin *cogitare* refers to the preliminary processes of considering and deliberating over a proposition. Although *intelligere* in a broad sense covers this kind of thinking, the term extends further to the grasping of a proposition, or the understanding of an object. Sometimes, when used narrowly, the term entails such success, in which case *understand* is just the right translation. Very often the term is used more broadly, however, in which case *understand* is misleading or even baffling as a translation. Hence it is sometimes important to choose something more literal but awkward.

Another frustrating term is *notitia.* As usual, it is clear enough what this term means: It is a very general term for all kinds of cognitive apprehension, with more of an implication of success than *cognitio* carries, and perhaps more of an implication of the intellectual. There are lots of English words that capture the meaning of *notitia* fairly well, including 'apprehension,' 'cognition,' 'perception,' 'comprehension,' and 'grasp.' But each of these except for the last needs to be used for its Latin cognate, and the last proves awkward in many instances.

Sometimes, *notitia* seems to match 'knowledge' in our broad modern sense. In fact, Henry of Ghent relies on *notitia* to define such a broad sense, proposing that "*scire* be taken broadly, for every certain *notitia* by which a thing is cognized as it is, without any mistake or deception" (Translation 4, p. 97). But this passage illustrates why the term can't generally be translated as *knowledge.* First, it obviously won't do to use the same English root to translate *scire* and *notitia* in this particular sentence. The definition would look hopelessly circular. Moreover, this is one of those clear cases, noted earlier, where *scire* simply must be rendered into English as *knowledge*. Further, Ghent makes it clear here that *notitia*, all by itself, does not mean *knowledge in the broad sense*. He stresses that knowledge in this sense extends only to those cases of *notitia* that are certain and mistake-free. Evidently, then, *notitia* picks out a broader class of cognition even than 'knowledge' in the broad sense.

Still, in Translation 10, where *scire* hardly occurs, I've concluded that it makes good sense to render *notitia* as *knowledge*. But in the other texts where *notitia* regularly occurs (Translations 4, 5, 8, 12), I've been able to find no better translation than *cognition*, even though *cognitio* also appears regularly in these texts and is translated by the same word. To me, this is immensely aggravating, but I hope it is fairly harmless to the reader. The terms, as used by these authors, do appear to be almost exactly synonymous.

All of the translations are based on modern editions, or at least modern transcriptions from the best available manuscript:

1 "Le traité de anima et de potenciis eius d'un maître ès arts (vers 1225)," ed. R. A. Gauthier, *Revue des Sciences Philosophiques et Théologiques* 66 (1982) pp. 27–55.

2 "Un Commentaire Averroïste sur les Livres I et II du Traité De l'Ame," ed. M. Giele, in *Trois Commentaires Anonymes sur le Traité de l'Ame d'Aristote* (Louvain: Publications Universitaires, 1971), pp. 21–95.

3 Bonaventure, *La Metodologia del Sapere nel Sermone di S. Bonaventura Unus est Magister Vester Christus*, ed. R. Russo (Grottaferrata: Collegium S. Bonaventurae, 1982), pp. 100–14.

4 Henry of Ghent, *Summa quaestionum ordinariarum*, ms. Paris Bibl. Nat. 15355, ff. 2r–3v, as transcribed by G. Wilson for his forthcoming critical edition.

5 Henry of Ghent, *Summa quaestionum ordinariarum*, ms. Paris Bibl. Nat. 15355, ff. 3v–7r, as transcribed by G. Wilson for his forthcoming critical edition.

6 Peter John Olivi, "Petri Iohannis Olivi Tractatus de Verbo," ed. R. Pasnau, *Franciscan Studies* 53 (1993) pp. 134–48.

7 William Alnwick, *Quaestiones disputatae de esse intelligibili* (*Bibliotheca Franciscana Scholastica* 10), ed. A. Ledoux (Quaracchi: Collegium S. Bonaventurae, 1937), Q1, pp. 1–29.

8 Peter Aureol, *Scriptum super primum Sententiarum*, ed. E. M. Buytaert (St. Bonaventure, NY: Franciscan Institute, 1952), Vol. I, pp. 177–217.

9 William Ockham, *Opera Theologica* vol.4, ed. G. Etzkorn and F. Kelley (St. Bonaventure, NY: Franciscan Institute, 1979), pp. 228–64.

10 William Crathorn, *Quästionen zum ersten Sentenzenbuch*, ed. F. Hoffmann, *Beiträge zur Geschichte der Philosophie und Theologie des Mittelalters*, NF29 (Münster: Aschendorff, 1988), pp. 67–151.

11 Robert Holcot, "A Revised Text of Robert Holcot's Quodlibetal Dispute on Whether

God is Able to Know More than He Knows," ed. W. Courtenay, *Archiv für Geschichte der Philosophie* 53 (1971) pp. 3–21.

12 Adam Wodeham, *Lectura secunda in librum primum Sententiarum*, ed. R. Wood (St. Bonaventure, NY: Franciscan Institute Press, 1990) vol. I, pp. 180–208.

The pagination of the Latin text is supplied within brackets – e.g., {53}.

Translations 2 and 12 are based on faulty manuscripts that demand frequent emendation, and I have made some suggestions beyond those of the original editors. Translations 3, 7, 8, 10, and 11 are based on extremely unreliable editions. In these cases I was forced virtually to reconstruct the text by working through and reassessing all the textual apparatus. Rather than bury this work within my translations, I have gathered it as endnotes, so that scholars working with the original texts can more easily consult my suggestions. Places where I have emended the text are marked within the translation by a degree sign: °.

ANONYMOUS (ARTS MASTER c. 1225)
THE SOUL AND ITS POWERS

Introduction

This short treatise was written around 1225, apparently by a professor of philosophy ("master of arts") at the University of Paris. It is not an original work, in that almost all the author's claims are taken from other sources. But the way these claims are compiled and assimilated is itself interesting, and would be highly influential on later authors. Moreover, this work vividly captures the state of the art of scholastic philosophy in the early thirteenth century, and puts in context the achievements of later and better known figures.

Our author's principal source is Aristotle, as interpreted by Avicenna and Averroes. Although Avicenna is mentioned more often, this work is notable for marking the beginning of Averroes's influence on the Latin West. Averroes's extended commentary on the *De anima*, composed around 1190, was translated into Latin by Michael Scot around 1220. In just a few years, then, the Commentator's reputation was becoming established at the University of Paris.

Most significant in this regard is the discussion of the rational power (sec. III.C). Though our author scrambles some of the terminology, he closely follows Averroes's account of a "passive intellect," inseparable from the body, and of a distinct "possible intellect" (equivalent to Averroes's "material intellect"). The treatise explicitly rejects Avicenna's treatment of agent intellect as separate from the soul, and seems to lean on Averroes in arguing that the agent intellect is "joined to the soul as its power." This makes an ironic debut for Averroes in light of how he would later be understood (see Translation 2).

The fact that its authorship is unknown should not be taken to imply that this work was obscure. It has survived in three manuscripts, more than can be said for most of the works translated in this volume. There are, moreover, definite allusions to the work in a great many later authors, including Albert the Great and Thomas Aquinas. Though not an "authority," and hence not worthy of explicit quotation, it is clear that this work was widely read during the middle years of the thirteenth century. It formed an important part of the now-hidden intellectual foundations on which medieval theologians built.

This selection breaks with the volume's general practice of supplying minimal notes on sources. René-Antoine Gauthier's edition of the text supplies detailed information on our author's sources, and it seemed important to supply some of this material, in translation, given that they are a large part of what makes the text interesting. By consulting these notes, readers will be able to see for themselves something of how the work was compiled.

For a discussion of this work's influence on the later thirteenth century, see the introduction to Gauthier's edition. For an overview of early thirteenth-century accounts of intellect, see CHLMP VIII.29, "The Potential and the Agent Intellect."

The Soul and Its Powers

[I. The Soul]

The soul is the first actuality of a physical body potentially having life.[1] When it is called an *actuality*, the soul's genus is stated. For it is a substance, and there are three kinds of substances: hypostasis, ousiosis, and ousia – or, in other words: matter, actuality (that is, substantial form), and the particular (*hoc aliquid*) (that is, the composite of {28} both).[2] So when it is said that the soul is *actuality*, it is differentiated from matter and the composite.

But there are two kinds of actuality, just as there are two kinds of form, substantial and accidental. Substantial form is defined in this way: "The substantial is what brings existence to the composition, from a certain composition." Accidental form is defined in this way: "Form is contingent to the composition, depending on the simple and invariable essence."[3] So

---

[1] Aristotle, *De anima* II 1, 412a27–28.
[2] Boethius, *Contra Eutychen* ch. 3 (p. 88): "So *ousia* is the same as essence, *ousiosis* the same as subsistence, *hypostasis* the same as substance." Though this is our author's remote source, he assigns quite different meanings to these Greek terms.
[3] *Liber sex principiorum* I 6, I 1.

since the substantial form brings existence to the composition (that is, to the composite), whereas an accidental form is contingent to the composition, the substantial form is accordingly called the first actuality, whereas the accidental form is called the second actuality. And so since the soul is called an actuality, it is differentiated from an accidental form by its being called *first*.

And because every actuality is the actuality of something, *of a body* accordingly follows. For the soul can be considered in three ways: as nature, as reason (*ratio*), and as actuality. It can be considered as nature insofar as it is the source of all the motions of an ensouled body *qua* ensouled. It can be considered as reason insofar as the body exists for the sake of the soul. For the soul does not exist for the sake of the body, but the body for the sake of the soul, inasmuch as the body's function (*ministerio*) is perfected by knowledge and morality.[4] It can be considered as actuality insofar as it is the perfection of an ensouled body *qua* ensouled.

And because some bodies are artificial, as an effigy is, the soul is accordingly called the actuality of a *physical* body (that is, a natural body), so as to distinguish it from an artificial body.

And because some natural bodies lack the disposition for life, as do the elements and some compounds of elements (this is a sign that they lack a soul, since life is the effect of the soul on the body)[5] *potentially having life* is added to exclude all these. This phrase should be understood of the potentiality that precedes the actuality of life, not the potentiality that precedes the disposition for life, as in blood and sperm. For these have life potentially, in a way that is neither actual nor dispositional, and so their perfection is not the soul but another form. But those bodies whose perfection is the soul have life potentially in a dispositional sense—that is, they always have life dispositionally, whether or not they have it actually. For some animals, such as giant frogs, [can] have a kind of life without the operations of life, such as nutrition, growth, and reproduction.[6]

And because the phrase *potentially having life* {29} has a primary and a derivative sense, in both fact and speech, in its application to plants and animals, Aristotle accordingly converts it into the phrase *organic*, which so applies in fact, but not in speech. (For although it is analogical in fact, it is

---

[4] Johannes Blund, *Tractatus de anima* §304 (p. 82): "The soul has its being in the body in such a way that therein it acquires its perfection by taking on virtue and knowledge."
[5] Alfred of Sareshel, *De motu cordis* (p. 5): "Life is the first effect of the soul on the body."
[6] Averroes, *In de anima* II 5 (p. 136).

univocal in speech.) Therefore this is the correct definition of the soul: *The soul is the first actuality of a physical, organic body*. And this accords with the exposition of Averroes.[7]

The translator Toletanus, however, understands each to be included in the soul's definition, in this way: *The soul is the first actuality of a physical, organic body potentially having life*.[8] *Organic* rules out nonorganic natural bodies, such as elements and compounds of elements, so that blood and sperm are ruled out by this differentia. And because the bodies of dead animals seem to be organic, *potentially having life* is added, to rule them out. This phrase is understood in the way said above.

But we prefer Averroes's account. For a dead body is not organic, since its parts are not organs: The eyes of the dead are not eyes. Hence Aristotle: "The eye is the matter of sight; if that is lacking, it is not an eye, except equivocally, as a stone eye, or a painted one."[9] {30}

[II. The Soul's Powers in General]

[A. The Definition of a Power]

Next, the soul's powers. A power is a principle of producing change in another, in the case of an active power, or of receiving from another, in the case of a passive power.[10] The natural powers of bodies require another that is substantially distinct, but here it is enough for there to be another that is conceptually distinct. For the intellect is acted on by what is

---

[7] Aristotle, *De anima* II 1, 412a28–b6; Averroes, *In de anima* II 6 (p. 137): "A body potentially having life is the first organic body."

On the primary and derivative application (*se habet secundum prius et posterius*) of 'organic' to plants and animals, see *De anima* II 1, 412b3: "The roots are like (Gr. *analogon*; L. *simile*) a mouth, since both take in food."

[8] Dominicus Gundissalinus, *De anima* ch. 2 (p. 40): "Aristotle defined the soul in this way, saying the soul is the first perfection of a natural, instrumental body potentially living."

[9] *De anima* II 1, 412b20–22.

[10] Aristotle, *Metaphysics* V 12, 1019a15–22: "A power is called a principle of motion or change in another *qua* other. . . . In virtue of a thing's being affected by something, we say that it has the power to be affected."

Ibid., IX 1, 1046a9–13: ". . . a principle of producing change in another *qua* other. For one is a power for being acted on, which in the thing acted on is a principle of passive change from another *qua* other."

Averroes, *In Metaphys.* IX.2 (107ra): "In one being it is a power for receiving something, and in another being the power for doing something."

intelligible, and the intellect itself is sometimes intelligible,[11] and in that case the intellect differs from what is intelligible only conceptually, because intellect is conceived of as passive (that is, receptive), the intelligible as active or moving. And it is called a *power* (*potentia*), as if it were *post-essence*, because it naturally follows the thing. For *being* is prior to *being able* – that is, being able to act or be acted on.[12]

[B. Distinctions among Powers]

According to Aristotle, there are five powers of the soul. For he says that "we say the powers are the vegetative, sensory, appetitive, locomotive, and intellective."[13] According to Avicenna there are three: the vegetative, sensory, and rational, because he includes under sensory the middle three of the above five.[14] {31}

But then a question arises: In virtue of what are the soul's powers distinguished? For they do not seem to be distinct in the soul's essence, since it is one and simple, nor through parts of the body, since not every power has a determinate part in the body (for example, intellect).[15] Moreover, it is not universally true for the soul's other powers that distinct powers exist in distinct parts of the body. Rather, some distinct powers do exist in distinct parts, such as sight in the eye, taste in the tongue, whereas distinct powers are also found in the same part, such as taste and touch in the tongue. Also, one power is found in different parts: For if a plant is divided, each part lives, and likewise there are some animals such that, if they are divided, each of their parts lives. Of these, there are of course parts that live only for a time, because no part thrives if it lacks the main organs such as the heart, the liver, or the like, whereas other parts can

---

[11] Aristotle, *De anima* III 4, 429a13–14: "If, then, intellectively cognizing is like sensing, it will, at least, be either something's being affected by what is intelligible or it will be something else of that sort."

    Ibid., III 4, 429b26: "If it, too, is itself intelligible."

[12] *Summa fratris Alexandri* (vol.2, p. 204b, n. 155, contra 1): "Power follows essence."

[13] *De anima* II 3, 414a31–32.

[14] *Liber de anima* I 5 (79–80): "We will say then that the animal powers (*vires*) are initially divided into three parts. One is the vegetative soul. . . . The second is the sensory soul. . . . The third is the human soul."

[15] Aristotle, *De anima* II 1, 413a7–8: "For the actuality of some [parts of soul] is that of the [body's] parts themselves. But yet with respect to some nothing prevents [such separation], because they are not the actuality of any body."

thrive. This is clear in the case of snakes.[16] Parts of animals whose parts are alike can each thrive in life, but the parts of the heart cannot, even though they are alike, because they do not have a shape like that of the whole.

We say in reply, therefore, that distinct powers are found in the same organ, as is clear in the main organs, and then one is material for the other, as the vegetative is for the sensory. For, according to Aristotle, "just as a triangle is in a square, so the vegetative is in the sensory."[17] For this reason, then, we say to the question of how the soul's powers are distinguished that some – those that exist in the same part of the body – are distinguished by natural order (that is, by being primary and secondary).[18] Others – those that exist in distinct parts – are distinguished by the natures of their distinct parts. So it should be recognized that the soul is one in subject and diverse through its powers: not like one apple that has within itself distinct actual qualities (like color, smell, flavor), nor like one genus that has within itself distinct potential differentiae, but in such a way that one power is the material for another, as was said above, and others are not. For life is the material for touch, and touch for the other senses. This is how the soul's powers are distinguished in real terms (*secundum rem*).

In terms of coming to cognize them, in contrast, powers are distinguished through acts, and acts through objects. Thus Aristotle: Acts precede powers in {32} account (*rationem*), and objects precede acts.[19] But I speak of an object as either that from which or that toward which the power is moved, just as color moves sight and what is willed is material for the will. For the object of a passive power is related to motion differently from how the object of an active power is: For the motion of a passive power begins from its object, and the motion of an active power terminates at its object, since the motion of a passive power is toward the soul, and the motion of an active power is from the soul.[20]

---

[16] Aristotle, *De anima* I 5, 411b19–25: "Plants seem to remain alive when divided, as do certain animals when cut up, inasmuch as they have specifically the same soul [in their different parts], even if not numerically the same. Indeed, each of the parts has sense and is locally moved for some time. And if they do not endure, this is in no way unacceptable: for they do not have the mechanisms with which to preserve their nature."

[17] *De anima* II 3, 414b31–32.

[18] Averroes, *In de anima* II 31 (p. 176): "For just as primary and secondary are found in shapes, and the primary exists potentially in the secondary, so it is for the soul's powers."

[19] *De anima* II 4, 415a18–20: "acts and actions are prior to powers in account; but if so, still prior to these are their counterparts (*opposita*)."

[20] Aristotle, *De anima* I 4, 408b15–17: "This occurs not through movement existing within it, but sometimes [through movement] up to it, and sometimes [through movement] from it: Sensation, for instance, comes from these [outside objects], whereas remembering comes from it [soul], toward the movements or states of rest that are in the sensory organs."

Powers cannot be distinguished through organs, as far as our cognition is concerned, because not every power has an organ, and because a single organ belongs to distinct powers and distinct organs belong to a single power. An organ is that through which a power goes into operation, and an instrument likewise. But they differ in that an organ is conjoined to a power, as the material eye is conjoined to the visible power through which it is an eye.[21] An instrument, in contrast, is conjoined to the operation and not to the power – an axe, for instance. And it is called an *organ* as if *from origin born* (*ab origine natum*), whereas it is called an *instrument* as if *in a pile of operations placed* (*in struem operationum positum*), or as if *instructing the mind* (*instruens mentem*).[22]

So, according to Avicenna, the human soul has three powers, vegetative, sensory, and rational, the first two of which should not be called souls in a human being, but powers of the soul. The soul of brute animals, in turn, has two powers, vegetative and sensory, and the first should not be called a soul in brutes. In plants, finally, there is only one power, the vegetative, which in this case should not be called a power of the soul, but the soul.

The vegetative soul that is in plants is said to be a substance, and so too is the sensory, but in a different way than the rational. For the former are substances in two respects: first, because they are not in a subject, as are accidents, but rather in matter; second, because they constitute the substance. The rational soul, in contrast, is said to be a substance because it can exist per se (that is, separate). For a rational power can be separate, as we will say below [III.C.2], whereas the others are inseparable. {33}

These three agree in moving, but the vegetative soul moves only by expanding the parts of its body from place to place in such a way that the whole does not move, as is clear in growth and generation. The other two, in contrast, move the whole body from place to place.[23] But these two differ because the sensory cannot [move] from affection toward some-

---

Alexander of Hales, *Glossa in Sent.* Bk.II d.39 (pp.378–79): "It should be said that there is motion from the soul and motion toward the soul. So through the soul's powers (*vires*) there is motion toward the soul, whereas through its powers (*potentias*) there is motion from the soul."

[21] Aristotle, *De anima* II 1, 413a2–3: "Just as the eye is pupil and sight, so too the animal is soul and body."

[22] Fanciful etymologies were de rigueur in the Middle Ages. But these must have been intended merely as teaching heuristics. It takes only a little familiarity with Latin to recognize that *instrumentum* derives from *instruo* (to build) which in turn derives from *struo* (to pile up).

[23] Avicebron, *Fons vitae* III 48 (p. 186): "The motion of the animal soul is the motion of the whole body and the movement as a whole from one place to another; the motion of the vegetative soul, however, is the motion of parts of the body without changing the whole from place to place."

thing spiritual, whereas the rational can. But still, the rational soul differs from an angelic intellect (*intelligentia*), because the only thing it moves is the body conjoined to it or else another through that conjoined body, whereas an angelic intellect moves other things. Moreover, the rational soul moves from form to form by reasoning,[24] whereas an angelic intellect does not.

The vegetative soul differs from the other two, however, in that it is not cognitive, whereas the other two are. But those two differ among themselves because the sensory soul cognizes bodily forms: Both what it cognizes and that by which it cognizes are bodily, the former as in its underlying matter, the latter not.[25] The rational soul, in contrast, cognizes spiritual things, either simply or in bodies (as it is said that "the intellect understands species in phantasms").[26]

[III. The Soul's Individual Powers]

So since we have distinguished the soul's three powers through the two things through which philosophers came to a cognition of them – namely, through moving and cognizing[27] – we should speak of each in turn. But first we should note that the vegetative and the sensory soul is each said to be both form and nature. For just as in ethics virtue is the same {34} as a disposition (*habitus*), but it is called a disposition insofar as it is the soul's form[28] and a virtue insofar as it is a principle of actions, and likewise in logic knowledge is the same as art, but it is called knowledge insofar as it informs the soul and is called art insofar as it is a principle of action,[29] so

---

[24] Isaac Israeli, *Liber de definitionibus* (p. 321): "Reasoning is to make the cause run toward what it causes."

  Johannes Blund, *Tractatus de anima* §337: "It belongs to intellect to compare its objects to one another and, by comparing them, to make judgments."

[25] Boethius, *Consolation of Philosophy* V pr. 4: "Sense [observes] shape constituted in its underlying matter."

  Aristotle, *De anima* II 12, 424a18–19: "Sense receives sensible species without their matter."

[26] Aristotle, *De anima* III 7, 431b2.

[27] Aristotle, *De anima* I 2, 403b25–28: "What has soul seems to differ from what does not have soul in two respects above all, in movement and sense."

[28] Peter Lombard, *Sentences* II, 27.2 (p. 482): "Some who are not uneducated hold that a virtue is . . . a form that informs the soul."

[29] Dominicus Gundissalinus, *De divisione philosophiae* (pp. 44–45): "Art and knowledge are one and the same thing. . . . It is called art . . . with respect to a teacher who constrains and limits (*artat*) us with his rules and precepts so that we act according to that art. Hence art is taken from limiting (*artando*). . . . But [that same thing is called] knowledge when it is already retained in the soul. For as Aristotle says, all knowledge is in the soul."

in the natural sciences form is the same as nature, but it is called form with respect to the matter that it completes, and nature with respect to the motions that it elicits (for instance, the form of fire).

Accordingly, the vegetative and sensory souls are called both forms and natures. This is clear from the fact that, according to Avicenna,[30] nature is spoken of in four ways.

- Strictly, nature is spoken of as a principle of moving in [just] one way, nonspontaneously, as in elements and compounds of elements (although in elements the nature is the form, whereas in compounds of elements it is part of the form: for every compound of elements takes its name from the nature of its predominant element).[31]
- In a second way, nature is spoken of as a principle of moving in various ways, nonspontaneously, such as the vegetative soul in plants.
- In a third way, nature is spoken of as a principle of moving in various ways, spontaneously, such as the rational soul in animals.
- In a fourth way, nature is spoken of as a principle of moving in one way, spontaneously, such as the mover of the heavens, which is an intelligence.

The first is the strict way of speaking of nature. But nature is defined more generally in the *Physics*, as the principle of motion and rest of that in which it exists per se and not by way of an accident.[32]

[A. The Vegetative]

We are focusing on the vegetative soul insofar as it is a nature. So conceived, it has three powers. This is proved by the fact that it has a relationship to two things: For because it nourishes, it is related to that which is nourished and to that by which it is nourished. That which is nourished is what has it – namely, that which is ensouled. That by which it is nourished {35} is twofold: the matter, food, and the instrument, heat. For food is digested by heat.[33] Now the matter of the vegetative soul, the food, can be considered in three ways:

---

[30] *Sufficientia* I 5 (f. 16vBC).

[31] Aristotle, *De caelo* I 2, 269a2: "Their motion is through the motion of the simple body dominating over them."

[32] Aristotle, *Physics* II 1, 192b20–23: "Nature is a principle and cause of moving and resting of something in which it exists first, per se, and not accidentally."

[33] Aristotle, *De anima* II 4, 416b20–29: "But because three things are involved – that which is nourished, that by which it is nourished, and that which nourishes – that which nourishes is the first soul, whereas that which is nourished is the body having this [soul], and that by which it is

• First, with respect to that which has the soul inasmuch as it is something particular (*hoc aliquid*) and a substance.
• Second, inasmuch as what has the soul is extended.
• Third, the food can be considered complete insofar as it can be changed into a substance of the same species as what has the soul.

In the first way it is called nutritive, in the second productive of growth, and in the third generative, materially speaking.[34]

Since acts are discerned through objects, and powers through acts, it is clear that with respect to food taken in these three ways there are three acts: nourishing, growing, and generating. Through these three acts we determine that there are three powers of the vegetative soul: the nutritive, the productive of growth, and the generative. And since the end is what is most worthy, and the first two powers exist for the sake of the generative power, the vegetative soul is accordingly defined through the act of the generative power. According to Aristotle, the vegetative is "generative of what is like it."[35]

[B. The Sensory]

Next, the sensory power. This is divided into the apprehensive and the motive. The apprehensive is divided into the apprehensive from without and the apprehensive from within.[36]

---

nourished is the nourishment. . . . That by which a thing is nourished, however, is one of two things. . . . It is necessary that all nourishment be able to be digested, and it is [something] hot that does the digesting. Thus everything with a soul possesses heat."

[34] Aristotle, *De anima* II 4, 416b11–17: "There are different [kinds of] being, however, for nourishment and for what is productive of growth. For [nourishment] is productive of growth inasmuch as what has the soul is something *extended*, whereas it is nourishment inasmuch as [what has the soul] is *something particular and a substance*. For [a living thing] preserves its substance and exists for as long as it is nourished. Yet it is also capable of producing *generation*, not of what is nourished, but of something like what is nourished. For that very substance already exists, and nothing generates its very self, but [merely] preserves [itself]."

[35] *De anima* II 4, 416b23–25: "Yet because it is right to name all things on the basis of their end, and the end [in this case] is to have generated what is like it, the first soul will be generative of what is like it."

[36] Avicenna, *Liber de anima* I 5 (p. 82): "The living soul . . . has two powers, motive and apprehending."

Ibid. (p. 83): "The apprehending power is twofold: One power apprehends from without, the other apprehends from within."

[1. The External Senses]

The apprehensive from without is divided into five senses, which we will discuss first. The five senses agree in being passive powers of the soul. For we sense by taking in, not by sending out. They also agree {36} in that each sense needs an object, a medium, an organ, and a spirit.[37] Hence the abstracted form is first in the medium, second in the organ, third in the spirit, fourth in the sensory power, and fifth in the rational power. They also agree in that the sensible object, when placed on top of the sense (that is, on top of the organ) is not sensed.[38]

But they differ in that touch and taste are necessary senses: touch to distinguish what harms the animal's body from what is good for it; taste to distinguish food that preserves the animal from what is harmful. Smell, hearing, and sight, in contrast, are not necessary, but are for the sake of what is better.[39] They also differ in that touch and taste have an intrinsic medium – namely, one that is part of the animal: flesh, or something of that sort. The other senses have an extrinsic medium, air or water.[40] Moreover, the medium of touch has by its nature certain forms of the same kind as tangible forms; as a result, it imparts only intense forms to the sense, such as water that is either hot or cold. And to the extent that the medium is more temperate, it more and better imparts to the sense even a form that is weaker.[41] Thus a human being has a better sense of touch than other animals, because he has a more temperate complexion,[42]

---

[37] Costa Ben Luca, *De differentia animae et spiritus* ch. 1 (p. 121): "Spirit is a kind of subtle body that in the human body is based in the heart. . . . It pulses in the veins so as to give the body life. It is likewise based in the brain and the nerves and brings about sensation and motion."

Avicenna, *Liber de anima* V 8 (p. 175): "So first we will say that the vehicle of the bodily powers of animals is a subtle, spiritual body diffused through their cavities; this is spirit."

[38] Aristotle, *De anima* II 7, 419a28–30: "When someone positions something that has a smell or sound on the sensory capacity itself, this will not bring about a single sensation." Cf. 421b17, 423b24–25.

[39] Aristotle, *De anima* III 12, 434b22–24: "These then are necessary for an animal . . . The others, however, are for the sake of the good."

[40] Aristotle, *De anima* II 11, 423b17–20: "Now it seems in general that, just as air and water are related to sight, hearing, and smell, so flesh and the tongue are related to [their] sensory capacity as each of those is."

Averroes, *In de anima* II.101 (p. 284): "[Taste] is a kind of touch, and for this reason it does not need to grasp its sense object through a medium that is an *extrinsic* body, but through a medium that is *part of the animal.*

[41] Aristotle, *De anima* II 11, 423b27–424a10.

[42] Aristotle, *De anima* II 9, 421a19–26: "But we have a more exact sense of taste because it is a kind of touch, and a human being has the most exact form of this sense. . . . Among mankind it is in virtue of this sense and no other that some are intelligent, some not intelligent. For those with hard flesh are mentally unfit, whereas those with soft flesh are well fit."

and in a human being the palm is better,[43] and even more the tip of the index finger. The media of the other senses, in contrast, do not naturally contain the sensible forms of these senses. {37}

[a. Sight]

Although touch is prior by nature, sight is prior in worth.[44] So we will begin with sight.

The object of sight is color. For color makes an impression on sight "in virtue of the actuality of what is luminous"[45] (that is, in virtue of light). For light within a luminous body is the light source (*lux*); in something diaphanous (that is, in something transparent) it is emitted light (*lumen*); in something smooth and dense, it is brilliance; in something mixed, it is formally color.[46] A ray adds to light (*lux*), because a ray is directed light (*lux*)[47] (just as virtue adds to grace, because virtue is grace directed toward action).[48]

The medium [of sight] is air. Its instrument is the eye, toward which extends the optic nerve containing visual spirit, which receives color from the crystalline humor of the eye (that is, from the pupil).[49] {38}

---

[43] Adelard of Bath, *Quaestiones naturales* 31 (p. 36): "The palm of the hand has temperate passions: hot, cold, and the like."

[44] Aristotle, *De anima* II 2, 413b4–5: "Of the senses, touch is first present to all."
   Aristotle, *De sensu* 1, 437a3–7: "Of these [senses], sight is better, both for what is necessary and in its own right."

[45] Aristotle, *De anima* II 7, 418a27–b1: "What is visible is color. . . . For every color is capable of moving [sight] in virtue of the actuality of what is luminous." Modern (and even later medieval) versions of this passage differ significantly.

[46] Johannes Blund, *Tractatus de anima* §123 (pp. 32–33): "Light is spoken of in relation to the thing that is translucent; color in relation to the thing that is colored. . . . The Commentator [= Avicenna!] distinguishes between *lux*, *lumen*, and brilliance. He calls *lux* the perfection of the translucent, *lumen* a passion generated in the translucent, as in air, brilliance a passion generated by some color in the thing that is translucent."
   See Avicenna, *Liber de anima* III 1–3.

[47] Averroes, *In de anima* II.80 (p. 253): "light is naturally suited to emerge from the luminous along direct verticals toward the part opposite to the luminous part, due to an illuminated body, as the authors of the *libri Aspectuum* state." See Alhazen, *De aspectibus* II 1 (p. 24).

[48] Peter Lombard, *Sentences* II 27.2 (p. 482): "Operating and cooperating grace can be called virtue."

[49] Avicenna, *Liber de anima* I 5 (p. 83): "Sight is a power established in the optic nerve for apprehending the form of what is formed in the crystalline humor from likenesses of bodies having color."

[b. Hearing]

The object of hearing is sound. Sound is produced in the air by a dense body's moving the air with a motion faster than its natural motion.[50] The dense body making the sound resists that [which strikes it],[51] and makes in the air a vibration that is continuous up to the ear,[52] like a sphere whose center is the origin of the percussion. As a result, a voice is "heard on all sides," as Priscian says.[53] But it generates a vibration that is constantly weaker in its circle until it dies out. Something like this appears when a stone is thrown into water.[54]

The medium for this sense is the air that is continuous with the air located within the ear's inner chamber.[55] Its instrument is the ear's tympanum,[56] toward which extends the nerve containing auditory spirit. Distinctive of this sense is that its sensible object has existence only in the medium,[57] and so it lacks a first abstraction [from its object]. {39}

[c. Smell]

The object of smell is odor. Within the thing that can be smelled it is called odor, whereas in the medium it is called a fume or vapor, which heat releases from what has the odor. This is why an object with a smell (such as an apple), when smelled often, rots more quickly.[58]

---

[50] Averroes, *In de anima* II 79 (p. 250): "Sound results only when the motion of what makes the percussion was faster than the division [of the air]."

[51] Avicenna, *Liber de anima* II 5 (p. 163): "[The body that is struck] resists the air that is in the medium and does not yield to it, and also resists that which strikes it."

[52] Aristotle, *De anima* II 8, 420a3–4: "What makes the sound moves the air as one, up to the sense of hearing."

Averroes, *In de anima* II 82 (pp. 255–56): "What brings about the sound moves the air as one, which is moved with one continuous motion until it reaches the sense of hearing."

[53] *Institutio Grammatica* I ii 4 (p. 6).

[54] Averroes, *In de anima* II 78 (pp. 248–49): "You ought to know that what is made in the air from the percussion of bodies against each other is like that which is made in water *when a stone is thrown into water*, from the circles: For in the air around the percussion there is made a spherical shape, or nearly spherical, *whose center is the origin of the percussion*."

Algazel, *Metaphysics* (p. 166): "A slight motion is made in the air like a circular overflow, and it doesn't stop being stretched and then weakened until it entirely *dies out*."

[55] Algazel, *Metaphysics* (p. 166): "internally within the ear's inner chamber."

[56] Costa Ben Luca, *De differentia animae et spiritus* (p. 127); Algazel, *Metaphysics* (p. 166).

[57] Avicenna, *Liber de anima* II 5 (p. 154): "Sound is not something stable in essence, nor does it have fixed being, in the way in which it is granted for whiteness, blackness, and shape that they have stable being, such that their being can be stabilized."

[58] Aristotle, *De sensu* 438b24–25: "Odor is a fumelike evaporation, which comes from fire."

Avicenna, *Liber de anima* II 4 (pp. 148–49): "Unless odor were diffused through something's being

Its medium is air, and its organs are two little pieces of flesh hanging from the brain like the nipples of two breasts,[59] toward which the olfactory spirit extends.

[d. Taste]

The object of taste is flavor. It exists within the thing bearing the flavor. The moisture of saliva,[60] when joined with that thing, makes an impression on it by means of the sponge-like flesh that is on the surface of the tongue and is the internal medium [of taste].[61] {40} That medium imparts flavor to the spirit that is in the internal nerve. Hence if the moisture of saliva has been infected with the bitterness of bile, the sense of taste judges all food to be bitter, as is clear in those who are sick.[62] The same holds for saltiness and other flavors. Accordingly, there are in effect two media in this sense, one internal (flesh) and another external (the moisture of saliva).

[e. Touch]

Touch can be numbered on the basis of that by which it is sensed, and in this way it is one sense.[63] It can also be numbered on the basis of the things that are sensed, and in this way it is not one but four senses. For it apprehends (i) hot and cold; (ii) dry and wet from which there is hard and soft; (iii) rough and smooth; (iv) heavy and light.[64] There is not one

---

discharged, heat (and whatever promotes heat due to friction, evaporation or the like) would not promote odors, nor would cold hide them. Therefore it is clear that odor reaches the sense of smell only on account of a vapor that evaporates from what has the odor, which is mixed with the air and diffused through it. Hence when an apple has been smelled for some time, it spoils because of how much has been released from it."

[59] Avicenna, *Liber de anima* I 5 (p. 84): "two little pieces of flesh of the anterior part of the brain, like nipples of breasts."

[60] Avicenna, *Liber de anima* II.4 (p. 143): "[Taste] needs a kind of medium . . . which is the moistness of saliva."

Algazel, *Metaphysics* (p. 166): "mediated by the moisture of saliva, which has no taste."

[61] Ali Ibn al-'Abbâs, *Liber regalis dispositionis* III 17 (f. 11vb): "The tongue is the instrument of taste and speech; it is composed from soft flesh and is like a sponge."

[62] Aristotle, *De anima* II 10, 422b8–10: "To those who are ill all things seem bitter. The reason is that they sense with a tongue filled with this sort of moisture."

[63] Avicenna, *Liber de anima* I 5 (p. 85): "Since they are collected in one instrument, they are accordingly judged to be one in essence."

[64] Aristotle, *De anima* II 11, 422b26–27 lists three tangible contraries: "hot and cold, dry and wet, hard and soft."

The Arabic translation of that passage by Ishâq ibn Hunain adds a fourth pair, "rough and smooth" (see Averroes, *In de anima* II 107 [pp. 294–95]; Avicenna, *Liber de anima* I 5 [p. 85]).

proximate genus of these qualities, in the way that color is the genus of all colors, and since they are not under one genus, in this respect touch is four senses. Thus Avicenna says that there are either five or eight external senses.[65]

[f. Differences among Media]

Note that air is the medium for sight in virtue of its being a diaphanous body. It is the medium for hearing in virtue of another unnamed disposition – namely, in virtue of its not having sound, but being capable of having it. It is the medium for smell in virtue of a third unnamed disposition – namely, in virtue of its not having odor, but being capable of having it.[66] {41}

[g. The Relationship between the Senses and the Elements]

The reason why there are five senses comes from the five elements (one of which, vapor, falls in between water and air). For sight is related to fire, since the medium of sight is luminous. Hearing is related to air and taste to water, since these are the media for these senses. Touch is related to earth, both since this is its medium (since flesh is earthy), and because touch can feel only what has the distinctive characteristic of earth, solidity. The sense of smell pertains to a fifth element, vapor,[67] because, though some claim that odor can reach the sense of smell by making an impression on the air without any fumes being discharged (as color reaches sight),[68] still it is more often released with such a discharge.

Algazel, *Metaphysics* (p. 165) adds a fifth: "heavy and light."

Our author includes hard and soft under dry and wet, thus preserving Avicenna's four-way division.

[65] *Liber de anima* I 5 (p. 83): "The senses apprehending from without are five or eight."

[66] Aristotle, *De anima* II 7, 419a32–b3: "The medium for sound is air, whereas [the medium] for smell has no name. For a certain state is common to air and water; what is [common] to each is [related] to something with smell just as being diaphanous [is related] to color."

[67] Ali Ibn al-'Abbâs, *Liber regalis dispositionis* IV 10 (f. 17ra): "The power of sight is more refined than the others, since its nature is fiery. . . . After sight the most refined is hearing, whose sense is airy. . . . After hearing the most refined is the sense of smell, since its nature is fumelike, and the fumelike falls in between the airy and the watery. . . . After the sense of smell, the most refined is taste, whose nature is watery. . . . Touch is the coarsest of all, since its nature is earthy."

The doctrine goes back to Plato, *Timaeus* 66DE, but is ridiculed by Aristotle, *De sensu* 2, 437a19–22, a passage our author was seemingly unaware of.

[68] Avicenna, *Liber de anima* II 4 (p. 148): "Some say that it is given off without the mixture of anything from its body and without making an impression on the medium."

We say that vapor is the element that falls in between water and air,[69] as regards the degree to which its substance is refined and dense: for it is more refined than water and denser than air. For though it comes from [other] elements, in that it is released from air and water due to the heat of the sun, and either remains shut up in the depths of the earth or is raised {42} more and less above the earth in keeping with the three regions of air,[70] it itself is a basis for other subsequent things.

That which is raised above the earth is the basis for comets and falling stars (be they stars or rocks), and of the circles that appear around the sun and moon, and of the rainbow, and also of the winds and the whirlwind, of thunder, flashes, lightning, clouds, the overcast, mist, hail, snow, hoar-frost, rainstorm (downpour or shower), and dew. These are the products of the first composition of elements.

That which remains in the depths of the earth is what heats springs in winter; it is the basis for the earth's motion. It generates mineral bodies such as sulfur (through whose combustion hot springs heat), stone, and quicksilver, {43} which is the basis for all seven metals:[71] lead, tin, bronze, brass, copper, silver, and gold. (For amber is not a simple metal.)[72] These are the products of the second composition of elements.

There are, however, some intermediary compositions of elements that are neither beneath nor above the earth, but are on the earth. Some of these, those born of the earth, are fixed in the earth: the plants, that is, trees and herbs. Others, the animals, are not fixed, unless because some fall in between plants and animals, such as sea sponges, which take in food through their roots, as do plants, and have the sense of touch, as do animals.[73] For these, too, vapor provides the basis: either per se, when plants are first generated from seed, or by means of rain. Things born of the earth are nourished by a mixture of earth and water. These fall into

---

[69] The remainder of this section summarizes Aristotle's detailed discussion in *Meteorology* Bks. I–III.

[70] Alfred of Sareshel, *In libros Meteorologicorum*, (f. 12ra, re. I 9, 346b16 ff.): "Note that there are three regions (*interstitia*) of air: the highest part that is continuous with fire, the lowest that touches the earth, and the middle that marks off the extremes of each [of the others]."

[71] Pseudo-Razi, *Liber de aluminibus et salibus*, cited in Vincent of Beauvais, *Speculum naturale* VII 63 (col. 465): "the view of the *Liber de aluminibus et salibus* – namely, that quicksilver is the element through which God created all minerals."

Avicenna, *De congelatis* (f. 115vb): "and so quicksilver is mixed with these bodies, since it is their subject."

[72] Isidore of Seville, *Etymologiae* XVI xvii: "There are seven kinds of metals: gold, silver, bronze, amber, tin, lead, and what dominates them all, iron." Isidore takes brass and copper to be species of bronze. Our author entirely omits iron.

[73] Aristotle, *De historia animalium* V 16, VIII 1, 588b20.

the third composition, in which the contrariety is somehow broken down that prevents the elements and the products of the first and second compositions of elements from having a soul. As a result, plants have a vegetative soul.

Since vapors are the basis for things born of the earth, from which the humors of animals are generated, and since through these humors animals are nourished and their seeds and eggs are formed, from which other animals are generated, it is clear that vapors are also the basis of both nonrational animals and human beings. These are the products of the fourth and fifth composition [of elements]. But in animals the contrariety is broken down more than it is in things born of the earth. As a result, they receive a loftier soul, one that is sensory. This is likewise the case for human beings more than animals, and as a result we receive the loftiest of souls, one that is rational, due to the supreme harmony of the human body. And because there could not have been a loftier perfection, it is clear that a human being is the final end of creatures.[74] Accordingly, as {44} the first rational creature, so the last. In this way, the end agrees with the beginning, as if this ordering of creatures were circular, so that from the perfection of the circle one may understand something of the perfection of the highest maker.

We have, therefore, rightly posited five elements, although four come first, initially.

[2. *The Internal Senses*]

Next, the internal senses. There are five internal senses: common sense, imagination, the imaginative or formative power (which in human beings is called the cogitative power), estimation, and memory.[75]

[*a. Common Sense*]

The common sense has three or four acts. For it sometimes turns itself toward the acts of an external sense, inasmuch as we say *I see that I see,* and generally, *I sense that I sense.*[76] It also discerns between sense objects of

---

[74] Aristotle, *Physics* II 2, 194a34–35: "We use everything as if it exists for our own sake. For we ourselves are in a sense an end."

[75] Avicenna, *Liber de anima* I 5 (pp. 87–90).

[76] Aristotle, *De anima* III 2, 425b12 ff.: "Now because we sense that we see and hear, it is necessary to sense that one sees either through sight, or else through a different [sense]."

different particular senses, such as between white and sweet, and it can do this inasmuch as it apprehends all the sense objects of the five senses. A particular sense such as sight cannot discern between white and sweet, because a power that discerns any two things also comprehends those two things, whereas sight, although it apprehends white, does not apprehend sweet.[77] Its third act, according to Avicenna, is to apprehend a thing as both somewhere it is not and somewhere it is – as if the same thing were in different places. For instance, it apprehends a drop of water falling from a roof as if existing in a continuous line from the roof to the ground, even though that drop does not exist higher up when it is lower down, and vice versa.[78] Its fourth act, according to some, is to apprehend common sense objects.[79] There are five of these: {45} motion, rest, number, shape, and size.[80] According to Themistius, the first three of these are common to all the particular senses; the last two are common only to two senses, sight and touch.[81]

[b. Imagination]

Imagination turns itself toward a thing's likeness as if toward the thing itself. This likeness is called an image or phantasm.[82] It receives it from the common sense and preserves it even in the thing's absence. It thus differs from the common sense in two respects: First, the common sense, like a

---

[77] Aristotle, *De anima* III 2, 426b12 ff.: "But since we distinguish both white and sweet, and any one of the sense objects relative to any other, by some means, and we sense that they differ, this then necessarily occurs by means of sense: for they are sensible things. . . . But we cannot by means of things that are separated distinguish that sweet is different from white. Rather, both must be made clear by means of some one thing."

[78] Avicenna, *Liber de anima* I 5 (p. 88): "When you want to know the difference between the job of an external sense, the job of the common sense, and the job of imagination, look at the state of a single falling raindrop, and you will see a straight line."

[79] Averroes, *In de anima* II 65 (p. 228): "Common sense objects, as will be explained, are proper to the common sense, in just the way that these [others] are proper to each of the senses."
   See also ibid., II 134 (p. 334).

[80] Aristotle, *De anima* II 6, 418a17–18: "The common sense objects are motion, rest, number, shape, size."

[81] Averroes, *In de anima* II 64 (p. 226): "Aristotle does not mean that each of these five is common to each of the senses. Rather, as Themistius understands him, and as seems to be the case, three of these sense objects – motion, rest, and number – are common to all the senses, whereas shape and quantity are common only to touch and sight." See Themistius, *De anima* II.6 (57, 36–58) – a work not translated into Latin until 1267.

[82] Image (*idolum*): Aristotle, e.g., *De anima* III 3, 427b20.
   Phantasm: ibid., 428a1–2: "If, then, *phantasia* is that in virtue of which we say that some phantasm is produced in us."

particular sense, needs the presence of an external thing (except while asleep), whereas imagination does not; second, the common sense receives a form but does not preserve it, whereas imagination receives and preserves all sensible forms. Hence Avicenna calls it the treasure chest of forms.[83]

[c. The Imaginative Power]

The third internal sense is the imaginative power, whose act is to move from one form placed within imagination to another, and to compound and divide them into chimeras and goat-stags.[84] This same power is called the formative,[85] with regard to {46} the formations that are produced in dreams. Things within dreams seem to be present, however, because forms are made to come back to the common sense.[86] For [a form] returns to the common sense just as easily as a flame rising from a candle returns to a recently extinguished candle placed above it. In human beings this is also called the cogitative power,[87] because through it, adorned by the light of reason,[88] a human being thinks of many things and plans for the future from a consideration of present or past events.

[d. Estimation]

The fourth sense is estimation, which apprehends intentions.[89] Form and intention differ in this context, because something is called a *form* when it falls under an external sense, as do common and proper sense objects. A

---

[83] Avicenna, *Liber de anima* I 5 (p. 88): "You should know that receiving is due to one power, which is distinct from the power responsible for retaining."
   In fact, the label 'treasure chest' (*arca*) is due to Algazel, *Metaphysics* (p. 170). Avicenna, *Liber de anima* I 5 (p. 89), uses 'storehouse' (*thesaurus*).

[84] Avicenna, *Liber de anima* I 5 (p. 89): "The power that is called the imaginative has the task of composing one thing from imagination with another, and dividing one thing from another, as it likes."
   For the goat-stag see Aristotle, e.g., *De interpretatione* 1, 16a16.

[85] Not according to the Latin version of Avicenna, in which 'formative' (*formativa, formans*) refers to the storehouse of imagination (*Liber de anima* I 5 [pp. 88–89]; IV 2, [p. 13]; V 8 [p. 183]).

[86] Averroes, *De sompno et vigilia* (pp. 98–99), quoted in Translation 8 n. 83.

[87] Avicenna, *Liber de anima* I 5 (p. 89): "After this is the power that is called the imaginative with respect to a living animal, and the *cogitans*, with respect to the human soul."
   Algazel, *Metaphysics* (p. 170): "in human beings this is standardly called the cogitative."

[88] Avicenna uses this phrase, but to describe the power of estimation (*Liber de anima* IV 3 [p. 40]).

[89] Avicenna, *Liber de anima* I 5 (p. 89): "Next is the power of estimation, which is the power . . . for apprehending the unsensed intentions that exist in individual sense objects."

thing is called an *intention*, in contrast, when it does not fall under any sense, but is nevertheless found in sensible and nonsensible things.[90] Hence it is better than a form; examples are goodness and badness, friendship and hostility, harm and help, honor and disgrace, and others of this sort. By this power a sheep judges a wolf to be hostile,[91] and a donkey judges a lion to be friendly and water harmful, because the water represents its horrid face or image – even though it would be killed by the lion and saved by the water.[92] So estimation apprehends these intentions from sensible things, and moves from one to the other.

[e. Memory]

The fifth sense is memory. It stands to estimation just as imagination stands to the common sense: for it receives intentions from estimation and {47} preserves them.[93] Hence it is "the storehouse of intentions."[94] It has one act as well: Through things that it actually attends to, it remembers what it has attended to in the past. It is in this respect that it is called the memorative power.[95]

[3. Sensory Motive Powers]

After the sensory and apprehensive powers, the motive powers follow. So it should be known that from an imagination and estimation of what is pleasant or painful, appetite or flight follows,[96] and from the difficult or easy, fear or daring follows. In this way, imagination or estimation goes from being cognitive to being affective,[97] and goes from being apprehen-

---

[90] Avicenna, *Liber de anima* I 5 (p. 86): "The difference between apprehending a form and apprehending an intention is this." See also IV 1 (pp. 6–8).
[91] Avicenna, *Liber de anima* I 5 (p. 89): "the power that is in the sheep for judging that it should flee from this wolf."
[92] Isaac Israeli, *Liber de definitionibus* (p. 314).
[93] Avicenna, *Liber de anima* I 5 (p. 89): "Next is the memory and reminiscing power, which . . . retains what the power for estimation apprehends of unsensed intentions that are in individual sense objects."
[94] Avicenna, *Liber de anima* V 8 (pp. 183, 89).
[95] Aristotle, *De memoria* 453a5–14.
[96] Aristotle, *De anima* III 7, 431a9–14: "But when something is pleasant or painful, [the soul], as if affirming or denying, seeks or flees it. . . . The powers for appetite and flight are not different from each other or from the sensory power, but they do differ in being."
[97] Robert Grosseteste, *De artibus liberalibus* (p. 1): "The works of our power consist either in the mind's attention or its affection. . . . First, its attention attends; second it verifies the things attended to or cognized; and once its agreeableness or harmfulness has been verified by the mind or attention, affection looks eagerly to embrace the agreeable or else to withdraw within itself and flee the harmful."

sive to being motive – that is, it is now *commanding* motion. For there are two kinds of motive powers: Some motive powers command, whereas others are commanded.[98]

Those that command are imagination and estimation taken as on the above account – that is, as affective, toward either possessing or fleeing. According to that account, each can be called concupiscible and irascible[99] (or desiderative, using the general term). Hence Aristotle says that imagination is for nonrational beings {48} just as reason is for human beings. This is also so for bestial human beings who are moved by order of the desiderative power, not by the judgment of reason.[100]

The commanded motive power is located in the muscles and nerves of the whole body, contracting and extending the tendons and ligaments by order of the irascible and concupiscible powers.[101]

So we say in short that there are two kinds of sensory motive powers, commanding and commanded, the first of which is called desiderative. That commanding power comes in two further kinds, irascible and concupiscible: One moves toward what is pleasant, the other moves away from what is painful.

[*C. The Rational Power*]

Having discussed the vegetative and sensory powers, the rational power follows. Reason is sometimes taken as cognitive, and sometimes as affective. More truly, it is one and the same power that is first called cognitive, with respect to the true, and then when it judges a thing to be good and is affected by it, it is called affective with respect to the good.[102] Hence the first reason is speculative, the second practical (that is, operative), because

[98] Avicenna, *Liber de anima* I 5 (p. 82): "The motive power is of two sorts, because either it produces motion in such a way that it commands the motion, or it produces motion in such a way that it brings about (*efficiens*) the motion."

[99] Avicenna, *Liber de anima* IV 4, (p. 57): "The concupiscible is that which wants the enjoyable and whatever is taken as useful to acquire. The irascible is that which wants to overcome and repel that which is taken to be harmful." See also Alexander of Hales, *Glossa in Sent.* Bk.II d.24 (p. 211).

[100] Aristotle, *De anima* III 10, 433a9–12: "These two things seem to produce movement, . . . appetite or intellect. . . . For many follow *phantasia*, beyond knowledge, and in other animals their intelligence is not reason, but *phantasia*."

[101] Avicenna, *Liber de anima* I 5 (p. 83): "The motive power considered as what brings about the motion is a power infused in the nerves and muscles, contracting the tendons and ligaments connected with the limbs toward the source, or relaxing and extending in length, and turning the tendons and ligaments in the other direction, against the source."

[102] Philip the Chancellor, *Summa de bono* (p. 141): "Since there is a power of the soul that contemplates the true . . . , there will be another likewise affected by the good."

it commands motion.[103] For this reason Avicenna defines reason as "a power moving the body toward individual actions"[104] with deliberation and judgment. With respect to its first action, to apprehend, it is sometimes spoken of as reason in the strict sense, and sometimes as intellect: *intellect*, when it apprehends the essence of a thing absolutely; *reason*, when it compares one thing to another.[105] {49}

[1. Material Intellect]

Beginning at a higher level, we say that the rational soul has two parts, one inseparable from the body and the other separable. The inseparable part is called rationality, and it is due to this that a human being is called rational.[106] It is also called the material intellect, which Aristotle calls "passive" (*passibilem*) and "corruptible."[107] This power falls in between the sensory power and the separable intellect. For the sensory power concerns phantasms and the separable intellect species, whereas this material intellect considers species in phantasms,[108] in such a way that it apprehends species with their accidents, distinguishing between the species and its accidents but without abstracting. In this way it materially prepares species for the separable intellect.[109] {50}

This solves the theological question of whether Christ was rational [during the three days after his death], taking *rational* as a differentia of *animal*.[110] For it is clear that if Christ was rational due to reason, he was

---

[103] Aristotle, *De anima* III 10, 433a13–15: "So both of these, intellect and appetite, produce locomotion. But this is the intellect that reasons for the sake of something and is *practical;* it differs in its end from *speculative* [intellect]."

[104] *Liber de anima* I 5 (p. 90).

[105] See note 24.

[106] Avicenna, *Liber de anima* I 1 (pp. 32–33): "Rationality here applies to a soul having two material intellects. This is not possibly so in the other case [viz., heavenly bodies] . . . , because their intellect is intellect in effect, and intellect in effect does not constitute the soul that is part of the definition of rational."

[107] *De anima* III 5, 430a24.

[108] *De anima* III 7, 431b2: "The intellective power understands species in phantasms."

[109] Averroes, *In de anima* III 20 (pp. 449–50): "By 'passive intellect,' Aristotle means the forms of imagination as acted on by the distinctively human cogitative power. For this power is a kind of reason, and its action is nothing other than to place the intention of imagination's form with its individual within memory, or to distinguish it from that within the formative power and imagination. And it is clear that the intellect that is called material receives these imagined intentions after this distinction. Therefore this passive intellect is necessary in their formation. . . . And without the imaginative and cogitative powers, the intellect that is called material understands nothing. For these virtues are like things that *prepare the material* of a craft for receiving the action of that craft."

Notice that Averroes *distinguishes* this "passive intellect" from the "material intellect." The latter, for Averroes, is what our author will call the possible intellect.

[110] Peter Lombard, *Sentences*, Bk. III Q22: "whether for the three days of his death Christ was a

not rational due to rationality, because rationality or the material intellect exists only in the soul's conjunction with the body.

[2. Separable Intellect]

Next, the separable intellect,[111] of which one part consists in cognizing what is true, the other in affection for what is good. The part that consists in affection for the good is called the practical intellect; the other part is called the speculative intellect. They are the same power, because the cognitive intellect turns into the affective intellect.

[a. Speculative Intellect]

[i. Agent Intellect]

The cognitive intellect is divided into two parts, one of which is called the agent intellect, whereas the other is called the possible intellect, which "is nothing actually before it operates (*intelligat*)."[112] {51} The relationship of the agent to the possible intellect is like the relationship of light (*lux*) to sight.[113] For just as light makes the species of a color jump from the colored object to the eye,[114] so the agent intellect abstracts species from the phantasms that the material intellect has prepared for it, and makes them in a way jump to the possible intellect. Thus the agent intellect has two acts: One is to abstract species from phantasms, the other is to arrange these abstracted species in the possible intellect.[115]

In this Avicenna erred, because he posited agent intellect as separate

---

human being." The issue is whether Christ, while separated from his entombed body, could still count as being human in virtue of possessing a human soul.

[111] Aristotle, e.g., *De anima* III 5, 430a17: "This intellect is separate."

[112] Aristotle, *De anima* III 4, 429b30–31: "Before intellect operates it is the intelligible things potentially somehow but it is nothing actually." See also 429a24.

[113] Aristotle, *De anima* III 5, 430a14–17: "There is intellect of the sort in which all things are brought about and, on the other hand, [there is] that by which it serves to bring about all things, as a sort of condition, like light. For in a way light, too, makes colors that are in potentiality into actual colors."

Avicenna, *Liber de anima* V 5 (p. 127): "Its relationship to our souls is like the relationship of the sun to our seeing."

[114] Avicenna, *Liber de anima* III 3 (p. 192): "Light is the cause of colors' being revealed and the cause of their *jumping (resultandi)* to another."

[115] Avicenna, *Liber de anima* III 6 (pp. 148–49): "Learning is nothing other than to seek the perfect aptitude for joining oneself to the agent intellect, inasmuch as from that results an understanding that is simple, from which emanates forms *arranged* in the soul by means of thought." This summarizes the account of arranging (*ordinans*) forms on pp. 138–44.

from the soul (that is, as an intelligence or angel), just as the sun is separate from sight.[116] But there is no doubt that this intellect is a power of the soul, because it is in the soul's power to use intellect when it wants to.[117] For it follows from this that, first, phantasms are always present to it and, second, the agent intellect, which abstracts species from phantasms, {52} is joined to the soul as its power.[118] This is clear through the contrasting case of sight, because we do not see white whenever we want to, because either light is not always present, or if light is for a time present, the white could itself be absent.

These are the things that have been said about agent intellect: that it has two acts, and that it is a power.

[ii. Possible Intellect]

Next, the possible intellect, which is initially called the possible intellect because it is a power of the soul and nothing actually.[119] An example of this is a bare slate without any picture or even aptitude for one more than another, but which is capable of having any one.[120] {53} This intellect, according to the various degrees to which it develops, receives different labels: Thus it is called the actual intellect, the dispositional intellect, and the achieved intellect. For when it has first received the quiddities of

---

[116] Avicenna, *Liber de anima* V 5 (p. 127): "Its relationship to our souls is like the relationship of the sun to our seeing." Ibid: "From considering these [particulars within imagination], the soul is suited to have abstraction emanate toward it from the agent *intelligence*."

  Algazel, *Metaphysics* (p. 175): "from one of the divine causes, which is called an angel or agent intelligence."

  Johannes Blund, *Tractatus de anima* §344 (p. 94): "that intelligence is said by many authors to be an angel, which ministers to the soul of a human being."

[117] Averroes, *De anima* III 18 (p. 438): "And it is important to add to the account: understand all things of itself and *when it wants to*."

[118] Averroes very often speaks of agent intellect as joined (*copulatus*) to us: e.g., *In de anima* III 5 (pp. 390, 404, 407, 411 [see note 123 below]), but without saying that it is joined to the soul "as its power."

[119] Aristotle, *De anima* III 429a18–22: "And so it is necessary, since intellect cognizes all things, that it be unmixed, as Anaxagoras says, in order to command – i.e., in order to have cognition; for something appearing within it will prevent and block what is outside it. That is why it has no nature at all but that it is *possible*."

[120] Aristotle, *De anima* III 4, 430a1: "It must be as it is with a slate on which nothing has actually been written."

  Averroes, *In de anima* III 14 (p. 430): "A slate having no actual picture nor a potential one close to actuality."

  Our author seems to have coined the phrase *tabula nuda*. Later in the thirteenth century it would become standard to speak of a *tabula rasa* – see, e.g., Translation 4, I.6.

things, it is then called actual intellect, because it can at that point act.[121] For from the quiddities of noncomplex [objects] it can form complexes, even of first propositions. Thus, having cognized what a part is and what a whole is, it can then form this complex:

> Every whole is greater than its part.

At that point it is called the dispositional intellect, inasmuch as it has within itself the principles of truth in the genus of the true.[122] And when beyond this, by ordering those principles, it has attained the knowledge of a conclusion, at that point with respect to that knowledge acquired from principles it is called the achieved intellect.[123]

These claims are enough regarding the possible intellect.

Yet since we have said above that the agent intellect abstracts species from phantasms and arranges them in the possible intellect, we should note here that there are some forms in the possible intellect that the agent intellect does not abstract from {54} phantasms, but that the soul acquires through the correct operation, such as justice and prudence.[124] There are other forms that it acquires through a higher illumination, such as some that are understood from God, in a divine mode.[125]

[*b. Practical Intellect*]

[i. Synderesis]

Next, the practical intellect, which is affected by the good. This is initially divided into two parts. One part is always naturally suited to be fixed on

---

[121] Aristotle, *De anima* III 4, 429b5–6: "But when this [intellect] knows each of them, it is said to be a knower in actuality."

[122] Avicenna, *Liber de anima* I 5 (p. 97): "The first intelligibles are propositions . . . , as when we believe that the whole is greater than its part. . . . And sometimes when an intention of that which is in effect is not acquired by it [intellect] except in this way, it is called dispositional intellect (*intellectus in habitu*)."

[123] Averroes, *In de anima* III 5 (p. 411): "When the material intellect has been joined inasmuch as it has been perfected by the agent intellect, then we are joined with the agent intellect, and this disposition is called achievement and achieved intellect (*intellectus adeptus*)."

[124] Aristotle, *Nicomachean Ethics* II 1, 1103a14–17: "There being two kinds of virtue, one intellectual and one moral, the intellectual comes mostly from teaching, in both its generation and growth . . . , whereas the moral comes from habit (*assuetudine*)."

[125] Dominicus Gundissalinus, *De anima* (p. 99): "For when this eye of the soul that is intelligence aims at the contemplation of the creator, it is infused by such a clarity of divine light – since God is light – that this inaccessible light seems to jump into that intelligence like a form onto a mirror."

higher things, whether it is a power or {55} a natural disposition,[126] naturally moving toward the good and abhorring the bad. This part is called *synderesis;* it never errs.[127]

[ii. Practical Reason]

The other part, which is called *reason*, is always connected to lower things, whether it is moved toward higher or toward lower things. This part is further divided into two parts, one of which is called the higher part of reason, the other the lower part of reason.[128] The first is named man, the second woman, which always errs in obeying the serpent – that is, sensuality, the desiderative power that above [III.B.3] we divided into the irascible and the concupiscible. The other part, which is called man, errs in consenting to the woman.[129] But synderesis always objects against the errors of these two parts,[130] and hence it sometimes calls them back from error to rightness.

---

[126] Alexander of Hales, *Glossa in Sent.* Bk. II d.40 (p. 380): "Whether synderesis is a power or a disposition."
   Ibid. (p. 382): "Formally, [synderesis] is called a connatural disposition."

[127] Alexander of Hales, *Glossa in Sent.* Bk. II d.40 (p. 381): "With respect to the motive power, there will be one power that always desires the good and detests the bad; this is synderesis."

[128] Peter Lombard, *Sentences* Bk. II d.24 (p. 453): "Reason is the higher power of the soul which, as we say, has two parts or differentiae, a higher and a lower."

[129] Peter Lombard, *Sentences* Bk. II d.24 (p. 455): "For just as there the serpent persuaded the woman, and the woman the man, so too in our case sensual motion, once it has conceived the enticement of sin, like the serpent's suggesting to the woman – that is, to the lower part of reason. . . . It then gives from the same to the man, the higher part of reason."
   Philip the Chancellor, *Summa de bono* (p. 147): "Synderesis will not be in reason, but above it, as intelligence. And that reason will be divided into two parts, one of which is compared to man, the other to woman."

[130] Alexander of Hales, *Glossa in Sent.* Bk. II d.24 (p. 217): "Synderesis *always objects* against sin."

2

ANONYMOUS (ARTS MASTER c. 1270) *QUESTIONS ON* DE ANIMA *I–II*

Introduction

This fascinating treatise seems to have survived in only one manuscript, anonymous and undated. As with the previous selection, the author is thought to have been a master in the Arts Faculty at the University of Paris. But these *Questions* date from the latter part of the thirteenth century, probably 1270 or shortly after. Judging from its repetitions and haphazard structure, this work seems to be a student's unedited report of a lecture. It is perhaps the most extreme example of the movement within the Arts Faculty known as *radical Aristotelianism*, whose proponents advocated the teachings of Aristotle without regard for how those views accorded with Christianity. Both of the best known members of this movement, Siger of Brabant and Boethius of Dacia, have been proposed as authors of the present treatise, but there seems to be no strong reason for accepting either attribution.

By far the most extreme and well-known part of these *Questions* is the author's argument that all human beings share a single intellect, and that the intellect is not united with the body in the way that form is united with matter (see I Q6, II Q4). This form of monopsychism matches Averroes's notorious interpretation of Aristotle; Siger of Brabant had also advocated the view in Paris. But our author goes one step further and simply embraces the absurdity that seems to follow: that in fact human beings do not themselves understand anything, and that it is only the separate intellect that truly understands (II Q4). Both the thesis of monopsychism and the seemingly absurd implication were among the thirteen propositions condemned by Bishop Stephen Tempier of Paris in 1270.

Given the controversial nature of his views, it is no wonder that our author did not himself publish these *Questions*. The practice of airing dangerous claims in private, in front of students, seems to have been widespread. Thomas Aquinas closed his caustic treatise against the thesis of monopsychism with this challenge to his opponents:

If someone exulting in this falsely named knowledge wishes to speak against what we have written, let him not speak in corners nor in the presence of boys who don't know how to judge such difficult matters, but let him reply in writing to this work, if he dares. (*De unitate intellectus* ch. 5)

In fact our author does reply to Aquinas's arguments: in II Q4 he works through those arguments in some detail, although without mentioning their source. Still, our author declined Aquinas's dare to make his views public. In that intolerant environment, who can blame him?

Although the discussions of intellect are the most startling and controversial, there is a great deal of other interesting material concerning the soul, its powers, and our knowledge of both the soul and the external world. Among the most notable are the discussions in Book II on the passivity of the senses (Q11), on the difference between sensation per se and sensation per accidens (Q14), and on whether the senses actually give us any knowledge of a world outside of our own sensations (Q17).

Because of the length of this treatise, and because of its disparate topics, some questions have been omitted, although the question titles have been retained so that readers can see what they are missing. On the dating and authorship of this treatise, see Giele (1960), as well as the introduction to his edition of these *Questions*. For the author's views on intellect, see Dales (1995), pp. 154–59. For a more general discussion of radical Aristotelianism, see Wippel (1994), van Steenberghen (1980), Ebbesen (1998), and CHLMP VIII.30, "Sense, Intellect, and Imagination in Albert, Thomas, and Siger."

Questions *on* De anima *I–II*

[Book One]

[*Prologue*]

Of things good and honorable . . . [402a1]. The soul has a science that is honorable and admirable and necessary for the cognition of many different kinds of beings. It has a science that is honorable, I say, because the soul is one of those beings that are honorable. It also has operations elevated far above what the elemental material powers can do. Thus it is said to have a science that is admirable, in that what is above the elemental material powers is admirable. For the soul has many operations whose cause cannot be supplied from the elements, such as hearing, seeing, etc. Thus it has a science that is honorable. For Aristotle says at the end of *Ethics* I [1101b10–2a4] that some beings are praiseworthy and some not praiseworthy but admirable and honorable. Those that are at our level are said to be praiseworthy; properly speaking, then, praise is owed to that from which something is acquired through our praise. But honor and admiration are owed to beings that are above us, such as the First Being and others. So it is not praise that is owed to God, properly speaking, but something better than praise: honor and admiration. But the soul is included among the sorts of beings that are above us, and for that reason it has a science that is honorable and admirable. Thus in *Physics* II, according to the interpretation of some, and according to Averroes, in *De anima* III, Aristotle holds that the soul is the final and ultimate perfection in material things – I mean the soul in actuality, speaking of the soul with respect to the part of it that is intellective, since this is the more noble and honorable perfection among material things {22} that can perfect matter (*yle*). Likewise, too, the science of the soul, at least with respect to this part, is the more honorable among the sciences of things having a form in matter. For as is written in *Metaphysics* VI [1025b3–26a32], a thing's state of being is just like its state in cognition. It should also be admired since, as I have said, it has operations (according to Aristotle in these books one [411a24–25] and two [417a2–b26]) the causes and reasons of which cannot be supplied from the elements, such as sensing, understanding, etc.

This science of the soul is also quite necessary for the science of natural things. Aristotle says this in the text [402a6]: for the soul is the actuality and perfection of natural bodies; therefore the soul's cognition is necessary for the cognition of natural bodies. It is also necessary for the science of separate [substances]. For separate being, which is the subject of first philosophy, is established on the basis of the soul's operations. Also, the science of the soul is necessary for all of moral philosophy and the positing of law (*legis positivam*). For virtues, works of virtue, and dispositions contrary to the virtues, all these exist in the soul, even if they are there with respect to different powers (*virtutes*) of the soul – given that chastity, prudence, bravery, etc. exist in different powers.

The science of the soul is therefore highly honorable and admirable, and very useful.

It should be understood as well that the science of the soul ought to teach two things: the soul's nature and its operations. It ought to teach its nature by considering whether it is abstract, etc. It ought to teach its operations by, for example, considering whether it is active or passive. And in this science of the soul we should recognize a like mode of proceeding not just for the soul in general, but also as regards all the soul's powers. As Aristotle says in *Ethics* I [1095a32–b3], on the authority of Plato, it makes a great difference whether in cognizing some being we are to proceed from things prior in being to things posterior in being or vice versa. It likewise matters greatly whether we are to proceed in this way or the other in presenting an account of the soul. For this is the logic proper to every special science: to know whether we are to proceed in this way or the other, as the Commentator says {23} on *Ethics* I. So there is no greater defect than when one has determined the way one ought to proceed in cognizing any being and then ignored it. For to ignore this poses the greatest of obstacles. But this is what the *Analytics* teach. Therefore we should consider what the mode of proceeding is for the science of soul – on what basis, that is, has the way been determined in presenting an account of the soul. For this is necessary, [if] logic is to be preserved. And what we should understand is that this universally is the logic, here and elsewhere: to proceed from things better known to us, whether they are prior or posterior in being.

And since the soul's operations are better known to us than is the soul's very substance, we should therefore proceed from these in determining whether a science of the soul is possible.

Question 1. Is a Science of the Soul Possible?

It seems that it is not, because every science has its root in the senses.[1] But the soul is not sensible with respect to its substance, nor with respect to its operations: for what appears of the intellect's operation is not sensible.

Also, science concerns only universals, according to Aristotle in *Posterior Analytics* I [87b38–39] and *Metaphysics* VII [1039b27–40a7]. But the soul is a particular. The proof of this is that each soul is the quiddity of what it is the form and species of. But the quiddity of any being is a particular, not a universal. For if the quiddity of a thing, considered as such, were a universal, then since a thing has existence through its quiddity, it would follow that things would have existence and quiddity only when they were

---

[1] Cf. Aristotle, *Post. an.* II 19, 99b35–100a9; *Met.* I 1, 980a22–981a12.

understood. For according to the Commentator, universals exist only when they exist in intellect.[2] Therefore, etc.

The opposite is clear from the account given by Aristotle [402a1–403a2].

[*Reply.*] It should be understood with respect to this question that there is a science of the soul because the soul has operations. These operations reveal its substance and allow us to ascend to the substance or nature of the substance from which these operations proceed. So in some manner the soul {24} is cognizable and has a science that reveals its substance; whence it is true that the soul's operations are cognizable. The reason is this, that from this [cognition of operations] the cognition of another being follows. For the soul's states (*passiones*) are not a being that subsists per se, but a being in another, and do not come from things that are naturally suited to subsist per se. For this reason they point to some other being. So if there were not these operations of the soul, we would know nothing of it; hence we cognize the soul not in its own right, but inasmuch as it is related to these. So we say that the soul is what makes *this* – that is, what makes hearing, seeing, understanding, etc.

From these results it follows that we have no knowledge of a soul or substance that has no operation apparent within us or in the things around us – not based on the mode of knowing that our logic teaches, via sense, memory, experience, etc.[3] For there is nothing that such beings teach, since if they are beings of such a sort, they are naturally hidden.

On this basis, we can reply to the arguments. *To the first*, when it is said that every science has its root in the senses, etc., this argument has two defects, both based on denying the minor. For I say that the soul has operations from which it is cognized. And this is so for two reasons. For even if understanding, the operation of the intellective soul, is not sensible, still the operations and motions of the lower powers that occur along with reason (such as those of the irascible power, etc., and also artificial operations) are sensible and reveal the intellective soul. This is to say that although the operations of the theoretical [intellect] are not sensible, still the operations of the practical [intellect] are sensible. Also, the operations of a craft reveal that the soul's substance exists. The other defect in the argument is this: It is true that we do not understand the intellect in its own right, but [we do understand the intellect] insofar as it is understanding – namely, through a species, insofar as it is something in actuality. This

---

[2] *In de anima* I 8 (p. 12).
[3] That is, the method described in the *Posterior Analytics*. See, e.g., II 19, 100a4–b5.

occurs through phantasms, and it does not understand except through phantasms. Hence it is understood only as it is understanding, etc. And since understanding is like this, it is clear that even if understanding is not sensible, still it is [intelligible], etc.

To the second it should be said that the argument fails, because it proceeds as if the universal and the particular cannot be based on the same thing, but as if they differ in their quiddity, as Plato was forced to say. But in fact this is not the case, because we have the same quidditative being under universal being and particular being. Therefore, etc. {25}

Question 2. *Should the Soul Be Examined Naturally?*

It seems that it should. For Aristotle says in book one [403a27–b19] that the physicist should examine the soul whose states do not exist without matter. But the soul's state of understanding does not exist without matter, nor without a body. Therefore, etc.

Moreover, Aristotle says in *Metaphysics* VI [1026a5–6] that it belongs to the physicist to examine the soul that does not exist without matter. So there is at least this particular conclusion: that it belongs to the physicist to examine some soul.

On the contrary, it is argued that it does not belong to the physicist to present an account of every part of the soul. For the naturalist does not get to make an examination of things that have existence separate from matter – this was written in book one [403b15] – because only the first philosopher gets to examine these. But the intellective soul is immaterial and unmixed, as is said in book three° [429a18–24]. Therefore, etc.

Question 3. *Should the Science of the Soul Be Separate from the Sciences of Bodies?*

It seems that it should not. For Aristotle says in book one [403b11–12] that to whomever it belongs to examine the form, to him it belongs to examine the matter. For example, since it belongs to a doctor to consider the form of health (or a form belonging to someone to whom health belongs), it likewise belongs to a doctor to examine the matter of health, such as the humors that make up one's [bodily] complexion. But the soul is the form of the body, {26} since it is its actuality and perfection, according to Aristotle in book two [412a20]. Therefore, etc.

Moreover, Aristotle [407b13–26] says against Pythagoras that it is absurd

Questions on De Anima I–II

to give and present an account of the soul and say nothing of the body capable of receiving it, by saying how it ought to be. For the soul does not use and inform just any body, but a determinate one. For it does not actualize just any one, indifferently, as in the Pythagorean fables, etc. Therefore, according to Aristotle, it is absurd to present an account of soul and say nothing of the body capable of receiving it. Therefore, if this science is of the soul itself, it will be not only of the soul, but also of the body, etc.

The opposite is argued as follows. When something has separate existence, its science ought to be separate. But there is a soul whose existence is separate, at least with respect to some part of it. Therefore etc. And this is argued universally for the soul: namely, that the science of the soul is universally separate from the science of the body. For this science of the soul is separate from [that of] the vegetative and animals. So since the books *De vegetabilibus* and *De animalibus* present an account of the ensouled body and all its conditions, it follows that no account of this sort will be given here of the body. Therefore this science has the soul alone as its subject, not the ensouled body.

To the first [Q2], I say and it should be understood that the physicist gets to present an account of things that have existence in matter. The soul has existence in matter, aside from doubts about the intellective soul. And it should be further understood that although the intellective soul is separate or has existence separate from the body (as will be explicitly determined below [Q6], by physical means, I say) and in this regard there is no natural science of the soul, still it is not separate with respect to the operations that it has. Instead, it shares with its body in the operations that it has only by means of the body. So there can be a natural science of the soul, on account of the operations that it shares with matter or its body. Through these operations, the soul's substance is revealed; this is so much the case that without the material and the physical, the intellective soul's existence is not established.

Through this the solution to the arguments is clear. For they go through on their own terms. {27}

In reply to what was asked secondly [Q3], whether the science of the soul is separate from the science of the body, it should be understood that I don't see anything doubtful here in this question, aside from what was touched on in the [initial] arguments. For as Aristotle says in book one [407b13–

26], it is absurd to say something about the soul while giving no account of the body capable of receiving it. So it is, then, that there will be no science of the soul that is not also of the body. Conversely, it seems that if this science of the soul is likewise of the body and its conditions, then this science seems not distinct from the science of the vegetative and plants. And notice that the science of the soul is certainly not separate from the body, if it concerns the ensouled body. If this science is separate, then it seems to concern the soul alone, etc.

[*In reply*] to this it should be understood that Avicenna says in his *Liber de anima* [prologue] and likewise Aristotle in *Physics* II [194a16–b15] that to whomever it belongs to present an account of the form, to him it belongs to present an account of what comes into it or up to it. I do not say that if it belongs to someone to present an account of the form, it belongs to him to present an account of the matter unconditionally, with respect to all its conditions. Rather, he who presents an account of the form presents an account of what comes up to it – that is, as regards those conditions by which the matter is made proper for that form. This is why Aristotle said later that it is absurd to say something about the soul while giving no account of the body capable of receiving it. And in this way Aristotle here, in presenting an account of the soul, likewise presents an account of the body as regards those conditions by which it is made the proper matter for the soul, but not as regards all the body's conditions. Thus Aristotle says in book one [409b18–411a25] that there are some operations of the soul that cannot be reduced to the elemental powers, such as hearing etc., but still do not occur without the body. But in the *De animalibus* he presents an account universally of all the conditions, powers, and properties of an ensouled body, and also in the *De plantis* – that is, an account of the whole complex: of what condition the eye is in, and so forth. Here, however, he does not give an account of the ensouled body in this way, but in the first way.

Through this it is clear how to solve the arguments, etc. {28}

Question 4. Is Knowledge Numbered among Good Things?

[. . .]

Question 5. Is Knowledge Honorable?

[. . .] {37}

Question 6. Is Any State Proper to the Soul Itself?

Next, concerning the passage "There is a puzzle," etc. [403a3 ff.], there is a question of whether any state (*passio*) is proper to the soul itself. For Aristotle puzzles over this in the text, whether any state of the soul is proper in such a way that it is separate.

It seems that there is, since that whose being is separate from the body also has an operation that is separate. For as it exists, so it operates. But the intellect is separate, as Aristotle says in book three [430a17, a22]. Therefore, so is its operation, and this seems to be nothing other than understanding.

Moreover, from the text, if any operation of the soul is proper, then the soul is separable [403a10–11], and if it is separable, then so is an operation of it. (Thus the major premise is convertible.) But the soul is separable "as the perpetual from the corruptible," according to book two [413b26–27]. Therefore, etc.

Also, Aristotle in book three [429a27–30], speaking with the thought in mind that the soul is separate, says that some rightly said that the soul is the locus of species, although the whole is not, but only the part of the soul that is intellect, because the other parts receive [species] in an organ. Therefore, understanding is proper to the soul.

Also, he says in book three [429a15–27] that just as matter is potentially all individual forms, likewise the possible intellect is all abstract material forms. And just as matter has no form, nor includes [any] in its essence, so neither does the intellect. Therefore it is not a power in a body, and therefore it has a proper operation beyond the body.

Moreover, every state in matter is individual, but the things understood are universal forms, and therefore abstract. And if so, then they are not states in the physical matter of animals.

On the contrary. The soul understands, which does not occur without phantasms, {38} [and so] it needs a body for its understanding. [But] according to Aristotle [431a16–17], all understanding is like this. Therefore understanding is not separate or proper.

Also, according to book two [414a12–13], the soul is that by which we sense, live, take in nourishment, and understand. Thus it is we who understand, and so it is not the soul that is said to understand or to sense, but that which has the soul, as Aristotle concludes in the same place [408b13–15]. Therefore understanding is not proper to the soul, but to the composite, etc.

A reply should be made to this, but since this will have more of a place below, in book three, we should go over it quickly here.[4]

It seems to some that an intellective substance gives existence to the body just as the others, the nutritive and sensory, in such a way that the soul as a whole (*universaliter*) is the perfection and form of the body. And yet there is a power of the soul that is separable, the intellect, and they say and acknowledge that its operation is separate. And that the soul as a whole is the actuality of the body, this is something they maintain because it is we who understand, and the soul is that by which we understand or are understanding, as Aristotle says in book two [414a13]. But that by which something operates formally is its form. Therefore, etc.

In actual fact this view cannot in any way be maintained. For an operation that is separate from matter and a power that is separate do not indicate that their substance is the form of a body. So if understanding is a separate operation, this does not indicate that the understanding substance is the actuality of a body.

Also, this view contains a contradiction. For it says that the way we understand is that understanding is a state in matter, since it says that we understand through the intellect, which is the actuality of the body. This contradicts the initial claim that understanding is a separate state. Hence this view cannot be maintained.

So we should reply to the question in another way. When it is asked whether there is an operation proper to the soul, etc., the puzzle seems to lie with the operation of understanding. I say to this that there are two ways we can understand the claim that the operation of understanding is common to the soul and to the body, or that the soul needs the body for understanding. It might mean [a] that understanding is a state in which the soul needs the body as the subject and matter in which, as in a subject, understanding has to occur – just as, in order to see, sight needs the eye, {39} in which it exists as in a subject. In this way the soul does not need the body; rather, understanding is in this way a state proper to the soul, given that it lacks a body that serves as subject and matter. For it does not need the body as an organ and subject in which it exists or has to occur as in a subject. For if that were the case then understanding would not be abstract. But [b] the soul does need the body as an object in order to understand, though not as its subject.

---

[4] No record has been found of the author's treatment of *De anima* III. But these issues are discussed in more detail in Bk. II Q4.

So if the question is asked in the first way, it should be said that it does not need the body. But if it is asked in the second way – Does the soul need the body as an object in order to understand? – I say that it does, since Aristotle shows [403a8–10] that understanding is not proper to the soul in this way, if the intellect is phantasia (as some said), or is not phantasia but in truth does not occur without a phantasm. And since it is phantasia, or does not occur without a phantasm, it will not occur without the body. For this shows that understanding needs the body or a phantasm as an object. So understanding is common in this way: in the way it does not occur without phantasia. For, as Aristotle says, phantasms stand to intellect just as colors stand to sight [431a14–15]. For the intellect is joined to us not because of intellect, but because (according to Aristotle in book three) the objects of intellect° are joined to us – not under the aspect of being objects of intellect, but under the aspect of phantasms. As Aristotle says (here for instance), phantasms are necessary as an object. In effect, he is saying that understanding is something common to the soul and the body, and that the soul, to carry out this operation, needs the body as an object.

So whoever wants the intellect to be joined to us as a form, in virtue of its substance, cannot arrive at this unless he holds, as Alexander did,[5] that the intellect is a generable and corruptible power. (We will investigate this later [Q18].) Likewise, he must necessarily hold that understanding is then joined to us as to matter. But for understanding and intellect to be joined to us through its object – this way of being joined is easy to understand. So those who argue against this manner of juncture are right to argue that we understand not as the subject of this operation, but as the things without which the intellect does not understand. Thus they have no argument against this manner of juncture except that it would then follow that {40} we do not understand. And they [themselves] certainly prove that we understand not in such a way that understanding is united to us as a form existing in matter, but in the aforesaid way. And this seems to be Aristotle's intent here.

It should also be understood that the joining of intellect to its objects – the phantasms through which it understands – is not entirely like the joining of sight to colors. And I say so for a specific reason: that the joining of sight to colors is accidental, whereas the joining of intellect to phantasms is natural. For it belongs to the nature of intellect to be at once united

---

[5] Alexander of Aphrodisias, *De intellectu.*

with phantasms, as soon as there are phantasms. For the union of sight with colors occurs in virtue of sight's being close to the colors; this occurs accidentally, given that there can be color and sight without sight's seeing. Thus the union of sight with colors occurs only when they have been brought close in position; but they are variable in their position, and so such a union is accidental. The joining of intellect to phantasms, in contrast, occurs essentially. For when the intellect (and in general every separate substance) is united with a body in any way, as its mover or otherwise, then it is (considered in itself) naturally and always united with that body. So, as Aristotle held,[6] all things that are moved in a certain way by a given substance are said to be moved by that given mover of themselves and naturally. For they are united with their movers by their nature: not by closeness or by a coming together of accidents, but essentially. They are moveable through their nature – that is, according to that nature by which they are moveable by these movers – and they are incorruptible by that same necessity. Thus Averroes says in book three [text 5] that although the agent and possible intellects are eternal, the speculative intellect is corruptible and generable, because for it the agent and possible intellects are not enough – phantasms are also necessary. Thus the speculative intellect is generated in phantasms, but in such a way that this intellect naturally, considered in itself, always understands – just as those separate substances, considered in themselves, always move. Hence phantasms are required, etc. And the reason for saying these things is that the intellect is not united with phantasms as sight is with colors.

All the arguments are solved through this.

When you say that it is separate in virtue of its substance, it is true that it is separate from matter that serves as its subject. In this way, then, its operation is also separate, and so in order to understand it does not need the body as its subject and matter. Still, it needs the body as an object. All the arguments for that first part fail for the same reason. {41}

You argue on the contrary that understanding is common, etc. This is true, but you have seen in what way.

You argue that we understand. This is true, and you have seen in what way: We do not understand as the subject of this operation but as the object, as was clear, etc.

---

[6] *De caelo* I 8–9, 276a18–279a11.

This account seems to be true according to the meaning of Aristotle, when rightly expounded.

Question 7. Does a Spherical Body Touch at a Point Applied to a Plane?

[. . .]

Question 8. Can a Spherical Body Move without Anything Pushing It?

[. . .]

Question 9. Can Matter Be Made Universal, and Can an Aggregate Be Made Universal?

[. . .] {46}

Question 10. Are the Things Signified by Utterances Actually in the Soul, or Not Only in the Soul But Actually Outside the Soul and Only Potentially in the Soul?

Spoken words retain their significations even when their significata do not exist outside the soul. Thus it seems that they signify something that exists only in the soul.

It should be said that there are some [things] that have existence only within the soul, and some that have existence per se only outside the soul, such as matter, and some that exist both within and outside the soul. So I say that spoken words signifying those that have existence only within the soul and have no existence outside the soul – and there are many such [things] – these I say signify something that exists only in the soul. So if that which they signify were not to exist in the soul, then it would not be possible for them to signify. Second intentions are of this sort: 'genus,' 'species,' etc.

Those, however, that exist only outside the soul, and are not intelligible per se, those considered as such do not have expressions signifying them, because what is not contained within the mind is not signifiable. As Aristotle says in *Metaphysics* VII [1040a10], someone who does not cognize a thing does not give it a name. {47}

Concerning those that have existence outside the soul and can exist in the soul, if you ask whether expressions signifying them signify something that exists in the soul or outside it, I say that such spoken words signify things containing each of those: both cognized being (*esse cognitum*) and also noncognized being is contained in them. A sign of this is that each [kind of] predicate holds true for terms of this sort:

> Man is a universal
> Man is a species

These are predicates that are truly said of something only when they exist in the soul. Therefore 'man' signifies something that exists in the soul. Also,

> Man runs

is true, even though the predicate applies only to something outside the soul. Therefore 'man' signifies something to which each of these may apply: existence in the soul and outside the soul. For [things such as] these to be signified, however, it is necessary for them to have existence in the soul, whereas they may exist outside the soul.

Question 11. Should We Posit a Smallest Body, in Terms of Action?

[. . .]

Question 12. Is the Soul in Motion per se?

[. . .]

Question 13. Is the Soul the Cause of Rest?

[. . .]

Question 14. Can a Thing Be Divisible, Even as a Being within Intellect?

[. . .]

Question 15. Do the Elements in a Mixed Body Have Harmony?

[. . .] {55}

Question 16. Is the Soul a Harmony?

It is, because when the body's harmony is corrupted, the soul is corrupted, and vice versa. This would not be so, if the soul were not a harmony.

On the contrary is the text [407b27–408a29].

[*Reply.*] It should be said that the soul is not a harmony, because some actions and states cannot be reduced to the composition, constitution,° or proportion that we call harmony, and consequently such a harmony does not suit the soul's actions. Consequently, if one considers only this composition or proportion of the elements – putting aside what comes after this composition – it will not yield the cause of the actions and states that appear regarding the soul. {56}

But the soul is a substantial nature that unites the elements and comes after this proportion. It gives the elements a single existence, an existence that had nothing from the elements. So there are actions belonging to the soul itself that are not reduced to the elements. For the soul neither is an element nor comes from the elements, and thus its actions are not reduced to the elements. Hence the soul is the substantial nature of those elements in a mixed body, whereas harmony is not any substantial nature of the elements. Therefore, etc.

You argue that when the harmony is corrupted, the soul is corrupted. It should be replied that this is not because that proportion is the soul. Instead, this occurs for another reason, that the soul is that existence or being in which the elements are proportioned. So it is that when the harmony is corrupted, the soul (or what comes after this harmony) is also corrupted – but not because the soul is this harmony.

Alternatively, it should be replied in another way, in other words that come down to the same thing, that that harmony, composition, or condition of those elements in a mixed body is the matter in which the soul has existence, just as a form has existence in its matter. But now just because once the matter is corrupted the form is corrupted that has existence only in that matter, it does not follow that for this reason the form is the matter itself, or vice versa. This likewise does not follow in the present case. Therefore, etc.

Question 17. Is the Soul United to the Body through a Medium or without any Medium?

It seems that it is through a medium, because one thing is not made from many unless there is something uniting them. The soul and the body are distinct. Therefore etc.

The contrary appears the case because of Aristotle in *Metaphysics* VIII [1045b7–24]. He says that some erred in looking for the medium by which form would be united to matter.

Moreover, things that are united through their nature as actuality and potentiality do not need any medium uniting them. Soul and body are of this sort. {57}

It should be replied that there is no medium uniting the soul with the body disposed for it which is its matter. The reason for this is that actuality and potentiality are by their nature one being. For if one thing comes from wax and its shape, this need not occur through any medium. So too, none is needed for one thing to be made from soul and body, according to Aristotle in book two [412b6–9]. Therefore soul and body are one by the unity, I say, of actuality. For in each and every thing, actuality is one: Thus the unity in a being comes from the unity of its actuality. For potentiality is not a being in its own right; instead, that which exists, exists through actuality. For this reason, if the actuality is one, it follows that the potentiality and actuality is one. And this is evident in the case of the bronze and its shape. Since they stand to each other as potentiality and actuality, if there were not any being in actuality other than shape, then the bronze and its shape would be entirely and unqualifiedly one being. But in fact it is the case that the bronze has an existence other than shape, and so they are one per accidens and not one unconditionally (*simpliciter*). But if you remove from the bronze that through which it is actually bronze and there remains only the potentiality for shape, then this thing would be entirely one, as potentiality and actuality. And this is what we seek in the present case.

Actuality and potentiality, therefore, are one being, because potentiality is not a being in its own right. Instead, that which exists, exists through actuality, and the actuality that belongs to potentiality belongs to its being (*sui entis*) in potentiality. And since actuality and potentiality are by their nature one being, it follows that when they do not have unity, they also do not have status as a being (*nec habet entitatem*). And so actuality is not a being unless, together with potentiality, it is one being. And so the separation of actuality or form from potential being is its corruption: Indeed, the separation of form from matter is the corruption of both, the matter and the form. For even if the matter is not corrupted in its essence through the form's separation from it, it is nevertheless corrupted as this being. So since they are by their nature one being, it follow that neither is being, where each with the other makes one being.

You argue that one thing is not made from many without a medium. It should be replied that where they exist as actuality and potentiality, there is one thing, as is clear from Aristotle in *Metaphysics* VIII [1045b16–24]. {58}

Question 18. Is the Intellect a Substance That Is Not Corrupted?

Why° does Aristotle say that the intellect is a substance that is not corrupted [408b18–19], and why do all say and presuppose this, when there are few who, when pressed, demonstrate it with certainty? For it does not seem that this *has* been demonstrated with certainty. Hence we ask about this, and we never cease to ask, for this is what we should never cease to place in front of our eyes, as the Commentator says.[7]

And it seems that the intellect is corruptible. [For] the intellect does not have existence abstracted from matter; therefore the intellect is corruptible. The inference is entirely evident through its converse: Aristotle shows in book two [413b26–27] that the intellect is incorruptible because it is not mixed with the body. Hence matter is such that privation and nonbeing are always mixed in with it, and so everything having matter is corruptible, as the Commentator says [79] and [Aristotle] concludes in *Physics* I [192a25]. Therefore this inference is evident, because it states the cause.

Proof of the antecedent: The objects of intellect do not have being abstracted from matter; therefore neither does the intellect. This inference is likewise clearly evident, because the objects of intellect are had only within intellect. Proof of this antecedent: That which is one with respect to form is divided only through matter, because that which is one by form is not divided by form, because then there would be something that was one and distinct in the same respect, which is absurd. So that which is one with respect to form is divided only by matter. I then argue: An object of intellect that is one with respect to form, remaining an object of intellect, is divided and multiplied into more than one object. The proof of this is

---

[7] *In de anima* I 12, p. 17.

that an object of intellect that is one with respect to form is understood by me, by you, and by Socrates, and that object is divided in me, in you, and in Socrates. For if not, then whatever I understand, you would understand too; for if this object were not divided in me and in you, then whenever I would be understanding through this object, you {59} would be too. Therefore an object of intellect is divided; therefore it is so by the matter of intellect; therefore it is corruptible. And this argument states the cause, as before. Proof of the minor, etc.

[*On the contrary.*] The objects of intellect have being abstracted from matter; therefore so does the intellect. Proof of this antecedent: One thing that can be in many, or one being with which being-in-many is not incompatible, is one with respect to form and is abstract. So that one thing that is such in its existence that with respect to that existence being-in-many is not incompatible with it, as it is one, that thing has abstracted existence. For something that is one in this way in its existence is a being and is one thing abstracted from matter. The proof of this is that a being that is not abstracted from matter in its existence is a being that cannot be in many. And the causal proof of each proposition is that what is one with respect to matter certainly cannot exist in many with respect to the same existence. But in fact it is the case that what is a being in this way, and one in this way, and not abstracted from matter, is undivided because of matter. Therefore that thing is one in its existence and not in many, because what is one in many is not one because of matter. Therefore, our proposition is clear: What is one in this way in its existence, with which being-in-many is not incompatible, that is one abstracted thing. Then I take up the minor premise: The object of intellect considered as the object of intellect, the universal, is one in its account (*ratione*); it exists in such a way as to be one thing such that being-in-many is incompatible neither with its unity nor its state of existence. Therefore that being, one in this way, was not one being through matter, but was abstracted from matter.

Also, form is multiplied in matter in this way: by a multiplication that is not opposed to the unity that it has in its existence as an object of intellect. Therefore, its existence as an object of intellect was not in matter, but was abstracted from matter. So since Socrates in his existence is a being and so one being − one through matter − being many through matter is incompatible with him, nor can° Socrates be found in many. Therefore if an object of intellect were one in matter, one through matter, it could not then be many. Therefore, since an object of intellect, considered as such, can be in many, it follows that it is not in matter. Therefore, an object of intellect is abstracted from matter. Therefore, the intellect also has the sort of existence that is separate from matter, sempeternal and incorruptible. Therefore, etc.

This should be granted. {60}

To the argument for the opposite, we reply as follows. The argument was this: The intellect does not have existence abstracted from matter; therefore it is corruptible. And the inference holds causally, because matter, since privation is mixed in with it, is the cause of the corruption of those in which it exists. The antecedent is proved, because an object of intellect does not have abstracted existence, or is not abstracted, and therefore neither is intellect. This inference is clear, because an object of intellect has existence only in the intellect, as form in matter.

The antecedent of this inference was also proved,° because with respect to form it is one thing only. If it is divided, it is divided only through matter, because what is one in every way, with respect to both form and matter, is one in the way that Socrates is. Something one in that way is not divided. But an object of intellect – one being with respect to form – is divided. Therefore it is divided through matter. But what is divided through matter, inasmuch as it is a being of this sort, is not abstracted. An object of intellect is of this sort; therefore it is not abstracted. But an object of intellect, remaining one being with respect to form, is divided, and the proof of this is as follows: One and the same thing, with respect to form, can be the object of my intellect, your intellect, and likewise Socrates's intellect. But it cannot be an object for me, you, and Socrates, unless it is divided. The proof of this is that if you say that that object of intellect is not divided in any way, but remains undivided in every way, then since it is through an object of intellect that I am formally understanding, and likewise you and others, and since according to you the object of intellect remains the same and undivided in all ways, as you say, it follows that whenever I would be understanding through this object, you would like- wise be understanding through that object and likewise Socrates. This is false. And this last inference is clarified through an example. For if a form, such as *human*, were the same for all in the same [respect], undivided, so that it is not divisible through matter, no more than through form, then whenever Socrates would be a human being through this form of human being, so likewise would Plato at once be a human being through that form of human being, since each is a human being. But this is false; therefore so is the first.

I reply to this argument by granting all the inferences apart from the last. The last I deny. {61}

Question 19. Is an Atom a Body?

[. . .]

Question 20. Is an Atom a Natural Body?

[. . .]

Question 21. Does an Atom Move Naturally or Violently?

[. . .] {64}

[Book Two]

What earlier philosophers proposed . . . [412a3 ff.] Concerning this second book it is asked first whether the soul is an accident.

Question 1. Is the Soul an Accident?

It seems that it is, because it is the actuality of an actual being; therefore it is an accident. The antecedent is clear, because the body, from the fact that it is a body, is an actual being, the actuality of which is the soul.

The opposite is maintained here by Aristotle [412a19], who says that it is a substance with respect to form. {65}

Also, the Commentator says here [II 2, p. 130] that it is a substance. His argument is that what is more noble in an ensouled body is substance, not accident. But this is the soul. Thus the Commentator says here that everything more noble in some respect is of less worth in nobility than the soul. And we grant this.

To the argument that it is the actuality of an actual being, because it is the actuality of the body, etc., I reply in two ways. First, a form is the actuality of its matter and of the aggregate. A substantial form, considered as the actuality and existence of the aggregate, is the actuality of an actual being, although considered as the actuality of its matter it is the actuality of a potential being. I then say that the existence that is the actuality of something actually existing as matter is an accident of it. The soul is not such an actuality – that is, of something actually existing as matter. But that existence that is the form of something actually existing as an aggregate is not an accident in this way.

Also, when you say that it is the actuality of a body as matter and that this is an actual being, I say that nothing keeps a substantial form from being the actuality of some actual being, not through its substantial form, but through some accident. But it is impossible for a substantial form to be the actuality of some being that is actual through [another] substantial form already giving existence to its matter. It is certainly necessary, however, for there to be certain dispositions, such as *organic, physical*, etc.

Question 2. *Is the Soul the First Actuality?*

It seems that it is not, because a being's first actuality is existence, as is written in the *De causis* [prop. 1]. Therefore an ensouled body has existence before it is ensouled, because there is some existence before there is soul, just as it is a being before being ensouled.

Moreover, the soul is the potentiality of the body; therefore it is not the actuality. For the text says [413a1] that the soul is the potentiality of the body, just as sight is the potentiality of its organ. {66}

Moreover, the soul is the body's actuality in the way that considering is an actuality, and so not in the way that knowledge is.[8] Therefore it is a second actuality, not a first. The major is proved: The ultimate form that comes to things with souls is the soul. Therefore it is the final actuality, not the first.

Moreover, when what exists in a thing suffices for the operation or passive reception (*passio*) distinctive of that being, it is impossible for that operation or action not to occur in that being (unless that which receives the action is missing), or for the distinctive reception not to occur (unless that which is active is missing). So since what is ensouled has a principle, the soul, that suffices for the action or passive reception, it therefore seems that the soul, unless it is impeded, should be in its final perfection.

Moreover, the nutritive soul is always in its final perfection, as the Commentator says [II 5, p. 136]; therefore so is the sensory soul.

---

[8] See Aristotle, *De anima* I 1, 412a22–23.

The opposite is stated by Aristotle [412a23–26]: for the sensory soul is the actuality of the body in sleep, but someone is not then actually sensing.

Question 3. Is the Soul the Actuality of a Body Having Life in Potentiality?

It seems that it is not, because life and soul are the same. Therefore the soul in actuality [is] life in actuality. Therefore what has a soul in actuality has life in actuality. Therefore the soul is the actuality of what has life in actuality, not in potentiality.

[*Reply to Q2.*] It should be said that the soul is the first actuality, and this is because a body having a soul certainly has it in such a way that those operations naturally suited to come from the soul do not [always] come from it. So, according to Aristotle [412a23–26], what has a soul is not always in its final perfection: It does not always sense or always understand – at least not with the intellect that the perfection of a human being consists in. So because the body has the soul in such a way that it is not always in its final actuality, the soul is accordingly called the actuality of what is potentially living.[9] Thus the body having a soul has life in potentiality not as semen or fruit does, nor in the final perfection {67} of life, but in an intermediate way. It is like someone who has knowledge dispositionally – not like someone who is entirely ignorant, nor like someone who is actually considering.

You argue that existence is the first actuality of being and that an ensouled body is a being; therefore existence is its first actuality. This is true, but the first actuality that is the existence of an ensouled body is nothing other than the existence that is the soul, and they are distinct only according to reason.

You argue that the soul is the potentiality of the body and therefore not its actuality. I say that nothing prevents the soul from being potential and actual in different respects: actual with respect to its matter, potential with respect to its operations, which are naturally suited to come from the soul even if they are not [now] coming. Sight, for example, is the actuality of an organ: for it exists in someone asleep differently from how it exists in semen, which is the source from which living comes.

You argue that the soul is the final perfection of an ensouled body,

---

[9] *De anima* II 1, 412a28.

indeed that it is even the noblest found in material things, according to the Commentator in book three. Therefore it is not the first actuality. I reply to this that the soul's being the ultimate perfection in material things should be understood of the soul as it is in its ultimate actuality, which is considering.

You argue: How will the soul exist in an ensouled body when an operation naturally suited to come from it (since it is the principle of operation) does not come? For it seems that the principle of action is missing in someone asleep, since he does not act, or that the passive principle is missing, since the agent is present (or vice versa). So necessarily, when the active and passive are present and not impeded, and their natures remain the same, they seem to act necessarily. Anyone who denies this denies everything I know. (I say this, to be sure, on behalf of the other view.)

It should be replied, however, that in someone asleep the principle from which the action is naturally suited to come exists only in accidental potentiality. For the person has that principle differently from how the semen does, nor does it require an essential transformation, as the semen does. So someone asleep has that principle, but it is impeded, just as a higher heavy object has a principle through which it ought to be lower, but it is not lower because it is impeded. For it is a principle capable of being impeded, but it is not so [impeded] everywhere. So I say that the principle of sense exists in someone sleeping, but it is impeded.

As for the question of whether the soul is the actuality of what has life in potentiality [Q3], this is clear from what has been said. {68}

Question 4. Is the Intellective Soul Conjoined to the Body with Respect to Its Substance in Such a Way as to Be Its Substantial Perfection?

Next there is a question of whether the soul is the actuality of the body in such a way that through its substance it is the form of the body. Second there is a question about the distinction among the soul's parts and powers [QQ5–6].

As regards the first, that which seems to be in doubt is the intellect. So it is asked whether the intellective soul is conjoined to the body with respect to its substance in such a way as to be its substantial perfection.

It seems that it is. [For] Aristotle says in *Metaphysics* IX [1047a24ff, 1049b13ff] that potentiality is revealed only through actuality. Thus we

know that a being that is heating and acting on other things is hot, and
we know that heat is its form. So what acts through the action of heat is
known to be hot. Now a form is a first actuality like knowledge, a
potentiality. For a first actuality is like a disposition and similar to a
potentiality. Therefore, it will be revealed only through its action. But
understanding (*intelligere*) is the actuality of a body. Therefore, the intellect
is the actuality of a body. The same is clear from the fact that it is the
human being who understands. For the soul is that by which we first
understand, as is said in the text [414a12–14]. Therefore if we are understanding, we are existing (*entes*) through intellect, just as if something is
heating, it is existing through heat (as fire is). Therefore [the intellect]
seems to be the actuality of the body, etc.

Also, this seems to be the truth according to Aristotle. For after he
defined soul in general "in outline" [413a9], he subsequently showed, in
distinguishing the soul through its powers, that through each of its parts
the soul is the actuality of the body. Therefore it seems according to this
principle to be the actuality of the body and the form.

On the contrary, it is argued as follows.

1. If the intellect were the first actuality of the body, then understanding
would be the actuality of the body and of matter. Although some have
wanted to deny this, it is entirely clear, regardless of whether understanding
is actuality or existence. For how will something be hot and not something
heating? How will it be a being through intellect formally and not understand in any way? But understanding is not the actuality of the body,
because it does not have an organ, {69} as will be said in book three
[429a24–26]. Nor should you say that what is true is that it does not have
a *determinate* organ. For it is also not the case that the whole body consti-
tutes the organ, in the way that the whole of the flesh does so for touch.
For the intellect does not belong to a mixed body, but is separate. Also, if
this were the case then the whole body would understand, and in every
single part.

2. The universality of the objects of intellect shows these objects to be
abstract. But if they are abstract, then so is the intellect. And this is what
Aristotle says [429b16–22]: that the intellect is a power abstracted from the
body, and therefore is not the perfection of the body.

3. Aristotle says here that the intellect is "a different kind of soul" and
is "separated," etc. [413b26]. Therefore, it is not the same substance as the
others. But if it were the perfection of the body, then the human body

would have multiple substantial perfections and then at least one of those perfections would have to be accidental to the body.

4. The intellect is separated from the body, and therefore is not the perfection and form of the body, because form is separated not in being but in concept (*ratione*) alone, as the Commentator says[10] and as is proved by reason as follows. Potentiality and actuality are one being, for as Aristotle says in *Metaphysics* IX [1046b28–47a30], that same thing that was in potentiality is later in actuality. Then I argue: Potentiality and actuality are one being through their nature; therefore when they are not one being, they are not a being; therefore they are corrupted. But a form separated from matter is not one being with the matter; therefore it is not a being.

5. Separate and nonseparate do not belong to the same species, nor even to the same genus, as Aristotle says at the end of *Metaphysics* X [1058b26–59a10]. Therefore much less do they belong to what is numerically the same. Therefore, since the intellect is separated, it will not belong to a single species with the body, and so much less with itself when united to the body. For that which is separate by its nature is not separate by accident. For there are some things that do not have existence by accident, and what is separate is not among those that inhere by accident. Therefore that which is separate is separate by its nature, nor does any impediment enter into such cases, as Aristotle says in the same passage. Therefore, by its nature the separate is never not separate, nor vice versa. Therefore since the intellective soul {70} is at some time separated from the body, it follows that by its nature it was *never* the form of the body.

6. Aristotle says [414a19–25] that they spoke well who said that the soul does not exist without the body, because it is the actuality of the body. Therefore if the intellect does at some time exist without the body, it was not its actuality or form.

Some say that, in its being, the intellect is the actuality of the body, just as form is the actuality of matter, but that in its operation it is a separate power. Aristotle says in the text [413a11–15, 415a18–20] that we should come to a cognition of the soul through its operations: These are posterior, but they are more known to us. How then does anyone say that the intellect's quiddity is the actuality of the body and matter, when its operation, which is to understand (*intelligere*), does not reveal this, nor does any

---

[10] *In Metaphys.* VIII 3.

other operation reveal it? For what within the intellect is more known to us? Certainly nothing of it is more known to us than understanding itself. Therefore, if understanding is not united to the body, but is a separate state, then certainly there is nothing that reveals the intellect, with respect to its substance, to be conjoined to the body. So what Aristotle says about the communication of intellect with body, this is understanding – if understanding is a state that is not in the body. Aristotle's intent therefore seems to be that the intellect is not conjoined to the body with respect to its substance. And they interpret Aristotle as saying in book three [429b4–5] that the intellect is separate as regards its operation, but not as regards its substance and essence. But this is not clear for Aristotle; indeed it ought to run in the opposite way for him, because otherwise the intellect's quiddity in us would be revealed only through the intellect's operation (*intelligere*).

The intention is to state that there are some operations separate from those that are forms of matter (for instance, that jet attracts straw, a magnet iron, and that jasper restricts blood) and that therefore likewise the soul can be the form of the body, whereas its operation will be separate.[11] This does not succeed, however, nor is it a demonstration. It is true that jasper does not restrict blood by the nature of its matter – as through the form and act that are the cause of this operation – and this is likewise true for a magnet with respect to iron, and so on. So in these cases it is clear that a cause cannot be supplied from the nature of the elements, if these come from a separate power. {71} But this is irrelevant to the issue. It is evident enough that jasper does not restrict blood through the nature of its matter (air, water, etc.), as it in fact does through the act and form through which that operation occurs. Still, the body of the jasper restricts blood inasmuch as it has a form, just as the eye senses because it has a form. But if they are right in the case of jasper, then I too am likewise right in the case of sight: Thus the organ of sight would not sense, because from the nature of the matter that belongs to the organ, no cause can be supplied as to why it senses as it does. Yet sight is not a separate power. So if I were to say that the eye senses only through its form, seeing would not for this reason be separate, would it? And if that had been right in the case of jasper, then likewise for the case of the eye; nor, as far as I am concerned, is there anything more as regards the subject heating and the jasper restricting. And

---

[11] Compare Thomas Aquinas, *De unitate intellectus* ch. 1 lines 469–99.

one can no more conclude that this operation is abstract than that the operation of sense is.

Also, I argue as follows. A magnet close to iron attracts the iron, since an agent attracts and acts at a definite distance. So it attracts iron when it is nearby, and when it is remote it does not. And likewise with jet and straw. Therefore this operation has something from both matter and form. For it has its nearness and distance from matter; therefore it does not have its operation from a separate form. For acting at one distance and not at another is due not to a separate form but only to the material.

If this is the case – that is, insofar as understanding is not a state in matter, but the objects of intellect are separate – and if the intellect is incorporeal, as Aristotle holds [429a24–26] and as all profess, then I say that it is not the actuality of the body as its substance, in the way that form is the actuality of its matter as its substance. For its operation does not teach this, that it is the actuality of a body. For we should always attend to the appearances, and from the appearances we should conclude this: that the intellect is not the form of the body. For potentiality is cognized only through actuality; therefore the substance of intellect, since it is a nature in potentiality, is cognized only through the act of understanding. And if the body is not engaged in understanding through intellect, in such a way that understanding exists in the body as in a substance and in matter, but instead understanding is abstracted from the body, then the intellect will not be that through which the body itself is actualized.

Reply to the arguments for the opposite. You say that it is the actuality of a body, and also that nothing understands through the intellect that is not a being through the intellect, and that we understand through the intellect. To these I reply that the intellect {72} is the actuality and perfection of the body – but not in the way that you want. Instead, it is a different kind of perfection from that of the senses. For I say to the argument that we understand and the intellect does not, as Aristotle says in book one [408b13–15], not in such a way that understanding is shared (*communicetur*) with the body as with its matter and subject, as matter shares in the operation of form, but in the way in which the intellect does not understand without a body naturally united to it, playing the part of object rather than subject. So it understands only through a phantasm belonging to the body – as its object, not because the intellect shares understanding with the body as its subject. And the appearances teach this about intellect:

for according to what Aristotle says in book three [431a14–17], phantasms are to intellect as color is to sight. And so Aristotle proved in book one [403a8–10] that the intellect is conjoined, because either it is phantasia or does not occur without a phantasm: for it shares with the body and needs the body as its object, not as its subject. Hence understanding is proper to the soul and not to the body – when the body is treated as its subject. But not otherwise. For in understanding the soul needs the body as its object, and rules the body in many of its actions. So although understanding is a state that is abstracted from the body as subject, it nevertheless is not abstracted from the body as object. Instead it has in this respect a natural conjunction with the body, because through the body's phantasms it understands, and with respect to the difference among phantasms in goodness and badness, human beings are ruled in different ways by intellect, some better and some worse. This is why Aristotle said in the *De somno* [464a17–b4] that the phantasms of the just are better.

It was then said that the soul – that is, the intellective soul – is not the actuality and form of the body. But from this the greatest of absurdities seems to follow.[12] For if this is so, then it follows that we do not understand; so from this it follows that human beings do not understand. Nor does the Commentator's way out succeed: He says that because the objects of intellect are joined to us, the intellect is also for that reason joined to us.[13] Against this way out are the following arguments:

1. According to Aristotle here [417b16–17], the first sensory impression comes from generation, but the second does not. Therefore if the intellect is joined to us {73} because the objects of intellect, phantasms, are joined to us and these are also joined to intellect, it then seems that the intellect is not joined to us through the first generation, just as intellection is not.[14]

2. Phantasms, inasmuch as they are within us, are material and not abstract. But inasmuch as they are actually understood, they are entirely abstracted from matter. Therefore, what is united to the intellect is not the

---

[12] For the following arguments, see Thomas Aquinas, *De unitate intellectus* ch. 3, lines 24–319.

[13] *In de anima* III 5 (p. 390).

[14] The senses are first actualized when the animal is generated, but they don't go into second actuality until they receive sensory impressions. One would expect the same to hold for the intellect, but on Averroes's account we come to have an intellect not when we are generated, but only when we have the appropriate phantasms. That is to say, we acquire intellect when we acquire an actual intellection: First and second actuality come at the same time.

same as what is united to us. Therefore, the intellect will not be united to us through those objects of intellect, and therefore we do not understand.

3. On the Commentator's account – that the objects of intellect are joined to us whereas the intellect, with respect to its substance, is not – it seems that we are understood rather than that we understand. So a person's phantasms are understood, but he will not understand, as is further clear on the Commentator's account. Nor does there seem to be another possible account on which someone understands through intellect, except that he is a being through intellect. Therefore if a human being is not a being through intellect, he does not understand through intellect.

4. If you say that one thing is made out of an intellect that moves and a body that is moved, then I ask whether 'human being' is a name (a) only for the body, or (b) for the aggregate of the intellect and the ensouled body, or (c) for the intellect alone. And however you reply, it is impossible for a human being to understand as long as he is not one thing made of intellect and body in the way that one thing is made of matter and form.[15] The proof of this is as follows.

4b. If you say that 'human being' is the name for an aggregate of an intellect that moves and a body that is moved, then since a human being is not one being, it will therefore not have one action; therefore human beings do not understand. In this same way, since a sailor and his ship are not one being, it does not follow that when the sailor understands the aggregate understands. Only the sailor does, because they are not one being. In the same way, it would not be the human being that sees through the eye, if the eye and the human being were not a single being. Therefore likewise in the present case.

4a. If you say that 'human being' is the name of the ensouled body alone, and not of the aggregate of body and intellect, then the same result will obtain. Aristotle holds in *Metaphysics* IX [1050a30–36] that there are some operations that do not pass into external matter, and some that do. His example of the second is building; his example of the first is understanding. So understanding is an operation that does not pass into external matter. But it would do so if it were the case that a human being understands because he is the external matter [of the intellect], {74} etc.

Also, when an operation passes into external matter, this is so only with respect to the opposite states and the opposite denomination: So on this

15 Compare Thomas Aquinas, *Summa theologiae* 1a 76.1c.

account a human being would be said to be understood and not to understand. I say this on the assumption that understanding is an operation passing into external matter in the way that the act of building passes into a house. For the house is said not to build but to be built. It is true that a thing sometimes produces motion because it is moved, and then it passes into external matter, and not with respect to the opposite denomination. A thing heats, for instance, because it is heated, and that into which it passes is likewise said to be heated and to heat. If it is said that understanding passes into external matter in this way, then on the contrary: the operation of a primary agent can pass into external matter (not with respect to the opposite denomination) only if the basis (*principium*) of that primary agent is produced in that matter. Heat, for instance, can pass into the aforesaid matter in the aforesaid way only if the basis of its being hot is generated in that matter. If this is what happens, then it is argued: If understanding passes in this way into the ensouled body that you call a human being, then the primary agent brings about within a human being the basis through which understanding occurs. But this is the intellect. And if this is what happens, then it would follow that human beings would understand only if they were to have that basis that is intellect as their form. This is the opposite of what we are supposing.

4c. If you say that 'human being' is the name for intellect and not for the aggregate or for the other part that is called the ensouled body, then the reply is as follows. [1.] It is described how for this reason Plato and certain other philosophers held that a human being just is the intellect.[16] But it is clear that, even on this view, a human being would not understand. [For] Aristotle holds in *Metaphysics* VII [1034a18–35b1] that animated matter, such as flesh and bones, belongs to the account and definition of a human being. So anyone who did not have flesh and bones in such a way as to be capable of their action would be a human being only equivocally. And one would not be capable of such actions if 'human being' were a name for the intellect. Therefore a human being is not the intellect; for when soul is deprived of body, a human being remains only equivocally.

Also [2], Plato says that the intellect uses the body as its mover.[17] But it is the mover of the body through the will, according to what Aristotle says in book three [433a21–25]. Therefore, the intellect is clothed with the

---

[16] Nemesius, *De natura hominis* ch. 1 (p. 5); ch. 3 (pp. 51–52).
[17] *Timaeus*, 34b–37c; cf. Aristotle, *De anima* I 3, 406b25–28.

body, as the body's mover, and clothes it in this way: that when it wants to it parts from it, {75} and when it wants to it moves it. And so over and over it would move and not move the same body, which is absurd.

From these arguments it is clear that those holding the above view feel that they understand nothing – like plants in this respect – knowing themselves to be unworthy of anything's being communicated to them.

This is a long speech, and it has a short solution. For when some absurdity is assumed without being proved, but is elsewhere presupposed, professed, and granted, then it is easy to reach many absurd conclusions. Now these men affirm that a human being does strictly understand, yet they do not prove this. It is from this supposition that they argue. But if that supposition is not true, then they have no argument. So I do not grant that a human being understands, strictly speaking. If that is granted, then I don't know how to reply. But I deny it, for good reason, and so I will easily reply. For as Aristotle holds in book three [429a24–26], and as his adversaries hold too, if understanding does not have an organ, but is instead abstract from matter, then it follows from this that strictly speaking human beings do not understand, not in the way that they sense.

You reply: Aristotle says in book one [408b13–15] that it is the human being and not the intellect that understands. Now the only way to ask whether a human being understands and not the intellect alone is to ask whether understanding is common to the soul and the body, rather than to the soul alone. But in fact Aristotle seems to decide in book one [403a5–10] that understanding is not proper to the soul, but to the soul and the body, and the way in which it is common to the body is that it does not occur without a phantasm. This is not because understanding is the perfection of a human being, however, but because it needs a human being as an object. So one should say that it is not the intellect that understands, but the human being, not because understanding occurs in matter, as seeing occurs in the eye, and consequently not as its perfection, but as it is separate from matter. Still, it needs a material body as its object, not as its subject, and to this extent one should say that a human being understands. Still, this is not the way we say that a human being senses. If you were to say that understanding belongs to a human being strictly, [I reply that] this has not been proved, and so it should be denied. Aristotle seems to think this in *De anima* I.

Now the union of intellect to these phantasms is natural. For Aristotle says in book one [408b5–8] that being joyful and sad belongs not {76} to the soul itself, but to the composite, because one is joyful in one's body. And he adds: "Understanding is something of this sort or perhaps something else" [408b9]. This claim is disjunctive in form. And as Themistius says regarding this same passage,[18] he said this inasmuch as the intellect was not yet clearly split off from sense. Hence his claim was cast in the form of a doubt. But once this communication of intellect with body is put in place, that it needs the body in the aforesaid way, you should not go looking for another communication in understanding by which a human being is said to understand. That is, you should not seek for the intellect to be united to the body as its perfection. It is due solely to the first communication that a human being is said to understand.

Moreover, the Commentator says in book two [15, p. 154] that "celestial bodies are clearly seen to understand." Aristotle also holds this, in *De caelo* II [292a18–22]. But they are said to understand because of the union of what understands to those bodies. It is not that what understands is united to them as form to matter, but solely as their mover. And if they are said to understand only on an abuse of the term, I do not care. It is in this way that a human being is said to understand.

You might ask why we say that a human being understands more than a ship does, given that the sailor is said to understand and he moves the ship. It should be replied that the cases are not alike. So I don't care that we don't say that the aggregate of a sailor and his ship understands, unless we thoroughly abuse the term. To be sure, I don't claim that human beings understand, unless the term is abused. But still I say that the cases are not at all alike, because the sailor is not by his nature united to the ship in such a way that he needs the ship for his understanding. But the opposite is so in the present case for the intellect with respect to the body.

You will say that I experience and perceive myself to understand. I say that this is false. Rather, the intellect is united to you naturally, as the mover and regulator of your body. It is what experiences this, just as the separate intellect experiences the objects of intellect to be in it. If you say that I, the aggregate of body and intellect, experience myself to understand, this is false. Rather, the intellect that needs your body as its object experiences this and communicates it to the aggregate in the aforesaid way. {77}

When you prove that a human being is not only the intellect [4c1], I grant this. I likewise grant that understanding is not an operation passing

---

[18] *In de anima* II 27,8–27,33.

into exterior matter [4a]. Understanding, then, is not an operation passing into external matter as into a subject. Instead, [it communicates with the body] in the way described.

To the other [4c2], I reply that the intellect moves and understands of its own nature. It is not actually understanding except through the will, and not of its own nature. But by its own nature it has the potential to move the body and to understand. So since it is not actually doing so of its own nature, it actually moves the body when it wants to and does not move it when it does not want to. You took this to be absurd, but I do not.

Question 5. *Is Each of These the Soul: The Nutritive, Sensory, Locomotive, and Appetitive?*

It should be said that none of these *is* the soul. Instead, each of these is always *part* of the soul, aside from the nutritive in some cases and also the intellective in some cases. But the sensory and the others are always in all cases a part of the soul. For whatever can exist without any other principle is called the whole soul, and a principle of life that cannot exist without another principle of life is called part of the soul. So the nutritive exists in plants without another° principle of life; likewise in immortal things the intellective is the whole soul, whereas in corporeal things the nutritive and sensory are parts of the soul, as is clear, and they are not separated. The sensory and the locomotive are universally parts of the soul in every case where they are found, because the locomotive does not occur without the sensory and the sensory does not occur without the nutritive. So each of those is always part of the soul and not the whole soul.

It should secondly be understood that the sensory in different animals – in brutes and in human beings, and in dogs and in horses, etc. – is distinct in species in the different cases. {78}

Question 6. *Are the Sensory, Nutritive, Locomotive, and Appetitive Distinct with Respect to Substance, in the Same Thing?*

It seems that they are distinct. The principle of a definition (*ratio*) is based on the principle of the essence. For the principle of being and cognizing is the same.[19] But as Aristotle holds in the text [413b27–29], the nutritive

---

[19] Cf. Aristotle, *Met.* VI 1, 1025b3–26a32.

and the other powers are principles of the soul that are definitionally distinct. Therefore since definitional distinctness is based on distinctness of essence (or in the essence), there will be distinctness in the soul's essence, etc.

Moreover, that which is prior to another through generation is distinct in substance from that same other. But as Aristotle holds,[20] the nutritive is prior in generation, even in the same thing, to the sensory. Therefore, they were distinct with respect to substance as well. For if they were the same in substance, then what is the same now would have been the same before.

Moreover, the Commentator says on *Metaphysics* II [10] that prime matter receives more universal forms and then less universal ones. Therefore since the nutritive is more universal than the sensory, it is received in matter before the others.

On the contrary. For one perfectible thing there is one perfection, with respect to substance. Therefore numerically one perfectible thing will also have numerically one perfection.

Also, these [parts] have been said to be distinct with respect to their powers and one in subject, as Aristotle [413b9–13] and the Commentator [II 20] hold.

Also, any two things that are distinct with respect to material substance are distinct in place and subject. The nutritive and sensory, etc., {79} are not distinct in an animal with respect to place and subject. Therefore, they are not distinct with respect to substance. For if they were distinct with respect to substance, then since souls that are material and distinct with respect to substance do not affect (*non compatiantur*) each other, they [would] require distinct matters. For they would not affect each other. Therefore, etc.

Reply. If [these powers] were distinct with respect to their substance, then each of them would be the whole soul and they would be distinct in place and subject and would be distinct in substance in terms of their species. And [then] one animal would be many animals. All of this is impossible. So they are one with respect to their actual form, one essence without qualification. For in the case of forms it is impossible to posit composition in existence and in reality, although composition can be posited in definition (*ratione*), as was seen elsewhere. So I say that the nutritive, sensory, etc., are one in substance and distinct solely in defini-

---

[20] *De generatione animalium* II 3, 736b2.

tion. And this is clear as follows. Although the principle through which there is sensation and through which there is motion is not distinct in substance, still this substance has a different definition and a different account (*intellectum*) as a result of its being sensible and productive of motion. Therefore, the principle of motion is also that from which the principle of sensation comes, because although the nutritive principle, etc., is one in substance, it still is possible that it have the definition of neither nourishing nor sensing, etc. So they are distinct only in definition, and this definitional distinctness made some believe that they were also distinct in substance. Aristotle, however, said that they are definitionally distinct [413b29].

You argue that principles distinct in definition are based on distinctness in essence. I reply that definitional distinctness can be based on either distinctness in essence or distinctness in existence. And in fact their definitional distinctness is based on that principle's distinctness in existence rather than in essence – that is, not because there is distinctness in its substance, but because there is this distinctness in the existence of certain properties and effects apparent to the senses.

The soul's powers in the body are not distinct in place and subject, as Aristotle proves of the nutritive, sensory, and appetitive powers in segmented animals.[21] But the visual and auditory powers, etc., are distinct in an animal. Still, if the former powers are taken with respect to that {80} by which they are principally carried out, then they are distinct in place and subject. For the nutritive exists in the instruments of that operation, such as the liver, etc., and the appetitive exists in the front part of the brain.

Question 7. Does the Semen from which Generation Comes Have a Soul?

[. . .]

Question 8. Does Semen Have a Soul with Respect to Its Substance?

[. . .]

---

[21] *De anima* II 2, 413b16–24, referring to worms and other animals whose parts can survive when cut apart.

Question 9. Is It True that the Nutritive Power Is the Power through which Living Things Generate What Is Like Themselves?

[. . .]

Question 10. Does Semen Belong to the Substance of What Generates It?

[. . .] {85}

Question 11. Is Sense a Passive Power?

It seems that it is not:

1. The power of sense is the power of a form, since it is a power of the soul, which is a form. But the power of a form is {86} an active power, not a passive one, as Averroes says on *Metaphysics* IX [2]. Therefore, sense is not a passive power, but an active one.

2. To sense is to act, to be sensed is to be acted on. Sense senses things that are sensible. Therefore, it acts on them.

3. Although the reception of sensibles within sense is a kind of being acted on within sense, nevertheless because the senses judge those sensibles and judging is a kind of acting, it follows, etc.

4. It is customarily argued – though not much to the point – that a menstruating woman infects a mirror, that a basilisk, by sight alone, kills a person, that a wolf, by sight alone, makes a person hoarse. This would not be so if sense were not an active power.

The opposite is maintained in the text [417b16–418a6], because otherwise sensation would occur without an outside object, as in the case of intellect, and further the senses would always sense.

Also, the senses are sometimes in potentiality, sometimes in actuality, and this is the condition of a passive° power, because an active power is always in actuality. Therefore sense is a passive power.

Reply. In the case of every power we ought to consider whether it is active or passive, as the Commentator says here [II 51]. And I say that active and passive powers differ because the being of a passive power is to be moved and acted on, whereas the being of an active power is to move and to act. I say that sense is a passive power, not an active one, as the arguments reveal.

But it should be understood that, as Aristotle maintains in book three

[428b10–17], sense is not in potentiality in such a way that it never acts. For sense, when it is actualized, is able to bring about another [action]. If it is called a passive power in sensing, still in bringing about phantasia, when it has been actualized, it is called active, as Aristotle says in book three [428b25–26]. So sense is passive in the operation of sensing, because that operation of sensing is made out of its being acted on and receiving. In this same way something is heated, receiving the action of heat, and the thing heated itself acts by heating another, so that it moves to produce heat because it is moved.

It should also be understood that sense is the sort of passive power to act through sensing that° is not the passive power of matter alone. {87} For a thing is not potentially sensing due to matter in the way in which sense is said to be something potentially sensing. This is clear, because the passive power of matter for sensing is brought to actuality not by what generates it, but by something sensible: Thus sense is potentially sensing in just the way that someone having knowledge is potentially considering. But there is a difference even here, because someone with dispositional knowledge goes into act whenever he wants to, whereas sense does not so act when it wants to, unless it is acted on by something external. Therefore, sense is potentially sensing, not through the potential of matter alone, like semen, but through the potential of a form, the soul. According to Averroes in book three [text 28], matter becomes actualized based on its mode of potentiality, with change and loss of the contrary state. But there is no change that is the loss of a contrary state when sense becomes actualized. So the two are distinct. Therefore, we hold that every sense is passive, but not in the way that matter is.

[Ad 1.] You say that the power of sense is the power of the soul, and therefore it will not be passive. This holds true just as it holds true for the power of prime matter.[22] But although [matter] is in a way formal and in a way actual, it still need not be *purely* active. Rather, it will *in a way* be active because it is formal; this conclusion is correct. So it is for having sense. For there is another way in which something actually has sense with respect to matter: with respect to [its presence in] semen. But although [semen] does in this way actually have sense, it need not be the sense's

---

[22] That is, the power (or potentiality) of prime matter would be purely passive insofar as prime matter contained no form. But the author goes on to indicate that he takes prime matter to have some minimal degree of form and hence to be minimally active.

final perfection. Thus Aristotle says that someone having sense has it in the way that someone having a dispositional grasp of medicine has knowledge [417b17–19].

Ad 2. To sense is not to act in the way that you suppose, but instead as the text states.

[Ad 3.] You say that sense judges what is sensible and so is active with respect to sensibles. I reply to this that the sense's reception just is the reception of the judge, so that its judgment just is the reception, not an action. For sense judges by receiving, and a sense has sensing because of its having been affected (*sua passione*), which stands to the sensing in such a way that the sense's having been affected just is the sensing itself, and not the form of the sensible in the sense. You will say that both the reception of the sensible and the judgment are there. I hold that the reception is actually there only if something actually sensed is there; moreover, the thing actually sensed within the sense just is the sensing – just as the thing actually understood within the intellect is nothing other than the understanding. And thus I say here that sensing is not a state of being affected that occurs on account of something already received within sense; it is instead nothing other than the sensing, etc. {88}

Ad 4. The eyes of a woman infect a mirror because of vapors from certain veins within the eye. The *De somno* [456b1] says of these that a vein is a blood vessel full of blood. So too for the basilisk, etc. This is not because sense is active, but because of a poisonous vapor coming from its eyes. So too for the other similar cases that you mention.

Question 12. Can Someone Have Dispositional Knowledge and Yet Not Be Actually Considering?

It seems that one cannot, because a disposition is a principle bringing about actual consideration. But a principle for action cannot inhere in something without the action, given that it is sufficient. Therefore, etc.

The contrary is maintained in the text [417a27–28] and is also apparent from what we experience within ourselves.

Question 13. Is Someone Who Possesses a Disposition Altered in Any Way When He Actually Considers?

It seems that he is not. According to the text [417b6–9], one should not say that someone wise is altered when he actually exercises wisdom.

On the contrary, someone who has knowledge, when he is actually considering, is in another state than before. Therefore he has been altered.

Reply to the first [Q12]. It is possible for someone to have dispositional knowledge but not to be actually considering, just as it is possible for something to have the form {89} of weight as a kind of disposition, not as an actuality. So too in this case, and Aristotle mentions this relationship in the text [417a24–28]. Thus it is possible for someone to have a form in its first perfection, in such a way as not to have it in its final perfection. This is possible for the two reasons mentioned in the text [417a25–29, b24]. For dispositional knowledge, even if it is the principle of actual consideration, is still not sufficient, because only if he wants to does the person having the disposition go from that dispositional knowledge to actuality (that is, to actual consideration). Likewise, someone with the disposition for building is able not to build, given that he does not have the will to build. So the will is the one thing that is required for bringing dispositional knowledge to actuality. Also, dispositional knowledge is the principle from which actual considering is born. But an impediment can block this principle, just as an impediment can block the form of something heavy that is up high, since it can be suspended up there. Now in this case, the impediment is a human being's preoccupation with external things – such as the necessities of food, or amusements and the like. Thus the text [417a25–28] says that someone with a disposition goes into act if he wants to, unless there is a cause that impedes him. For there are some principles of action that can be impeded, and some that cannot.

This solves the [initial] argument.

If you ask what this disposition is, I say that it is revealed only through its act. But a disposition is a kind of potential for considering whenever someone wants to.

Reply to the second [Q13]. When someone with a disposition is actually considering, he is altered broadly speaking. For there are four modes of alteration.

• One occurs when a thing is changed from contrary to contrary in such a way that something is removed from it. Such a state is an impairment, etc.
• Also, when someone unknowing is made knowing, one speaks of alteration in this regard. This is nothing other than going from potentiality to actuality.

• The third mode occurs when someone is changed into having actual knowledge – coming not from ignorance but from error. This mode does not go from there being no knowledge to there being knowledge, because there was knowledge already. Instead, this person acquires the final perfection of knowledge, whereas before he had the first perfection.[23]

A person is more altered by the first alteration, then, because something is removed from him. By the second alteration to someone, in contrast, he is not so altered, because nothing at all {90} is removed from him. And someone is even less altered by the third alteration than by the second, because in the second case there is a change from there being no knowledge to there being knowledge, whereas this is not so in the third case.

There is also, beyond the modes mentioned, another mode of alteration in virtue of which someone is said to be altered with respect to the dispositional knowledge that he has, so as to be made actually considering. This [fourth] mode of alteration entails even less of an alteration than the others, etc.

Question 14. *Why Are the Common Sensibles, Rather than the Accidental Sensibles, Said to Be Sensible per se?*

The common sensibles are said to be sensible per se. The son of Diarius and such sensibles are said to be sensed per accidens. There is a question of why the common sensibles (such as size, shape, and motion), rather than the son of Diarius and the like, are said to be sensible per se.

It is argued that the son of Diarius and the like are not sensible per accidens. For although white is accidental to the son of Diarius, still if he is not sensed through the sensation of white, then he will not be sensible per accidens. But he is not sensed per se, because he is not then sensed per accidens nor through the sensation of white, because the senses are affected by nothing from the son of Diarius in sensing his whiteness, and therefore neither is he cognized through the sensation of white. Thus the son of Diarius is sensed in no way, and therefore neither is he sensible per accidens.

---

[23] These last two sentences are puzzling. First, it seems wrong to say that the person in error has knowledge (*scientia*). What he has, unlike in the second case, is a belief. But since it is a false belief, it should not count as knowledge. Second, it seems wrong to say, "whereas before he had the first perfection." Having a belief, even a wrong one, seems a step in actuality beyond the mere first perfection. The first perfection would consist in having merely the cognitive capacity to form a belief.

The Commentator offers two reasons why the one kind is sensible per se, the other per accidens.[24] For although the common sensibles are common to the particular senses, they are nevertheless not common to the common sense; instead, they are sensed per se by the common sense. Also, the common sensibles are the subjects of the proper senses, whereas the son of Diarius is not, etc.

But it seems that this claim of the Commentator cannot stand. And first it seems that the common sensibles are not proper to the common sense, because the common sense is altered by all; therefore these common sensibles will be no more proper to it than any of the others. {91}

Also, even if they are proper to the common sense, it still does not follow that they are proper to a particular sense; therefore neither do they seem to be sensed per se by a particular sense.

So we hold in a different way that the common sensibles are sensible per se. And this is clear, because things that make a difference to an impression on the senses are sensible per se. This is because the senses receive by being acted on and being changed. Things then° that do not make distinct impressions on the senses are sensed per accidens. But regardless of whether whiteness is accidental to the son of Diarius or to something else, such as a wall, the sense is always acted on and impressed in the same way. Thus the text [418a22–24] says that the senses are in no way acted on by the son of Diarius. Also, the senses are acted on in different ways by the differing species of the active [quality]. But the common sensibles make no difference in this way; their differences come in the way [a sensible species] acts. For in what way does a species making an impression on the senses make that impression? By its being far off or close, and so on in other cases. It is in this way, then, that the per se sensibles make distinct impressions on the senses, whereas the per accidens sensibles do not, as was said.

Also, for something to be sensed per accidens it must be cognized by the one sensing, for the reason that it accidentally applies (*ut accidit*) to what is sensed per se, so that it is cognized by that means. That which cognizes it can be a cognitive power grasping this individual under such a species or some such common feature (such as *this human being*), or it can be the estimative power cognizing the individual, not under such a species (as the sheep cognizes this wolf and this grass). Now it can be the case that at once, without difficulty, when the per se sensible is perceived by the

[24] *In de anima* II 65 (pp. 227–28).

senses then something else is perceived. This and only this should be called sensible per accidens. For from things sensed per se, some [perceptions] occur at once and some with great difficulty. The first that is had at once from a sense is called sensible per se, but something is called sensible per accidens that is sensed along with the sensible per se, but where the power grasping it is not the sense, but either the estimative or the cogitative power or another.

To the argument I say that what is sensible per accidens need not be sensed by the sense. Instead, it suffices for it to be sensed by some sensory power. Hence, as Averroes says,[25] some individual intentions are perceived by not just any animal, but by an intelligent animal. {91}

Question 15. How Is Light Necessary for Seeing Colors?

[. . .]

Question 16. What Does Sound Exist in as Its Subject?

[. . .] {94}

Question 17. How Does Sense Know that the Object Sensed Has a Different Being from Its Being that Is Conjoined to Sense?

There is still a question regarding the above. Sensible things have their actual sensed being in the senses, so that their actual sensed being is the being of the senses, and conversely. But the being of those sensibles outside the senses is not their sensed being. There is a question, then, of how the senses know that the object sensed {95} has a different being from its being that is conjoined to sense. In what way does it know that it has a being different from sensed being, a being under which it is not in the senses?

It is not enough to say that just as a sense concerns its sense object (e.g., color), so a sense concerns that which is distant from us. For even if this is so, I still ask as before how you know that that distant object is different from what is actually sensed, as it is existent in the sense. For this is the same question as the main one.

Reply. Aristotle holds at the start of *Physics* II [193a3] that it is ridiculous

---

[25] *In de anima* II 63 (p. 225).

to try to demonstrate [the existence of] nature. For something must be cognized per se, and as the Commentator says regarding that text [II 6], the kind of human being that does not know to distinguish what is from what is not known per se (rather than on account of something other than itself) could never do philosophy. From this it is clear, then, that cognition does not go on to infinity. Instead, some things are known per se, and when we come to these, we should not go on any further; instead, we should believe these things in themselves (*per se*).

To the question, then, I say that someone who doubts how he knows that an object of sense has a being other than what appears does not believe that the senses are true per se of their sense objects. And I say that anyone who denies this knows nothing for himself. This [answer] cannot be proved, because it is known per se. For we believe the senses per se, concerning how their proper objects appear to them. So, too, it is only through the senses that we believe the things we understand. But we believe the senses per se, nor can this be proved except through the senses. And just as you would deny that first sensation, so, too, for that which you take from sensation in your argument. It was in this way that Aristotle spoke against Zeno in *Physics* VIII. Zeno had denied that motion exists, seeking for himself a reason beyond this, even while his senses say that motion does exist. And Aristotle says there that we do not need a reason in cases where we have something worthier than reason, such as the senses. {96}

Question 18. Why Is the Form of Luminosity Corrupted When the Luminous Body Is Corrupted?

[. . .]

Question 19. Why Do Phosphorescent Things Appear Colored during the Day, Whereas at Night They Instead Appear Luminous?

[. . .]

Question 20. Does an Odor Impress the Medium with a Fumelike Evaporation in the Medium?

[. . .]

Question 21. Does Sound Multiply Itself through the Medium up to the Sense of Hearing All at Once or Successively?

[. . .]

Question 22. Does Light Multiply Itself in the Medium and in the Organ All at Once or Successively?

[. . .]

Question 23. Does Color Produce Itself in the Medium at Once or Successively?

[. . .]

Question 24. If Light Were Held to Multiply Itself through a Medium that Is Infinite, Would It Multiply Itself through that Whole Medium?

[. . .]

Question 25. Is Light Produced in the Medium in Such a Way that It Is Generated by the Medium?

[. . .]

3

BONAVENTURE
CHRIST OUR ONE TEACHER

Introduction

St. Bonaventure (1217–1274) is in many ways the most influential theologian of the Franciscan order. As a young man, he wrote admired works of technical scholastic theology, including an influential *Sentences* commentary. In his later years he turned increasingly to popular and highly innovative treatises defending a conservative Augustinian perspective. He was, in all respects, one of the leading public intellectuals of his day.

This beautiful sermon reveals a different side of medieval philosophy. Here Bonaventure addresses a university audience, but in the form of a sermon rather than a classroom lecture or debate. Because his audience is highly educated, the argument of the sermon moves on an elevated plane. But because of the religious context, Bonaventure pays more attention to exhortation than to analysis.

Still, this is a substantive philosophical text, and provides a useful introduction to the distinctive character of Bonaventure's philosophical-theological thought. The topic of the sermon is a verse from Matthew in which Jesus says that Christ is our one master or teacher (*magister* in Latin). The verse is particularly apt for a university audience, because *magister* was the very word used to refer to university professors such as Bonaventure himself. In developing his theme, Bonaventure spells out the place of divine illumination in faith, reason, and spiritual contemplation (2–14), and then goes on to address how this sort of Augustinian account is compatible with Aristotelian empiricism (18). The second half of the sermon spells out our duties to Christ (20–23) and the special duties of those that teach in Christ's name (24–28).

On the theory of divine illumination, see CHLMP VI.21, "Faith, ideas, illumination, and experience," and Pasnau (1999a). For a more technical, analytic presentation of Bonaventure's illumination theory, see the fourth of his *Disputed Questions on the Knowledge of Christ*. For detailed notes on this sermon, with special attention to Bonaventure's sources, see Madec (1990).

Christ Our One Teacher

1. *Christ is your one teacher* (Matthew 23:10). This verse identifies the foundational source of cognitive illumination, Christ, *who being the brightness of glory and the figure of his substance, upholding all things by the word° of his power* (as is said in Hebrews 1:3), is himself the origin of all wisdom, according to Ecclesiasticus 1:5: *The foundation of wisdom, the word of God in the highest.* Moreover, Christ is himself the foundation of all right cognition, because he is *the way, the truth, and the life* (John 14:6). Indeed, cognition that is certain and correct has three levels, according to Hugh of St. Victor in *De sacramentis* I.x:

These are the three levels of progress in faith, by which one's growing faith ascends to perfection: first, to choose through piety; second, to approve through reason; third, to apprehend through truth.

Accordingly, it is evident that there are three modes of cognizing: first, through the belief of pious assent; second, through the stability of certain reasoning; third, through the clarity of pure contemplation. The first concerns a state of virtue, faith; the second concerns the state of a gift, understanding; the third concerns a state of blessedness, purity of heart. So cognition comes in these three different kinds – believing, reasoning discursively, and contemplating – and Christ is accordingly the source and cause of them all: He is the source of the first insofar as he is the way, the source of the second insofar as he is the truth, and the source of the third insofar as he is the life.

[Faith]

2. Insofar as he is the way, Christ is the teacher and source of the cognition that comes through faith. This cognition is achieved in two ways: through revelation and through authority. For as Augustine says {102} in *De utilitate credendi* [ch.11], "what we understand, we owe to reason; what we believe, we owe to authority." But there would be no authority unless revelation had come first. Accordingly, in II Peter 1:19, *we have the more stable, prophetic discourse, to which you do well to attend, as if to a lamp shining in a dark place.* With this he suggests the authority of prophetic discourse, and he goes on to give an explanation: *for prophesy is never conferred by human will; rather, holy human beings spoke of God when inspired° by the Holy Spirit.*

So since it is in these two ways that one is able to reach cognition by faith, this can occur only through the gift of Christ, who is the source of all revelation in virtue of his advent into the mind, and the ground of all authority in virtue of his advent in the flesh.

3. He came into the mind as a light revealing all prophetic visions, according to Daniel 2:22: *he reveals what is deep and hidden, and knows what is kept in darkness, and light is with him.* This is the light of divine wisdom, which is Christ, according to John 8:12: *I am the light of the world; he that follows me does not walk in darkness,* and 12:36: *While you have the light, believe in the light, so that you may be the children of light.* For as is said in John 1:12, *he gave to them the power to become the sons of God, to them that believe in his name.* Without this light, which is Christ, no one can penetrate the secrets of the faith. For this reason, in Wisdom 9:10, *Send her* (speaking of wisdom) *from your holy heaven and from the throne of your majesty, so that she may be with me and work with me, so that I may know what is accepted by you. For what human being could know the counsel of God, or think of what God wills?* And so on,[1] up to [9:17]: *Who will know your meaning unless you provide wisdom and send your Holy Spirit from on high?* From this we are given to understand that one can attain the certain revelation of faith only through Christ's advent into the mind.

4. He also came into the flesh, as the word that confirmed all prophetic speech, according to Hebrews 1:1: *God, who at many times* {104} *and in many ways in the past spoke to the fathers in the prophets, has in these days of late spoken to us in his Son, whom he has appointed heir of all things, through whom he also made the world.* For since Christ is the discourse of the Father, full of power – according to Ecclesiastes 8:4: *His discourse is full of power, nor can anyone say to him, Why do you do this?* – he is also the discourse full of truth, or rather he is the truth itself, according to John 17:17: *Sanctify them in truth,* since *Your discourse is the truth.* According to the Common Gloss, *in truth* means *in me, who am the truth,* which is made evident by what follows: *Your discourse is the truth,* which is to say: *I am the truth.* In Greek, *logos;* in Latin, word (*verbum*). Therefore, since authority is accredited to discourse that is powerful and truthful, and since Christ is the Word of the Father, and hence *the power of God and the wisdom of God* [1 Cor. 1:

---

[1] Bonaventure probably would have recited the whole passage when delivering this sermon. But our two surviving manuscripts often abbreviate longer Biblical passages in this way, relying on the reader to supply from memory the elided verses. When necessary for the sense of the argument, I supply what is missing.

24], so the stability of all authority is founded on him, stabilized by him, and consummated in him.

5. Thus all of authentic scripture and its preachers are focused around Christ's coming into the flesh, as the foundation of the entire Christian faith, according to 1 Corinthians 3:10: *According to the grace that has been given to me, as a wise architect, I have laid the foundation. For no one can lay another foundation, aside from the one that has been laid, which is Jesus Christ.* For he is the foundation of all authentic teaching, apostolic or prophetic, according to each law, new and old. For this reason, in Ephesians 2:20, *You have built on the foundation of apostles and prophets, with Jesus Christ as the chief corner stone.*

Therefore it is clear that Christ is the teacher of cognition by faith, and this insofar as he is the way, in virtue of his two advents, into the mind and into the flesh. {106}

[Reason]

6. He is also the teacher of the cognition that comes through reason, and this insofar as he is the truth. For cognition that is knowledge necessarily requires immutable truth on the part of what is known, and infallible certainty on the part of the one that knows. For everything that is known is necessary in itself and certain to the one that knows it. For we know when we take ourselves to recognize the cause of why a thing is, knowing that it is its cause and that it° is impossible for it to stand otherwise.[2]

7. So the thing known requires immutable truth. But created truth is not like this, unconditionally and absolutely, because everything created is changeable and mutable. What is like this, instead, is the creating truth, which has full immutability. For this reason it is said in Psalm 101:26:[3] *And in the beginning, Lord, you founded the earth, and the heavens are the works of your hands. They will perish but you remain, and all of them will grow old like a garment. And like clothing you will change them, and they will be changed. But*

---

[2] Cf. Aristotle, *Posterior Analytics* I 2, 71b9–12.

[3] Latin versions of the Psalms joined together psalms 9 and 10, decreasing by one (compared to the Hebrew Bible) the numeration of subsequent chapters. I've retained the Latin numbering scheme.

    Throughout, Bonaventure relies on the sometimes unreliable Vulgate text. His quotations will often differ notably from those found in modern Bibles, and I've made no attempt to update his texts. Occasionally, he refers to an alternative, non-Vulgate text, not because he supposes it better, but because he supposes that more than one translation can capture God's authoritative word.

you yourself are the same, and your years will not fail. This (as the Apostle says in Hebrews 1:10) is said of the Son of God, who is the word, art, and reason of the omnipotent God, and hence is the eternal truth, according to Psalm 118:89: *Your word, Lord, endures for eternity, and your truth, into the age of ages.* Therefore, since things have being in their own kind, in the mind, and in eternal reason, and since their being is not wholly immutable in the first and second ways, but only in the third − namely, as they exist in the eternal Word − the result is that nothing can make things perfectly knowable except for the presence of Christ, Son of God and teacher. {108}

8. For this reason Augustine writes in *De libero arbitrio* II [xii.33]:

You have in no way denied that there is an unchangeable truth, containing all things that are immutably true, which you could not call yours or mine or anyone's, but which is present and shows itself in common to everyone who discerns what is unchangeably true.

This very same thing is found in *De trinitate* XIV [xv.21]:

Given that the impious see the rules in keeping with which we all ought to see, where do they see them? Not in their own nature, since these rules are undoubtedly seen with the mind itself, and their minds are clearly mutable, whereas whoever can see this in these rules sees that the rules are immutable. Not in a disposition of one's mind, either, because those rules belong to justice, where even someone unjust recognizes what is just and discerns that what he does not have ought to be had. So where are they written, unless in the book of that light that is called the truth, from which every just light is copied and from which justice is transferred to the human heart, not by relocating, but as if by impressing itself?

The same is said in *De vera religione* [xxx.56−xxxi.57], *De musica* VI [xii.36], and in the *Retractationes* [I.iv.4].

9. The second thing such cognition requires is certainty on the part of the knower. This cannot involve what can be deceived, or a light that can be obscured. Such light [as is required], however, is not the light of a created intelligence, but of the uncreated wisdom that is Christ. For this reason, in Wisdom 7:17, *God gave me the true knowledge of things that are, so that I would know the disposition of the whole world, the powers of the elements, the start, finish and middle of time.* And {110} later [7:21], *Wisdom, the maker of all things, taught me.* And the reason for this is added later [7:25]: *For [wisdom] is a vapor of the power of God, and a kind of pure emanation of omnipotent God, and so nothing defiled comes to her. For she is the brightness of eternal light, and the unspotted mirror of God's majesty. She is more beautiful than*

the sun, and above every disposition of the stars; though compared to light, she is *found before it. She reaches therefore from end to end mightily, and she orders all* *things sweetly.* Hence John 1:9 says, *That was the true light that illuminates* *every human being coming into this world.* Here the Gloss says that "what illuminates not through itself, but through something else, is not the true light."

10. So the light of a created intellect does not suffice for a certain comprehension of any thing without the light of the eternal Word. Thus Augustine, in *Soliloquies* I [viii.15]:

Just as in the case of the sun one may notice these three features: that it exists, that it shines, and that it illuminates, so too in the innermost part of God there are these three: that it exists, that it understands, and that it makes others understand.

Hence he remarks a little earlier,

Just as the earth cannot be seen unless it is illuminated by light, so it must be believed that the subjects of the various fields of study – though everyone grants, without any doubt, that they are understood to be most true – cannot be understood unless they are illuminated by him, as if he were their sun.

Again, in *De trinitate* XII, last chapter [xv.24], speaking of the boy who without a teacher replied rightly about geometry, Augustine rejects as false the Platonic° view that souls are filled with knowledge before being introduced into their bodies.

We should rather believe that the nature of the intellectual mind is so constituted that, when it is subjected to intelligible things in the natural order, as its maker has arranged, it sees them in an incorporeal light of its own kind, in just the way that the eyes° of the flesh see their surroundings in a corporeal light, a light that the eyes were created to receive, and to which they are adapted.

As for what this light is, Augustine says {112} in *De libero arbitrio* II [xiv.38]:

That beauty of truth and wisdom is not exhausted by time, nor does it change places, nor is it interrupted by night or covered by shadow or exposed to the bodily senses. Throughout the world, it is near to all those who have turned toward it and love it, and it is eternal to them all. It has no place, but it is never absent. It warns outwardly and teaches inwardly. No one judges it, but no one judges well without it. And through this it is clear, without any doubt, that it is better than our minds, which are individually made wise by it alone, and which judge not it but other things, through it.

He says this very same thing in *De vera religione* [xxx.56], *De trinitate* VIII [iii.5], and in *De magistro* [xi.38], where he proves throughout the conclusion that Christ is our one teacher.

[Contemplation]

11. Finally, insofar as he is the life, Christ is the teacher of contemplative cognition. The soul engages in such cognition in two ways, according to two kinds of nourishment: internally in divinity and externally in humanity. Accordingly, there are two modes of contemplating, going in and going out, which one can attain only through Christ. Thus he himself says in John 10:9: *I am the door. Through me, if anyone enters, he will be saved. He will go in and go out and find nourishment.*

12. We go into Christ inasmuch as he is the uncreated Word and the food of angels, of whom it is said in John 1:1, *In the beginning was the Word.* Of this going in, Psalm 41:5 says, following an alternative translation, {114} *I will go into the place of the wonderful tabernacle, up to the house of God, with a voice of joy and praise, the sound of one feasting.* This was said of the heavenly Jerusalem, into which no one goes to contemplate unless brought there through the uncreated Word, which is Christ. Hence Dionysius, in *The Celestial Hierarchy* ch.1,

Calling upon Jesus, then, the light of the Father, that which is true and that *illuminates every human being coming into this world* [John 1:9], through whom we have access to the principal light, the Father, we will attend as much as possible to the illuminations conveyed by the Father° through the most sacred of phrases. From these phrases, we will consider, as much as we can, the hierarchies of celestial minds, made clear to us symbolically and anagogically, attending with the mind's immaterial and steadfast eyes to the principal and more-than-principal divine clarity of the Father.

13. We go out to the incarnate Word that is the milk of the young, of which John 1:14 says, *The Word was made flesh and dwelt among us.* Of this going out, Song of Songs 3:11 says, *Go out, daughters of Zion, and see King Solomon wearing the diadem with which his mother crowned him on the day of his betrothal and of gladness in his heart.* This diadem, with which the true, peaceful Solomon was crowned by his mother, is the immaculate flesh, which he assumed from the Virgin Mary, and which is called the diadem of betrothal, because through it he betrothed himself to the Church, which

was formed from his side, just as Eve was formed from the side of a man. So through this [immaculate flesh], the whole ecclesiastical hierarchy is purified, illuminated, and perfected. Hence it should be viewed as the living nourishment of the whole Church, in accordance with John 6:55: *My flesh is food indeed, and my blood is drink indeed.* For this reason he adds, *He who eats my flesh and drinks my blood has eternal life.* {116}

14. This is what is said in *De anima et spiritu* [ch.9]:[4]

The soul has two lives, one by which it lives in the flesh and another by which it lives in God. For there are in fact two senses in a human being, one internal and one external. Each has its own good in which it is renewed: the internal sense in the contemplation of divinity, the external sense in the contemplation of humanity. It was for this reason that God was made human, so that he would beatify the whole human being within himself, with the result that, whether going in or out, one might find nourishment in one's maker: external nourishment in the flesh of the Savior and internal nourishment in the divinity of the Creator.

But this going into divinity and going out to humanity is nothing other than the ascent to heaven and the descent to earth that is made through Christ as through a ladder. Regarding this ladder, in Genesis 28:12, *Jacob saw in his sleep a ladder standing on the earth, with the top of it touching heaven, and with angels ascending and descending on it.* By the ladder we understand Christ, and by the ascent and descent of the angels we understand the illumination of contemplative men ascending and descending. We also understand these two modes of contemplation in the internal and external reading of the book written within and without, as in Revelation 5:1: *I saw* (John says) *in the right hand of him sitting on the throne a book written within and without, sealed with seven seals.* And he adds there that *no one was able, neither in heaven nor on earth, nor under the earth, to open the book or look at it.* Then he adds, *the lion of the tribe of Judah has conquered, he who is worthy to open the book and break its seven seals.* So if he who opens the book and breaks its seals is the one who should properly be called a doctor, and if the only such one is Christ, who was the resurrected lion and the slain lamb, it is therefore evident that Christ is our one teacher, in every kind of cognition, inasmuch as he is the way, the truth, and the life. {118}

---

[4] For a while, this twelfth-century work was attributed to Augustine, and hence had considerable authority. Bonaventure was aware of the growing doubts regarding its authorship. Today the author is thought to be Alcher of Clairvaux, or perhaps Peter Comestor.

[Achieving Wisdom]

15. From the aforesaid, then, it is evident in what order and from what master one achieves wisdom. For the order is that one begins with the stability of faith and advances through the serenity of reason, so as to achieve the sweetness of contemplation. Christ suggested this, when he said *I am the way, the truth, and the life*. In this way, Proverbs 4:18 is fulfilled: *The path of the just goes on, like a shining light, and grows into a perfect day*. The saints held to this order, attending to Isaiah 7:9 in an alternative translation: *Unless you believe, you will not understand*. The philosophers ignored this order: Neglecting faith and grounding° themselves entirely on reason, they could in no way achieve contemplation. For as Augustine says in *De trinitate* I [ii.4], "The weak focus of the human mind is not pierced by so excellent a light, unless it is purified by the justice of faith."

16. It is also° clear who our doctor and master is: that it is Christ, who is the director and guide of our intelligence, not just in general as in all works of nature, nor as specifically as in works of grace and meritorious virtue, but in a way that is intermediary between the two. To understand this, notice that in creatures one finds three modes of conformity to God. For some are conformed to God as a vestige, some as an image, and some as a likeness. A vestige implies a relationship to God as causal source. An image implies a relationship to God not only as source, but also as motivating object. For as Augustine says in *De trinitate* XIV [viii.11], "The soul is an image of God {120} by being receptive of him and able to participate in him" (that is, through cognition and love). A likeness has reference to God not only by way of his being source and object, but also by way of an infused gift.

17. So in those operations of a creature that are of God inasmuch as they are a *vestige*, such as all natural actions, he cooperates as the source and cause. In those that are of God inasmuch as they are an *image*, such as intellectual actions by which the soul perceives the unchangeable truth itself, he cooperates as an object and motivating basis. In those that are of God inasmuch as they are a *likeness*, such as meritorious operations, he cooperates as a gift infused through grace. And for this reason Augustine says in *De civitate dei* VIII [iv] that God is "the cause of being, the basis of understanding, and the order of living."

18. His being called the basis (*ratio*) of understanding certainly should

not be understood[5] as his being the sole or plain (*nuda*) or whole basis of understanding. For if he were the sole basis, then cognition that is knowledge would not differ from cognition that is wisdom, nor would cognizing [a thing] in the [Divine] Word differ from cognizing [it] in its own kind. Further, if he were the plain and open basis of understanding, cognition in this life would not differ from cognition in heaven, which is certainly false, because the one is *face to face*, the other *through a mirror in obscurity* [1 Cor. 13:12], since our understanding in this life occurs only through phantasms. Finally, if he were the whole basis, we would not need a species or [any sort of] reception in order to cognize things. We plainly see that this is false, because if we lose one sense, we must necessarily lose one kind of knowledge.[6]

So although the soul is, according to Augustine, tied to the eternal laws, because it somehow attains that light {122} through agent intellect's highest focus and through the higher part of reason, nevertheless it is undoubtedly true, in keeping with what the Philosopher says,[7] that cognition is generated in us through the senses, memory, and experience, from which the universal is assembled in us, which is the source of art and knowledge. Hence Plato, who shifted all certain cognition to an intelligible or ideal world, was rightly rebuked by Aristotle:[8] not because he was wrong to say there are ideas and eternal reasons, since Augustine, the greatest of doctors,° praised Plato for this,[9] but because, disdaining the sensible world, he wanted to trace all the certainty of cognition back to those ideas. In making this claim, though it might seem to stabilize the way of wisdom that proceeds according to the eternal reasons, Plato nevertheless destroyed the way of knowledge that proceeds according to created reasons, the way that Aristotle, conversely, stabilized, while neglecting that higher way. So it seems that among the philosophers, the discourse of wisdom was given to Plato, and the discourse of knowledge to Aristotle. For the former looked chiefly to higher things, whereas the latter looked chiefly to things that are lower.

19. Augustine, as the leading expositor of all scripture, received each of

---

[5] *sane intelligendum est non quia sit* This might also be translated: "His being called the basis of understanding should be understood in a reasonable way, not as if he were . . ."

[6] These are Aristotelian commonplaces. On phantasms, see *De anima* III 7, 431a14. On losing a sense, see *Posterior Analytics* I 18, 81a37.

[7] *Posterior Analytics* II 19, 100a3–9.

[8] See, e.g., *Metaphysics* I 9, XIII 4–5.

[9] See, e.g., *De civitate dei* VIII.v–vi.

these discourses, of wisdom and knowledge, from the Holy Spirit. And, as is clear from Augustine's writings, he received them in quite an excellent way. But they were in Paul and Moses in an even more excellent way: in the one as in the minister of the prefigured law, in the other as in the minister of the law of grace. For it is said of Moses in Acts 7:22 that he was *instructed in all the wisdom of the Egyptians;* and it was further said of him on the mountain, *Look and act according to the exemplar that was shown to you on the mountain* [Ex. 25:40]. Regarding Paul, he himself says that when among the simple he presents himself as *knowing only Christ and him crucified,* whereas he spoke *wisdom among the perfect,* as is said in 1 Corinthians 2:6. {124} He learned this wisdom when he was *carried up to the third heaven* (2 Corinthians 12:2). But in the most excellent way, each was in the Lord Jesus Christ, who was the principal lawgiver and at the same time the perfect wayfarer and comprehender. Hence he alone is the principal teacher and doctor.

[What We Owe Christ]

20. As the principal teacher, Christ should be principally honored, heard, and asked. He should be principally *honored,* in such a way that the dignity of a teacher is conferred upon him, in keeping with Matthew 23:8: *Do not be called rabbi, because you have one teacher, whereas you are all brothers.* For he wants to reserve for himself the dignity of the teacher's role, in keeping with John 13:13: *You call me teacher and Lord, and you do so rightly, for so I am.* But he should be honored not just vocally, in speech, but also in reality, by imitation. For this reason he adds, *If then I, your teacher and Lord, have washed your feet, you also ought to wash one another's feet.* For, as is said in Luke 14:27, *whoever does not come after me cannot be my disciple.*

21. He should also be principally *heard,* through the humility of faith, in keeping with Isaiah 50:4: *The Lord gave me a learned tongue, so that I would know how to uphold by word someone who is weary. In the morning he arouses, in the morning he arouses my ears, so that I hear him as a teacher.* He says "arouses" twice, because it is not enough for our ears to be aroused to understand, unless they are also aroused to obey. For this reason Matthew 13:43 says, *He who has ears to hear, let him hear.* For Christ teaches us not only by word, but also by example, and so one hears perfectly only when one fits understanding with words and obedience with deeds. For this reason, Luke 6:40 says that *everyone will be perfect, if he is as his teacher.*

22. He should also be principally *asked*, out of the desire for learning, not like the curious and disbelieving who ask in order to tempt, as in Matthew 12:38: *Some of the scribes and Pharisees replied, saying "Teacher, we want to see a sign from you."* Certainly, they had seen signs and were seeing them, and yet they still sought a sign. This shows {126} that human curiosity has no limit and does not deserve to be brought to the truth. Thus he replied to them that *a sign will not be given to them, except the sign of Jonas the prophet.* Jesus should be asked not in this way, but earnestly, as Nicodemus asked him. It is said of Nicodemus, in John 3:2, that *he came to Jesus at night and said to him: "Rabbi, we know that you are a teacher, come from God, since no one can produce the signs that you produce, unless God has been with him."* And it is added there that Christ revealed to him the mysteries of the faith, because he asked not for signs of power but for lessons in the truth.

23. We should ask this teacher regarding knowledge, discipline, and goodness, according to the Psalmist [118:66]: *Teach me goodness, discipline, and knowledge.* For knowledge consists in a grasp of what is true, discipline in wariness of what is bad, and goodness in the choice of what is good. The first concerns truth, the second sanctity, the third charity.

So° we should ask regarding the truth of knowledge, but not from the desire to tempt him, as the students of the Pharisees tempted him at Matthew 22:16: *Teacher, we know that you are truthful*, etc. And because their intention in questioning° him was bad, he replied to them, *Why do you tempt me, hypocrites?* But because their question was good, he gave them a true reply: *Render therefore to Caesar the things that are Caesar's, and render to God the things that are God's.*

Second, we should ask regarding the sanctity of discipline, as the young man asked him at Mark 10:17: *Good teacher, what should I do to receive eternal life?* Christ replied to him that he should observe the commandments and, if he wished to be perfect, that he should observe the counsels in which perfect moral discipline consists, being wary of what incites us° to sin.

We should also ask regarding {128} the charity of benevolence, on the example of the doctor of the law, at Matthew 22:36: *"Teacher, what is the greatest commandment in the law?" Jesus said to him, "Love the Lord your God from your whole heart, and with your whole soul and mind. This is the greatest and the first commandment. And the second is similar: Love your neighbor as yourself."* Here he shows that *love is the fulfilling of the law* [Rom. 13:10].

[The Teaching of His Ministers]

24. Therefore it is these three that we should ask Christ about, as a teacher, and to these the whole of Christ's law is directed. Thus the teaching of a ministering doctor should be directed to these three, so that under that supreme teacher the office of teaching can be worthily authorized to function. For a ministering teacher should focus on knowledge of the truth of the faith, according to 1 Timothy 2:7: *I speak the truth and I do not lie; a doctor of the gentiles in faith and in truth.* Accordingly, in 2 Peter 1:16: *For we have made known to you the truth and foreknowledge° of our Lord Jesus Christ not by following ignorant° fables, but by being made witnesses to his greatness.*

25. He should also focus on the discipline of the mind's sanctity, according to 2 Timothy 1:11: *I, Paul, have been appointed preacher and apostle for this gospel, and for this reason I suffer these things.* For, as is said in Proverbs 19:11, *The learning of a man is known by his suffering.* For just as it is not right° for the unwise to teach wisdom, so it is also not right° for the unsuffering to teach suffering or for the undisciplined to teach discipline. For where morals are concerned, examples carry more weight than words.

26. He should also focus on the benevolence of charity for God and neighbor, as in the last chapter of Ecclesiastes [12:11]: *The words of the wise are like goads and like nails deeply driven, which are given, through the counsel of teachers, by one pastor.* These words, I say, are the words of divine love, which penetrate the depths {130} of the heart. They are said to be *given, through the counsel of teachers, by one pastor* because, though divine love is praised and extolled by the words of many (through the lessons of both testaments), it is nevertheless inspired by the one sole Word, which is the repast and pastor of all. Hence all those words come from and tend toward the same Word, and for this reason they are expressly said to be given through the *counsel* of teachers – that is, through the *same* point of view.

And since all doctors of Christian law should in the end focus on the bond of charity, their viewpoints should therefore agree. For this reason, in James 3:1, *Do not, my brothers, become many teachers.* He does not say this so as to prohibit them from communicating the gift of knowledge. For Moses says, in Numbers 11:29, *Who will let all the people prophesy, and let the Lord give them his spirit?* And 1 Peter 4:10, *Each one, as he receives grace, administering it to another.* Rather, he says this so that they would not have various alien viewpoints, but would all say the same, as in 1 Corinthians 1: 10: *I beseech you, brothers, in the name of our Lord Jesus Christ, that you all say*

*the same thing, and that there be no schisms among you, but that you be perfectly
of the same meaning and the same viewpoint.*

27. For dissenting viewpoints have their roots in presumption, according to Proverbs 13:10: *Among the proud there are always disputes,* and yield
confusion, according to 1 Timothy 6:3: *If anyone teaches otherwise and does
not consent to the sound discourse of our Lord Jesus Christ, nor to teaching that
accords with piety, he is proud, knowing nothing, but languishing over questions
and verbal disputes. Out of this, envies, contentions, blasphemies, evil suspicions,
and conflicts take root among those who are corrupt in mind and deprived of the
truth.*

28. Therefore since these three are what impede us from coming to
perceive the truth – namely, presumption regarding meanings, dissenting
viewpoints, and despair of discovering what is true – Christ stands in the
way of these, {132} saying: *Christ is your one teacher.* He says that Christ is
the *teacher,* so that we will not be presumptuous regarding our knowledge.
He says that he is the *one,* lest we dissent over meaning. He says that he is
yours, ready to assist us, lest we despair over our foolishness° – especially
since he is willing and knowing and able to teach us, by sending that spirit
of which Christ says, in John 16:13: *When that spirit of truth comes, he will
teach you the whole truth.*

May he who lives and reigns with God the Father and the Holy Spirit in
the age of ages deign to bestow this upon us. Amen.°

4

HENRY OF GHENT
CAN A HUMAN BEING KNOW ANYTHING?

Introduction

Henry of Ghent (c. 1217–1293) was an immensely influential and re-spected theologian at the University of Paris. Unlike every other theolo-gian represented in this volume, Henry was an independent (or secular) cleric, neither a Franciscan nor a Dominican. His two major works are his *Summa quaestionum ordinariarum* and his *Quodlibeta*, both massive collections of questions written and debated over the same extended period of time, from the mid-1270s until his death. Active in formulating the notorious Condemnation of 1277, Henry was in general a conservative voice in Paris, resistant to the growing Aristotelianism of his day, sympathetic to the Augustinianism of Bonaventure.

But Henry was no dull reactionary. He begins his *Summa* with an extended treatment of the scope and limits of human knowledge, which occupies the first thirty-nine questions of the first five articles. After Henry it became standard to begin theological treatises with this sort of episte-mological inquiry, but at the time his approach was unprecedented. Even more startling, Henry begins the very first question, translated here, with a detailed discussion of the merits of skepticism. This was entirely novel territory in the thirteenth century: Though the arguments of the skeptics had a prominent place in the writings of Augustine, earlier scholastics seem nevertheless to have regarded the issue as closed and settled, not worthy even of serious discussion. In reopening these issues, and positioning them so prominently, Henry can be seen as a precursor to the increasingly skeptical tone of much fourteenth-century philosophy (see, for instance, Translation 10) – even though his intention is to refute skepticism soundly.

This and the following selection present the first two questions from the first article of Henry's *Summa*. The seven initial arguments in favor of skepticism (section I) draw on standard ancient arguments, and in replying to these arguments (sections III and IV) Henry relies heavily on the antiskeptical strategies employed by Aristotle, Cicero, and Augustine. But the discussion is by no means entirely derivative. Henry begins, for instance, with an important remark about what knowledge is, remarking that in the broad sense, to know (*scire*) is to have a certain grasp of anything that is true. This should not be taken as an attempt to articulate a precise criterion for knowledge: Medieval philosophers had little interest in that project. The remark is important, instead, because it extends the field of epistemology into the realm of ordinary empirical knowledge, putting aside the narrow Aristotelian conception of *scientia* as solely the product of a demonstrative syllogism. In this way, too, Henry is laying the groundwork for the growing empiricism of the fourteenth century and beyond.

For further reading on Henry of Ghent's epistemology, see Marrone (1985).

Can a Human Being Know Anything?

Summa Quaestionum Ordinariarum a.1 q.1

I. Arguments that a Human Being Cannot Know Anything

1. Based on the mode of knowing, it is argued as follows. Whatever a human being knows he knows from something prior and better known to him (*Posterior Analytics* I [71b20–23]; *Physics* I [184a10–20]). But a human being can know something in this way only by knowing it through something prior and better known than it, and (for the same reason) by knowing this through something else that is prior and better known than it, and so on to infinity. But one can know nothing at all by approaching knowledge in this way, according to the Philosopher in *Metaphysics* II [994a1–b30]. Therefore, etc.

2. Based on the means by which a thing is known, it is argued as follows. All human intellective cognition has its origin in the senses (*Metaphysics* I [980a26]; *Posterior Analytics* II [100a11]). But "pure (*sincera*) truth shouldn't be sought from the bodily senses," according to Augustine (*Book of 83 Questions*, Q9). Therefore a human being cannot know pure truth through intellective cognition. But one can know only by knowing pure truth, since nothing is known but what is true (I *Posterior Analytics* [71b25]) and according to Augustine (*Book of 83 Questions*, Q1) it is not the truth unless it is pure – that is, clear (*pura*) of falseness. Therefore, etc.

3. From the same premise, those who denied knowledge argued as follows (as is said in *Metaphysics* IV [1009b1–10]). The senses apprehend nothing of what is certain concerning a thing. For if something appears to one person concerning some thing, its contrary appears to another concerning that same thing. And when something appears to a given person at a given time and in a given condition, its contrary appears to the same person at a different time and in a different condition. Therefore, since the intellect apprehends nothing if not through the senses, it can apprehend nothing of what is certain concerning anything at all. But there can be knowledge only by apprehending something certain and determinate, according to the Philosopher in *Metaphysics* VI. Therefore, etc.

4. Based on the knowable, according to *Metaphysics* IV [1010a7–14], they have a similar argument, as follows. There is knowledge only of what is fixed and stable, according to Boethius in *Arithmetic* I [ch. 1]. But {1v} there is nothing fixed or stable in the sensible things from which, by means of the senses, all human cognition is drawn. This is so according to Augustine, who says in his *Book of 83 Questions* Q9 that "what is called the sensible changes without any intervening time." Therefore, etc.

5. Based on the knower, there is the argument of the *Meno*, at the beginning of the *Posterior Analytics* [71a29], by which he denied that there is knowledge. As the Commentator says on *Metaphysics* IX [5], no one learns unless he knows something. This accords with Augustine, in *Contra academicos* III [iii.5], and with the Philosopher, in *Metaphysics* IX [1046b35]. But someone who knows something isn't learning, because learning is a movement toward knowing. Therefore there is no one who learns anything. But no one who has not learned anything can have learning, according to Augustine in the same passage. Therefore, etc.

6. From the same premise, by forming the argument in another way, it is argued as follows. Someone who knows nothing learns nothing; but someone who learns nothing cannot have learning; therefore someone who knows nothing cannot have learning. Every human being at first knows nothing, because the human intellect, before it receives species, is like a blank slate on which nothing has been drawn, as is said in *De anima* III [430a1]. Therefore, etc.

7. Based on the object, it is argued as follows. One who doesn't perceive the essence and quiddity of a thing, but only its image, can't know (*scire*) the thing. For one who has seen only a picture of Hercules doesn't know (*novit*) Hercules. But a human being perceives nothing of a thing, except only its image – that is, a species received through the senses, which

is an image of the thing and not the thing itself. For "it is not the stone but a species of the stone that is in the soul."[1] Therefore, etc.

II. Arguments to the Contrary

1. The Commentator's argument on the beginning of *Metaphysics* II [1] goes as follows. A natural desire is not pointless. But according to the Philosopher in *Metaphysics* I [980a21], a human being desires by nature to know. Therefore a human being's desire to know is not pointless. But it would be pointless if he were unable to know. Therefore, etc.

2. From the same premise, by forming the argument in another way, it is argued as follows. It is possible for what a person naturally desires to come to him, according to what Augustine says in *Contra Julianum* IV [PL 44, 747]: "Nor would all human beings wish by natural impulse to be blessed unless they could be." A human being naturally desires to know. Therefore, etc.

3. From basically the same premise, there is this further argument. Anyone can attain the perfection to which he is naturally ordered, because [his being so ordered] would otherwise be pointless. Knowing is the perfection of a human being to which he is naturally ordered, because according to the Philosopher, in *Ethics* X [1177a17], one's happiness consists in speculative knowledge. Therefore, etc.

4. The Philosopher says in *Metaphysics* III [999b9–12] and IV and in *De caelo* II [292b17–21] that it is impossible for what cannot be completed to be begun by an agent through nature or reason, because every movement has an end and a completion on account of which it exists. But according to the Philosopher, in *Metaphysics* I [982b20–27], human beings philosophized and first began to investigate prudence for the sake of knowing and understanding and escaping ignorance. Therefore, it is possible for a human being to know and to understand.

5. According to Augustine, in *De vera religione* [xxxix.73], anyone who doubts whether someone can know something doesn't doubt whether he is doubting – he is certain of that. But he is certain only of something true that he knows. Therefore anyone who doubts whether he knows must necessarily concede that he knows something. But this wouldn't be so unless he happened to know something when he happens to doubt. Therefore, etc.

[1] Aristotle, *De anima* III 8, 431b29.

6. Along basically the same lines, the Philosopher and his Commentator argue as follows in *Metaphysics* IV [1008a7–b31, 1012b14–22]. Anyone who denies that there is knowledge says by this that he is certain there is no knowledge. But he is certain only of something that he knows. Therefore anyone who denies that there is knowledge and that a human being can know must necessarily concede that there is knowledge and that a human being can know something. And this argument is similar to the argument by which the Philosopher concludes in *Metaphysics* IV that anyone who denies that there is speech must necessarily concede that there is speech. {1vB}

[III. Reply]

If 'to know' is taken broadly for every certain cognition (*notitiam*) by which a thing is cognized as it is, without any mistake or deception, and if the question is understood and proposed in this way, then it is manifest and clear – contrary to those who deny knowledge and every perception of truth – that a human being can know something and can do so in every mode of knowing and cognizing. For someone can know something in two ways: either through another's external testimony or through one's own internal testimony.

That one can know something in the first way Augustine says in the *Contra academicos* and in *De trinitate* XV.xii [21]:

Let it be far from us to deny that we know what we have learned from the testimony of others. Otherwise we do not know of the ocean, nor do we know there to be the lands and cities that famous reports describe. We know of the existence neither of the people nor of the deeds of those people which we have learned about through historical reading. Finally, we don't know from what place or what people we came, since we have learned all these things through the testimony of others.

But that in the second way one can know something and perceive a thing as it is is clear from things we experience within ourselves and around ourselves, through both sensory and intellective cognition. For in sensory cognition a thing is truly perceived as it is, without any deception or mistake, by a sense that during its own action of sensing its proper object is not contradicted by a truer sense or by an intellection received from a different truer sense, whether in the same or in another [person].[2]

---

[2] Compare Aristotle, *De somno* 3, 461b3.

Nor concerning something that we perceive in this way should one be in doubt whether we perceive it as it is. Nor need one search in this matter for any further cause of certainty. For as the Philosopher says,[3] {2r} it is a weakness of intellect to search for reason in cases where we have sensation, since one should not search for a reason for the thing we possess that is more valuable (*dignius*) than reason. For the test of true words is that they agree with what is sensed. Hence Augustine says, in the same place:

Let it be far from us that we doubt to be true those things that we have learned through the bodily senses. For through them we have learned of the sky and earth, and the things in them that are known by us.

Hence also Cicero, in his *Academics* [II.vii.19], wanting to prove against the Academics that one can know something with certainty, says the following:

Let us begin with the senses, from which judgments are so clear and certain that, if one were allowed to choose one's own nature, I do not see what more would be sought. In my judgment truth exists in the senses above all. And if they are healthy and in good condition and all the things are removed that oppose and impede them, then a glance itself engenders faith in their judgment.

Concerning faith in intellective cognition, however, since through it one can in this way truly know something as it is, he immediately continues the same passage [vii.21]:

These things that we say are perceived by the senses are such that others follow that are not said to be perceived by the senses – for example, *This one is white*, [therefore] *This one is old*. Then greater claims follow, for example, *If something is a human being then it is an animal*. On the basis of claims of this sort the cognition of things is given to us.

So through intellective cognition, as has already been said about sensory cognition, a thing is truly perceived as it is, without any deception or falseness, by an intellection that in its proper action of intellective cognition is not contradicted by a truer intellection, or by one received from a truer sense. Nor should there be any more doubt regarding such an intellection than there is regarding the senses. Thus Augustine, in the same passage as before [*De trinitate* XV.xii.21]:

Since there are two genera of things that are known, one of which the mind perceives through the bodily senses, the other through itself, those philosophers (i.e., the Academics) raised many complaints against the bodily senses, since they were utterly unable to call into doubt certain perceptions of true things that in themselves are most firm. Of this sort is 'I know that I live.'

With respect to this we don't need to worry that we are deceived by some likeness of what is true. For it is certain that anyone who is deceived is alive. Thus nor can an Academic say that perhaps you are asleep and do not know it, and are seeing in your dreams. For no one can be mistaken in that knowledge through dreams, since sleeping and seeing in dreams both belong to the living. Nor can that Academic say that perhaps you are crazy and don't know it, because the visions even of the crazy are like those of the sane. For anyone who is crazy is alive, nor does the Academic dispute this. Therefore someone who said that he knows he is alive is not deceived, nor can he be lying.

Nor concerning this should another proof be required beyond that which is used for training the intellect, and through evident *a posteriori* signs, of the sort that will be set out later. {2rC}

Seven errors have endured from ancient times against this view, based on both the senses and intellect. The Philosopher refutes five of these in *Metaphysics* IV, in particular the error of those who deny knowledge by denying this principle of knowledge: For any thing, either its affirmation or negation is true, and not both at the same time in the same respect.

The sixth error, from the *Meno*, denies that a human being can learn. Aristotle refutes this at the start of the *Posterior Analytics* [71a25–b9]. The seventh belonged to the Academics who denied perception of the true. Augustine and Cicero refute this in their books on the Academics.

But as for those whose errors the Philosopher argues against in *Metaphysics* IV, some said that all things are false, whereas others said that all things are true. Still others said that all things are true and false at the same time. Of those who said that all things are false, some based their view on the things themselves, as for example Anaxagoras and Xenocrates,[4] who said that everything is mixed with everything, since they saw that everything is made from everything. They said that that mixture is neither being nor nonbeing and, in a way, neither of the extremes, but rather, by cancellation, a medium between them. Hence they said that it is impossible to judge something truly; rather, all judgments are false. And for this reason they said that there is no knowledge of anything, since knowledge is only of things that are true (as is said in *Posterior Analytics* I [71b25]).

---

[4] Though this is the manuscript reading, and though Aristotle occasionally discusses Xenocrates, his contemporary, the correct reference is to the pre-Socratic Xenophanes (cf. *Met.* IV 5, 1010a6)

These men erred by not distinguishing potential from actual being. For contraries and contradictories exist at the same time potentially, but not actually. This is because the distinction among contraries and contradictories holds only for beings in actuality. Only here, in other words, is something determinately this and not that. Through this, there is determinate truth and knowledge that a thing is what it is and not something else.

But others said that all things are false, taking their argument from the senses. Democritus and Leucippus, for example, said that the same thing is sensed by some people as sweet, and by others as bitter, and that these groups differ only in that the one is larger, the other smaller, since there are many healthy people to whom it seems sweet, and a few sick people to whom it seems bitter. Therefore nothing, as they said, is in actual truth determinately this or that. Rather, each thing is neither this nor that, and for that reason nothing is true; instead, all things are false, and there is no knowledge at all. The reason for their error was their judging that the intellect and the senses are the same, and that knowledge is grasped by the senses. So when they saw that sensible things have different conditions within the senses, and that nothing of what is certain is sensed, they believed that nothing is known with certainty.

Associated with their views was the view of the Academy. Augustine says that they affirmed that human beings can perceive nothing true or certain, but not that human beings ought to stop inquiring into the truth. They did say, however, that either God alone knows the truth, or perhaps also the disembodied soul of a human being. They directed these remarks only to things pertaining to philosophy, not caring about other things. Their reasoning, according to what Augustine recounts [in *Contra academicos*], was this: They said that what is true can be recognized only by signs that cannot have the character (*rationem*) of what is false [II.v.11], so that "the true is discerned from the false by distinct marks" [II.vi.14] and "does not have signs in common with what is false" [III.ix.18]. Thus what is true "cannot appear false" [III.ix.21]. But they believed it impossible that such signs could be found [III.ix.19, 21], and so they concluded that, "because of a certain darkness on the part of nature," the truth either does not exist or, "obscured and confused" [II.v.12], is hidden from us. Thus Democritus, as *Metaphysics* IV [1009b12] recounts, said that either nothing is entirely true or else it is not shown to us.

Others, such as Protagoras and his followers, said that everything true and false exists simultaneously. They said that there is no {2v} truth outside the soul, and that what appears outside is not something that exists in the thing itself at the time at which it appears; instead, it exists in the one apprehending. Thus they completely denied that things have existence outside the soul, and so they had to say that two contraries are true at the same time: not only relative to different people apprehending through the same sense but also relative to the same person through different senses and through a [single] sense in different conditions. For what appears sweet to one person through taste will appear not sweet to another through taste; what appears sweet to someone through sight will appear not sweet to that same person through taste; what appears to be a single thing to the eyes will appear to be two things when the position of the eyes is changed. From this they concluded that nothing appears determinate, that nothing is determinately true, and that therefore there is absolutely no knowledge.

Still others, such as Heraclitus and his followers, said that all things are true and false at the same time, since they supposed that only sensible things are beings and that they are not determinate in their existence, but constantly changed. For this reason they said that nothing about them remains the same in actual fact; rather, being and nonbeing belong to them at the same time and in the same respect. For motion is composed of being and nonbeing, and every change goes between being and nonbeing. Accordingly, they further said that one needn't reply yes or no to a question. And thus Heraclitus[5] at the end of his life believed that he needn't say anything, and he moved only his finger. From this they were led to say that there is nothing a human being can acquire knowledge of.

The view of the *Meno* and of certain of the Platonists was that no one can learn anything, and that therefore no one can know anything, as was said above in the fifth and sixth arguments [I.5–6]. The defect in the reasoning of these views will be clear at once when we solve the arguments. {2vD}

To deny knowledge is to destroy all faith and the whole of philosophy, as the Philosopher says in *Metaphysics* IV. For this reason it is impossible to dispute their main view by demonstrating that there is knowledge and that something can be known, because they deny all the principles of knowing. The only thing that should be used against them in defense of knowledge is true and extremely well established (*probabilibus*) assertions that they cannot deny. So it was by means of such assertions that Cicero refutes them in his *Academics* through three obvious absurdities that follow from

---

[5] In fact, the reference should be to Cratylus; see *Metaphysics* IV, 1010a12.

their claim. The first of these is taken from craft-based knowledge, the second from acts of virtue, the third from the conduct of human affairs. Cicero explains the first in this way:

Every craft is based on many perceptions. If you were to take these perceptions away, how would you distinguish a craftsman from someone who is ignorant? For what is it that can be accomplished through craft if the one who is to practice the craft has not perceived many things? [II.vii.22]

Thus Augustine says in *De vera religione* [xxx.54] that "common craft is nothing other than the memory of things experienced." Cicero explains the second in this way:

How can that good man who has decided to endure every torture rather than neglect his duty or faith, how can it happen that he accepts every suffering unless he has assented to things that cannot be false? [II.viii.23]

He explains the third in this way:

How will someone dare to undertake anything or to act with assurance, if nothing of what follows is certain to him, and he is ignorant of the ultimate good by which all things are reckoned? [II.viii.24]

The Philosopher gives a good example of this in *Metaphysics* IV [1008b15–19]: Someone who is walking walks and does not stop, because he believes that he should be walking. And along the way he does not fall into a well that stands in his path, but he avoids it. For he knows that falling into a well is bad.

[IV. Reply to the Initial Arguments]

So the arguments proving that someone can know something [II.1–6] should be granted. But we should reply individually to the arguments for the other side [I.1–7]. {2vE}

To the first – that all knowledge comes from something prior and better known, etc. – one ought to say that that mode of acquiring knowledge should be understood to apply only to the knowledge of conclusions. For principles are cognized first, immediately, and through themselves, not through other things, because they don't have anything else better known than themselves. Therefore, the infinite regress and nothing's being known is an issue for no one other than those who don't distinguish what is known through itself from what is known through another. {2vF}

To the second – that pure truth shouldn't be sought from the bodily senses – one ought to say that this is true everywhere and in all things, when one follows the senses' judgment. This is because of two claims based on which Augustine argues that certain judgment is not established in the senses: first, the changeability of sensible things; second, the fallibility of the senses themselves. But from an apprehension made through the senses, by turning away from the senses so that a judgment is made in reason (which Augustine urges us to do especially when inquiring into the truth), pure truth should indeed be sought from the senses. This is so to the extent that it can be discerned either by purely natural means through the judgment of reason in a pure, natural light, or else absolutely through the judgment of intellect in the clarity of the eternal light. Augustine speaks in these very terms of this purity in the judgment of reason following the senses, as we will see below with regard to the two ways of examining the truth.[6]

So pure truth certainly should be sought from the senses in a certain way, as the origin of truth. For a proper sense has the most certain cognition of its proper object, unless it is impeded either in itself, by the medium, or by something else. But when every impediment is lifted, there is no chance (*nec contingit*) that it will err or apprehend its proper object otherwise than as it is – though such a cognition is not stable, because of changeability on the part of either the object or the sense itself. Hence truth that is certain can't be grasped for long by depending entirely on the judgment of the senses. Nevertheless, truth that is entirely certain is grasped through the senses, by abstracting that which was apprehended by an undeceived sense and forming a judgment in intellect where what was apprehended remains as if unchanged, unable to be obscured by truthlike species of phantasms. And for us the most certain knowledge is that of sensible things, when we can trace it back to sensory experience.

Hence those letting go of the senses and thoroughly denying their judgment, deceived by sophistical arguments, frequently fell {3r} into the most absurd errors of intellect. Take Zeno, for example, who said that nothing can move, and all those who said that all things are moved by a single motion. Thus one should always believe a particular sense when it is not impeded, unless it is contradicted by some other worthier sense (either in the same person at a different time or in a different person at the same time) or by a higher power perceiving that the sense is impeded. For the senses are not in equal good condition in everyone or in the same

[6] See Translation 5, pp. 118, 124.

person at different times, and so one should not believe their judgments equally – as is clear with the healthy and the sick. For we should believe the taste of someone healthy more than the taste of someone sick, and someone who sees something up close more than someone who sees it from a distance, and someone who sees a thing through a uniform medium more than someone who sees it through a varying medium, and so on for other conditions of this sort. {3rG}

To the third – that the same thing often appears in different ways to the same person or to different people – one ought to say that it doesn't follow from this that no sense should be believed. For, as was said, in a case in which one [sense] is deceived, another frequently indicates what is true; or in a case in which [a sense] is deceived in one condition, in another condition it indicates what is true. It's clear in this way how the reasoning of Democritus was deficient. For though sensible things have different conditions within the senses, a thing is still determinately perceived through an undeceived sense, at the time at which it is not deceived. And sensations differ not only as there are fewer and more who sense it [that way], but also according to the greater and lesser worth of the senses when it comes to sensing.

The defect in the reasoning of the Academics is similarly clear. For their claim is not true, that nothing is determinately perceived through signs and that signs do not show what is true in things. Instead, those signs that are the proper sensibles of a given sense display that which they are to their proper sense, assuming that sense is neither deceived nor impeded, and can bring intellect to a determinate cognition of a thing's truth. And hence the Academics themselves, more than others, were devoted to inquiring into the truth through signs of this sort, although their view was that they could never find the truth. In this respect their view was like that of someone who runs to grasp a thing he never will grasp – this is how the Philosopher reproves them in *Metaphysics* IV. Other issues concerning their view will be spelled out further in the next question.[7]

It's clear for the same reason that the assumption of Protagoras – that things follow the appearances of the senses – is false, because sensations, whether true or deceived, can be derived only from things, since a sense is a passive power. So even though the same thing appears in different ways to the same or different [senses], this happens only on account of a

---

[7] Translation 5, pp. 121–23.

sense's being deceived or impeded. In this case one needn't believe that sense. But one should not, on this account, say that no sense is to be believed, because an undeceived sense ought to be believed completely. As for which sense is such, the intellect above all else has to judge this on the basis of many prior experiences concerning what the senses can be deceived or impeded by. {3rH}

To the fourth – that all sensible things are in constant change – one ought to say that the Heracliteans, whose argument this was, believed that only sensible things are existent. And this was the error of all the philosophers up to the time of the Italians: They unanimously denied that there is knowledge, on account of the changeability of natural sensible things. Perceiving their error, later philosophers asserted that there is knowledge and that something can be known of natural sensible things. But they were divided as to how one knows and acquires knowledge. Pythagoras, the first of the Italians, believed with his predecessors that one can't have knowledge of natural things through the things themselves, because of their changing. But to preserve in some way the knowledge of natural things, he brought mathematical facts into nature, proposing them as the principles and causes of natural things both in existence and in cognition. For mathematical facts are in a certain way unchangeable, through their abstraction from sensible and changeable matter.

But Plato, coming after Pythagoras, saw that in reality mathematical facts inhere in natural things. So however much they are abstracted from natural things, mathematical facts are really changed along with them, and no fixed knowledge of natural things can be had through them. Plato proposed ideal Forms as the causes and principles of natural things, both in existence and in cognition, entirely separate from natural things and without any change. In this way, through them, there can be unchangeable knowledge of what is changeable. {3rI}

Aristotle, however, saw that a thing has existence and can be cognized only through something that exists within it (*in re*). And he saw that, due to their changing, there cannot be knowledge of singulars through themselves. So he claimed that universals – that is, genera and species – are abstracted by intellect from the singulars where they have true existence. For a universal is one in many and of many. And though they are changeable as they exist in singulars, they are unchangeable as they exist in intellect. Accordingly, he claimed that we do have fixed knowledge of changeable, particular, sensible, natural things, through their universals existing within intellect.

Augustine was imbued with the philosophy of Plato. If he found in it things suitable to the faith, he took them into his own writing. The things he found that were adverse to the faith he interpreted in a better light to the extent that he could. Now as Augustine says in his *Book of 83 Questions*, Q46, it seemed to be "sacrilege" to believe that the ideas of things are located outside the divine mind – ideas that the divine mind contemplates so as to establish what it establishes. So for this reason, even though Aristotle attributed this view to Plato, Augustine said that Plato located these ideas in the divine intelligence and that they subsist there. As he says in *City of God* VIII.iv,

> What Plato thought about these matters – that is, where he thought or believed that the end of all actions, the cause of all natures, and the light of all reasons exist – I don't believe should be rashly decided. For it may be that those celebrated by fame who praise Plato above all others perceive something about God so as to find in God the cause of subsisting, the reason for understanding and the direction for living.

Thus Augustine, interpreting Plato's pronouncements more soundly than Aristotle did, claims that the principles of certain knowledge and of cognizing the truth consist in eternal, unchangeable rules or reasons existing in God. It is by participating in them, through intellective cognition, {3v} that one cognizes whatever pure truth is cognized in creatures. Consequently, just as by his being he is the cause of the existence of all things insofar as they exist, so too by his truth he is the cause of the cognition of all things insofar as they are true. In this way there can be certain and fixed knowledge of changeable things no matter how changeable they are. Accordingly, Augustine says in *De trinitate* XII [xiv.23]:

> It is not only for sensible things located in space that intelligible and incorporeal reasons endure, apart from local space. Those same intelligible, nonsensible reasons stand, apart from any passing of time, for the motions that pass by in time. Few attain these through keenness of mind, and when they are attained insofar as they can be, the one who has attained them does not endure there. Hence a transitory thought is formed of a thing that is not transitory. Nevertheless this transitory thought is committed to memory through the training by which the mind is educated, so that there is someplace to where a thought can return after it is forced to pass away. For if the thought were not to return to memory and find what it had placed there, then as if never educated it would once again be led just as it once had been, and would find it where it had first found it, in the incorporeal truth. And from there it would again, as if written down, be formed in memory.

But there will be a fuller discussion of this in the question immediately following.[8] {3vK}

To the fifth and sixth – that one can't know because one can't learn – one ought to say that the assumption is false. For one can indeed learn, as will be clear below.[9] But it should be realized that 'to learn' can be taken in two ways. In one way, generally, learning extends to every new acquisition of knowledge. In this way it needn't be the case that every learner knows something. For someone learning to cognize first principles acquires this through no preceding cognition. In another way, strictly, learning extends to a cognition only of conclusions, which one acquires in actuality from a prior cognition of principles in which the conclusion lies hidden, in potentiality (as will be clear below). In this way, someone who is learning knows something.

To the seventh – that a human being perceives nothing of the thing to be cognized except the image alone – it should be replied that one can perceive a thing's image in two ways. In one way, it can be perceived as the object of cognition. In this way it is true that someone perceiving only the thing's image does not cognize the thing: For example, someone seeing an image of Hercules painted on a wall does not thereby either see or cognize Hercules. In another way, it can be perceived as the basis (*ratio*) of cognizing, and in this way the claim is not true. For a thing is truly cognized through just a perceived species of it – as a stone is truly seen through its sensible species alone, received in the eye, and is truly understood through its intelligible species alone, received in intellect.

But perhaps you will say that that species is something sensible received by a sense and that therefore, because it is an accident and the likeness of only an accident, it doesn't lead to a cognition of the thing's quiddity and substance. To this one should reply that even if the intellect first receives intelligible species of sensible and corporeal things as they are sensible, and first understands them through those species, nevertheless secondarily, out of those species of sensible things, by means of the investigation of natural reason, it conceives cognitions of nonsensible things through itself. These are the quiddities of substances, for instance, and others of the same sort that don't have their own species in intellect. And this is what Augustine says, in *De trinitate* IX.iii [3]:

---

[8] See Chapter 5.
[9] See *Summa* 1.6: "Can one human being acquire knowledge through the teaching of another human being?"

That power by which we discern through the eyes, whether it is rays or something else, we are not able to discern with the eyes, but we seek with the mind, and (if possible) we comprehend with the mind. The mind itself, then, just as it collects cognitions of corporeal things through the bodily senses, so it collects cognitions of incorporeal things through itself.

He calls things corporeal inasmuch as they are sensible, and calls incorporeal whatever is not sensible, whatever it is – such as mathematical things, the quiddities of substances, [composed of] matter and form, and others of this sort. The mind, through the efforts of natural reason, puts together a cognition of such things from out of the species of sensible things, on the basis of a natural connection between the sensible and the nonsensible – as if by digging under the species something sensible presents to it. It's in this way that a sheep by natural instinct makes an estimation through a sensed species about something not sensed – as when through the sensible species of a wolf, imagined or seen, it makes an estimation that the wolf is harmful and hostile. And so one speaks of understanding (*intelligere*), as if it were reading from within (*ab intus legere*).

5

HENRY OF GHENT
CAN A HUMAN BEING KNOW ANYTHING WITHOUT DIVINE ILLUMINATION?

Introduction

In the previous selection, Henry of Ghent considered and rejected the ancient skeptical arguments purporting to show that human beings can know nothing at all. His strategy there was to define a broad sense of knowledge (*scientia*) on which ordinary sensory experience could count as a sufficient ground, and then to establish a criterion for picking out those circumstances in which the senses should be trusted. All of that was, in a sense, merely a warm-up exercise for the far more complicated discussion contained in the present selection. Whereas ancient skepticism must have struck Henry as a tired and antiquated issue, the present question – divine illumination – clearly lies at the heart of his own interests, and indeed of thirteenth-century epistemology in general.

For medieval philosophers up until Henry's time (the last quarter of the thirteenth century), it was commonplace to assume that true knowledge requires some kind of special illumination from God. (Bonaventure offers a classic statement of the doctrine in Translation 3.) But later thirteenth-century authors began to question this doctrine and then reject it entirely. Thomas Aquinas supported the theory of illumination, but denied that it should be conceived of as a special ongoing event: He thought human beings were born with a certain sort of illumination (*Summa theologiae* 1a 84.7). Later scholars, in particular John Duns Scotus, were even more critical of the theory, and by the fourteenth century the theory was entirely discredited. Henry of Ghent, then, should be read as the last great defender of divine illumination.

In this selection, Henry works to spell out precisely what kind of knowledge requires a special divine illumination. As Henry points out (section II.A), all parties to the debate agree that God provides a kind of general and constant illumination to all of creation, without which nothing could exist or function in any way. What is at issue is whether God does something further in certain cases to permit certain human beings to have a special kind of knowledge. Henry argues in the affirmative, and explains that without such illumination no one could have this special kind of knowledge. He characterizes such knowledge as knowledge of the pure truth, as compared to knowledge of what is true. The latter requires merely that one "apprehend a thing just as it has existence in itself" (section II.B), and this is possible for human beings naturally, even at the sensory level. Knowledge of the pure truth, in contrast, requires a composite judgment whereby one concludes that this is a true thing – for instance, that this particular shade of color is a true instance of a certain kind, or that this particular animal is a true instance of a certain species of animal. That requires an insight into the true species and kinds that lie behind particulars, something that is available – Henry argues – only through access to the "divine exemplars." This, of course, is possible only through divine illumination.

For further discussion of Henry's argument, see Pasnau (1995). On divine illumination more generally, see CHLMP VI.21, "Faith, ideas, illumination, and experience," and Pasnau (1999a).

Can a Human Being Know Anything without Divine Illumination?

Summa Quaestionum Ordinariarum a.1 q.2

[I. Initial Arguments]

[*A. In Favor of Divine Illumination*]

Concerning the second, it is argued that a human being cannot know anything through natural effort alone, without a special divine illumination (*illustratione*).

1. The Apostle says in II Corinthians 3:5, *We are not sufficient to cognize something from us as if from us, but our sufficiency comes from God.* But the truth is perceived only through cognition. Therefore it is only through God that we possess the sufficiency to perceive the truth. But this does not occur except through a special illumination of some divine light, since everything that is perceived is perceived in a light. Therefore, etc.

2. Commenting on I Corinthians 12:3 – *No one can say "Lord Jesus"*

unless in the Holy Spirit – Ambrose says that the true, no matter who speaks it, comes from the Holy Spirit. But whoever knows something true speaks it through the word of his mind. Therefore he both knows it and speaks it through the Holy Spirit. But this happens only through a special illumination. Therefore, etc.

3. Augustine says in *Soliloquies* I [viii.15]:

God is intelligible, as are the observable facts of the sciences. Nevertheless they differ in many ways. For the earth is visible, as is light, but the earth cannot be seen unless it is illuminated by light. And therefore with regard to those things that are passed on in the sciences – which without any doubt everyone concedes to be most true – it ought to be believed that they cannot be understood unless illuminated by something like their own sun.

But that additional thing that is like the sun can only be the divine light, according to what Augustine says in the same place:

Just as there are three things in this sun that may be observed – that it exists, that it shines, and that it illuminates – so too {4r} there are such things in that most secret God: that it exists, that it understands, and that it makes other things be understood.

Therefore, etc.

4. Augustine says in *The Lord's Sermon on the Mount* II [ix.32] that

When any rational soul thinks and reasons, even if blinded by desire, whatever in that reasoning is true should be attributed not to it but to the very light of truth by which it is touched, however lightly.

But that light belongs to nothing other than a special divine illumination. Therefore, etc.

5. Augustine says in *Confessions* XII [xxv.35],

If we both see that what you say is true, and we both see that what I say is true, then where (I ask) do we see it? I at any rate don't see it in you, nor you in me, but we both see it in the unchanging truth that is above our minds.

But since that truth exceeds the limits of our nature, we see something in it only through a special divine illumination. Therefore, etc.

[B.] *On the Contrary*

1. Augustine says in *Contra academicos* I [v.14] that "no way is found that better leads to the truth than diligent investigation into the truth." But

investigation would be pointless unless through it a human being could attain the truth without a special divine illumination. Therefore, etc.

2. The Philosopher says at the start of the *Metaphysics* [980a22] that "All human beings naturally desire to know." But they desire naturally only things that they can know through nature. Therefore, human beings can know something through nature. But for this a special divine illumination is not required. Therefore, etc. {4rB}

[II.] Reply

[*A. Knowledge in a Broad Sense*]

Consider all the objects of cognition, standing in an ordered relation to each other so that the last is always suited to be cognized through a preceding one. If a cognition of the first of those could be attained through intellect by purely natural means without any special divine illumination, then likewise a cognition of all the later ones could be attained in the same way. For if a human being by purely natural means without any special divine illumination could attain a cognition of the first theoretical principles, then likewise by purely natural means without any special divine illumination he could attain a cognition of all the conclusions following from those principles. For although the cognition of principles is a kind of illumination toward the cognition of conclusions, nevertheless if someone could attain such a cognition by purely natural means then there is not said to be any special divine illumination in cognizing conclusions through those principles.

In contrast, if in the case of some interrelated objects of cognition the first of them cannot be attained by someone by purely natural means, but only through a special divine illumination, then likewise neither can any of those that come later. For the later ones are cognized only by reason of the first. But now it is undoubtedly true that in the case of some objects of cognition, the first of them cannot be cognized or known by purely natural means, but only by a special divine illumination. This is so in the case of those that are held by the faith in themselves, unconditionally (*per se et simpliciter credibilia*). And so in such cases, it ought to be granted unconditionally and absolutely that it is not possible for a human being to know anything by purely natural means, but only by a special divine illumination. We will establish this later [*Summa* art. 5, q.3].

But some want to extend this mode of knowing to everything that is knowable: They say that nothing true can be known by a human being by purely natural means, without a special divine illumination infused by some supernatural light. And they believe this to be Augustine's view in all his works, wherever he claims that whoever sees something true sees it in the first truth, or in the eternal rules, or in the eternal light. As he says in *City of God* XI.x,

It is not inappropriate to say that the soul is illuminated by the incorporeal light of God's simple wisdom, just as a body of air is illuminated by a bodily light.

Those who speak in this way greatly degrade the worth and perfection of the created intellect. For matched with every natural thing that is perfect in its form there ought to be some natural action or operation that is proper to it and through which by purely natural means it can attain the good natural to it. This is clear in the case of all other natural things. In keeping with this, Damascene says in *Sentences* Bk. I that of things whose natures are different, their operations are also different. For it is impossible for a substance to lack its natural operation. And in the *Liber de duplici natura et voluntate Christi*, ch. 4: It is impossible for a nature to be established outside of those natural characteristics that are proper to it – e.g., living, rational, voluntary. For someone that does not reason is not a human being, since no human being has been made that does not reason, either well or badly. But as is said in *De anima* I [403a8], knowing and understanding are the intellect's proper operation, "above all else." For this reason, then, if knowing is not possible for someone by purely natural means, then neither is any operation at all; such a person would hence be inferior to all creatures, which is absurd. As the Philosopher says in *De caelo* II [292a22–b12], a thing well completed by the whole of goodness does not need an operation by which it is good, and it is the first cause of everything from which every other thing receives its goodness. So [every other thing] needs its proper operations, through which it is moved toward that [first cause] so as to participate in its divine existence insofar as it can. For all things desire it, and whatever they do by nature they do because of it.

At this point, perhaps it will be said in defense of the above view that it clearly is true that understanding and knowing what is true are the proper and natural operation of intellect and the human soul, and that through which it acquires its goodness. Still, because of that act's eminence and worth, one needs a special illumination for it, even though other beings

carry out their actions by purely natural means. For they do so because of
the imperfection of those actions – and it is not absurd that one thing
should need more to carry out a more perfect action, whereas another
thing needs less to carry out a less perfect action.

It is utterly absurd to say this, and is highly derogatory to the worth of
the rational soul. For if {4v} other inferior things are by purely natural
means capable of some operation corresponding and proportionate to their
nature, then it is absurd to deny this of the rational soul. The result would
be not just that it is not capable by purely natural means of an eminent
operation exceeding its nature, but also that it would not even be capable
of some operation agreeing with and proportionate to its nature. For it is
highly absurd that God would have made the human soul among natural
things and not have prepared for it the natural instruments by which it
would be capable of any natural operation suited to it, given that he
prepared those instruments for other inferior things. For God, much more
than nature, does not do anything pointless, or fail to provide a thing with
what is necessary for it. But the proper natural operation of the human
soul is nothing other than knowing or cognizing. Therefore it must absolutely be granted that a human being through its soul without any special
divine illumination can know or cognize something, and can do so by
purely natural means. For to hold the contrary is highly derogatory to the
worth of the soul and of human nature.

(When I say 'by purely natural means,' I am not excluding the general
influence of the first intelligence – which is the first agent in *every* intellectual and cognitive action. Just as in every movement of every natural
thing, the first mover produces the movement, so too the general influence
that helps with cognition does not preclude that cognition's being said to
be brought about by purely natural means. For a human being has that
influence assisting him while he cognizes all the things he cognizes naturally, and for this reason it should be said that he attains by purely natural
means the cognition of all the other subsequent things that he attains
through that influence.)

So if we take 'to know' broadly for every certain cognition (*notitiam*) of
a thing, so that it includes even sensory cognition (*cognitionem*), then (as
was said in the preceding question) to the extent that it comes from the
senses and sensory cognition, it is clear that we ought to say unconditionally and absolutely that one can know and cognize something through a
sensory cognition that is certain, as was shown in the preceding question
[p. 97]. Further – and this pertains to the present question – this can

occur by purely natural means, because the primary sensible objects make an impression on the senses by purely natural necessity, and it is through these sensibles, again by natural necessity, that all subsequent sensible objects make an impression on both the external and internal senses. {4vC}

[B. Knowledge of the Truth]

A distinction must be drawn, however, with respect to intellect and intellective cognition: It is this cognizing, strictly, that is called knowing. For although nothing is known unless it is true (according to Augustine in his *Book of 83 Questions* [Q54]), still it is one thing to know of a creature what is true with respect to it, and another to know its truth. So there is one cognition by which a thing is cognized, another by which its truth is cognized. For every cognitive power that through its cognition apprehends a thing just as it has existence in itself, outside the cognizer, apprehends what is true in it. But through this it does not apprehend the thing's truth. For the senses even in brute animals apprehend well enough concerning a thing what is true in it – for instance, a true human being, true wood, a true stone, and especially the proper objects with respect to which the senses are necessarily true. But still they apprehend or cognize the truth of no thing, because they cannot judge regarding any thing what it is in actual truth – e.g., concerning a human being, that it is a true human being, or concerning a color, that it is a true color.

So through the intellective cognition of something created, one can have two kinds of cognitions. By one, someone knows or cognizes through a simple understanding solely what a thing is. By the other, someone knows and cognizes the truth of the thing itself, through an understanding that composes and divides. In the case of the first cognition our intellect entirely follows the senses, and there is no concept in intellect that was not first in the senses. Insofar as it is of this sort, then, such an intellection certainly can be true – by conceiving or cognizing the thing as it is – just as the sense that it is following can be. But it doesn't conceive or understand the thing's very truth through a certain judgment by perceiving of it what it is – for instance, that it is a true human being or a true color.

There are two reasons for this, one pertaining to the intellect itself, another pertaining to what is intelligible. The reason that pertains to the intellect is that it conceives the truth not by a simple understanding, but only by composition and division (as the Philosopher claims in *Metaphysics*

VI [10727b18–32] and as will be explained below). Hence just as a sense is called true because of grasping a thing as it is, not because of grasping its truth, so too a simple understanding following a true sense is called true because of grasping a thing as it is, not because of grasping its truth.

The reason that pertains to what is intelligible is that the intention of the thing by which it is that which it is and the intention by which it is called true are two different things, even though – since every being is true and vice versa – these intentions coincide in each and every thing and are convertible with one other. For as the first proposition of the *Liber de causis* says, the first of created things is existence, and so the first intention capable of being grasped by intellect is the notion *being* (*ratio entis*). One can understand this notion without understanding any other intention pertaining to *being*, because it includes none of the others in itself, and is included in all the others. For although the intention *being* is understood only under the notion *true*, which is the per se object of intellect, it is nevertheless not the case that *true*, as the notion from which *being* is understood, is the object of intellect in the way that *being* is. For the notion *true* is the notion of intelligibility in all things. But the object [of intellect] is *true being*, or *true good*, and so on for the other intentions of things. {4vD} Hence, the intention *being* is included in all the other intentions of things, both universal and particular, because what is not a being is nothing. For this reason, the Commentator claims regarding the first proposition of the *Liber de causis* that existence is characterized by its adhering to the thing more vehemently than do the other intentions in that thing.

The next most proximate intentions in the thing, after the intention *being*, are these universal intentions: *one, true,* and *good*. This is so in various ways, in order, because {5r} anything existing under the intention *being* can be considered in three ways:

• First, insofar as it has in its nature a determinate existence by which through its form it is in itself undivided but divided from everything else. In this way the intention *one* holds of it. For everything is one insofar as it is, in itself, formally undivided, but divided from everything else. For as the Philosopher says in *Metaphysics* III [999b33], something is one that exists by itself and alone.

• Second, insofar as it has in its own existence what its corresponding exemplar represents it as having. In this way the intention *true* holds of it.

For each thing is true insofar as it contains in itself what its exemplar represents.

· Third, insofar as it holds of the end to which it is directed. In this way the intention *good* holds of it. For every thing is good insofar as it aims toward an end that is good.

So *true* indicates an intention concerning the thing relative to its exemplar. And since this is not first but secondary, whereas *being* indicates the first, discrete intention concerning the thing, it follows that the intellect can indeed apprehend that which is a being and is true in the thing, without apprehending the intention of its truth. For the intention of truth in a thing can be apprehended only by apprehending its conformity to its exemplar. The intention *being*, on the other hand, is apprehended in the thing discretely, without such a relation. But in a second cognition, by which the truth of the thing itself is known or cognized (without which it is not a complete human cognition of the thing), the cognition and judgment of intellect altogether exceed the cognition and judgment of the senses, since (as has been said) the intellect cognizes something's truth only by composing and dividing, which a sense cannot do. Hence such an intellection can cognize a thing in a way that the senses cannot, nor can even an intellection that is an understanding of simples: Such an intellection can apprehend by a certain judgment concerning a thing that in actual truth it is such or such — for instance, [that it is] a true human being, a true color, and so on.

[C. Different Kinds of Exemplars]

So with respect to this mode of knowing and cognizing something through intellect, by which the truth of the thing is known (this is knowing in the strict sense), it is still in doubt whether a human being can know anything by purely natural means, without any special divine illumination. {5rE} We should say the following. It was said already [II.B] that the truth of a thing can be cognized only by cognizing the conformity of the cognized thing to its exemplar. For as Augustine says in *De vera religione* [xxxvi.66], "true things are true insofar as they are like their one source." Also, Anselm says in *De veritate* [ch. 7] that "truth is the conformity of a thing to its most true exemplar" and, in the same passage: "What is, truly is, insofar as it is what is there." For this reason, then, inasmuch as there are two kinds of exemplars of a thing, a thing's truth has two ways of being cognized by a human being, with respect to two exemplars. For according to what Plato holds in the *Timaeus* [27d–29a], there are two exemplars: one kind made and constructed, the other kind perpetual and unchangeable. The first exemplar of a thing is its universal species existing within the soul, through which the soul acquires a cognition of all the individuals it stands for. This exemplar is caused by the thing. The second exemplar is the divine art containing the ideal formulations of all things. Plato says that God established the world from this exemplar (just as an artisan builds a house from an exemplar of the artistry in his mind) and not from the first exemplar.

We should know, then, that in examining that first exemplar, there are two ways in which a human being can go about it:

• First, so as to examine the cognized object depicted outside the cognizer – as by examining a person's image painted on a wall in order to recognize that person;
• Second, so as to examine the basis (*rationem*) of cognizing depicted in the cognizer – in that the species of sensible things are depicted in the senses and the species of intelligible things in the intellect.

In the first way it is impossible to cognize a thing's truth by examining its exemplar. One can have only an imaginary apprehension of the thing, an apprehension of whatever sort someone's imaginative power happened to be able to form for him. Thus, as Augustine says in *De trinitate* VIII [v.7], someone would marvel if a person he had imagined but never seen were to appear before him [just as he imagined]. Also, through that imaginary apprehension taken from a painted image, if someone were to learn the name of the person in the image, then he could come to an estimative judgment of that person – if that person were to appear before him. At that point he could for the first time, on the basis of the thing itself seen in its own form, cognize its truth, and on that basis make a judgment as to whether that image is a true one, corresponding to the person seen. It was in this way, one reads, that Queen Candace had a painted image of Alexander made for herself before she had ever seen him, and she recognized him immediately when she saw him, even though he pretended to be someone else.[1]

So in the second way – that is, by examining the exemplar taken from

---

[1] *Historia Alexandri Magni*, III.19–22.

the thing itself, so as to examine the basis of cognizing in the cognizer himself – the truth of the thing itself can indeed be cognized in a way: by forming a mental concept of the thing, conforming to that exemplar. It was in this way that Aristotle held that human beings acquire knowledge of things and a cognition of truth by purely natural means – and this with respect to natural, changeable things. Aristotle held that such an exemplar is acquired from things through the senses as the primary basis of art and knowledge, according to what he says at the start of the *Metaphysics* [981a5–7]: "Art results when from many things understood through experience, one universal judgment is made regarding similar cases." And in *Posterior Analytics* II [100a4–8]:

Memory is produced from sense, and from a memory often produced, experience. And from experience – a universal existing in the soul – the one [is produced] over the many. That is the basis of art and knowledge.

This accords with what Augustine says in *De trinitate* XI.iii [6]:

If the species of a body that is sensed by a body is taken away, its likeness remains in the memory. Through this the will turns the mind's attention so that it is formed internally by that, just as it was formed externally by the body that was its sensible object.

And so, as he says in *De trinitate* VIII.v [7], {5v} things we have not seen we think of according to generic or specific cognitions, either naturally innate or gathered from experience. So through the universal cognition that we have within ourselves, acquired from different species of animals, we form a cognition, regarding whatever appears to us, of whether it is an animal or not, and through the specific cognition of a donkey we form a cognition, regarding whatever appears to us, of whether it is a donkey or not.

[D. Infallible Knowledge of the Truth Requires Illumination]

But through such an exemplar, acquired within us, it is altogether impossible for us to have an altogether certain and infallible cognition of the truth. There are three reasons for this: The first draws on the thing from which such an exemplar is abstracted, the second on the soul in which such an exemplar is received, the third on the exemplar itself that is received in the soul from the thing.

The first reason is that such an exemplar, because it is abstracted from a changeable thing, necessarily has some of the characteristics of a changeable thing. So since natural things are more changeable than mathematical things, the Philosopher claimed that our knowledge of mathematical things has more certainty than our knowledge of natural things, through their universal species. This can be only because of the changeability of the species themselves existing within the soul. Hence Augustine, taking up this cause of the incertitude of the knowledge of natural things (the cause due to sensibles), says in his *Book of 83 Questions* Q9 that "pure truth shouldn't be sought from the bodily senses" and that

We are warned for our own sake to turn away from this world and toward God – that is, toward the truth that is understood and apprehended in the inner mind, and that always remains and is of the same nature – and to make this turn with all haste.

The second reason is that because the human soul is changeable and undergoes error, nothing that is equally changeable or more so can correct it so that it is not bent by error, and so that it persists in the correctness of truth. Therefore, every exemplar that the soul receives from natural things, since it is of a lower grade of nature than the soul, is necessarily equally changeable as the soul or more so. It therefore cannot correct the soul so that it persists in infallible truth. This is the argument of Augustine in *De vera religione* [xxx.56] by which he proves that the unchangeable truth through which the soul has certain knowledge is above the soul:

It is clear enough that the law of all arts, since it is utterly unchangeable – whereas the human mind, to which it has been granted to see such a law, can suffer the changeability of error – is the law above our mind that is called the truth.

Only this is sufficient to correct our changeable and bendable mind with infallible cognition. The mind does not have the ability to judge this law, but through it it judges everything else. For the mind is more able to judge anything lower than itself than it is able through that to judge another, as Augustine concludes in the same passage.

The third reason is that an exemplar of this sort, since it is an intention and species of a sensible thing abstracted from a phantasm, has a likeness with the false as well as with the true. So as far as the species is concerned, they cannot be distinguished. For it is through the same images of sensible things that (a) we judge in sleep and in madness that the images are the things themselves, and (b) when awake we judge the things themselves. But the pure truth is not perceived unless it is discerned from what is false. Therefore it is impossible through such an exemplar to have certain knowledge and a certain cognition of the truth. Thus if we are to possess certain knowledge of the truth, the mind must turn away from the senses and sensible things and from every intention, no matter how universal and abstracted from the senses, and turn toward the unchangeable truth existing above the mind. This truth "does not have an image of the false from which it cannot be discerned," as Augustine says in his *Book of 83 Questions* Q9, where he discusses this argument. {5vF}

[E. The Academics]

So in this way it is clear that the truth is of two sorts and that there are two ways of knowing the truth, ways that Augustine suggests in reconsidering what he had said in *Soliloquies* I [i.2] − "God, you willed that only the pure know what is true" − when he says [*Retractations* I.iv.2]:

It can be replied that many people, even the impure, know many true things. For it was not defined here what that true is that only the pure can know, and what it is to know.

It is also clear that if a human being can have a cognition of certain knowledge and infallible truth, this is not possible for him by examining an exemplar abstracted from a thing through the senses, no matter how much it is purified and made universal.

It was for this reason that the first Academics denied that anything is known at all. They were imitating the claim of Plato (since as Augustine says in an epistle [n. 118] to Dioscorus, the Academics are the same as the Platonists), and opposing the Stoics, who claimed that there are only sensible things in the world. The Academics' argument was based on their understanding of the cognition of pure truth: They claimed that every cognition of pure truth concerning anything can be had only by examining the second exemplar. {5vG} Nevertheless they were well aware that some cognition of the truth could be perceived through the senses and, mediated by the senses, through intellect. But they judged that this wasn't worthy of being called knowledge, according to what Augustine says in *Contra academicos* III [xi.26]:

There are those who grant that all the things that the bodily senses attain can result in opinion. But they deny that this can result in knowledge, which they want to be confined to one's intelligence and to dwell in the mind, far removed from the senses.

For as Augustine says in book II [v.11–12], it seemed to them that "nothing is more shameful than holding an opinion" and that "nothing can be perceived." They therefore concluded that "a wise man would never approve of anything," but would follow what appears "plausible" and "truthlike." It was for this reason that they didn't distinguish between a certain cognition by which what is true in the thing is perceived through either sense or intellect, and a cognition by which the truth of the thing itself is known. They did not even distinguish, in this connection, between those cognitions of the truth that are clear and pure, and those that are imaginary and obscured by phantasms and images of things. Instead, as it seemed from their words, they unconditionally denied that anything can be known.

Thus the later Academics, holding to the words of their predecessors' position, but ignoring their intent, completely denied all knowledge and perception of the truth – not only as regards the intellect's perception of the cognition that pertains to wisdom, and of things pertaining to philosophy, but also as regards sensory perception, {6r} as was explained in the previous question [p. 100]. But the reason why those first Academics unconditionally denied all knowledge and cognition of the truth, at least verbally, was to conceal until an opportune time Plato's true view about the cognition of pure truth, until at last the time was right. {6rH}

The third group of Academics made this public, according to what Augustine says in *Contra academicos* II [x.24]: "They seem to me to have needed to do this in order both to hide their position from the slow and to signify it to the vigilant." For "the Academics had certain knowledge of the truth and did not wish rashly to reveal it to others who were ignorant or impure" [xiii.29]. And as he says in book III [xvii.37],

Why did it please such great men to carry on in such a way that knowledge of what is true would seem unavailable to everyone? Listen a little more carefully, not to what I know, but to what I think. Plato was the wisest and most erudite man of his day, and it is certain that he believed there were two worlds: an intelligible world where the truth itself resides and another world, this sensible one, made in the image of the first. Plato also held that the truth about the intelligible world is polished and brightened, as it were, within a soul that knows itself, whereas opinion about this world, rather than knowledge, can be generated in the souls of fools. These and other views of this sort seem to have been preserved among his successors as much as they could, and to have been guarded as mysteries. For these theories are not easily perceived except by those who cleanse themselves from all vices and restore themselves to another, more than human way of life. And whoever knows these theories and is willing to teach them to any and all men grievously sins.

For this reason, when Zeno, the founder of the Stoics, [claimed that] nothing at all exists beyond this sensible world and that nothing in it is acted upon except by a body (for he took God to be fire), it seems to me that Arcesilaus, when that evil was widely spreading, very prudently and advantageously concealed thoroughly the knowledge of the Academy, and buried it as if it were gold to be found by posterity. So since people are rather prone to rush into false opinions, and, through their familiarity with bodies, they very readily but dangerously believe that all things are bodily, that most ingenious man undertook to uneducate those that were badly educated, rather than to educate those he did not consider educable.

For, as Augustine says in the epistle [n.118] to Dioscorus,

Although the Epicureans said that the bodily senses are never deceived, whereas the Stoics conceded that they sometimes are deceived, still they both proposed a rule for grasping the truth within the senses. With those groups contradicting each other, who would listen to the Platonists if they were to say not only that there is something that cannot be perceived by bodily touch, smell, or taste, nor by the ears or eyes, and cannot be thought of by any imagination, but also that only what is unchangeable and sempeternal truly exists and truly can be perceived, and that it is perceived only by the intelligence through which the truth, however it can be attained, is attained? So since the Platonists believed such things, things they did not teach to those devoted to the flesh, and since they did not have enough authority among the people to persuade them to believe until their minds were led to that state in which they were won over, they chose to conceal their view and to defame those who boasted that they had discovered what is true. For those people had located that discovery of the true in the senses of the body.

"From this," as Augustine says in *Contra academicos* III [xvii.38], "all those things were born that are attributed to the New Academy." For the New Academics, not knowing that mystery, said that the old Academy had utterly denied knowledge. In this way they cruelly disgraced those Academics to whom the later Academics were resolutely opposed.

For Carneades first gave up the audacious deception by which he saw that Arcesilaus had been greatly defamed. Because of this Carneades is said to have been the leader and founder of a third Academy. Then (finally) Antiochus, a pupil of Philo, began to open the gates, as it were, now that the enemy was in retreat, and to call the laws and the Academy back to the authority of Plato. Metrodorus had previously tried this: He is said to have been the first to admit that it was not exactly welcome to the Academics that nothing can be comprehended, but that it was necessary to take up a weapon of this sort against the Stoics. After these times, however, all the stubbornness and arrogance died down. Once the clouds of error had been dispersed, Plato's countenance, the clearest and brightest in philosophy, shone forth, especially in Plotinus – so much so that Plato was believed to have lived again in him. [*Contra academicos* III.xvii.39, xviii.41]

[F. *Two Ways of Knowing the Eternal Exemplar*}

So, as was said [II.D], the pure truth can be conceived only in an eternal exemplar. {6rI} But we should realize that the pure truth can be known by examining this exemplar in two ways. In one way by examining it as if it were the object cognized in it – that is, by seeing what is exemplified. For "someone who intuits the exemplar surely does confirm the image," as Augustine says in *Contra academicos* III [xviii.40]). In another way by examining that exemplar as merely the basis (*ratio*) of cognizing.

In the first way we cognize that an image of Hercules is his true image by seeing Hercules. In so doing, by noticing the correspondence between the image and the exemplar, we know that it is a true image of him. In this way the truth of anything made to an exemplar is perfectly cognized when its exemplar is seen. And so since every creature is a kind of image of a divine exemplar, the truth of every creature is cognized most truly and completely in its quiddity by seeing the divine essence uncovered. Augustine accordingly says in *City of God* XI [xxix] that

Those holy angels, through the very presence of the unchangeable truth, know a creature better there, in the art by which it has been made, than in the creature itself.

Hence not only is the image suited to be cognized *a priori*, through an exemplar, but also conversely the exemplar is suited to be cognized *a posteriori*, through the image. For this reason, then, Augustine teaches us to learn through creatures to cognize what the art of the divine exemplar is like. As he says in the *Treatise on the Gospel of John* [I.ix],

Human beings notice an amazing piece of work and are amazed at the plan of the maker. They are astounded by what they {6v} see, and love what they do not see. If therefore the plan of men is praised on the basis of some great piece of work, do you want to see how great the plan of God is – that is, the Word of God? Notice this piece of work, the world. See the things that are made through the Word, and recognize how great it is.

So in this way, from a collected cognition of all creatures that is like a single complete image of the divine art (as complete as it could be in creatures), the philosophers claimed that a complete cognition of God is possessed to the extent it could be by purely natural means, as will be seen below. But a human being cannot by purely natural means attain such a cognition of the divine exemplar without a special illumination, and in this life not even by the light of communal grace.

In this connection, Augustine says in *De fide catholica* I, speaking to God,

'You can be called essence and species and form. It is that which is, whereas others are not that which are. This most truly can say "I am who am." This is so great and lofty that in this life, as regards a vision of it, the human mind dares to claim nothing for itself. For you reserve this reward for your chosen alone, in a remuneration to come.'

Accordingly, regarding the text *He inhabits inaccessible light, which no men have seen nor can see* [I Tim. 6:16], it is said that it refers to this life, and that afterwards that light will be seen. And it is true that it cannot be seen in this life – unless through the gift of a special grace by which a human being is seized and drawn away from the senses. In this way Moses and Paul saw God in this life in his essence, as Augustine says to Paulina in *On Seeing God* [epistle n. 147]), and in this way blessed Benedict saw the whole world in one ray, as Gregory says in *Dialogues* IV [ch. 8]. For without a special divine illumination a human being cannot come to see an exemplar of the divine nature by purely natural means, nor come to know any truth in creatures by examining this nature.

If, however, the pure truth were known by examining the divine exemplar [in the second way], by examining the basis (*rationem*) of cognizing, this would be how Plato claimed that all truth is cognized – by examining an eternal exemplar – according to what Augustine says in the epistle [n. 118] to Dioscorus, invoking in this connection the authority of Cicero:

Notice this: how Cicero shows Plato to have established the truth, the end of the good, the causes of things, and the security of reasoning; and how Cicero shows quite clearly, and in many ways, that Plato did this not with a human wisdom, but with an evidently divine one (by which the human is in a way directed), with that same unchangeable wisdom that remains ever the same. Notice too that those that were attacked by the Platonists, under the name of the Epicureans and the Stoics, were the ones that placed the end of the good, the causes of things, and the security of reasoning within the nature of either body or mind.

These errors remained,

whether they concerned ethics, or the nature of things, or the character of the truth to be investigated, up until the Christian era. But now we see that they have been quieted. From this it is understood that the philosophers themselves, even those of the Platonic school, after changing the few things that Christian

teaching refutes, must bend their devout necks to Christ, the one unconquerable
King. He commands, and what they had feared even to utter is believed.

So Augustine pursued this view of Plato, as he says at the end of the
Contra academicos [III.xx.43]: {6vK}

No one doubts that there are two weights, authority and reason, impelling us to
learn. What is certain for me, then, is never to depart at all from the authority of
Christ, for I do not find anything more powerful. But as for what can be obtained
by the most subtle reasoning (for I am now so disposed that I desire to apprehend
what is true not only by believing, but also by understanding), and as for what is
not incompatible with our religion, I am confident for now that I will find this
in Plato.

And this is the thesis that he maintains in all his books, and that we hold
with him, saying that no certain and infallible cognition of the pure truth
can be had from anything except by examining the exemplar of uncreated
truth and light. Hence those alone prevail in recognizing certain truth
who prevail in viewing it in that exemplar, which not everyone prevails
in doing, as Augustine says in *De trinitate* VIII [vi.9]. But few prevail
through keenness of wit in transcending all changeable things and in
judging changeable things through changeable rules, concerning which no
one judges and without which no one judges with certainty, as he says in
De libero arbitrio II [xii.34]. Thus he says in *De trinitate* IX [vi.10],

When we rightly approve or disapprove of something, we are shown within
ourselves to approve or disapprove of the forms of corporeal things, through
altogether different rules that unchangeably remain above our mind. These forms
are drawn up through the senses and are somehow infused into memory, and
from them we think of things we have not seen, with an invented phantasm,
thinking of them either otherwise than as they are or by chance as they are.

And, in the same place [IX.vi.11–vii.12],

When I recall to mind a beautiful and evenly curving arch that I saw in Carthage,
something announced to my mind through the eyes and transferred to memory
makes an imagined appearance. But with my mind I conceive something else: It
is according to this that that work pleases me, and it is on this basis that if it were
unpleasant, I would amend it. And so we judge these things according to that
conception, and discern them through the rational mind's intuition.
    But we touch things that are present [with the senses] of the body, or we
remember images of absent things fixed in memory, or we imagine such things of
similar ones. We do this in one way by shaping in the mind images of bodily
things or, through the body, seeing bodily things, and we do it in another way by
grasping through a simple intellection the natures and the ineffably beautiful art
of such shapes above the mind's eye. So in that art in which all temporal things

have been made, we look through the mind's eye to the form in virtue of which we exist, and in virtue of which something is done with a true and right nature, either in us or in bodies. {7r} And so conceived from this we have a truthful cognition of things, like a word within us, which we give birth to by speaking internally.

This is the case not only with respect to such corporeal things, but also with respect to incorporeal things, as Augustine says in an epistle [n. 13] to Nebridius.

That which we call intellection comes into the mind, and it is produced in us in two ways: either internally, by the mind and reason itself, of themselves; or by a suggestion from the senses. Of these two ways, we understand that God must be consulted on the first – that is, concerning what is within us. But God must also be consulted on the second, concerning what is reported by the body and the senses.

In this way, as Augustine says in the *De magistro* [xi.38], "with respect to all the things we understand, we consult the truth internally present to the mind itself." It is with respect to this truth that everything glimmers that shines forth to the rational mind, as Augustine says in *Soliloquies* [I] ch. 14. How this happens will be spelled out in the next question. {7rL}

[G. The Divine Impression]

But for now, the account (spelled out further in the next question) is that in order for a true concept of the truth of an external thing – the pure truth – to be in us, the soul must be like the truth of the external thing, insofar as it is informed by the truth. For the truth is a kind of adequation of thing and intellect. So because the soul in itself is changeable from truth to falsity, as Augustine says in *De libero arbitrio* II [xii.34], it is therefore not – as it is in itself – informed by the truth of anything, although it is able to be informed. But nothing can give form to itself, since nothing can give what it does not have. Therefore it must be informed by some other pure truth concerning the thing. But this cannot occur through an exemplar taken from the thing itself, as was shown earlier [II.D]. Therefore, it is necessary for it to be given form by an exemplar of the unchangeable truth, as Augustine claims in the same passage. This is why he says in *De vera religione* [xxxvi.66] that "just as all things that are true are true by his truth, so too they are alike by his likeness."

It is therefore necessary for that uncreated truth to impress itself on our concept and to transform our concept in accord with his character. And in this way he informs our mind with the express truth concerning the thing, through the likeness that the thing itself has within the first truth. Accordingly, Augustine says in *De trinitate* XI [v.8], "an image is fully expressive of that [truth] when no nature lies between them." And he explains through a metaphor how this expressing occurs, saying in *De trinitate* XIV [xv.21]:

Where are those rules written by which what is just and what is unjust is recognized, if not in the book of that light that is called the truth? It is from here that every just law is taken down and transferred onto the human heart – not by changing its location but as if by making an impression. In just this way an image passes from a ring into the wax without leaving the ring.

This is the informing of that light by which (i) to the extent that it shines, a human being is made truthful in his intellect, and (ii) to the extent someone touches it, that person is made just in his affections. Augustine accordingly says of the first, in his *Treatise on the Gospel of John*, sermon 39 [viii],

Your eye was made to take part in this light. Is it closed? Then you have not diminished this light. Is it open? Then you have not enlarged it. But [if] the soul is truthful then the truth is within God, and in it the soul takes part. If the soul were not to take part in it, then every human being would be deceitful.

He says of the second, in a sermon [n.341] on the exposition of sacred scripture,

In the case of God, everything that is said is that very thing. For power, prudence, strength, justice, and purity are no different within God, because these belong to souls that that [divine] light somehow fills and affects by its qualities. It is as when visible light dawns. If that light were removed then there would be one color for all bodies, which should instead be called no color. But once it arises and illuminates bodies, though it is of one kind, it nevertheless casts a varying lustre upon the different qualities of bodies. Thus do those affections belong to souls that surely are affected by a light not itself affected, and given form by what is not given form.

So, as was said, we are completely informed by the truth only through a likeness of the truth concerning some object of cognition impressed on the mind by that first exemplary truth. For every other [likeness] impressed by any exemplar abstracted from the thing itself is incomplete, obscure, and foggy, and hence no certain judgment regarding the truth of a thing can be had through it. On this account Augustine compares the first [likeness] and judgment through it to the clear air above the clouds, and compares the second [likeness] and judgment through it to the foggy and obscure air beneath the clouds. Thus he says in *De trinitate* IX vi [10–11]:

It is clear that judgment from above regarding the truth and his law, based on the most incorruptible rules, is firm, even if it is covered by a cloud, as it were, of corporeal images. But it makes a difference whether I am under or in that gloom as someone shut off from the clear heavens, or whether, as may happen in the highest mountains, I am among both, enjoying the fresh air and observing both the clearest air above and the densest clouds below.

One should also know that the above way of cognizing the truth is common both to the cognition of principles, as above in argument three of this question [I.A.3], and to the cognition of conclusions, as is clear from everything already introduced. Thus dispositions are generated in us through this way of acquiring a cognition of the truth concerning the true arts. These are stored away in memory so that from them we again form like concepts, pertaining to dispositions for both principles and conclusions. We understand Augustine accordingly, in *De trinitate* IX [vii.12]: {7v} "In that eternal truth we perceive things seen by the mind, and conceived from this we have a truthful cognition of things, like a word within us." This is conceived in the disposition of memory, so that one's intelligence, returning to it, again forms a [mental] word and holds it with certain knowledge, even regarding things that are changeable. Accordingly, Augustine says in *De trinitate* XII [xiv.23], "not only for sensible things located in space" etc., as quoted above in the preceding question, in the solution to the fourth argument [p. 106].

This way of acquiring knowledge and a cognition of the truth is therefore truer than the way Aristotle defends, based only on the experience of the senses – if in fact Aristotle did think in this way and did not agree with Plato on this matter. But in fact it is closer to the truth to believe that even if he opposed Plato in his way of speaking, concealing the divine doctrine of his teacher as did other earlier Academics, nevertheless Aristotle held the same view as Plato regarding the cognition of truth. He seems to have implied this when, speaking of cognizing of truth, he says in *Metaphysics* II [993b23–30] that what is most true is the cause of the truth of what comes later, and that therefore the state of anything in being is its state in truth. On this account Augustine says at the end of the *Contra academicos* [III.xix.42],

As regards erudition and teaching, and the morality by which one counsels the soul, there has been no lack of very sharp and skillful men who teach in their disputations that Aristotle and Plato agree with each other, but do so in such a way that to the unskilled and less attentive they seem to dissent over many contentious points. But nevertheless the teaching of the truest philosophy is, I believe, clear. For it is the philosophy not of this world, which our religion detests, but of another intelligible world. Souls blinded by the manifold darkness of error would never be led to this world through even the most acute reasoning unless God the Highest, due to a sort of general pardon, were to bend the authority of the divine intellect down even to the human body. Souls, aroused not only by divine precepts but also by divine deeds, would be able to return to themselves even without a clash of disputations.

For as he says in the epistle [n.118] to Dioscorus,

From the beginning of the Christian era, faith in invisible and eternal things was announced, through miraculous visible things, for the purpose of salvation for human beings who could neither see nor think about anything beyond the corporeal.

So in this way, someone who understands something of the pure truth, with mind transcendent, understands it within the conceptions (*rationibus*) of the first truth. But as Augustine says in *On Seeing God* [epistle 147, ch. 42]), "this is certainly difficult, because due to the habit of a carnal life, the turmoil of phantasms rushes into our inner eyes." These phantasms, as he says in *Contra academicos* III [vi.13]), "strain to deceive and delude us, due to the habit for corporeal things, even when we hold the truth and have it almost in our hands." So as he says in *On Seeing God* [epistle 147, ch. 29],

Let anyone who is not able to do a thing pray and act so that he is worthy of being able. And let him not assail a human disputant so as to read what he does not read. Rather, let him assail God the Savior so that he becomes capable of what he is not capable.

So by purely natural means, excluding all divine illumination, a human being can in no way know the clear truth. {7vM}

[H. The Original Question]

Still the question remains of whether someone can know the pure truth by purely natural means. For if a human being by purely natural means can attain that illumination of divine light, and through that know the pure truth, then it ought to be said that someone can know the pure truth by purely natural means, even though one cannot know it without that illumination. In the same way, if by purely natural means one can attain the first principles of the sciences, and through them know other things, then he is said to know them by purely natural means, even though he could not know them without the first principles. If, on the other hand, one cannot by purely natural means attain that illumination, then one should also not through that illumination be said to know the clear truth by purely natural means, as was said at the start of this reply.

But it is in fact the case that a human being cannot by purely natural means attain the rules of the eternal light, so as to see in them the pure truth of things. For although it is certainly true that purely natural things do attain these rules − for, as was said already [II.G], a rational soul is created so as to be immediately informed by the first truth − nevertheless natural things cannot act on their own so as to attain them. Rather, God offers them to whomever he wants and takes them away from whomever he wants. For it is not by any natural necessity that these rules bestow themselves so that a human being sees the truth in them. This is the case for corporeal light, so that one sees colors in it, but it is not the case for the bare divine essence itself. For as Augustine concludes in *On Seeing God* [epistle 147, ch. 18], "If he wants to be seen, he is seen; if not, he is not."

Thus God sometimes bestows the eternal rules on bad people, with the result that in these rules they see many truths that the good cannot see, given that foreknowledge of the eternal rules is not bestowed on them. Accordingly, Augustine says in *De trinitate* IV [xv.20],

There are some who could extend the keenness of their mind beyond every creature and reach, in however small measure, the light of the unchangeable truth. They derided Christians, living on faith alone, who could not yet do so.

Sometimes, too, God takes these same rules away from such people and allows them to fall into error. Accordingly, with reference to Job 36:32 − *In his hands he hides the light* − Gregory says in *Moralia in Job* XXVII [13] that {8r}

Monstrous are those who praise themselves with boastful thoughts. But from them the light is hidden, since the cognition of truth is too much denigrated by the arrogance in their thoughts.

But as Augustine says in *Soliloquies* I [xiii.23], it is granted to all others, "for their salvation," to behold this light.

It should be said absolutely, therefore, that there is nothing concerning which a human being can have pure truth by acquiring a cognition of it by purely natural means. Such truth can be had only through the divine light's illumination. Consequently, although someone fixated on the purely natural may attain this light, he still cannot naturally, by purely natural means, attain it. Instead, God bestows it, through free will, on whomever he wants. {8rN}

[III. Reply to the Initial Arguments]

[A. To the Arguments for Illumination]

Something should be said in reply to the individual arguments.

So [*to the first,*] when it is argued that our sufficiency in cognizing comes from God [I.A.1], one should reply that this is true as regards a special illumination in the cognition of pure truth. But in the case of every other cognition of thought this is true only as the result of his universal movement, as was said already [II.A]. And this suffices, with respect to the Apostle's intent, to counter those he is arguing against there, those who said that the faith has its origin in us. For if cognition has its origin not in us, but in God, as the first mover for every action, natural and cognitive, then much less does faith have its origin in us. For faith requires a special illumination as its origin, which is not the case for the origin of cognition – unless (as was said) it is a cognition of the pure truth. {8rO}

To the second – that *no one can say "Lord Jesus"* etc. [I.A.2] – one should reply that this is true with respect to the complete word for which the will's consent is required. For there is a complete word when the delighted will rests in that which the mind cognizes. Hence Augustine says in *De trinitate* IX [x.15] that the complete word is "cognition with love." Hence just as the will, based on its own natural capacity, cannot rise up into the good without the help of a special grace, so too nor can it rise up to say such a word. But it doesn't follow that one couldn't say a simple word of impure truth without any special illumination from the Holy Spirit. Hence the Gloss says that the Apostle properly referred there to *saying* this word, signifying the speaker's will and intellect. And with respect to what belongs to the pure faith, someone can say such a saying only from faith. Thus it is said in Matthew 7:21, concerning another simple saying, *Not everyone that says "Lord, Lord" [shall enter into the kingdom of heaven].* {8rP}

To the third – that "the observable facts of the sciences cannot be understood unless illuminated by something like their own sun" [I.A.3] – one should say that this is true for the pure truth and for entirely infallible cognition. But in another way these facts can be understood in the light of a natural light, as was said above. Augustine accordingly says in *De trinitate* XII [xv.24],

> It should be believed that the nature of the intelligible mind has been established so as to see in a kind of *sui generis* incorporeal light the things that, by the creator's plan, have been placed under intelligible things in the natural order – just as the eye of the body sees things that lie near it in this corporeal light which it has been created to receive and to which it is matched. {8rQ}

To the fourth – that whatever the soul thinks of or reasons about "should be attributed to that light by which it is touched" [I.A.4] – one should reply that this is true for those things that it thinks of or reasons about in cognizing the clear truth. Otherwise this needn't be true, as has been said.

{8rR} One should reply in the same way *to the fifth*. Or one should reply that our seeing what is true in the first truth can mean either (i) in that which is the object first seen, or (ii) in that which is solely the basis of seeing. (This distinction will be developed in the following question.) In the first way, every truth is seen in the first truth, just as every good is seen in the first good. For whoever sees this or that true thing sees the true unconditionally in the universal, which is God – as Augustine says in *De trinitate* VIII [iii.4] and as will be set out below. But in the second way only the purely seen truth [is seen in the first truth], as was said [II.D].

We should pay attention to these two ways of cognizing the true, good, beautiful, and others that by nobility are in God, and that apply to creatures. For Augustine speaks of these in various places. Sometimes he says in the one way that the good, beautiful, true, and so on are cognized in creatures only through the true, beautiful, and good in the creator. Sometimes he speaks in the other way. But all his statements on this subject converge on one of these two ways. {8rS}

[B. To the Arguments for the Contrary]

The two arguments to the contrary [I.B] do indeed prove that some truth can be known and cognized by a human being without a special divine illumination. But they do not prove that the pure truth can be known. Or, if we wish, we can say (and perhaps this is better) that (i) a human being by purely natural means without any supernatural illumination from an assisting divine light or exemplar can cognize through intellect, by following the senses, only what is true of a thing – as was said above [I.B].

(But the intellect discerns what is true more clearly than the senses do, because it apprehends more subtly and is infused with the substance of what it receives more than the senses are, which perceive external things only according to their surfaces, as Avicenna says in *Metaphysics* IX [7, p. 512].) [We then also say] that one cannot perceive the truth itself of a thing – neither to a lesser nor to a greater extent – without the illumination of the divine exemplar, and that an exemplar abstracted from the thing is not sufficient to do this on its own. Instead, the concept of a thing must be worked out for an exemplar taken from the thing, through the divine exemplar. So if one were to see in that concept the clear and pure truth, then the intellect would be more clearly illuminated by the divine exemplar. And if [one were to see the truth] in any way, however slight, then again the intellect would be slightly {8v} illuminated by it. And if one were illuminated by it in no way, then in no way would the intellect see the truth itself.

So we say that in the common course of this life, though the presentation of such an exemplar may be forsaken without reason, and though the soul's natural [capacities] are not so ordered that by their natural operation they can attain it, still, on God's part, it is presented equally to all. Hence each is illuminated by it, according to his condition and capacity, unless someone by displaying great malice merits that it be taken away from him altogether. Such a person, as a result, would not see any truth at all, but would be completely made a fool of in the case of everything cognizable, so that for any given thing he would not see the truth in it, but would dissipate into the error that he deserves. And so, in keeping with the conclusion of Augustine, no truth at all is seen except in the first truth. And this is natural for a rational creature: that by purely natural means he can attain a cognition only of what is true of a thing, and cannot go beyond this to the cognition of the truth itself, unless illuminated by a divine exemplar. As was said above [II.B], this is because of the eminence of the act of understanding that truth.

In this way, in reply *to the first* argument to the contrary – that unless a human being by purely natural means could attain a cognition of the truth, investigating it would be pointless [I.B.1] – one should say that without that illumination a human being would not succeed in investigating it so as to be able, investigating by purely natural means, to arrive at a cognition of the truth. One would succeed in this only with the help of that illumination (assuming that the rational soul exists as it does, created in its natural state). {8vT}

To the second – that a human being naturally desires to know, and therefore can know by purely natural means [I.B.2] – one should reply that this is true. But it is not true in the sense that someone sees through the truth itself, by purely natural means (as was said). For, indeed, by natural appetite a human being desires to know even those things that must be cognized supernaturally. And these cannot be attained through a common illumination from the divine exemplar without a more special illumination, as will be said below [*Summa* art. 5, q.3].

6

PETER JOHN OLIVI
THE MENTAL WORD

Introduction

Peter John Olivi (1247/8–1298) was a brilliantly original thinker from the south of France. His theological and philosophical writings were twice suppressed by his own Franciscan order, in large part because of his outspoken criticism of mainstream Franciscans for an alleged laxness regarding their vow of poverty. Though many of Olivi's ideas were later developed by others, his writings have still not recovered from that early attempt at censorship, and Olivi himself remains an undeservedly obscure figure.

The selection translated below is an excerpt from the beginning of Olivi's *Lecture on the Gospel of John*, written sometime during the early 1280s.° In standard medieval fashion, Olivi is working through the text literally: sentence by sentence, word by word. In the passage below, he's still working on the opening phrase of John 1:1:

> *In the beginning was the Word,*

but he's gotten as far as the last word of that clause. In commenting on the significance of 'Word' (*verbum*), Olivi begins by making some straightforward exegetical remarks that rely heavily on early commentators. The discussion comes into its own only in the sixth and last section, which is significantly longer than the other five sections combined. There Olivi takes up the question of how a word in the human mind compares to the Word in the mind of God. This requires him to give a philosophical analysis of what a mental word is.

Medieval debates over the mental word are in large part debates over how intellect represents conceptual features of the world. Where modern authors speak of concept formation, medieval authors spoke of the formation of a mental word. Earlier selections have invoked this mental word, and discussed its relationship to the second person of the Trinity (see, in particular, Translations 3 and 9). But here, more than elsewhere, we are given a sustained and explicit analysis of what a mental word is. Olivi takes the unorthodox position that a mental word is simply an act of thought. On this account, conceptual thought does not require the formation of a mental word; the thought itself is the mental word. In his later *Sentences* commentary, he offers this summary:

Some maintain that a kind of concept, or word, is formed through an abstractive, investigative, or inventive consideration, in which real objects are intellectively cognized as in a mirror. For they call this the first thing understood and the immediate object; and it is a kind of intention, concept, and notion of things. This [sort of intermediary concept] ought not to be called a word, nor can it be anything other than the act of consideration itself or a memory species formed through that act – as I proved in the beginning of the *Lecture on John*, where the eternal Word of God is discussed. (Q74, pp. 120–21)

Many earlier theologians, most notably Thomas Aquinas (see his disputed questions *De potentia Dei* 9.5c), took roughly the position that Olivi is criticizing. In eliminating the mental word as something over and above the act of thought, Olivi is advancing his broader project of eliminating all intermediaries in his cognitive theory, at both the sensory and intellectual levels, whether those intermediaries be referred to as sensible species, intelligible species, or mental words.

On Olivi's eliminativist program in cognitive theory, see Pasnau (1997), chs. 5, 7, 8, and the introduction to Pasnau (1993). For an overview of Olivi's thought, see Pasnau (1999b).

The Mental Word

Lectura super Iohannem, excerpt from ch. 1

[1. John Begins with the Word]

Word. Note that [John] begins with the Word, rather than with the Father, because he was setting out chiefly to relate an evangelical account of the Word. Also, the order in which he did this is well suited to our guidance. For just as our natural reason attains an understanding (*notitiam*) of nature's most hidden causes only through the effects that are better known to us of those causes, so, in keeping with the order of reforming grace, we are brought through the incarnate Word to an understanding of the Father. Also, a general sort of understanding of the Word, taken from the creation of things, leads us to an understanding of the Father. That is, it leads to a distinct (*propriam*) understanding of the Word insofar as it is distinctly and personally engendered by the Father and within the Father – in the way that an understanding of the three Persons through their individual features (*appropriata*) leads to an understanding of their distinctive features (*propriorum*).

[2. The Greek Term Is *Logos*]

Note also, second, that where we have 'Word,' it is *logos* in Greek. According to Jerome, this signifies *word, cause, notion* (*rationem*), and *number* or *computation*.[1] From this it seems that it properly signifies the *mental word*, which is the cause and causal notion behind things that are made artificially or by design (*a proposito*), and behind the number of the whole, or the distinction among their parts. For although the perceptible word uttered vocally by a physical mouth is similar in a way to a mental word and the Eternal Word – to the extent, namely, that it is expressive of things that are in the mind, and is engendered and formed within the mouth of the speaker, and this without the speaker's being physically corrupted – still the mental or intellectual word is incomparably more similar to the Eternal Word. So it is from this that the term 'word' is more fully and properly extended to the divine realm. {135}

[3. *Logos* Is Given an Article]

Note third, according to John Chrysostom,[2] that *logos* in Greek is given an article – as if one were to say "the *logos*," or "the word," or if in our common language one were to say *"la paraula."*[3] From this it is clear that John is speaking about some discrete primary Word in particular.

---

[1] *Epistulae* 53, p. 449.
[2] *Homiliae in Joannem* II.4, pp. 14–15.
[3] Latin does not have definite or indefinite articles, so Olivi is straining to convey in Latin the meaning that such an article would give the text. What he actually writes is "le logos" and "le verbum."
   'La paraula' is Provençal, the medieval language of Olivi's southern France.

[4. Why John Did Not Say "the Word of God"]

Note fourth, according to Origen, why [John] did not say "the Word of God," but spoke absolutely and without qualification. The reason, Origen replies, is to establish that just as truth and wisdom, taken in the most absolute and abstract sense, are solitary and highest, so too is the Word that pronounces truth and wisdom.[4]

It can also be said that [John] was not concerned to attach a qualification because he was supposing it to be commonly known and understood among the Greeks to whom he was writing, even through the Platonic philosophers, that there was one primary and antonomastic Word through which all things have been made.

Also, third, perhaps [John] did this so as to intimate from such a manner of speaking that this Word is hypostatic and fully subsistent in its own right. But from the fact that it was a Word it was readily apparent that it was the Word of some speaker. And on that basis it was clear that such a sublime and transcendent Word could only be of the highest speaker – that is, the highest God.

[5. Why John Signifies the Son by the Term 'Word']

Note fifth why [John] signifies the person of the Son by the term 'Word' rather than by the term 'Son.' There are, for now, four reasons to be given.

[5.1. To Match the Opening of the Old Testament]

First, so that the opening of his Gospel would match the opening of the Old Testament, where God is said to have created all things by speaking, or through {136} the Word. It is in this connection that the Psalmist later recalls that *By the word of the Lord the heavens were established* [Ps. 32:6]. In this it also matches all the law and prophets. For in the law it is continually said that *the Lord spoke to Moses* [Lev. 4:1, 6:1, etc.]. And the prophets, in nearly every one of their prophesies, say *Thus says the Lord* [Is. 37:6, 49:7, etc.], as if they were always introducing the Eternal Word of God the

---

[4] *Commentaire sur Saint Jean*, II §§37–41.

Father. For a saying and a speech are the same as a word. Also, they often introduce the term 'word' – for example, in Isaiah chapter 2, *The word that Isaiah saw*, and chapter 9, *The Lord sent a word into Jacob*. And Jeremiah, chapters 1 and 2, says a number of times *And the word of the Lord came to me*, and he says the same in chapters 7, 10, 11, and a number of times again later. Ezekiel, too, time after time says *And the voice of the Lord came to me* [6:1, 7:1, etc.], and in numerous chapters it is said *And the word of the Lord came to me* [Ez. 1:3, 11:14, etc.]. Hosea also begins in this way: *The word of the Lord, that came to Hosea.* And Joel, Micah, and Zephaniah did the same. Amos too often says *Hear the word* of the Lord [Am. 3:1, 4:1, etc.]. Jonah too, on his twin missions, begins *And the word of the Lord came to Jonah* [1:1, 3:1]. Zachariah also says a number of times *And the word of the Lord came to me* [Zach. 4:8, 5:9, etc.].

[5.2. To Suit Greek Philosophy and Literature]

Second, because this term was better suited to the philosophy and literature of the Greeks, to whom and in whose language he wrote this Gospel. For the Platonists held that there is one exemplar and one word that is primary. But they did not call this the Son of God, because they denied {137} that it is consubstantial with the highest God. For this reason both Arrius and Origen gathered from these [Platonists] that the Word of God was a creature and less than the highest God.

[5.3. It Is More Easily Conceived as Coeternal]

Third, because it is easier to conceive of an intellectual word's being coeternal with a mind having the most actual wisdom than to conceive of a son's being coeternal with his father. Also, it is easier to conceive that the word through which a craftsman plans what has to be made exists at the start of his craftsmanship than to conceive that from the start that craftsman has a son through whom he makes all his crafts. Also, the intellectual, unchangeable, and incorruptible generation of the only-engendered God is more purely and clearly expressed and conceived under the term 'Word' than under the term 'Son.' Also, it is easier to conceive that what is engendered is always within the one who engenders it by using the term 'Word,' which [refers to something that] always remains in the mind, than by using the term 'Son,' which in our case [refers to something that] visibly subsists outside the person of the one who engenders him. So by speaking in this way, [John] rendered himself better able to instruct and more intelligible to our reason, and at the same time he took advantage of the fact that 'Word' is better suited to his purpose. For it was part of his purpose here to establish that the person of the Word was coeternal and intrinsic to God the Father, and was intellectually engendered by Him, and that through the person of the Word all things have been made, and moreover that this was the intellectual light of human beings. But the term 'Word' is more clearly well suited to all of these things than is the term 'Son.'

[5.4. *It Brings Us More Easily to the Proper Nature of the Son*]

Fourth, because in connection with the divine, we are brought to a proper notion of the Son (as it properly is in the divine) through the general notion of a word more easily than we would reach a notion of the Word through the general notion of a son. (This is readily apparent from things said in [my] questions on the Trinity [I *Sent.* QQ 5–6].) Therefore it was more fitting for [John] to have first {138} expressed the person of Christ with the term 'Word,' and later with the term 'only engendered son' – below, for instance, when he says *we saw his glory, the glory as it were of the only engendered of the Father* [John 1:14].

[6. How Our Mental Word Applies to the Son]

Note sixth under what notion or construal of our mental word the term 'word' is extended to designate the person of the Son of God.

[6.1. *Some Say Our Mental Word Follows an Act of Thought*]

For some say that our mental word is something following an act of thought or actual consideration and formed by that act, and they say that in the end, after it has been formed, the external thing is clearly understood or inspected in that word, as if in a mirror. They call this word the *primum intellectum* – that is, that which is first understood by intellect and is its first object. The external thing understood through it, they call the *intellectum secundum*.

But when it is asked of these people how this word is required for an act of intellect, given that an act of thought from that [intellect] precedes this word as its effective cause, they say that the external thing – present in itself or in a phantasm – is first thought by a simple apprehension. After that, the intellect forms the word within itself and then, when the thing is absent, it thinks of the thing as in a mirror. Therefore the first thought precedes the word, the second follows it. And so because the blessed see God as immediately present and not in any created mirror, as if absent, they say that the blessed don't see God through any word of their own and that they don't form within themselves a word of God when he is seen.

Therefore these people say on this subject that the son of God is called the Word as a concept formed or produced by the actual intellection of the Father. For if a word is produced by our actual intellection, then much more is it produced by the actual intellection of God the Father.

[6.2. How This Position Is Deficient]

[6.2.1. It Contradicts the Saints]

This position is deficient in four ways. First, because it contradicts the express words of the saints. For Augustine, in a great many places, says that our word is our actual thought, and vice versa. Thus in *De trinitate* book IX, chapter vii, and in the five following chapters, he says that actual understanding, conceived and {139} begot by us with love, is our word and the offspring of our mind, as if engendered by the mind, like a parent. Thus he says at the end of book IX [xii.18]:

This is a kind of image of the Trinity: the mind itself, its understanding (which is its offspring and its word of itself), and thirdly love. Nor is the offspring less than the mind, while it understands itself to the extent to which it exists. Nor is the love less, while it cherishes itself to the extent to which it understands and exists.

Also, in book XV, chapter x, based on the book of Wisdom, where it is said *They have said, thinking within themselves, but not rightly* [2:1], Augustine proved that to say within oneself is the same as to think. And later, based on the Gospel where the scribes (speaking of Christ's saying *Your sins are forgiven you*) said *within themselves: He is blaspheming* [Mat. 9:2–3], Augustine proved that there was nothing they "said," except by thinking. And so it is immediately added: *And Jesus, seeing their thoughts, said: Why do you think evil in your hearts?* [Mat. 9:4] Similarly, speaking of that rich man whose *land brought forth plenty of fruit*, Christ said *and he thought within himself, saying*, etc. [Luke 12:16–17]. Based on these passages Augustine concludes [XV.x.18]:

Therefore some thoughts are speeches of the heart, and the Lord showed that the mouth belongs to the heart, when he said *But the things that proceed out of the mouth, come from the heart, and those things defile a person. For from the heart come evil thoughts*, etc [Mat. 15:18–19].

And in the same place Augustine adds: "Nor is it the case that, because we say that speeches of the heart are thoughts, they consequently are not also visions rising from visions of understanding." For

In the mind, seeing and hearing are not two different things. So although an external speech is not seen but rather heard, nevertheless the Evangelist said that internal speeches – that is, thoughts – are seen by the Lord, not heard.

For after having stated that

They said within themselves: He is blaspheming, the Evangelist added: *And Jesus, seeing their thoughts* . . . Therefore Jesus saw what they said. So whoever can understand this (the word of our heart) can see some likeness of that Word of which it was said *In the beginning was the Word*, etc. For it is necessary, when we speak a word, that through the knowledge that we hold in memory {140} a word is born that is of entirely the same kind as that knowledge from which it is born. For surely the thought formed from that thing that we know is the word that we speak in our heart.

Also, in chapter xi, Augustine says,

We must reach the human word that precedes all the signs by which it is signified, and that is engendered from the knowledge that remains in the mind, when that same knowledge is spoken inwardly just as it is. For the vision of thought is entirely like the vision of knowledge.

Also, in chapter xii,

The word is entirely like the thing that is understood, from which it is engendered when the vision of thought arises from the vision of knowledge.

Also, in chapter xvi, showing how the Word of God is not voluble as is ours, for which reason it should not be called a thought as is ours, Augustine concludes,

Therefore the Son of God is not called the thought of God, but the Word of God. For surely our thought, reaching to that which we know and from there formed, is our true word.

In chapter xv, however, Augustine says that the unformed core (*acies*) of our mind, which can be formed into various thoughts, is a word when it is formed into an actual thought. But this passage has no force, because that core formed in this way is not called a word on account of itself, but only on account of the thought by which it is then informed.

Also, in his sermon on the birth of John the Baptist, Augustine says, "the sacred scriptures define a word to be that which we conceive mentally within the silence of the spirit (*animi*). They define the word to be that thought that remains kept within the hidden parts of our conscience." And a little later: "An utterance (*vox*) is a sound and an index of thought. A word, on the other hand, is the thought itself."[5]

Also, Anselm says in *Monologium*, chapter 33, that "the mind, when by thinking it understands itself, has along with itself an image born of itself – that is, a thought of itself toward its own likeness, as if it were formed by its own impression. This image is its word." And he says the same a little later, in the same chapter. {141}

Also, in chapter 48, where the Son must be not only the intellection of the Father's memory, but also the memory of the memory, he says

The word seems to be born from memory, which is perceived more clearly in our mind. For because the human mind is not always thinking of itself, in the way that it always remembers itself, it is obvious when it does think of itself that its word is born from memory. For to think of a thing whose memory we have, this is to say it in mind. And the word of the thing is the thought itself toward its likeness, formed from memory.

[6.2.2. *It Contains Obvious Absurdities*]

Second, it is deficient because it contains within itself obvious absurdities and thus contradicts sound reason. For the word that they postulate either is something that remains in the mind after the act of every thought, or it remains only while we actually think. If the first, then it seems no different from a memory species that is retained in memory after the act of thought. But it is absurd to call this the word. For, in keeping with Augustine, that [species] is rather the "parent" of the thought formed from it. Further, no one says that a human being, while thinking of nothing at all, speaks something within himself. But it is clear that the word of the mind is the same as the speech of the heart. If, however, the word were claimed to

---

[5] Augustine (pseudo), *Sermones* n. 196, 2114b.

remain in the second way only, then they would contradict themselves. For they hold that the word serves as first object not for the thought through which it is formed, but instead for another thought which comes after that first one.

Also, the word that they postulate is either some act or action, or it is a disposition (*habitus*) or some dispositional state. But if it is an act then it can be only an act of thought or an act of conversion preceding the thought through which intellect is moved and turned toward thinking something. But to say that it is a conversion of this sort is utterly absurd, and no one says this. If, however, it is a disposition or something dispositional then it is not constantly engendered in the way that a word and a thought are. Also, since a disposition of intellect is for expressing or generating some act of understanding or of believing, it follows that the word is what engenders and expresses, rather than what is engendered and expressed. Moreover, it is clear to everyone that every speech is a kind of action of the one speaking, made and formed by the one speaking. It's plain, however, that the word is the same as a speech. {142}

Also, the ultimate perfection of our intellect consists in an act of vision. This is clear first because its highest and actual glory consists perfectly and properly in the act of a vision of God. Second, because that through which it ultimately, completely, and most actually attains its object is solely an actual vision. Third, because all of its dispositions and conditions are in potentiality for that vision or for some other act of thought, and they are directed to this as to their end. Therefore it better fits the perfection of the Word for the term 'word' to be extended to it from the act of intellective vision than from anything else that is in intellect.

Also, if the word is formed from some prior thought, then it is either a kind of likeness of the thought, a likeness engendered by that thought (which is ridiculous to say), or it is some likeness of the thing being thought, made through a prior thought. This is the same as to say that the word is a memory species.

Also, according to them, the intellect thinks of a thing in the word it forms, as if in a mirror image of that absent thing, and the thing thought about through the word is not made the object of intellect first and immediately, but only the word is. Therefore, if Augustine's teaching is true, they have to say that the word is nothing other than a species existing in memory. For Augustine holds that when we think of an absent thing, our intellect is turned toward the species that is in memory, as to its first object from which some other species or image is engendered in it.

Also, the word is either in memory or in the core of intellect. The first is denied, even by those who hold this view. If, then, it is in the core of intellect, how is that core turned toward it as to the first object from which its thought is formed and which it first sees – even though it sees it only as a mirror and image of a thing that is absent?

[An Evasion: The Word as a Conception of Terms]

But perhaps it will be said, as some say, that the word is a kind of conception of complex terms – i.e., of propositions or explicit definitions – formed through reciprocal comparisons (*mutuas collationes*) of various simple thoughts or apprehensions, and various simple terms. {143}

Against this are not only many of the arguments already set out, but also others. First, that reciprocal comparison of various [thoughts and terms] is nothing other than a kind of thought or consideration that is able to compare those various things and apprehend all at once their reciprocal relationships. Therefore if a word is formed through this comparison, that word is preceded by a full and actual apprehension of the complex and of the correlation between the various terms mentioned. But they posit the word as the prior object and the mirror of this sort of complex (or complex-forming) apprehension. So on this account the word is posited to occur *before* its cause and to be the *cause* of its cause.

Second, in such a comparison and complex-forming consideration two things alone suffice: namely, the reciprocal coordination of various memory species, which are species of various terms or things, and the actual inspection and consideration of those species coordinated in such a way, or of the things insofar as they are represented in these [species] so as to be connected to one another in such a way.

Third, why is no word posited for simple terms apprehended simply, when the contrary is expressly gathered from many of Augustine's words?

Also, against their claim that the word takes the place of the first and immediate object in which an absent thing is intellectively cognized, on account of which (as they say) a word is formed of no thing insofar as it is presently and immediately cognized – against this, I say, is what Augustine says many times in *De trinitate* IX: that the actual understanding by which the mind understands itself is the mind's offspring and word. And, as is clear in the last chapter of the same book, he speaks of the understanding that has its own mind for its present, first, and immediate object. Also, in chapter x, he holds that all actual understanding, loved in this way only, is a word. But as he says in the same place, even that which is displeasing is in a way a word. He proves this through the word of Christ, who said *Not everyone that says to me, "Lord, Lord," shall enter into the kingdom of heaven* [Mat. 7:21]. For the saying or word which, or by which, such people say "Lord, Lord" is certainly not with love or charity.

Moreover, it is utterly absurd to say that in the glorious vision of the Eternal Word there is no more perfect an image of the Trinity and of the Word itself {144} than there is now in us, when we actually cognize God or ourselves. Augustine, however, in *De trinitate* IX, chapter xi, says that the actual understanding that we have here of God, when° it is suitably loved, is the word and a kind of likeness of God. Therefore much more is that [understanding] by which the blessed see God and his Eternal Word a more perfect word and a more perfect likeness of the Eternal Word.

Moreover, don't the blessed, in seeing that God exists, say in their hearts and, by saying, assert that God exists and that God is seen by them? Also, don't they praise him with all their heart and, in praising him, speak? Indeed, it is certain that they always cry "Holy Holy Spirit, Lord God of the Heavenly Hosts." It is plain, however, that such a saying, speech, or cry is truly a word.

[6.2.3. Supported by No Argument]

Third, it is deficient as regards its support, because it is supported by no argument. For there is no necessity or usefulness in postulating such a word. For the things and their real relationships that the intellect cognizes are present to intellect either in themselves or in memory species. So regardless of whether the things and their relationships are present to intellect in themselves or are themselves absent but are presented to intellect through memory species, there is no necessity for another mirror serving as object in which the external things are presented to intellect itself. Instead, that would be an impediment.

It might be said to the contrary that this position is supported by two arguments. First, by experience: For we experience in ourselves that we form in our mind new concepts both of many propositions and of conclusions. These concepts remain in us later and we return to them when we want to remember such propositions – as if we want to see reflected in them (as if in a mirror) the truths of such propositions. It is clear, however, that a concept is the same as a word conceived in the mind.

The second argument is that from individuals seen or imagined by us we abstract and form notions (*rationes*) of their universal features. When we do this, we conceive and form such notions within ourselves, and we come back to them when we want to view such universal features.

One can easily reply to the first that whatever we conceive first and *per se* through the actual consideration of our intellect, we conceive in the act itself of considering. Indeed, {145} not only is the act itself conceived in its internal conception and formation, but so is its object, insofar as it exists intentionally or representatively in that act. And this is the concept that we first experience within ourselves. But when such an act has passed, the memory of that act and of its object remains within us. For that reason we experience secondarily that something remains in us through which we can remember the act that has passed and its object. Augustine calls this a memory species, and this can certainly be said to be conceived and formed within us to the extent that it has been formed and caused through the force of the act that has passed, and received and retained in the matrix of our memory. But it doesn't for this reason properly deserve to have the name 'word' – just as the shape that remains in the wax after the actual impression of a copper seal should not be called an action or actual impression, but ought to be called only the form brought out from the wax through the actual impression of the seal. For 'word' does not signify *whatever* the speaker expresses: For if this were so then every thing we speak of – what we express when speaking – would be our word. Instead, 'word' refers only to what is expressed in such a way as to be the actual expression itself. For it is that itself that is our actual and expressive speech – whether it is taken for the external vocal expression of our mouth or for the mental speech of our heart.

The reply to the second is also clear. For the first abstraction of universal notions occurs only in an act of abstractive consideration attending to and considering the real notion of the common or specific nature without the notion of its individuation. Through this, however, nothing serving as an object is really abstracted or formed that differs from the act of consideration already mentioned. But this consideration does cause a kind of species within memory that remains in us later, once the act has passed; we return to that species when, in the absence of the things that we first had considered intellectively and presently, we later want to remember them.

[6.2.4. *Unsuitably Applied to the Divine*]

Fourth, it is deficient as regards the present subject, because it unsuitably and perhaps erroneously applies and carries over to divine things the name and notion of a word. For the Word of God the Father is not formed by the Father as if a kind of mirror and a kind of first object in which and through which the Father reflects on the things that he intellectively cognizes. It is on the contrary clear that the Word of God emanates from the Father as a kind of most actual wisdom expressive of the whole actual {146} wisdom of the Father. But according to those under discussion, the word doesn't refer to any actual wisdom or consideration in us, but rather to something following that and caused by it or left over, and to a kind of first object of some other succeeding consideration. Or, as it is said (all the more impossibly), it refers to the first object of the same consideration from which it is produced and formed. It is easily clear to anyone that this claim is full of contradictions.

[6.3. *'Word' Is Extended Only in Respect of Perfections*]

Therefore, following the lead of the saints and of the truth, we should know that the term 'word' is extended from our word to the Son of God only in respect of the perfections that it contains in itself, throwing out every defect that it has in us. Consequently the power of wisdom and intellect by which and through which it is generated in us is extended to signify the Father's power of wisdom, through which he generates the Word – but only in respect of the perfection that it has in us, throwing out every defect connected to it in us.

[6.3.1. *The Perfections of Our Word*]

Our word has at least three perfections. The first is in respect of imitating or expressing: For it imitates and expresses in a marvelous way the wisdom or understanding from which it comes. The second is because it is characterized by the ultimate actuality of knowledge or understanding. For if the actual consideration or understanding that is called the word is taken away, then we utterly lack the full actuality of knowing, however great our dispositional knowledge is. For such [a state] is like sleeping. Thus beatitude can never occur without actual understanding. The third is because it has a living and intellectual state of being. For it is a kind of living act and living understanding, and because it is in itself pure form, it is to that extent also pure life.

But in these areas it is also lacking. It is lacking with respect to the first because there is an essential difference in its imitation. For it has an essence that is different from the essence of its cause: not just different in number, but in species and genus as well. Such a difference is incompatible with the most perfect conformity and uniformity.

As regards the second, it lacks an actuality that is powerful and ultimate. Thus our act is not the power and force itself of our intellect, through which we are capable of understanding not just one thing but {147} many and all; it is, instead, only a kind of partial action and determination of our intellective power, determining and determined toward a determinate object. Thus it certainly lacks some of the lofty perfections of our power and our dispositions.

As regards the third, it lacks the substantial and independent, or permanent and fixed character of being and existing. For it has an accidental existence that inheres in and rests on its subject. As a kind of action, it is also in constant flux from its cause, and so constantly depends on that cause and necessarily needs it.

So if you exclude these three defects and add their contraries to the initial perfections, you will then have properly applied the term 'Word' to the Son of God – once you add a fourth perfect characteristic possessed by our word, which is that it is intimate to what engenders it, and within that is intimately and also most calmly and brightly engendered and conceived, without any corruption on the part of what engenders it.

[6.3.2. *The Perfections of Our Power of Wisdom*]

Our power of wisdom or intellect, through which our word is engendered, also has three perfections. The first concerns the permanence and stability of its being and existing. This is of course lacking in that it is not our whole substance and person, nor entirely substantial. Rather, it includes some accidental dispositions or conditions connected to it.

The second is the perfection of formal actuality, since both the form of our intellect and the form of its dispositions are kinds of formal acts in the genus of things intellectual and wise. Yet they lack the actuality of wisdom properly implied by that actual understanding that is called the word. Compared to that, then, [these forms] are potential or possible, rather than actual, on which account they are potentially ordered to that [actual understanding] as to one of their perfections.

The third perfection is its causal power for generating a word. This power is of course lacking, because to do this it needs some object toward which and onto which it is turned – with the one exception of when by thinking of itself it generates a word. But even then it has one causal power in respect of which it is properly the efficient cause of the word, and another in respect of which it is {148} the objectlike, terminating cause of the word and of the efficient cause's causal attention.

So if you exclude these three defects and attach their opposites to the three perfections just mentioned, you will then properly have God the Father's power of wisdom or paternal wisdom, through which he generates the Word – at least once you attach certain things that can easily be gathered from what has been said.

So since nothing of ours is likened to the divine in respect of its defects, but only in respect of its perfections, Augustine, as someone insightful and ingenious in grasping these matters, calls our word not only our vision and wisdom, but also our power of wisdom, which is the cause of our word. Thus, as he says, vision has its origin in vision, and wisdom in wisdom.[6] In keeping with this, he turns his attention to the divine, where actual vision clearly does not have its origin in a potential or dispositional vision. Instead, this most actual vision has its origin in the most actual vision, and the substantial or hypostatic vision has its origin in a vision that is subsistent and hypostatic in its own right.

---

[6] See *De trinitate* XV.xii–xxi.

7

WILLIAM ALNWICK
INTELLIGIBLE BEING

Introduction

William of Alnwick was a master of theology at both Oxford and Paris during the first quarter of the fourteenth century. He died in 1333. Hailing from the north of England, William became a member of the Franciscan order, and studied closely with John Duns Scotus. William played an important role in transcribing his master's lectures and, after Scotus's untimely death, in editing his work. But despite this close relationship, William in his own writings was by no means a slavish disciple. The discussion translated here illustrates his independence.

William's *Disputed Questions on Intelligible Being* considers what it means to say that an object exists in the mind of a person thinking about that object. Following the usage of Scotus (*Ordinatio* bk. I q.36) and Henry of Harclay (Maurer 1961), William refers to this sort of existence as intelligible being (*esse intelligibile*), represented being (*esse repraesentatum*), and cognized being (*esse cognitum, esse intellectum*). William's particular interest, in these questions, is the intelligible being of creatures in the mind of God. This gives dramatic force to the philosophical problem, since such being would have existed from eternity. But many of the same considerations apply to the fleeting sort of intelligible being that objects have within human minds, and William is also interested in those cases.

The first, foundational question (translated here) asks whether intelligible being is something over and above the being of whatever in the mind gives rise to the representation. He considers two versions of what he regards as the same question:

1. Is the intelligible being of an object equivalent to the mental form (the intelligible species or divine essence) that represents the object?

2. Is the intelligible being of an object equivalent to the act of intellect that represents the object?

William takes the trouble to distinguish these two questions because of disputes over whether there are such things as representing forms within intellect. Those who deny the reality of intelligible species and similar representing forms must at least grant that there are acts of intellect (as in Translation 6). In answering each question in the affirmative, William is clashing with certain "modern" authors – in particular, Jacob of Ascoli (see Yokoyama 1967). William also seems to be moving away from Scotus, his teacher, inasmuch as the argument presented here seems contrary to Scotus's interest in giving intelligible being some sort of independent status in the mind.

But it is far from clear what Scotus and others really meant in speaking of intelligible being. One of the merits of William's discussion is that it clearly sets out his opponents' view and then examines in detail the consequences of that claim. William is often accused of being tedious and overly subtle. Even the editor of the selection translated here remarks that "he has the late scholastic defects of being excessive in his polemics and in his use of logic." Too logical? In many ways, William's work reads like what gets published in philosophy journals today.

For further discussion of intelligible being, see Perler (1994) and Pasnau (1997), ch. 2.

Intelligible Being

Question 1

[I. Initial Arguments]

Regarding the intelligible being that belongs to a creature from eternity, it is asked first in general:

> *Is the represented being of a represented object the same in reality as the representing form?*

And (same question):

> *Is the cognized being of a cognized object the same in reality as the act of cognizing?*

[A.] *It Seems that It Is Not*

1. That which belongs to a represented object insofar as it differs from the representing form is not the same in reality as that representing form,

because no thing [A] is the same as some thing [B] that belongs {2} to another [C] insofar as it [C] differs from that [A]. For if so then the same thing would be the basis of identity and diversity. But represented being [=B] belongs to a represented object [=C] with respect to that object's proper being, by which it differs from its representing form [=A]. For a species distinctly representing a rose represents it with respect to the rose's proper being, which is distinct from the representing form. Therefore the represented being of an object is not the same in reality as the representing form.

The same argument can be made for cognized being and cognition. For a cognized object, with respect to its cognized being, is not the cognition pertaining to the cognized object, insofar as that object differs from the cognition, because no thing [A] is the same as another [B] through that [C] which belongs to it [A] insofar as [A] is distinguished from that other [C]. But cognized being [=C] belongs to the cognized object [=A] with respect to the object's proper being, by which it is distinguished from the cognition [=B]. For someone intellectually cognizing a rose distinctly cognizes it with respect to its proper being, which is distinct from both the cognizer and the cognition. Therefore an intelligible object, with respect to its cognized being, is not the same in reality as the cognition.

2. If two things are the same in reality, then whatever produces one produces the other. But an object made in intelligible being by agent intellect produces an intelligible species, either as the total cause of that species or at least as a partial cause along with agent intellect. Yet [this object in intelligible being] does not produce the object in represented being (as will be proved). Therefore the object, with respect to its represented being, is not the same in reality as the representing species. And one can argue in the same way for cognized being relative to cognition.

I prove the minor premise in two ways. First, the same thing does not produce itself. But the stone in intelligible being due to agent intellect is the same as the stone in represented being due to an intelligible species representing it. Second, that which produces something by a real action is related to what it produces by a real relation. But an intelligible object is not related by a real relation to the same object in represented being, because as such it does not have real being, and a real relation necessarily requires a real end-term. Therefore an intelligible object does not produce that object in represented being. {3}

[B.] *On the Contrary*

1. That which exists, and is not a being of reason, if it is not distinct in reality from another, is the same in reality as that other, because *same* and *different* are the first differentiae of being (according to *Metaphysics* X [1054b18–23]). But the represented being of some object is not a being of reason, because it does not depend on an act of intellect, and it is not distinct in reality from its representing form, because if so then it would have subjective being and not only objective being. Therefore represented being is the same in reality as its representing form. And the same argument can be made for cognized being – if it is caused by a direct and not a comparative act of intellect.

2. Avicenna (*Metaphysics* V ch.1) distinguishes three ways in which a thing has being: (1) in the soul, (2) in its own proper existence, and (3) being that is indifferent to each. This last is the being of essence (*esse essentiae*), which can be in the soul and in the external world. But represented being is clearly not (3) the quidditative being of the thing, because it does not belong to the quiddity of the thing that is represented. It is also not (1) being in the soul, by which the thing cognized is within the cognizer, because it precedes being in the soul.° Therefore, it is (2) real external being (*esse reale in effectu*), and is nothing other than the being of what is representing, not of what is represented, because something can be represented without its existing. Therefore represented being is the same in reality as its representing form.

[II. Solution]

[A. One Modern View]

On this question, some modern authors say that 'the represented being of an object' signifies an entity distinct from {4} that which represents it, and that 'the cognized being of an object' implies an entity distinct from the cognition. In virtue of this represented being, through the divine essence, and this cognized being, from the cognizing divine intellect, a creature cognized from eternity has had some being or existence (*entitas*) actually distinct from God, beyond the operation of [God's] intellect.

They establish this as follows.

1. Wherever something is said univocally of two things through a greater univocation than the univocation of genus or species, there each is a being through its own proper existence (*entitas*). For things are univocal when they have a single substantial nature (*ratio*), whereas a being and something entirely not a being have no single substantial nature. But 'stone,' when said of a stone in cognized or represented being and of a stone produced in real being, is said with greater univocation than the univocation of genus or species (as will be proved). Therefore, a stone, with respect to its cognized and represented being, has its own proper existence (*entitas*), just as it does with respect to its external being. Consequently, a stone in cognized and represented being differs from the cognition and from that which represents it, just as it is distinct from these in its produced being in {5} effect.

The minor is proved in this way. That which is said univocally of two things due to numerical unity° is said of them with greater univocation than the univocation of genus or species. But it is in this way that 'stone' is said of a stone in cognized being and of a stone in external reality (*in effectu*), because a stone produced in external reality either is or is not the same as the stone cognized by intellect. If it is, then we have our conclusion. If not, then the stone produced in external reality is neither cognized nor represented, which is false.

2. Based on what they say, I argue further as follows. That which is a lesser state of existence (*entitas minor*) than real existence (*entitas realis*) and is greater than the existence of reason is an intermediary state of existence distinct from each – both from real existence and from the existence of reason. But the represented being of an object is a lesser state of existence than real external existence, because it is a diminished state of existence (*entitas diminuta*), and it is a greater state of existence than the existence of reason, because the latter exists through an act of reason. Represented being, in contrast, does not exist through an act of intellect or of reason, but rather precedes the act of intellect, as when an intelligible species represents an intelligible object and the divine essence represents a creature prior to an act of intellect. Therefore, the represented being of an object is a positive being or existence (*esse sive entitas positiva*) distinct from the real existence of that which represents it.

One can argue in the same way for an object cognized by a direct act: This [cognized being] is a lesser being than real being and greater than the being of reason, because that cognized being, from a direct act, is not caused by a comparative° act of intellect.

3. Based on what they say, I argue further as follows. There can be a distinction between two things in represented being without there being a distinction in what represents them. Therefore the represented being of those two things will not be the same as what represents them. The inference is clear, because the same thing cannot be at the same time distinct and not distinct. The antecedent is proved: For if one species represents a human being and a donkey distinctly, then these are several and distinct in represented being – otherwise the species would not represent them distinctly. But that species has no distinction within itself. Therefore two things represented by a single representation can be distinct in represented being, without there being any distinction within the {6} representation. The same can be argued for cognized being with respect to a cognition by which several things are distinctly cognized.

But what sort of being is this? And what sort of distinction is this between represented (and cognized) being and the representation (and cognition)? Those who hold this view answer that there are three sorts of being in the universe: real being, intentional being, and the being of reason.

Real being is that which belongs to a thing as it exists formally and in its proper nature. Such being belongs only to something singular or to what has being within something singular, because only the singular exists in its proper nature per se and primarily. Universals, in contrast, exist only as they have being within singulars. It is this being that the Philosopher has in mind in the *Categories* [2b5]: "If those that are primary are destroyed, it is impossible for any of the others to remain."

Intentional being is what belongs to a thing as it has representational or represented being within some other real being. And since to be represented objectively in some other thing belongs equally° to both the universal and the singular, it follows that intentional° being no more assumes universal being for itself than it assumes singular being (and vice versa). It also follows that such intentional being is weaker than real being and so is always founded on it, though objectively.

The being of reason belongs to a thing as it has conceived being solely within the consideration of a working intellect. Such being, since it is diminished being, always presupposes one (*alterum*) of the two preceding beings.

Therefore they say that intentional being is not real being, because it can belong to a thing that does not exist in its proper nature. But neither is it the being of reason, because existing in reality (*in re*) is incompatible with the being of reason, {7} whereas it is not incompatible with what has represented being in something and objective being in the soul. Hence this intentional being is intermediary, as they say, between real being and the being of reason.

They likewise distinguish between distinctions: For just as there are three kinds of being, so there are three kinds of resultant distinctions: real, intentional, and of reason. A real distinction is that by which things are distinguished as they exist in their proper natures in real existence. An intentional distinction is that by which things are distinguished in representational being, when a thing is represented in different ways. A distinction of reason is that by which things are distinguished solely through the operation of intellect.

Accordingly, they say that an intentional distinction is intermediary between a real distinction and one of reason, because there can be an intentional distinction between things in represented being even though there is not a real distinction between them in real being – for things can be distinctly represented and so distinct in represented being even though they do not have real being in the natural world. So this distinction is less than a real distinction and yet it is greater than a distinction of reason, because the one exists only through an act of intellect, whereas the other exists in represented being before an act of intellect.

In this way, then, they claim that represented being (and cognized being) is intentional being, distinct by an intentional distinction from the representing form (and from the cognition).

They offer the following proof that an intentional distinction is not a real distinction, and that things can be distinct intentionally without a real distinction. If there were numerically one species distinctly representing several things (say, a human being and a donkey), then the several things distinctly represented within that species – in such a way that they would have represented being there – would not have any real distinction in the species, because by assumption the species is numerically one. {8} Consequently, the things represented in that species do not have any real being either, only intentional being. Yet those several things distinctly represented within that numerically one species necessarily are distinct intentionally from one another and from that species. Otherwise,° the species would not represent them distinctly – unless they were to have some distinction within that representing species. For it is impossible for things to be distinctly represented within something unless they have some distinction there. As a result, to say that things are represented distinctly within something and that they have no distinction there is to run together opposite claims (*oppositum in adiecto*).

From these considerations, they conclude that an intentional distinction is greater than a distinction of reason, because things that are represented distinctly in a single species are distinguished more objectively or representationally in that species than are those that are distinguished only through an operation of intellect. Therefore an intentional distinction is intermediary between a real distinction and one of reason: It is greater than the one and less than the other.

[B. *Against This View*]

It does not seem to me that these claims are true. So I show that represented being is the same in reality as the representing form, and cognized being the same in reality as the cognition.

1. Every positive entity (*entitas*) not dependent on the soul is a real entity, because such an entity would have being even if the soul were not to exist. Thus the Philosopher and the Commentator, in *Metaphysics* VI [1026a34–b1], make a first division of being into being in the soul and being outside the soul. They say that being outside the soul is real being, because they divide it into the ten categories, each of which is a real being or real entity. For it is clear that [if] no thing exists [then] nothing exists. Therefore it is clear that {9} being that is not dependent on the soul is real being. But represented being is positive being and a kind of positive entity, as they too grant, and it is not dependent on the operation of intellect or soul, as they also grant, because the species would represent even if the intellect were not cognizing. Therefore, if that which is represented is a real being or a real entity, it is nothing other than the entity of what represents it. For if it were a different real entity outside the soul, it would have subjective being distinct in reality from what represents it. Therefore, represented being is the same in reality as the representing form.

The same argument can be made of cognized being and cognition, because a cognition is a true thing perfecting the soul, since that is its proper state. Then I argue as before. Every entity (*entitas*) not dependent on a comparative act of the soul either° is some entity perfecting the soul or else is outside the soul. But the cognized being of an object cognized by a direct act is a positive entity not dependent on a comparative act of intellect. For it can belong to a cognitive power other than the intellect and also can belong to the intellect itself, cognizing through a direct act before its comparative act. Therefore, cognized being is real being and it is not distinct from the cognition. Therefore, it is the same as the cognition.

2. I argue secondly as follows. Whatever follows a real entity by natural necessity is truly a real entity, because if the causal antecedent is real then what follows by natural necessity is real. But by natural necessity represented being necessarily follows the representing form (and cognized being [likewise follows] the cognition). Therefore, since the representing form is a real entity (and likewise the cognition), the represented° being is also a real entity (and likewise the cognized being). But the latter is not distinct from the reality of the representing form (and the cognition), because if so it would be a real subjective being distinct in reality {10} from the representing form (and the cognition), which is false and denied by those who hold this view. Therefore they are the same in reality as the representing form and the cognition.

3. The outcome of a real and natural production has real being. But the agent intellect, by a real and natural action, produces the intelligible° being of an object, or produces the object in intelligible being: for its role is to make something actually intelligible from what is potentially intelligible. Therefore, the intelligible being it produces is some real being. Yet it produces nothing but an intelligible species. Therefore, the intelligible being of the object, which is its represented being through the species, is the same being in reality as the representing species. This is to argue as follows: The agent intellect makes something actually intelligible from what is potentially intelligible, as the Commentator says at *De anima* III [18]. But the agent intellect makes nothing but an intelligible species (or an act of intellectual cognition), because whatever it might be supposed to make in the faculty of imagination or phantasia would be material and extended the length of the material or corporeal faculty's organ. Therefore, the intelligible being of the object is the same in reality as the representing intelligible species (or the cognition). But represented being through the species (or through the cognition, if posited) is the object's intelligible being, not its subjective being. Therefore, represented being is the same in reality as the representing form.

4. The Philosopher shows in *Metaphysics* IV° [1003b22–30] that "being

and one are the same in reality and one nature [. . .] because they are not separated in generation and corruption." For when a person is generated, a person with *being* is generated, and *one* person is generated. Likewise when a person is corrupted, a person with *being* is corrupted, and *one* person is corrupted. From this it is clear that two things are the same in reality when it is entirely impossible for one to be generated or corrupted without the other. But it is impossible for there to be a representing form unless there is the represented being of something. Nor is it possible {11} for there to be a cognition unless there is the cognized being° of something.° Likewise it is impossible for one of those not to exist unless, necessarily, the other does not exist. Therefore, they are the same in reality. So by all the means by which it is necessarily proved that two things are the same in reality it can be proved that represented being is the same in reality as the representing form. For when one is posited then necessarily the other is posited, and when one of the two is destroyed then necessarily the other is destroyed. Therefore, they are the same in reality.

5. Every entity that is neither first nor formulated by an act of intellect comes from another as its efficient cause. But the represented being of a creature through the divine essence does not come from the divine essence as its efficient cause. Therefore, the represented being of a creature through the divine essence is not an entity that is not first. Therefore if it is an entity, it will be the first entity, which is the divine essence.

I prove the major premise as follows. An entity that is neither first nor formulated through an act of intellect is either of itself a necessary being, and then it *is* the first entity, or it is a possible being, not of itself, and if such a thing has being it comes from another as its efficient cause.

The minor premise is proved as follows. Whenever the divine essence is the effective principle of a thing by means of its essence, it effectively produces that thing naturally, to the full extent of its power. Such a thing necessarily has real external being. But the represented being of a creature does not necessarily have real external being, because if so then the thing would exist externally from eternity. Therefore the represented being of a creature does not come from the divine essence as its efficient cause.

6. If represented being is a positive entity distinct from that which represents it, then it is an entity having either subjective or objective being. Not the first, because then there would be a real external entity distinct from what represents it, which is false and denied even [by them]. Not the second, because that which° has objective being in the representing form is the end term of the representation, and that which has objective being

in the cognition is the end term of the cognition,° whereas represented being is not the end term of the representation, and cognized being is not the end term {12} of a direct act of cognition. Therefore, represented being is not a different entity from what represents it, nor is cognized being a different entity from the cognition.

7. Everything naturally prior to something absolute can, without contradiction, exist without the other. And insofar as the one that is naturally posterior belongs to a lesser state of existence (*minoris entitatis*), the one that is naturally prior can exist that much more without it, because it depends that much less on the other. But if represented being and cognized being are their own states of existence, distinct from the representing form and the cognition, then the latter are naturally prior to the former, because then represented being would naturally follow the being of what represents it, and cognized being would naturally follow the being of the cognition. Therefore that which represents an object could exist without the represented being of that object, and the cognition of an object could exist without the cognized being of that object. That involves a contradiction.

8. If represented being is a positive entity (*entitas*) beyond the operation of intellect and distinct from the representing form, then it is a distinct entity either absolutely or relatively. Not the first, because then it would be either a substance or a quantity or a quality – and whichever is proposed, it would be a real being. If the second is proposed then, on the contrary, it is not *only* the relationship, since (according to *De trinitate* VII [i.2]) "everything spoken of relatively is a thing, the relation aside." So beyond the relationship it involves something absolute, and according to you it does not involve the absolute thing that represents it nor does it belong to the thing represented. Therefore, as before, it involves something absolute [in the category] of substance, etc. Whichever is proposed, it would be a real being and would not be distinct in reality from what represents it; for if it were distinct it would possess subjective being. Therefore, it is the same entity in reality as what represents it.

9. If represented being is a positive entity (*entitas*) distinct from what represents it and beyond the act of intellect, {13} then in virtue of that represented being a creature is related to the divine essence that represents it. The consequent is false, therefore so is the antecedent. The inference is clear:

· First, because everything possessing being distinct from God and beyond the operation of intellect is related to God in virtue of that being, because it depends on God in virtue of that being.

• Second, if represented being is a distinct entity from what represents it, then since it is possible to understand represented being as such only when one also understands the being of what represents it, represented being would involve a relation to the being of what represents it.
• Third, if represented being is distinct from what represents it and beyond the operation of intellect, then that which is represented in represented being will be assimilated to its representing° form and consequently that which is represented would be related, in virtue of its represented being, to what represents it.

That the consequent is false, I prove as follows. The relation would be either a relation of reason or a real relation. Not the first, because it is beyond the operation of intellect, just as its foundation is too. For, as they concede and as is true, the represented being of that creature, through the divine essence, is beyond the operation of intellect. Not the second, because then from eternity there would have been a real relation from the creature to God. Also, a real relation requires a real foundation, because a relation does not possess a more perfect existence (*entitatis*) than does its foundation. Thus a creature having represented being from eternity would have a real existence from eternity, which is false and they deny.

Nor can one suppose that it is an intentional relation intermediary between a real relation and a relation of reason. For according to those who hold such a view, intentional being is represented being or cognized being. But from the fact that something represents an object, it does not represent the relation of the represented object to the representing species – just as from the fact that a species represents an intellectually cognized object it does not represent the relation of that object in {14} represented being. Also, an intellect cognizing an object represented by a species would by that very fact cognize the relation of that represented object and consequently it would also cognize the representing species. Each of these is false. Also, a species in the eye, from the fact that it would represent some visible object, would represent the relation of that object in represented being to the species. As a result, someone seeing a visible object through a representing species would by that very fact see, through his corporeal eye, a relation that is in fact not visible through corporeal vision. Therefore, from the fact that an object has represented and cognized being, it does not follow that the relation of that object has represented and cognized being, which you call intentional being. Therefore represented being is not distinct from what represents it.

10. If represented being is a positive entity (*entitas*) distinct from the

species that produces it, then it is produced by a distinct production – otherwise it would be a necessary being. Therefore it is produced either by (i) the representing species or by (ii) something else producing it. Not the first (i), because then God could concur in the production of the species without concurring with the species in the production of the represented being. This is false, because then the species could exist without the represented being of its object. Not the second (ii), because then it is produced either by a producer other than what produced the species – which cannot be the case for the same reason: that then God could concur in the production of one without concurring in the production of the other – or it is produced by the same thing that produced the species, as a concomitant end product, accidental to that production. This cannot be the case for two reasons.

• First, because God can influence its production and operation so that it has the essential (*per se*) end product as its end, without influencing it so that it has the accidental end product as its end. For the blessed can see the divine essence without seeing any creature.
• Second, the end product of a production – not just its essential (*per se*) but even its accidental end product – has something real as its necessary concomitant. This is clear for a relation that is produced accidentally with the production {15} of its foundation. But, according to those in question, represented and cognized being is not real being; it is, as they say, less than real being. Therefore, etc.

[C. Main Reply]

1. I reply to the question that the represented being of an object is not a thing distinct from the representing form. The represented being of Caesar, for instance, represented by a statue, does not differ from the representing statue except in mode of signifying. For when I say that a stone is represented by a species (or by the divine essence) and cognized, this description (*denominatio*) is based on either an intrinsic or an extrinsic form. But not on an intrinsic form inhering in the stone, because then represented being would have real subjective being in the stone. This cannot be the case because [represented being] belongs to the stone even if the stone does not exist. It also would follow that the cognized being of a stone would have being formally inhering in the stone. As a result, our intellect, in understanding the stone, would be the cause of a form's inhering in the stone,

which is false. Therefore, when I say that a stone is represented or cognized, this description is based solely on an extrinsically describing form, which is nothing other than the form that represents it or the form of the intellection. So when a stone is said to be in a place (*locatus*), this is an extrinsic description, based on the surrounding place (*loco*), whereas when a stone is said to be positioned (*ubicatus*), the description is based on the position (*ubi*) inherent in the stone. Likewise, when a stone is said to be represented or cognized through a species, this description is based solely on the representing species and on the cognition having the stone as its ultimate object. And just as, when a stone is said to be in a place, being-in-a-place is nothing other than the place as it surrounds and coalesces with the stone, so when a stone is said to be {16} represented or intellectively cognized through a species, its represented being is no other entity than that of the species signified in a kind of coalescence with the stone, and the intellectively cognized being of the stone° is nothing other than the intellection of the stone signified in a kind of coalescence extrinsic to the stone.

2. I establish this conclusion in the following way as well. A thing that has been or° can be created possesses being in the divine essence perfectively inasmuch as that essence eminently contains all perfections. Second, it possesses being in the divine power virtually inasmuch as that power contains all causality. Third, it possesses being in the divine essence in a representational mode insofar as that essence distinctly represents and expresses all other things. Fourth, it possesses being in divine knowledge insofar as that knowledge cognizes all other things. So just as a thing that has been or can be created is nothing other than the divine essence, inasmuch as it is perfectively and eminently contained in the divine essence, and is nothing other than the power of God, inasmuch as it is virtually contained in God, so it is nothing other than the representing divine essence, inasmuch as it has represented being in the divine essence, and is nothing other than the knowledge of God, inasmuch as it has known or cognized being in the knowledge of God.

3. All these conclusions are confirmed by the blessed Augustine, in *On Genesis* V [xvi.34], where he says, speaking of God, "he possesses all things from the start, just as he himself exists." Augustine proves this as follows:

He would not have made them unless he had known them before he made them, he would not have known them unless he had seen them, he would not have seen them unless he had possessed them, and he would not have possessed what had not yet been made unless in the way that he himself exists without being made.

So Augustine says two things: that God would not have seen other things unless he had possessed them, and that inasmuch as he possesses them, they are God himself. For he says, "he would not have possessed what had not yet been made unless in the way that he himself exists without being made." From these two claims I make the following evident argument: God would not have seen anything unless he had possessed those things, but to possess them only perfectively and not in a representational mode would not have sufficed to have cognized them. For however much {17} and however eminently God might possess the perfections of other things, he would not represent those things, nor would this be sufficient for cognizing other things. So what Augustine means is that unless God had possessed other things perfectively *and* in represented being, he would not have seen them. And he secondly says that as he possesses them, they are God himself. Therefore creatures as possessed by God in a representational mode and perfectively are God himself, whose essence represents all things.

Augustine says in the same place that a creature, according to its cognized being from God, is God himself: "Before things had existence from God, they existed within him, known in such a way as to live eternally and unchangeably and to be life [itself]" [xv.33]. Therefore, as they possess known being from God, so they are eternal and unchangeable life, which is nothing other than God. Augustine also says in the same place,

All these things, before they existed, were within the knowledge of the one who made them, and indeed were better where they were more true, and where they were eternal and unchangeable. [xv.33]

Therefore, inasmuch as they exist in the knowledge of the one who made them, in virtue of their known being, they are eternal and unchangeable and more true, and consequently they are nothing other than God and his knowledge.

Also, Anselm says (*Monologion* ch. 34):

Just as a work made in keeping with some art is always within that art and is nothing other than what the art itself is, so all things that have been made are always within the highest spirit: not what they are in themselves, but what is the same as that spirit.

But art is representational, relative to the thing made through that art. Therefore, a thing, inasmuch as it exists in virtue of its represented being within what represents it, is the representing form itself. So too all things, inasmuch as they exist in the Word that represents and says all things, are the Word itself – as Anselm said above. {18}

Also, according to Anselm (in the same work, ch. 35): "Just as all things are life and truth within the Word, so are they within his knowledge." But they are within his knowledge as what is cognized is within a cognition. Therefore, all things other than God, in virtue of their cognized being, are the same as God's cognition and knowledge.

[D. Reply to the Earlier Arguments]

1. To the first argument for the other view [II.A.1], when it is argued:

> When something is said of two things through a greater univocation than the univocation of genus or species, each of those is a being through its own proper existence; but so 'stone' is said of a stone in cognized being and a stone in produced being,

here I will first show that this argument reaches a conclusion that is false and contrary to their view. Second, I will reply to the form of the argument.

I show the first as follows. I take this as the major premise:

> *If something is said of two things through a greater univocation than the univocation of genus or species, then each of those things is a real being.*

I prove this major premise in the same way as he proves his own: for things are univocal that have the same substantial nature (*ratio*). But that which is a real being and that which is not a real being but purely nothing (such as something that *could* be created) do not have the same substantial nature. For example, the soul of Peter and the not-yet-existent soul of the Antichrist do not have the same substantial nature, because the soul of the Antichrist has no quiddity, as I suppose with him. Next, I take this as his minor premise:

> *'Stone,' said of a stone in cognized being and of a stone in external reality, is said with greater univocation than the univocation of genus or species, because it is said according to numerical unity.*

Therefore a stone in cognized being is a real being, which is false and contrary to his own view. And if it is said [in reply] that something *is* univocal to a being and a nonbeing (for instance, that 'human being' is said univocally of a nonexistent Caesar {19} and an existent William),

then the proof of his major premise collapses, when he says that a being
and something entirely not a being have no single substantial nature.

Alternatively, I take this as his major premise:

> *If something is said univocally of two things through a greater univocation than
> that of genus or species, then each of those things truly is the thing said univocally
> of them in this way.*

But, according to you, 'stone' is said in this way of both a stone in
cognized being and a stone in external reality. Therefore the stone in
cognized being truly is a stone. Then I argue: The stone in cognized being
existed from eternity, and the stone in cognized being truly is a stone.
Therefore a stone existed from eternity. The conclusion is false; therefore
one of the premises is false. Not the major; therefore the minor.

Therefore, [second,] I reply to the argument by granting the major and
denying the minor. For 'stone' is not said univocally, through the univocation of species, of both a stone in cognized being and a stone in external
reality. Consequently, it is also not said of them through a *greater* univocation than the univocation of species, because being-in-cognition, like
being-in-opinion, is a diminishing modifier (*determinatio diminuens*). Thus
a stone in cognized being is a stone in a qualified way (*secundum quid*), just
as the being of Homer in his poetry is the being of Homer in a qualified
way.[1]

To the proof [of the minor], when it is argued:

> *'Stone' is said of both a stone in cognized being and a stone in external reality
> due to numerical unity, because a stone produced in external reality is the same as
> a stone in cognized being,*

I reply as follows. Something broken apart (*distractum*) is not broken relative to what breaks it, but relative to a third [term] it is broken when
qualified by what breaks it. In the same way, something diminished is not
diminished relative to its diminishing modifier, but relative to a third
[term] it is diminished when modified by what diminishes it. For example:
A human being is not modified° by 'dead,' because according to the
Philosopher [*De int.* 11, 21a22], to speak of a dead human being is to put
together opposites, from which a contradiction follows. But the contradiction would not follow unless 'human being,' when matched with 'dead,'
refers to a human being without qualification. For it is the same human

---

[1] See Aristotle, *De interpretatione* 11, 21a25–28.

being, {20} without qualification, who did exist externally and was living and is dead. Hence a true human being is dead, not a qualified human being. Therefore, something broken apart is not broken relative to what breaks it, but relative to a third [term] it is broken when informed by the property that breaks it. So relative to an adjacent third [term] (such as 'human being' or 'animal'), a human being modified by 'dead' is broken.[2]

So when 'stone' is taken in itself and matched with 'being in cognition,' it refers to a stone without qualification. Otherwise it would not be diminished from that state, because it is not diminished from diminished being but from the unqualified being of a stone. But relative to a third [term], a stone as modified by 'being in cognition' is a stone in a qualified and diminished way. Therefore I grant that the stone is numerically the same in external reality and in cognized being. The same stone that in reality and without qualification exists externally is in cognition as well, because relative to a third [term] the stone is diminished through being-in-cognition. So it does not follow that 'stone' is said univocally or due to numerical unity of both a stone in cognized being and a stone in external reality.

2. To the second argument [II.A.2], when it is argued that represented being is a state of existence (*entitas*) intermediary between real being and the being of reason, I say that absolutely speaking there is no such real intermediary state, because every state of existence is either of first or of second intention. For there is no intention intermediary between first and second intention. But if this existence is of second intention, then it is the existence of reason, whereas if it is of first intention, then it is real, because then it is put into being by a first intention of nature and not one of reason.

To the proof, when it is argued that the represented being of a stone is not the existence of reason because it precedes the act of intellect, I grant

---

[2] In other words, whereas it is a contradiction in terms to speak of *a dead human being*, it is not contradictory to say that

A dead human being is not a human being

or

A dead human being is not an animal.

In these latter cases, when we add "a third term," the words 'human being' take on a new "broken" meaning. We are now speaking of a human being in a qualified sense, as a corpse or perhaps as a separated soul.

These two examples are offered at this point in one of our two manuscripts, but the text is so disjointed that the printed edition prefers the other manuscript.

this. And when it is further argued that it is not real existence, because it is {21} diminished being, I reply that although represented being is the diminished being of the represented stone, nevertheless it is real being, the same in reality as the being of the representing form. Analogously, although being-in-opinion is the qualified being of the opinion-holder, it is nevertheless a true thing, an act of cognition in the intellect of the opinion-holder.

But it should be noticed here that although represented being is not absolutely a being intermediary between real being and the being of reason, nevertheless, with respect to the represented object, this being is intermediary between that object's real being and the being of reason. Analogously, although there is no absolute intermediary between good and bad, nevertheless there can be an intermediary in some such respect, as a hermit who is good or bad in himself is neither good nor bad with respect to society. Thus the represented being of an object is not that object's real being. It is also not the being of reason of that object, because represented being does not belong to the object through an act of reason. So with respect to the represented object, represented being is neither real being nor the being of reason, because although absolutely speaking it is being either of first or of second intention, nevertheless with respect to this object it is being neither of first nor of second intention. For it is judged a first or a second intention not with respect to this object but in itself, according to its proper nature. From this it is clear that not every being that is in the soul objectively is the being of reason. For being that is in the soul through a direct cognition is not, nor is being that is in the soul with respect to apprehensive powers other than intellect (such as being that is in the imagination), since such being does not occur through a comparative operation of intellect. It is also clear that if a creature possessed represented being from eternity in such a way that from eternity this represented being was the creature's diminished being, still it would not from eternity have possessed its own proper existence (*entitas*), neither with nor without qualification, because represented being is not a proper existence distinct from the existence of its representing form, as was shown above. {22}

Perhaps you will say that represented being has a real relation with what represents it, because this relation is beyond the operation of intellect, since the representation itself is beyond the operation of intellect; but the end terms of a real relation are distinct in reality and their being is distinct in reality; therefore represented being and the being of what represents it are distinct in reality.

I reply that when that which is represented is a true thing, then there *is* a real relation of what is represented to what represents, especially with respect to the representing divine essence. In that case the end terms of that relation and also the being of those end terms are distinct in reality from one another. In that case, then, that which represents and that which is represented are distinct in reality, and the being of that which represents and the being (formally and intrinsically) of that which is represented are also distinct in reality. But represented being is not formally and intrinsically the being of what is represented, and so it does not follow that represented being is distinct in reality from the being of what represents it.

But perhaps you will still argue: A relatum is distinct in reality from its correlative in virtue of the being by which it has that real relation. But when that which is represented° is a true thing, it has a real relation to what represents it in virtue of represented being: Otherwise the thing represented, as represented, would not be related to what represents it. Therefore, represented being is distinct in reality from what represents it.

I reply that something relative is sometimes said to be related to its foundation (related foundationally), and sometimes to the relation itself (related formally). For example, something is said to be like another in one way by *whiteness*, and in another way by *likeness*. Therefore, when one takes this as one's major premise:

> *A relatum is distinct in reality from its correlative in virtue of the being by which it has that real relation,*

the reduplication[3] can be on account of the foundation or on account of the relation. If the first then this premise is true, but then the minor premise is false, when it is said that what is represented is related to what represents it in virtue of represented being *foundationally*. {23} For the foundation of the relation between what is represented and what represents is not represented being but the absolute nature of what is represented, since its absolute nature is what is represented by the divine essence.

If the reduplication is meant in the second way, on account of the relation, then the major premise remains true, because the relation of what is represented is distinct in reality from the representing divine essence.

---

[3] That is, the phrase 'in virtue of.'

But then one must draw a distinction regarding the minor premise, when it is said that what is represented has a real relation to what represents it in virtue of represented being.

- For in one way, 'represented being' signifies the relation itself by which what is represented is related to what represents it. Then the minor premise is true and rightly accepted alongside the major: for this relation in virtue of which what is represented is formally related to what represents it *is* distinct in reality from what represents it and formally exists in the represented thing when that exists outside the soul.
- In another way, 'represented being' signifies the representation itself in a kind of coalescence (*concretione*) extrinsic to the thing represented, just as 'being white' signifies whiteness in a kind of coalescence extrinsic to its subject. In this way the minor premise is false, because represented being is not in this way distinct from the representing intention, nor does the thing represented° have a real relation to what represents it in virtue of represented being that is the same as the representing form.

This reply can be clarified by a comparison. For an agent is said to be an agent due to two kinds of actions.

- One is in the genus of action, and in virtue of this action an agent brings the thing acted on into some state. As the author of the *Liber sex principiorum* [ch. 2] states: "An action is that in virtue of which we are said to act on that which is the receiving subject." According to many, this action is not in the agent as its subject but in the thing acted on.
- Another is a relation in the mode of a capacity (from the second mode of relatives),[4] in virtue of which an agent {24} is formally related to the thing acted on or produced. This action exists formally in the agent, just as a relation exists formally in its relata.

In just this way, when a creature represented by the divine essence has external being, it has two kinds of represented being:

- First, insofar as 'represented being' signifies the representation by way of an extrinsic description; this is in the representing form.
- Second, insofar as 'represented being' signifies the relation of the thing represented to the representing divine essence; this is in the represented creature.

---

[4] See Aristotle, *Metaphysics* V 15, 1021a15–26.

But in this question we speak of the represented being that belongs to an object regardless of whether it exists; we are asking whether *this* being differs from the representing form. When the represented creature does not have external being, then represented being belongs to it only through an extrinsic description and not insofar as it implies a real relation, because a real relation requires an actual subject.

3. To the third argument for the other view [II.A.3], when it is argued:

> *There can be a distinction between two things in represented being without there being a distinction in what represents them. Therefore the represented being of those things is not the same as what represents them,*

I reply by denying the antecedent insofar as represented being implies an extrinsic description. This becomes clear in replying to the proof of the antecedent. When it is argued:

> *If one species were to represent distinctly a human being and a donkey, then these are several and distinct in represented being – otherwise it would not represent them distinctly,*

I say that just as if several bodies were in the same place those several bodies would have the same being-in-a-place through an extrinsic description based on that same place, so if several objects are represented by the same species they have the same represented being, based on the representation described extrinsically, even though there are several things represented. So such a species distinctly represents several things in represented being, but it does not represent them in distinct° represented beings. These remarks will become more clear in replying to the following argument. {25}

To the argument made as part of the prior view, when it is argued:

> *If several things are distinctly represented by one species, then the things distinctly represented in this way do not have a real distinction in that species, because that species is numerically one. Yet the things distinctly represented in this way necessarily are distinct intentionally from one another and from such a species: otherwise that species would not represent them distinctly,*

I reply first by showing that the argument does not go through. For a species posited to be numerically one and to represent several things distinctly (as some say of the species by which an angel cognizes)[5] is in itself numerically one intentionally just as it is numerically one in reality,

---

[5] See, e.g., Thomas Aquinas, *Summa theologiae* 1a 55.3, 58.2.

since it is in itself one intention and not several. Therefore just as you argue that several things represented by that species are not distinct in reality in that species, because that species is numerically one in reality, so it follows that the things represented by that same species are not intentionally distinct in that species, because the species is numerically one intention. So I say that if several things are represented by the same single species and do not exist in nature, then just as they are not distinct in reality in that species (since the species is not itself distinct in reality) and just as the things represented are not distinct in reality from one another, so they are not intentionally distinct in that species (since the species is numerically one intention), nor do the things so represented (if they do not exist in nature) have being other than the being of the representing species. Consequently, their intentional being is the same in reality as the intention that represents them.

[Second], to the proof, when it is argued:

> *If that representing species represents several things distinctly then they have some distinction within what represents them,*

I reply that if in the antecedent the adverb 'distinctly' modifies the things represented, then it is not universally true – for instance, when the things represented do not exist. For, on this reading, it does not distinctly represent {26} things that are not distinct. On the other hand, if it modifies the verb 'represents,' then the antecedent is true, because such a species distinctly – that is, not confusedly – represents several things. But, on this reading, the inference does not hold, because the divine essence represents distinctly and discretely that which it contains in a unified way, and consequently it distinctly represents things that have no distinction within it.

But to the major statement in the reply I just made, consider the following objection. If some species or form represents several things then it represents distinct things; but not things that are distinct in reality, because they are not distinct in reality if they are not established in nature. Therefore they are distinct intentionally or in represented being. Then the argument made earlier comes back, that things are distinct in represented being without any distinction in their representing form [etc.]. And one can argue in the same way for a cognition and cognized being. For if several things are cognized by a single cognition, then they are cognized distinctly by a single cognition. But they are not cognized distinctly in subjective being. Therefore they are distinct in cognized being and yet the cognition remains one. Therefore things are distinct in cognized being without there being any distinction within the cognition. Therefore, the cognition and cognized being are not the same in reality (*ex parte rei*).

I reply that there are two ways in which things can be distinct in cognized or represented being.

· In one way, *formally*, so that cognized being is distinct in them in virtue of some formal account° – just as we say that two opposite species are distinct in their natures and differentia. In this way we deny that things are distinct in cognized being when they are cognized by a single cognition, and we deny that they are distinct in represented being when they are represented by a single form, just as they are not distinct by cognition.
· In another way, things can be understood to be distinct in cognized being *objectively*, because the same cognition has these things as its distinct end-terms, or has the distinction between them as its end-term, as when distinct things are cognized as distinct. {27} In this way it is true that things are distinct in cognized being even when they do not exist. For they are cognized by a single cognition in virtue of their naturally distinguishing quiddities, and the same is true for what distinguishes them in cognized being. But it does not follow from this that they are distinct in reality, because cognized being is a diminishing modifier. Hence so too are they distinct within cognition. Therefore, it is clear that when several distinct things are cognized by a single cognition, their cognized being is not made to be several, no more than the cognition is, although they are made several in cognized being objectively. And much the same should be said for represented being.

This reply is clarified by a comparison. If two bodies are put in the same place, these bodies are distinct in their containing place not formally, on account of place, [but objectively]. Likewise, two species are distinct in their genus not actually but potentially, through the differentiae contained potentially within the genus. So, as the foregoing has made clear, the claim that 'things are distinct in something' is equivocal.

[III. Reply to the Initial Arguments]

1. To the first of the initial arguments [I.A.1], when it is argued:

> That being which belongs to a cognized and represented object insofar
> as it is distinct from the cognition and the representing form is not the
> same in reality as the cognition and the representing form,

I say that this is true if it belongs to it formally and intrinsically, but not –
as in this situation – if it belongs to it by an extrinsic description (as has
often been said[6]). For example, being-in-a-place belongs to a body in a
place insofar as the body is distinct from the place, and yet being-in-a-
place is nothing other than the place's surrounding the body in that place,
just as being-white is nothing other than whiteness's describing a subject.
In the same way, cognized being belongs to a stone insofar as the stone is
distinct from divine cognition, because God cognizes a stone° insofar as it
is distinct from him, and nevertheless the cognized being of the stone from
eternity is nothing other than God's cognition. Much the same should be
said for represented being and the representing form. Another appropriate
example concerns honor and being honored, and praise {28} and being
praised. For honor and praise are within the one honoring and praising,
and yet they describe the one praised and honored insofar as that person is
distinct from the one praising and honoring.

2. To the second [I.A.2], when it is argued,

> *An object given intelligible being by agent intellect does not produce the object in
> represented being through a species,*

I say that if the intelligible species is impressed on intellect by the object
and by agent intellect, then since the species representing the object and
the represented being of the object are the same, the proposition is false.
For although the intelligible object does not produce the represented
object, still it produces the object with respect to represented being – or,
to put it more accurately, it produces the represented being of the object.

To the first proof, when it is said,

> *The same thing does not produce itself; but the object that is intelligible due to
> agent intellect is the same as the object in represented being through the species,*

I say that the same thing does not produce itself with respect to one and
the same being. Nevertheless, a thing with respect to one being can
produce its being in another respect – or, to put it more accurately, it can
produce another being belonging to itself but accidental and extrinsic to
itself. In this way, although a human being cannot make himself, he

---

[6] See II.C.1 and II.D.2–3.

nevertheless can make himself in a place, and with being-in-a-place. Thus although the same object does not produce itself, it nevertheless can produce itself in represented being by producing the species in which it is represented, and this is nothing other than to produce the represented being of that object.

To the other proof, when it is argued,

> *That which produces something by a real action is related to what it produces by a real relation,*

this is granted. And when it is said,

> *An intelligible object is not related by a real relation to the [same] object in represented being,*

I deny this, if the intelligible object impresses the species [on intellect]. And when you say,

> *the object in represented being does not as such have real being, and a real relation requires a real end-term,*

I reply that although the object does not have real being in represented being, nevertheless the produced represented being is a real being, {29} just as the representing species is real. As a result, the intelligible object has a real relation to its represented being, just as it has a real relation to its representing species, if it produces it in intellect and impresses it on intellect.

PETER AUREOL
INTUITION, ABSTRACTION, AND DEMONSTRATIVE KNOWLEDGE

Introduction

Peter Aureol (c. 1280–1322) was one of the most influential and original philosophers of the early fourteenth century. A member of the Franciscan order, Aureol became a master of theology at the University of Paris in 1318. The following selection is taken from the prologue to his major work, his commentary on Lombard's *Sentences*.

The official topic of this question concerns divine illumination: specifically, whether God could illuminate someone in this life with the articles of faith in such a way that this individual would have *knowledge* of these propositions. On its face, this might seem unlikely, because such articles – regarding the incarnation, the Trinity, etc. – are supposed to be held by faith alone in this life. (In the next life, in the "light of glory," matters will be quite different.) But Aureol wants to know whether it would be possible, if only in principle, for God to provide illumination that would provide a "wayfarer" (someone in this life) not just with a stronger faith, but with genuine knowledge. Aureol accepts the standard medieval account of knowledge (*scientia*) as requiring a demonstrative proof. (To stress this point, we sometimes translate *scientia* as "demonstrative knowledge.") So the present question raises the problem of whether illumination could conceivably supply this sort of demonstrative evidence. In other words, could someone granted illumination in this life ever *prove* the mysteries of the faith? Aureol's answer is Yes.

Although the question is cast in terms of divine illumination, Aureol's real interest is in the nature of knowledge. In the course of his affirmative answer, Aureol has to distinguish knowledge from faith. This leads him to Scotus's influential distinction between two kinds of cognition (*notitia*), intuitive and abstractive. Scotus had claimed that intuitive cognition always takes as its object something that is present to the cognitive agent. Aureol objects to this account by describing various cases of nonveridical perception, such as afterimages and double vision, where there is no object corresponding to what is being perceived. Aureol's own proposal is that an intuitive cognition, at both the sensory and intellectual levels, is a cognition that is direct (not inferential), and that makes the object appear present, actual, and existent.

Lurking in the background is Aureol's theory of *apparent being*, which is what he takes to explain how objects – even nonexistent objects – can appear to be present before one's mind. This will be the topic of Translation 9.

For further reading on this subject, see CHLMP VI.21, "Faith, Ideas, Illumination, and Experience," and VI.22, "Intuitive and Abstractive Cognition." Regarding Aureol in particular, see Tachau (1988) and Pasnau (1998a).

Intuition, Abstraction, and Demonstrative Knowledge

Scriptum, prooemium, Q2[1]

In the present section, since Master Lombard puts his trust in divine help, the question can therefore be rightly asked:

Can God provide to a wayfarer some light in virtue of which theological truths are demonstratively known (*scientifice cognoscantur*)?

Initial Arguments

1. Arguments for Such a Light[2]

6. It seems that God could provide some light that energizes and elevates the intellect, under the influence of which we would clearly understand the articles of faith in such a way that conclusions deduced from articles so understood would be cognized as knowledge. For God can provide a light that elevates and strengthens the intellect in such a way that everything passively knowable in propositions is brought to actuality; for to every

---

[1] Translated in collaboration with Charles Bolyard.
[2] See Henry of Ghent, *Quodlibet* 12.2. (See also Translation 5, for Ghent's more general views on illumination.)

passive potentiality there is possibly a corresponding active potentiality. Therefore for everything passively knowable it is possible that a light be correspondingly made, which would play an active clarifying role. But in propositions formed from the articles of faith, their passive knowability and cognizability lie hidden. For such propositions are either immediate, in which case they are cognizable at once, or they are mediate. In the latter case, given that between two terms (predicate and subject) there cannot be an infinite number of intermediaries, {178} it is possible to reach immediate propositions that will be cognizable in themselves. Therefore God can provide a light by which the articles of faith are sufficiently cognized.

7. Moreover, between species maximally distant from one another, God can produce an intermediary. But the light of glory and the obscure light of faith are maximally distant from one another in species. Therefore God can provide an intermediary light, less than the light of glory, but more than the light of faith, in which the articles of faith are demonstratively known.

8. Moreover, any thing that can be cognized in three ways – by faith, as knowledge, or intuitively – can have three corresponding lights in which the thing is in these three ways cognized.° For example, when one hears from an astronomer that a future eclipse will occur at a certain day and hour, one cognizes this through faith. But if one knows it through astronomical calculation, one cognizes it as knowledge. And if one intuits it visually by the moon's position, one cognizes in a higher way, intuitively. Accordingly, there are three lights: the first being the least, the third the greatest, and the second intermediary. But with regard to the [theological] truths we believe, one can have the first cognition and the first light; this is the obscurity of faith. One can also have the third cognition and the third light; this is the clarity of heaven. Therefore, one could have had an intermediary cognition that would be knowledge and an intermediary light in which such truths are known.

9. Moreover, with respect to these truths God can provide the light of knowledge: a light that comes with necessary arguments, since knowledge stems from necessary arguments. But according to Richard of St. Victor (in *De trinitate* bk.I, ch. 4), to explain those beliefs that are necessary [for salvation], "there is no lack of arguments that are plausible, indeed even° necessary, although it sometimes happens that they escape our scrutiny." Therefore, with respect to such truths God can provide some light in which they are known.

10. Moreover, knowing whether something is possible in God is the same as knowing whether it is necessary. For in the case of divine truths, whatever is possible is entirely necessary, since God is a necessary being to the highest degree (according to Avicenna in *Metaphysics* I [chs. 6–7]). But God can provide a light by which such truths are known to be possible, because if their impossibility is inferred from some syllogism, it will be mistaken either in matter or in form.[3] But every mistake in matter can be detected through one of the various branches of knowledge, whereas a mistake in form can be detected through logic, assuming logic and the various branches of knowledge are perfectly grasped. {179} Therefore, since God can perfectly provide these kinds of knowledge, he can also provide a light with which one would refute every syllogism proving that the truths we believe are impossible. Indeed, by this light one will as a consequence know these truths to be possible. Therefore, by the same light, one will know how to separate what is necessary from what is impossible.

11. Moreover, anything God can provide suddenly and in passing, he can provide for a long time, enduringly. But God gave the light of the highest faith to the prophets in passing, suddenly. Therefore, he could provide a similar light to the faithful enduringly, for a long time.

12. Moreover, cognizing a conclusion is the effect of the premises. But God can provide every effect of a secondary cause without that cause. Therefore God could provide a clear and luminous cognition of the truths we believe without the premises' being grasped, and as a consequence these truths would be cognized by a higher light than the obscure light of faith.

13. Moreover, a cognition of the terms is distinct in reality from a cognition of their connection and combination, as is self-evident. Therefore, [God] could clarify one's cognition of the combination and connection of the terms without clarifying one's simple cognition of the terms. Thus he could provide a clear cognition of the proposition *God is three and one*, even while one has an obscure and enigmatic cognition of both terms, 'God' and 'three.' Such a light and such a cognition are higher than faith, but lower than the beatific vision in which God and the trinity are intuitively cognized. Therefore, God can provide such an intermediary light. [14] This is confirmed by the fact that God can provide a cognition that is certain of the proposition *The Antichrist will exist*, even given that a

---

[3] That is, either one or more of the premises will be false, or the form of the syllogism will be invalid.

human being does not have a simple cognition clearly of the Antichrist, as regards his form and person.

15. Moreover, it is neither plausible nor safe to say that the saints have spoken falsely and boastfully of themselves. But Saint Augustine, in his *Contra epistulam fundamenti* [sec. 14], says "I profess the Catholic faith, and through this I am confident of achieving certain knowledge." Richard also says (where quoted above), "Our efforts in this work are, for the things we believe, to bring forth arguments that are not merely plausible but even necessary." Also, Augustine often says that the light in the faithful and wise is different from the light of simple faith.[4] Therefore it seems that such a light absolutely should be posited. {180}

2. *Arguments for This Light as an Abstractive Cognition*[5]

16. It further seems that God could provide a light that is nothing other than a clear and distinct abstractive cognition of the quidditative notion of deity, from which all truths concerning the persons and their attributes and other intrinsic features can be derived as knowledge. For whenever the memory of some object remains in any intellect from a prior intuitive act, this intellect can have an abstractive cognition of that object. This is clear, because the memory of an object is an abstractive cognition, because it abstracts from the presence (*praesentialitas*) of the thing. But from the intuition of deity that Saint Paul suddenly had, the memory of deity, as suddenly seen, remained in his intellect. So he himself testifies in II Corinthians 12:2, that he was *suddenly carried off to the third heaven*. According to Augustine, this should be understood as referring to a vision of deity. And in the same place the Apostle adds that he *heard secret words that human beings are not permitted to speak*. Therefore it seems that there was an abstractive cognition of deity in his intellect, even while he was a wayfarer. Hence God can similarly provide this to any of the faithful.

17. Moreover by whatever kind of cognition one cognizes an act and its relationship to an object, through that same kind of cognition one can cognize the object. But one can cognize abstractively both the act by which one cognizes God and the relationship to God as cognized, because these are wholly created. Therefore the object, God and his proper essence, could also be cognized abstractively.

---

[4] See n.39 below.
[5] Cf. Scotus, *Quodlibet* 7.19–28.

18. Moreover, it seems to be possible for there to be two cognitions of God that are no different with respect to the object that is cognized, and that differ only with respect to the cognitive agent and to the mode of cognition. For although {181} no diversity should be posited within God, nevertheless there is nothing absurd about different modes of cognizing God. But intuitive and abstractive cognition do not differ with respect to the object that is cognized, because the very same thing that is cognized intuitively can be cognized abstractively. In fact, we can abstractively cognize the existence of a thing when we see a lesser part of it: for we can imagine how the rose exists on the branch [that we now see]. Therefore, one can have abstractive and intuitive cognition of God, because they are simply two diverse modes of cognizing the same object.

19. Moreover, anything whose essence differs conceptually from its existence can be cognized abstractively. For the concept of essence without existence will be an abstractive concept. But God's essence differs conceptually from his existence, although there is no real difference. Therefore, it seems that God can be conceived abstractively. And this is confirmed by the fact that essence can be conceived without truth, goodness, or any other attribute, and so likewise without existence, it seems.

20. Moreover, an abstractive cognition is said to be that which concerns an absent thing, and which abstracts from the thing's presence. But deity can be conceived without its presence to us, since such presence is nothing other than a relation of reason, and deity can be conceived apart from every relation of reason. Therefore, it seems that deity could be conceived abstractively.

21. Moreover, a creature is not cognizable by us in more ways than God is, it seems. For each thing is cognized insofar as it is an actual being, according to *Metaphysics* IX [1051a22–33], and so to the extent a thing is more actual it is more cognizable, and in more ways. But a rose and any other created quiddity can be cognized intuitively and abstractively by us. Therefore, so can deity.

22. Moreover, what is conceptually prior (*prius per intellectum*) can be detached from anything posterior. But since deity is "a sea of infinite substance" according to Damascene,[6] it is prior to existence, to presence, and to every attribute. Therefore it can be conceived without existence and presence, and as a result it can be conceived abstractively.{182}

---

[6] *De orthodoxa fide*, ch.9.

3. Arguments against Knowledge by Illumination[7]

23. On the contrary, it seems that no light elevating the intellect to knowledge of our beliefs could be provided by God. For if such a light were possible, it would have been provided to the blessed Virgin, the apostles, the holy doctors, or masters in theology. But no one has ever been provided with such a light:

- Not the Virgin, because she walked through faith. According to Church teaching, *faith* resided in her on Holy Saturday; no one says that *knowledge* of our beliefs resided in her on that day.
- Not the apostles either, because Paul testifies in II Corinthians 5:6–7 that he *went away from the Lord, walking through faith and not through sight.*
- Nor was it provided to Augustine and the other holy doctors, because if they had possessed this knowledge they surely would have passed it on to us in their books on what is to be believed – something we don't find them doing.
- It is also not provided to masters in theology: for no matter who is asked, however great he is, he does not say at death that he has knowledge of what is to be believed, but that it suffices for him to believe.

Therefore, such a light is not possible.

24. Moreover, if it were possible for a wayfarer to possess such a light, it ought to have been infused during baptism. For just as nature does not fail in what is necessary, but rather provides at the point of natural origin everything that contributes to achieving natural perfection, so such a light ought to be provided during the renewal of baptism, because it is necessary for achieving a great spiritual perfection – a knowledge of our beliefs. But this light is not provided during baptism: For no one has experienced it, and it is impossible for the loftiest dispositions to be possessed and be concealed from us. Therefore, such a light is not possible for a wayfarer.

25. Moreover, it is impossible for a wayfarer to possess what cannot coincide with faith, because faith is the condition of this life, as the light of glory is the condition of heaven. But such a light cannot coincide with faith. First, it would take away from the merit of faith. Also, they would be contradictory, because faith contains darkness and obscurity, since it concerns *things that appear not*, according to the Apostle in Hebrews 11:1, whereas this light would contain the appearance, and would supply evi-

---

[7] Cf. Godfrey of Fontaines, *Quodlibet* 8.7.

dentness and clarity. Also, faith and opinion are incompatible.[8] Also, that light would provide demonstrative knowledge, but such knowledge can in no way coincide with faith; otherwise, a mathematician could have faith in the conclusions {183} that he knows. Therefore, such a light is not possible for a wayfarer.

26. Moreover, if this light were possible, it would be intermediary between the light of faith and the light of glory, by either participation or negation. But not by participation, because then it would be more excellent than either one. For a mixture contains its ingredients virtually; thus a human being is loftier than the elements between which flesh is intermediary (according to *De anima* III [429b15]). Nor can it be claimed that the light is intermediary by negation, because then it could be separated from faith and infused in an infidel. Therefore, it is not possible, it seems.

27. Moreover, it is impossible to provide an evident cognition of a principle without providing a cognition and distinct cognition of its terms, because this is necessarily required for the evident cognition of a principle. But no light apart from the state of glory can provide a distinct cognition of the terms 'God' or 'trinity of persons,' because beatitude consists in a distinct cognition of each. Therefore, such a light cannot be provided.

28. Moreover, it is impossible to adhere primarily to the same truth through two different dispositions. But the faithful always adhere to and hold onto articles through faith. Therefore, they cannot be provided with another light through which they primarily hold onto these articles.

4. Arguments against This Light as Abstractive[9]

29. It further seems that a light could not be provided when it is taken as an abstractive cognition of deity under a proper and distinct notion. Such a cognition is impossible for a wayfarer. For every cognition of the divine essence is beatific. But such an abstractive cognition would be of his essence, clearly and distinctly. Therefore, it would be beatific.

30. Moreover, an abstractive cognition is either more perfect than an intuitive cognition, or less perfect, or equally perfect. It is not less perfect, because then God's {184} cognition of creatures would be less perfect

---

[8] And so, *a fortiori*, faith and knowledge must be incompatible. By *opinion*, Aureol means the assent to a proposition with some doubt about whether it is in fact true. In the previous question [nn. 96–111], Aureol had argued at length for the incompatibility of opinion and faith.
[9] Cf. Hervaeus Natalis, *Quodlibet* 2.5.

when they do not exist than when they do. For he has an abstractive
cognition when they do not exist, whereas he intuits them when they
exist; hence the existence of a creature would make divine knowledge
more perfect, which is impossible. So it is either more perfect, in which
case it would be more beatific, or it is equally perfect, in which case it
equally beatifies. Therefore, such an abstractive cognition is not possible
for the faithful while remaining wayfarers.

31. Moreover, cognitions that concern the same object under the same
aspect (*ratione*) are so related to one another that if one is beatific so is the
other. But an intuitive cognition concerns God under the aspect of deity,
and in the same way so does this supposedly possible abstractive cognition.
Therefore, since the intuitive would be beatific, so likewise for the abstractive, and so it would be impossible for a wayfarer. This is confirmed by
the fact that beatitude seems to consist in God's being clearly and sheerly
cognized through his essence, either abstractively or intuitively.

32. Moreover, a single relation of reason added to a cognition does not
make it beatific, for a human being is beatified only in the highest essence,
and therefore not in a relation of reason. But an intuitive cognition does
not grasp more of deity than an abstractive cognition would, except for a
single relation° of reason — namely, presence. For the whole of deity is
cognized abstractively except that it is not conceived of as present, whereas
through an intuitive cognition it is seen as present. Therefore, the intuitive
will not be beatific unless the abstractive is also beatific. Hence it cannot
be provided in this state of life.

33. Moreover, when the quidditative concept of a thing includes existence, it cannot be conceived abstractively. For an abstractive cognition
abstracts from existence and nonexistence. But existence is included in the
quidditative concept of deity, because God is necessary existence.
Therefore deity cannot be conceived abstractively.

34. Moreover, an abstractive cognition presupposes an intuitive one.
For the universal is abstracted only insofar as the singular has been under
sense and intuition. But God cannot be cognized by a wayfarer intuitively,
and therefore not abstractively.

35. Moreover, whatever wayfarers cognize abstractively they cognize
by abstracting from a phantasm. But God is not a phantasm. Therefore, as
before.

36. Moreover, if God could be cognized abstractively, that cognition
would either extend immediately to the sheer essence of God or {185}
extend to some representation of it. But not to a representation, because

then deity would not be cognized in itself and in its proper aspect, but rather in its likeness, and also because deity cannot have a sufficient representation. So it remains that such a cognition would extend to God's sheer essence as it is in itself. Therefore, it would be intuitive.

37. Moreover, it seems improper to say that there is an intuitive cognition within intellect, because such a cognition is material inasmuch as it concerns a thing's presence, which is one of the material conditions under which sensory cognition occurs. Further, the phrase 'abstractive cognition' seems fictitious and improper. Therefore, deity is not open to being cognized in these ways.

Main Reply

38. In replying to this question, I will proceed in the following order. First, I will present views opposed to those of two doctors. Second, I will present a modern way of speaking and will investigate its truth. Third, I will make some remarks so that we may see the point of the question. Fourth, I will say what, it seems, ought in truth to be said regarding this question.

Article 1. Against the Views of Two Doctors

1. Henry of Ghent (Quodlibet 12.2)

39. Regarding the first, then, we should consider that some have wanted to say that God can provide a light by which the articles of faith can be cognized in this life more clearly than through the light of faith, so that through this light theologians can have demonstrative knowledge of truths about God. But this view, even if it could be confirmed through the nine arguments introduced above (in what was argued in the first place [nn.6–15]), is still mainly supported by authoritative texts from the saints, who seem to place such a light beyond the light of faith. Hence Augustine[10] says of John 1:4 – *the life was* {186} *the light of men* – that there are many who cannot yet be raised to a spiritual understanding of the phrase *In the beginning was the Word*. "For an animate human being does not perceive

---

[10] *Tractatus in Evangelium Iohannis* I.1–2.

this." He adds that when the Prophet says *Let the mountains obtain peace for the people, and the hills justice* [Psalm 71/72:3], he understands by 'peace' the wisdom by which greater minds are illuminated, and by 'justice' the faith by which those lesser are illuminated. But the lesser would not receive faith unless the greater had been illuminated by wisdom itself. Also, in a letter to Consentius [120.2], Augustine speaks in these terms:

(As for the unity of deity and the distinction of Persons,) in which our faith chiefly consists, see to it that you believe by authority alone, and that you do not seek to understand the reason for it. For although I undertook to see the meaning of this secret, I could not have arrived at it in any way unless God had aided my intellect.

Augustine makes many similar remarks about a double light.

40. These claims not withstanding, it should be said [in reply] that this light can be understood in one way as that by which the articles of the faith are more clearly cognized as regards their terms. Neither the connection nor any discord between these terms would be seen through this light; the light would instead remove any discord arising from arguments to the contrary or from a defect in the plausible arguments conveying an understanding of the articles. With respect to a light of this kind, God certainly can provide it to the greatest degree, beyond what can be provided to some degree through both natural ingenuity and the study of theology (as discussed in the previous question).[11]

Alternatively, such a light can be understood as that by which the connection between terms in the articles of faith is seen and not merely believed. This can happen in two ways. First, it can happen under the concepts of the terms that we possess in this life of 'God,'° 'three,' etc.; these are of course not proper and distinct concepts of deity and the trinity of persons. Second, it can happen under the *proper* concepts of deity, trinity, etc. If the light is proposed in this last way, as that by which these sorts of° proper concepts of terms are possessed and their connections are seen, then it certainly is possible for such a light to be provided. But this coincides with and is the same as an abstractive cognition, something not understood by the proponent of this light, [Henry of Ghent,] but understood by the modern doctor who will be discussed in the second article, [John Duns Scotus]. The result, then, is that this doctor understands such a light in the second way under discussion – namely, that it happens under

---

[11] Prooemium Q1, esp. nn. 92–95 (ed. Buytaert, pp. 159–60).

the concepts of terms that are either of the same kind as every wayfarer has, or at least not proper to deity {187} and the divine trinity, and that the connection and the combination of these terms are seen in the articles of faith. When the light is understood in this way, it cannot possibly be posited.

41. This conclusion can be established in many ways. For it is impossible to see the connection and combination of any terms unless one sees the foundation of the connection and the founding nature (*ratio fundandi*). For a connection is a kind of relation; but one cognizes a relation only once one cognizes the foundation, the relatum, and the founding nature. Certainly, it is impossible to cognize the conformity of two things unless one cognizes that quality in which they conform. But no concept whatsoever, except that which is proper to deity and the trinity of persons, is the foundation of the connection and combination in *God is three and one*. For if some other concept were such a foundation, then either (1) it will be a disparate concept, concerning a being other than God, and then such a being will be three personally and one essentially, which cannot be allowed; or (2) it will be a common concept proper to God, such as that of the first actuality of being, or pure actuality, or something similar. And it is certain that such conceptions are neither the foundation nor the founding nature of this connection, because the trinity of persons is within God through the proper nature (*rationem*) of deity. Therefore it is impossible to see this connection clearly through any light unless one possesses proper concepts of this kind.

42. Moreover, if such a connection [between terms] is seen, it is seen either immediately, or in the terms, or through other principles and propositions seen first. It cannot be said that it is seen through the terms because these, as so [improperly] conceived, are not the cause of that connection. Nor can it be said that it is cognized through prior propositions, because either (1) they would go from the universal to the lower in concluding that there is a trinity of persons in God, which cannot be because the trinity is in God not through a common nature (*rationem*) but through a proper one; or (2) they would reach this conclusion *a simili*. But this too cannot be. First, because there is more dissimilarity than similarity between any given thing and the trinity of persons, according to Augustine in *On the Trinity* XV [xx.39]. Second, because the argument *a simili* is a sophism, as Aristotle suggests in *Topics* I [103a6–23], unless in each of the similar° objects there is a universal nature to which applies the predicate that, through one of the similar objects, is proved of the other. So the soul of

Socrates is proved immortal because the soul of Sortes is immortal. This
would not have held if immortality did not apply to both souls through a
common nature. {188} But there plainly is no common nature through
which the trinity applies to God and to something else. The third principle
option – on which one immediately sees and cognizes the connection in
the articles of faith – is also unacceptable. For a thing can be cognized
only as it is naturally suited to be cognized, as is clear from *Physics* I
[184a17–21]. But the connection [between terms] does not in fact have
the character of being primarily cognizable or being a first truth. It is
instead a resultant truth and is secondarily cognizable. Therefore no power
could provide a light by which this connection is cognized immediately
and at first. Therefore such a light is impossible.

43. Nor does it help if one says that sometimes the connection is known
and yet the terms are not known. For example, without knowing the
figure and form of the Antichrist, someone can know and cognize that at
the Second Coming the Antichrist will appear.[12] This does not help,
because it is not a case of clearly cognizing or seeing, but only of believing
and firmly adhering. It is possible to adhere through faith to the connection between terms without clearly cognizing those terms.

44. Moreover, God cannot take an act directed at an object and split
off the basis (*rationem*) by which it is formally directed at that object. For
instance, if one sees a wall through its color as the formal basis, then it is
impossible for the apprehending of color to be split off from the seeing of
the wall. The same goes for choosing the means to an end and intending
the end. But the formal basis by which the intellect cognizes and is
directed at the connection between terms is the proper concept of each
term in the immediate propositions. For we cognize principles insofar as
we cognize their terms (*Posterior Analytics* I [72b23–25]). Therefore principles are cognized through their terms, just as the means to an end is
desired° through its end and, likewise, conclusions are cognized through
principles. Therefore, without the proper concepts of the terms, it is
impossible for a light to be provided by which one cognizes the connection or combination of any proposition whatsoever.

45. Nor does it help when some say that cognizing the terms is the
efficient cause of cognizing the principle and its combination, and when
they say that cognizing the premises efficiently causes a cognition of the

---

[12] Cf. n. 14 above.

conclusion.[13] This is undoubtedly true for a cognition by which the terms are cognized separately. But that cognition by which the connection [between terms] is cognized includes a cognition of the terms not efficiently but formally — just as was proved in the present question [n. 44] for a conclusion, relative to {189} its principle, and for the desire for the means to an end, on account of the end.

46. Moreover, anyone who clearly cognizes and knows some connection [between terms] cognizes it as necessary and impossible to be otherwise. But a connection can be conceived as necessary and impossible to be otherwise only through its terms. For a connection derives its necessity from its terms, since of course no relation is a necessary being through itself; rather, its necessity is based on something else. Therefore, the connection cannot be known unless one preconceives the terms under that account by which they underlie the connection.

47. Moreover, as the terms when vocalized stand to the proposition when uttered, so the concepts of the terms stand to the total concept of the principle. But it is impossible for a proposition to exist as an utterance without the terms being there, as spoken words. Therefore it is impossible for the concept of a principle to exist, with a cognition of it, without the concepts of the terms being there, as parts of this principle, with a cognition of these same [terms]. But they are not parts under a confused and common concept, but rather under a proper concept. For a proposition that is immediate under a proper concept is not immediate under a common concept. For this is immediate:

> *A triangle has three angles*

whereas this is not:

> *A shape has three angles.*

Instead, the latter can be proved from a lower proposition, and this precludes its being immediate, according to the Philosopher in *Posterior Analytics* I [72a6–9, b19–22]. Therefore it is impossible to cognize clearly and sheerly the combination of any proposition without having the proper concepts of its terms.

48. Moreover, just as the connection [between terms] stands to its proper terms qua existence, so it stands qua being cognized. But it is impossible for a connection to exist without its proper terms. Therefore,

---

[13] Cf. n. 12 above.

it is impossible for it to be conceived without the proper concepts of these same terms.

49. So from the above it is clear that a light by which the connection [between terms] is seen and clearly cognized cannot be granted. But a light can be granted by which the terms are more clearly cognized, by which all discord among the terms (arising from contrary arguments) is removed, and which nourishes the connection between these terms in the minds of the weak, who on account of such doubts strongly resist [the faith] unless they have plausible arguments in favor of the connection. This light is the theological disposition discussed above;[14] all the authoritative passages {190} from Augustine concern this light, not that fictitious light that cannot possibly be posited.

2. *Godfrey of Fontaines* (Quodlibet *8.7*)

50. On this account, others say that such a light is impossible, and for this there are the six arguments introduced in the third section above [nn. 23–28]. This position maintains its conclusion above all because such a light, if granted, could not coincide with faith. But though such a claim is true as regards its conclusion, still its means of argument do not go through, as will become clear when I answer them [nn. 140–46]. Also, the claim that such a light is incompatible with the faith needs scrutiny. But this has more of a place in book III of the *Sentences*, and so it should be passed over for now.

Article 2. A Modern Account

1. *The View of Scotus* (Quodlibet *7.19–28*)

51. With respect to the second article, then, it should be noted that some, coming closer to the truth, said that God can provide {191} a light by which the terms of the articles of faith are cognized under their *proper* concepts. 'God,' for example, would be cognized under the notion of deity, properly and distinctly. This light would be nothing other than an abstractive cognition of the sheer and unmixed essence of deity. And these doctors present four arguments, in sequence.

---

[14] Cf. n. 40, and also Prooemium Q1, esp. nn. 92–95 (ed. Buytaert, pp. 159–60).

52. First, they explain what abstractive and intuitive cognitions are. An intuitive cognition is that which concerns the presence and existence of a thing and has as its terminus the thing as existing in itself. An abstractive cognition is said to be that which abstracts from being and nonbeing, existing and nonexisting, and from the thing's presence. In this manner I intuit a rose when I grasp its presence, whereas I cognize it abstractively when I consider its quiddity and nature. Each of the two are possible for the intellect. For it is certain that an angel intuits a rose, when it exists, whereas when the rose does not exist the angel considers its essence abstractively.

53. Second, they prove that the divine essence can be cognized abstractively, just as can every quidditative nature. For God can do through his will alone whatever he can do by means of his essence. But by means of his essence he moves the intellect of the blessed to a clear and sheer cognition of himself. This is of course an intuitive cognition, in that the intellect has as its terminus God's essence as truly present and existent, since it moves [the intellect] in this way. Therefore God could move that intellect to a cognition of his sheer and clear essence through his will alone. But it is certain that such a cognition has as its terminus the divine essence under the same notion under which the intellect is moved toward it. But it is moved not through the presence and existence of the divine essence, but through the command of God's omnipotent will. Therefore, such a cognition will have as its terminus God's essence not as existing and present, but solely by abstracting from existence and presence. Accordingly, it will not be an intuitive cognition, but rather an abstractive one.

54. Third, they prove that this kind of cognition is possible for a wayfarer. For every cognition is possible for a wayfarer that does not put him in a beatific state of understanding. But an abstractive cognition of the divine essence is not beatific. Rather, only an intuitive cognition is: first, because to see God through his essence, which is beatific, is to know him intuitively. Also, because there could be an abstractive cognition even supposing *per impossibile* that God did not exist – in the way that the quiddity of a rose {192} is cognized abstractively when the rose does not exist. Therefore, this kind of cognition is possible for a wayfarer.

55. Fourth, they prove that through this cognition theological truths could be demonstratively known, even *a priori*. For whoever cognizes a subject under its proper and quidditative account (*ratione*) can cognize all the truths contained virtually within that subject. For the truth of the conclusion is contained virtually in the truth of the principle, and the

cognition of the other term of that principle (the predicate) is contained virtually in the account of the subject. For according to the Bishop of Lincoln [Robert Grosseteste] in *Posterior Analytics* I [ch. 4], principles belong to the second mode of *per se* predication when in them a proper attribute (*passio*) is predicated of the defining account of the subject, on which depends a cognition of the attribute. Hence all demonstrative truths are reduced to the defining account of the subject. But this is an abstractive cognition, because demonstrative knowledge abstracts from the subject's being and nonbeing. For it remains when the thing is destroyed, and for this reason there can be no knowledge of singulars, only estimation (according to the Philosopher in *Metaphysics* VII [1039b27–40a7]). Therefore, since an abstractive cognition of the quidditative notion of deity could be provided to the intellect of a wayfarer, as was stated [n. 54], it follows that a light could be provided to a wayfarer by which he would know the articles and truths of faith – those truths, I mean, that are by the nature of things necessary, not voluntary° and contingent. And this way of positing [such a light] seems entirely rational, beautiful, and subtle.

2. Against Scotus (Hervaeus Natalis, Quodlibet 2.5)

56. To some this view seems unreasonable in both its conclusion and its proof. In its conclusion it seems unreasonable because every first cognition, which no other precedes, seems to have as its terminus the thing as it is in its existence (*entitate*), and consequently it is an intuitive cognition. For if it is first then the intellect forms through it a determinate concept of the thing – not under this or that posterior notion, but {193} under the existent (*entitativa*) reality of it, which is both prior and fundamental, and from which other concepts are formed under secondary notions. But a cognition of the divine quiddity is immediately first; nothing else precedes it. For if something else precedes this cognition, either (1) it is a cognition of something other than God, in which God is revealed, which cannot be because it is impossible for deity to be revealed in anything created that is cognized objectively; or (2) it is a cognition of God himself, and then either (a) it would concern the existence of God, which cannot be because then existence would precede essence, and the cognition of existence would precede the cognition of quiddity; or (b) it would concern the quiddity itself – in which case we have our conclusion: that it is first. Therefore a cognition of the divine quiddity always has as its terminus the thing as it is in its existence, and consequently it will always be intuitive.

57. Moreover, if one has an abstractive cognition of God's quiddity, one grasps either the nominal quiddity alone or the real quiddity (*quid nominis aut quid rei*). It cannot be said that one grasps only the nominal quiddity, because then one would not have a greater cognition than one has of fictitious entities. Therefore, it remains that it is a real quiddity. But it is impossible to cognize the real quiddity of a thing without cognizing that it is a certain nature actually existing in the natural world, or that it possibly exists. But someone who perfectly and evidently cognizes the divine essence cognizes it as actually existing, not as naturally suited to exist and as merely possible. Therefore someone who cognizes the divine essence always cognizes it as actually existing and as a consequence cognizes it intuitively.

58. Moreover, it is impossible to cognize a real quiddity without cognizing whether it exists – actually and potentially, in the case of things other than God, but in God's case [the existence must be] actual. This is clear, because the question *What is it?* presupposes the question *Does it exist?* (see *Posterior Analytics* II [92b4–8]). But an abstractive cognition concerns God's real quiddity – what he really is. Therefore, it necessarily concerns whether he exists, and as a consequence it will be an intuitive cognition.

59. In its proof, the view seems unreasonable in three ways. First, it falsely supposes that God imprints a vision on the beatified intellect as if he were bringing it about naturally and acting from the necessity of his nature.[15] This is of course not true, because whatever God does in creatures he does through free choice and not by natural necessity, according to the truth of the faith.

60. Second, if this assumption is true, then the proposition by which the entire proof is supported is destroyed – namely, that whatever God can do by reason of a naturally moving object, he could {194} do through his will alone [n. 53]. But if God moves by natural necessity then this proposition is false. For those things that are contained in God by the necessity of his nature are not within his will. For example, it is not within the will of the Father to generate the Son or to be God.

61. Third, by parity of reason it is concluded from this proof that God

---

[15] This is suggested by n. 53, where the claim is that God would produce an abstractive apprehension of himself through his will, and an intuitive apprehension through his essence, directly. So it might seem that in the latter case, the will isn't involved at all, and hence that "God imprints a vision on the beatified . . . from the necessity of his nature."

could bring about an intuitive cognition without the presence of an existing object moving [the intellect] by its own reality. This follows from the
claim that he can bring about by will alone whatever he brings about
through the movement of his essence [n.53]. For by his will alone he will
make an intuitive cognition exist without that which moves [the intellect]
– something that is rejected by those who advance this proof.

3. Defense of Scotus

62. But these objections not withstanding, the position of the earlier
Subtle Doctor still remains, unless another objection is raised. For the first
three arguments [nn. 56–58] are supported by a false supposition and a
shaky foundation. For they assume that the existence and actuality of a
thing cannot be cognized abstractively, which appears false in many ways.

63. First, an astronomical cognition, since it counts as demonstrative
knowledge, certainly counts as abstractive. But an astronomical cognition
can concern the existence and actuality of a thing: first, in the future,
because an astronomer knows that the actuality and existence of an eclipse
will come at a certain day, hour, and minute; second, in the past, because
the astronomer knows that an eclipse did occur at a certain time; third, in
the present, because even if he is in a closed vault, he would know to say
at the time of the eclipse: "Now it begins, now it is at the halfway point,
now it ends." Yet it is clear that he does not intuit it. Therefore, an
abstractive cognition can concern the existence and actuality of a thing.

64. Moreover, memory and its act (the act of remembering) fall within
abstractive cognition. But memory pertains to the existence and actuality
of a thing. For we recollect only the actual occurrences of things that have
happened. Therefore an abstractive cognition can concern the actuality of
a thing. {195}

65. Moreover, imagination is an abstractive cognition directly contrary
to intuitive cognition. But imagination reaches directly toward the existence, presence, and actuality of a thing. For example, someone within a
vault can imagine that there is an eclipse now, or someone hearing the
voice of a man without seeing him can imagine that he is a certain sort of
man. Therefore, as before.

66. Moreover, a cognition that comes via a demonstration is knowledge
and is consequently abstractive. But an astronomer demonstrates that the
actual earth is round and that the heavens are spherical, and a medical

doctor who sees urine infallibly cognizes that there is a certain disease in the body. Therefore, an abstractive cognition, preeminently, can concern the actuality, presence, and existence of a thing.

67. So the three arguments do not work. The first [n. 56] does not, because granted that a cognition of God's quiddity has as its terminus the reality and existence of God, it nevertheless has its terminus not intuitively but abstractively, in an imaginary like way (*quasi imaginarie*) – just like the cognition with which the astronomer in his vault imagines and knows that an eclipse is actually occurring at this time. In the same way the second argument [n. 57] also fails, because through an abstractive cognition one cognizes the real quiddity of God and that he really exists. But the whole is cognized abstractively, in an imaginativelike way, as was said of the eclipse. And it is clear for the same reason that the third argument [n. 58] does not go through.

68. The other three arguments [nn. 59–61] proceed from two false suppositions. The first of the two is that the Subtle Doctor means to say that the divine essence moves the intellect of the blessed naturally and by the necessity of its nature, not freely and from the power of the will. He does not say this. For it is clearly one thing for the divine essence to move the intellect as the executive cause (*executive*), through a command of the will directing it toward such motion. (It is in this way that the *nature* of a human being is said to generate another human being, even though this occurs only through the will's direction.) It is another thing for the divine essence to move the intellect by the necessity of its nature. This is certainly false, and was never said by this Doctor.

69. Therefore, the first argument [n. 59] shows that the divine essence, with respect to moving the intellect of the blessed, acts through divine free choice, directing God's essence toward this kind of motion. Nor does it show anything but that this motion comes from his essence immediately, as the executive cause. {196}

70. The second argument [n. 60] would go through if the Doctor had accepted that God's essence produces movement by the necessity of its nature. But he accepts the opposite, namely that God's essence, in producing movement, is under the control of will. And so it is reasonable to conclude that God can do immediately through his will alone that which he can do by means of his essence, as the executive cause.

71. The third argument [n. 61] is supported by a [second] supposition that is not true according to this Doctor: namely, that an intuitive cogni-

tion is a thing by itself (*solum quid*) and absolute, not implying anything relative (*ad aliquid*) or an actual relationship to the existence of the object. And so it should be said that, on his [Scotus's] view, it is a contradiction that an intuitive cognition could be separated from its actual relationship to the object's actuality and existence. For this relationship exists formally within an intuitive cognition, and on his view this is what differentiates it from an abstractive cognition. But if a relationship to an object is posited, then it is necessary for that object's actuality to be posited. Therefore if an intuitive cognition is posited, then it is necessary for that object's actuality to be posited.

72. So when this Doctor asserted that whatever [God's] will can bring about by means of his essence it can bring about immediately [n. 53], he was explicitly referring to whatever is not relative to another. Thus he indicated that [God's will] could not bring about that which implies a relationship to and is relative° to his essence and its actuality, like an intuitive cognition. If he had in fact said this, then the proposition in question would be false. For God cannot bring about any relative thing without the presence of its relatum: He cannot bring about the Father without the Son, and so too in other cases. But he can bring about an abstractive cognition, because it does not involve a relationship to his essence and its actuality.

Article 3. Further Remarks on Scotus's Position

73. As for the third article, we should consider that the subtle and modern Doctor's position is true {197} in two respects: first, that there can be an abstractive cognition of deity [n. 53]; second, that this is not beatific and so is possible for a wayfarer [n. 54]. From this it follows, third that God can provide such a light by which theological truths are demonstratively known [n. 55]. Yet in two other ways he seems to speak less truly [n. 52]: first, when he says that an intuitive cognition cannot be separated from the actuality and presence of its object; second, when he defines an intuitive cognition as that which has as its terminus the actuality, presence, and real existence of an object, whereas he defines an abstractive cognition as that which abstracts from these things, and does not have them as its terminus.

1. *Intuitive Cognition of Absent Things*

Scotus's view

74. The first of these errors, that an intuitive cognition can occur only when its object is actually existing and present, seemingly can be proved. For no relational designation° can be posited without its proper relatum: for it is impossible to posit the Father without positing the Son. But an intuitive cognition seems to be said relatively, designating the existence and actual presence of its object. For when one says

I see Peter,

it seems to follow that

Therefore Peter exists,

insofar as *to see* entails the existence of that which is seen, as its relatum. Therefore, it is impossible for an intuitive cognition to occur without the object's being present. This is confirmed by the fact that an actual relationship to an existing object is in reality the same as an intuitive cognition, even if not formally the same.

75. Moreover, it is impossible for an intuitive cognition to occur without the differentia that distinguishes it from an abstractive cognition, both because a differentia cannot be separated from its object and because it would occur and then in time cross over into an abstractive cognition. But the differentia by which an intuitive cognition is distinguished from an abstractive is that it requires the existence of its object. For they do not differ with respect to their objects; rather, everything actual, existent, and present – everything that is cognized intuitively – can be cognized abstractively. They are instead distinguished on account of what is required, since an intuitive cognition requires {198} the existence of the thing cognized, which an abstractive cognition does not require. Therefore, an intuitive cognition cannot be separated from the existence of the thing cognized.

76. Moreover, just as an abstractive cognition is related to an object placed in cognized being, so too an intuitive cognition is related to an object placed in real being. But an abstractive cognition cannot exist unless there is an object in cognized being. Therefore, an intuitive cognition cannot exist unless the object is in cognized *and* real being.

77. Moreover, touch, taste, and the other senses no more require an

object's presence than sight does. But it is possible to touch or taste only that which is present. Therefore, so too for seeing or intuiting.

78. Moreover, something is necessarily required for intuition if, when it is withdrawn, we are said right away not to intuit. But when the object is removed we are said right away not to intuit, but to be deceived – as is clear in the case of those who are tricked (*ludificatis*). Therefore, as before.

79. Moreover, if an intuitive cognition did not necessarily require the actuality of its object, then (since an intuitive cognition of God is beatific) a beatific cognition could occur without God's actuality and existence. But this is an absurd conclusion to reach. Therefore, the assumption is also absurd, it seems.

Aureol's View

80. But these arguments not withstanding, it should be said that an intuitive cognition can occur when the object is absent and not actually present. This can be shown in two ways.

81. First, by way of experience, which we should adhere to before adhering to any logical arguments. For knowledge has its origin in experience and, according to the Philosopher in *Metaphysics* I [981a7], the common judgments that are the principles of art are also taken from there. Thus a sign that words are true is that they agree with what is perceived. But experience teaches that an intuitive cognition in the senses and a sensory vision do not necessarily require the thing's presence. There are five experiences to show this.

82. The first occurs in visions left over from something intensely visible. Augustine discusses this in *De trinitate* XI, ch. ii [sec. 4]:

Commonly, after we have looked at the sun or anything luminous and then closed our eyes, certain bright colors continue to hover (so to speak) in our vision, variously changing and becoming less bright until they completely go away. They should be understood as remnants of the form produced in the sense.

And he concludes,

it was there even while we were seeing, and it was clearer and more distinct, but it so coincided with the species of the thing discerned that it could not in any way be distinguished from it. This was our vision.

{199} Thus it is clear that a vision of the sun or of other luminous objects remains in the eye when the object recedes, according to Augustine and to every experience.

83. The second experience is in sleep and dreams. The Commentator discusses this near the middle of his treatise *De somno et vigilia* [pp. 98–99]:

While asleep a human being sees and senses through the five senses without any external sense object's being there. But this happens through a motion contrary to what occurs while awake. For while awake external sense objects move the senses, and the common sense moves the imaginative power. But in sleep the imagined intention will be turned around: It will move the common sense, and the common sense will move the particular power. So it happens that someone grasps sense objects even though they are not external, because their intentions are in the organs of the senses, and it makes no difference whether the intentions come from within or without.

Thus it is clear that sight is in the eye of someone who dreams he is seeing, and hearing in the sense of hearing, and touch in the sense of touch – all in the real absence of objects.

84. The third experience appears when people are afraid. Disabled by fear, they hear sounds and see terrible things. The Commentator attests to this (ibid.), saying that "this happens to those who are afraid and to those who are sick, because of a weakness in the cogitative power, which is disabled. As a result, such a thing happens to them."

85. The fourth experience occurs in those who are tricked. It is clear and known to all that they see things that are not there, such as camps, dogs, rabbits, etc.[16]

86. The last experience occurs in those who have soft eyes. In their case, when they see something red, the vision of red remains, so that everything they see appears red.

87. These experiences can therefore prove the thesis [n. 80]. For an intuitive cognition within intellect requires the object's presence no more than does an intuitive cognition within sense. This is clear from the fact that the term 'intuitive cognition' comes to intellect as derived from the senses. Further, the intellect is more abstract and independent than the senses. But multiple experiences have proved that sensory intuition can be separated from the real presence of the object. Therefore the intellect's intuition could be separated all the more. {200}

88. Moreover, God is more powerful than either art or nature. But a

---

[16] It is clear from n. 88 below that the *ludificati*, here and elsewhere, are people who have been purposefully deceived by illusions, hence tricked. This then is just one category of deception. In Translation 9 (p. 235), Ockham suggests that this sort of deception is often brought about by an evil demon.

vision is produced through art without the presence of the visible object, as is clear from those who are tricked. A vision is also produced through nature, in those who are asleep, afraid, and sick (as both the Commentator and Augustine taught above [nn. 82–84]). Therefore God can produce this all the more.

89. But perhaps it will be said against these experiences first that such visions are false, deceptional, and errors, and from errors and deceptions one should make no arguments about true visions. Second, one might say that they are not visions, but a judgment of the common sense, through which we judge ourselves to see (as is clear in *De anima* II [425b20–24]). Hence those who are tricked do not *see* such things; rather, it *seems* to them that they see, when the common sense judges that they do.

90. But these rebuttals do not block the demonstrations given above. The first does not rebut but rather confirms the point. For there is no act within the visual power that does not share the specific nature of vision. But such [illusory] acts are in the eye, as both Augustine and the Commentator explicitly say. Augustine concludes, "this was our vision" [n. 82]. The Commentator says that "a human being senses through the five senses" [n. 83]. Therefore, such experienced apprehensions share the specific nature of vision. Therefore, *no* vision, by its specific nature, requires the presence of the object.

91. Moreover, true and false apply to numerically the same cognition without its undergoing any change, with only a change in the object (as is clear according to the Philosopher in the *Categories* [4a21–27]). Hence the assessment that Sortes is sitting is true when he is sitting but at once becomes false when he stands up, though the assessment remains numerically the same. But appearances of the above sort are false visions and errors, according to this rebuttal. Therefore, they can be true while remaining numerically the same – or at least they are of the same species as true visions. As a consequence, the reality of the vision does not require the real presence of an existing object, although the truth of a vision requires this, since truth adds to the reality of a vision the relationship of conformity to the thing.

92. The second rebuttal also does not go through, first because it clashes with the Commentator and Augustine, who explicitly say that such appearances occur in a particular sense [nn. 82–83]. Also, the common sense is never actualized except through the particular senses' {201} coming into actuality (as is clear from *De anima* II [425b12–19]). Also, if the common sense judges that the eye sees then there must be something in the eye that

it judges – namely, the appearance of the thing. But the appearance of a thing existing in sight just is the vision itself. Also, the common sense does not judge anything external. But, on this proposal, things that appear external are judged. Also, even granted that this occurs in the common sense, our conclusion is still reached, because there is an intuitive cognition without the object's presence. Therefore, the thesis is clear by way of experience, which produces knowledge.

93. The second way proceeds *a priori*. For it is certain that God can do whatever does not imply a contradiction, even preserve the foundation of a relation after the relatum is destroyed and the relationship is no more – as Sortes is preserved after his son Plato is destroyed and Sortes's being a father is no more. But an intellective vision, a sensory vision, and in general every intuitive cognition are something absolute, the basis of a relationship to the thing intuitively cognized. Therefore, God could preserve an absolute intuition of this sort, even after the relationship is destroyed and there is no present object.

94. Nor does it help when some say that such a relationship is in reality the same as the absolute entity, differing from it only formally, and consequently that they cannot be separated from one other, because they are the same thing. This clearly does not help, because it is impossible. For it is impossible for a thing that is dependent in reality and a thing that is independent in reality to be the same thing in reality. Nor is it enough for them to be distinct formally; rather, they must be distinct in reality. For having the status of a real predicate requires a real distinction in the subject, just as a formal predicate requires a formal distinction, a predicate of reason a distinction of reason, a relational predicate a relative distinction, and an absolute predicate an absolute distinction (as is clear from the Philosopher's discussion of large and small in the *Categories* [5b15–6a11]). The reason for this is that a real predicate inheres only in the nature (*ratione*) of the thing, and its first subject is the thing, not a formality – otherwise the subject would have less being than would that to which it is made subject. Therefore, however much formal difference there is in the subject, still, as long as it is the same reality, it is impossible for a real predicate that inheres in that reality to be denied of it without contradiction. Thus a thing that is dependent in reality and a thing that is not {202} dependent are not the same thing. But an intuitive cognition is independent in absolute reality from everything else formally outside it, even if it efficiently depends on God and on its object. The relationship within it to the intuited object, however, is a thing dependent in reality on its object, as its final term,

because every relationship requires a relatum for its reality. Therefore it is impossible for the absolute basis of an intuitive cognition to be the same thing as° its relationship to the actuality of its object. Therefore, they could be separated by divine power, as was said.

95. Moreover, God can preserve any thing without any other thing on which it does not depend, or on which it depends only efficiently. For he can suspend the efficient causality of any creature while preserving its effect. But the absolute basis of an intuitive cognition is a certain thing from the category of quality (according to those who posit such cognitions), and as a consequence it does not depend on its object, except only efficiently. For if, as a matter of its quiddity, something were required formally and essentially for its reality, an object serving as its relatum in just the way that the real existence of a relation essentially requires a relatum – if, I say, this were so regarding° the absolute reality of an intuitive cognition – then it would follow that it would not be a reality from the category of quality, nor would it have the character of something absolute. Therefore it is necessary to say that God can preserve that reality, which is there absolutely, without the presence of the object.

96. Nor are the above arguments to the contrary decisive. The first [n. 74] is not, because it assumes that an intuitive cognition is a wholly relational designation and not something absolute, the opposite of which has been said [nn. 93–95]. Further, it is not true that an intuitive cognition is said relatively – unless relatively to the object as it is intuited.

97. The second argument [n. 75] also does not go through, because it is not true that requiring the object's real existence is the distinctive differentia between abstractive and intuitive cognition. For an intuitive cognition requires only° that something *appear* to the senses.

98. Nor does the third argument [n. 76] go through, because it is not true that an intuitive cognition requires an object with real being; it is enough for it to have intuited being, as will be evident below [nn.102–11].

99. The fourth argument [n. 77] also assumes something false, that in the cases of taste and touch, tasting and touching cannot occur in the absence of the objects. {203} The opposite is clear in the case of someone dreaming about flavors and various tangible qualities.

100. Nor does the fifth argument [n. 78] stand. We do not say that those who are tricked see, but rather that they are deceived and that it seems to them that they see. But we say this not because there is no vision in them, but because it is a false vision. Similarly, when someone has an

understanding that is not true, we customarily say that he does not understand, although it is clear that in his intellect there is an intellection pointed at something false.

101. The final argument [n. 79] also does not go through, because an intuitive cognition of God cannot be of him if he is nonexistent. This impossibility arises not because God's actuality is required as the object of the cognition, but because God's actuality is required as what causes and preserves the cognition.

2. *The Correct Account of Intuitive and Abstractive Cognition*

102. It is clear from the foregoing that abstractive cognition is not well defined as a cognition that does not have as its terminus the existence and actual presence of its object, but instead abstracts from these things. For it was proved above, at the end of the second article [nn. 62–72], that the actuality, presence, and existence of an object can be cognized abstractively. It is also clear, through the arguments introduced just above [nn. 80–101], that intuitive cognition is not well defined as a cognition that requires the presence of its object. And so we have to see what the difference is between these cognitions, and how each can be defined. {204}

103. It is very difficult to reach an understanding of intuitive cognition, above all due to our lack of appropriate terms. But philosophical authority teaches that one should coin words so that reality is not subject to speech, but speech to reality, as Hilary advises.[17] So an intuitive cognition can be properly described in these words: as° a direct presentive cognition° of what it extends to, objectively actuating and (so to speak) positing existentially.[18]

104. In explanation of this, notice that all these [qualities] are most apparent in sensory vision, from which the name is carried over to intellectual vision. Therefore we should recognize that imaginary cognition, which is completely abstractive, and ocular cognition, which is completely intuitive, do not in any way differ with respect to their object. For everything visible is imaginable: Just as color, straightness, distance, presence, and existence can be viewed ocularly, so they can be apprehended imaginarily. They differ, then, only with respect to *how* they cognize. For

---

[17] See *De trinitate* bk. II, ch. 7.
[18] . . . *ut dicatur quod est cognitio directa praesentialis eius super quod transit obiective actuativa et quasi positiva existenter.*

four conditions come together in how an ocular cognition extends to an object, and these four are lacking when an imaginary cognition extends to that object.

105. The first condition is directness. For the imagination neither extends to nor apprehends the existence of the thing immediately, but does so as if discursively from its cause, effect, or sign. This is clear in the case of the astronomer in a vault who imagines, through calculations, the actual occurrence of an eclipse, and also in the case of a doctor who imagines a disease in the stomach through a sign that appears in the urine. An ocular cognition, in contrast, extends directly and immediately, not discursively, to the existence of the thing.

106. The second condition is presence. For however much the imagination extends to the presence of a thing (by imagining, for instance, that there is an eclipse present now to such a degree, with all the surrounding details), one still imagines that thing as something absent, with respect to the way it is grasped: For one reaches toward something present in an absentlike manner. An ocular cognition, in contrast, reaches toward something present in a present manner, and even reaches toward something absent in a present manner, as is clear in those who are tricked and in all the experiences introduced above [nn. 82–86]. For though the objects are absent, if the vision is in the eye it reaches toward them in a present manner, as is clear.

107. The third condition is the actualization of the object. For however much the imagination reaches toward the actuality of the thing (as when one imagines {205} the actuality of an eclipse) it still does not extend in an actualizing manner, as if to put the eclipse in actual being through its own power. An ocular cognition, in contrast, has such an attendant actualization that it makes the object appear in its actuality, even if it does not actually exist, as is clear in the case of those who are tricked.

108. The fourth condition is its positing existence, which comes down to much the same point. For an ocular cognition makes even those things that do not exist in reality appear to be existing in reality.

109. Therefore, it is rightly said that an intuitive cognition is a direct cognition as opposed to a discursive one [n. 105], that it is present as opposed to the absent mode in which the imagination reaches even toward things that are present [n. 106], and that it actualizes the object [n. 107] and posits its existence [n. 108], since it makes the object's real existence and actual position appear, even if the object does not exist. And in contrast it is clear that an imaginary cognition lacks and abstracts from these four conditions. It extends to its object neither directly nor presently,

nor by actualizing or positing° existence, even if one imagines the object to exist and be actual, and even if it is present.

110. Extending these remarks to intellect, there are these two modes of cognition. First, there is that which makes the presence, actuality, and existence of an object directly appear. Indeed, this cognition is nothing other than a kind of present and actualizing appearance and direct existence of the object. This mode of cognition is intuitive. Second, there is that which makes things appear neither directly, nor of themselves, nor presently, nor actualizingly. This mode of cognition is abstractive.

111. From the foregoing we can gather how abstractive and intuitive cognition differ, and what the nature (*ratio*) of each is. For there are two modes of formal appearance, given that an intellection is nothing other than a certain formal appearance by which things appear objectively. In one appearance, things appear as present, actual, and existent in reality, whether or not they exist. This is intuition. In the other appearance, whether or not a thing exists, it does not appear as present, actualizing, and existent in reality, but in an imaginary and absentlike manner. Hence this cognition could be called *imaginary* more properly than *abstractive*. For the Philosopher (in *Metaphysics* XII [1072a30]) and the Commentator (in the same place [XII 37] and in *De anima* [Book I] 3) use this word for intellect, calling such a cognition an "imagination {206} through intellect." Also, the phrase 'abstractive cognition' seems appropriate for the cognition of universals, which occurs through abstraction. Also, there is this way of speaking about intellective cognitions: that one kind is intuitive and present, in the manner of a sensory vision, whereas the other is imaginary and absent, in the manner of imagination, which reaches toward the thing as absent. Therefore, by whatever° name it is called, it is nevertheless more properly spoken of in this way. Their difference, in brief, consists in presence and absence. These do not refer to whether the cognized object exists, because imagination extends objectively to absent and present things, and intuition also extends to both. (The case of trickery proves that it reaches toward absent things.) Rather, 'absence' and 'presence' refer to the mode of cognizing and reaching toward an object.

3. A Poor Definition of Intuitive Cognition

112. The definition that some assign to intuitive cognition is therefore not a good one.[19] They say that it is a cognition by which one cognizes a

---

[19] Gerard of Bologna, Quodlibet II, question 6.

thing with complete immediacy, mediated neither by a species or exemplary image, nor by an object other than the thing itself, having the presence of the thing as its terminus.

This definition fails for two reasons. First, the vision or intuition that occurs in a dream is mediated by a species and comes to the eye through imagination. It does not have the true presence of the thing as its terminus, because its objects are absent. Yet this truly is an intuitive cognition, as was evident° above in many ways [and] stated in the claims of Augustine and the Commentator [nn. 82–83].

Second, this whole definition fits an imaginary cognition, which does not occur through the mediation of any exemplar or image or any other object that the person imagining views in cognizing. Otherwise the Rome that is imagined by the founder of Rome would not be Rome itself, but rather a kind of replica of it. Nor {207} would a house in the mind of its builder be the same as the house in the real world, which is the opposite of what the Philosopher says in *Metaphysics* VII [1034a23–24]. Thus it is clear that someone imagining a thing reaches toward it without any medium serving as object, although perhaps imagination occurs through a species serving as a formal medium, just as someone seeing sees through a species. And if species are rejected in the case of sight, then it is not clear why they could not be rejected for imagination. Then imagination will be an immediate cognition reaching toward its object, without any species, image, or exemplar, or any sort of medium serving as object. Yet it will not be an intuition, because it reaches its object in an absentlike manner. Therefore, that definition is poorly assigned.

Article 4. Reply to the Question

113. Finally, as to the question itself, we should state what seems to be the case, in four propositions.

1. Intuitive Cognition Is Possible within Intellect

The first proposition is that intuitive and imaginary cognitions are possible within intellect.[20] [114] Certain things seem to preclude this, however. For

---

[20] Here context requires taking the section title (this sentence) to be part of Aureol's original text. Other section titles in Buytaert's edition, though present in the best manuscript, appear to be later additions to the text; hence our translation follows them only loosely.

a material cognition should not be posited within intellect, since the intellect abstracts from the here and the now. But an intuitive cognition seems to be material, both insofar as it is present and so involves simultaneity of duration and the now, and insofar as it actualizes and posits existence, and so involves the here. Therefore it is not possible within intellect.

115. Moreover, a cognition that would always put the intellect in error is not suitable for intellect. But an intuitive cognition puts the intellect in error. For it is agreed that every cognition can be preserved for a long time within intellect, since it is immaterial and incorruptible. Therefore the intellect will be tricked and deceived for as long as an intuitive cognition is within it, unless the object is in truth present. But the intellect {208} will not be able to detect its presence. Therefore, it will be deceived by this sort of cognition. Therefore, it should not be postulated within intellect.

116. This is confirmed by the fact that, given the above remarks, God is now deceived by having an intuitive cognition of future events. Through this cognition, of course, he judges that a thing to come exists at present – which is false.

117. These objections notwithstanding, the proposition is true. This is evident as follows: It is clear that an intuitive cognition is loftier than an imaginary cognition, for many reasons. First, because it is more desirable. For one who imagines something desires to see it, whereas one who sees has no desire to imagine it. Second, because it is more enjoyable. For it is more enjoyable to see a rose or something loved than to imagine it. Third, because it is clearer. For one who imagines something still experiences that he remains somewhat in the dark relative to that thing, whereas one who sees the thing experiences being in the most thoroughly clear of cognitions. Fourth, because it is more certain. For a vision is an experiential cognition, whereas imagination is not. And for this reason *De anima* II [428a11] attributes truth to the senses, but deception and fallibility to phantasia. Fifth, it follows from these remarks that it is more perfect and ultimate. Thus it ultimately and most perfectly unites with its object. So if intellective cognition is loftier than sensory cognition, then it is necessary to posit within it the loftiest mode of cognizing, and consequently a mode that is intuitivelike. But there is no doubt about the other mode in question – namely, imaginary cognition. Therefore, each cognition should be posited within intellect.

118. Moreover, a face-to-face cognition seems to be the same as an intuitive and present cognition. But Scripture posits a face-to-face cogni-

tion within intellect. For the Apostle says in I Corinthians 13:12 that *now we see through a glass, darkly* (that is, imaginarily), *but then face to face* (that is, intuitively). Therefore these cognitions should be posited within intellect.

119. Nor do the two arguments introduced above preclude this. The first does not [n. 114], because the materiality of sensory vision arises from the fact that presence, directness, and actuality, which are posited as its conditions [nn. 105–7], are taken materially and locationally (*situative*). Vision, for example, involves the object's locational directness, because everything seen is directly seen, along a direct line, imaginarily directed from the eye to the thing seen, as is clear from the first proposition of the book *De speculis*. Its presence too is locational, because all things are seen as they are locationally opposed and set apart (*obiecta*). Also, its actualization is material, because everything seen {209} is judged to exist actually here and now – that is, at the present time and at a given location.

Yet as applied to the intellect's intuitive cognition, these conditions are not locational and material. For the intellect does not intuit along a direct line, at the end of which the object is located; nor does it judge the object to be locationally present. For it abstracts from all of this. But it judges its object to be present by a spiritual presence, which is not the concurrence of two things located together, nor is it even based on location, but simply on reality. So it is a presence without distance and closeness, without inside and outside, and without here and there, as will become clear elsewhere. In light of this, then, it should be said that such an intuitive cognition is immaterial and abstract, and possible for the intellect.

120. The second objection [n. 115] too does not, with respect to the natural order, preclude an intuitive cognition from being impressed on intellect by an object and preserved by that same object – just as light is, by the sun. And this does not cause the intellect to err, because once the object is absent the intuitive cognition at once ceases to be. This is not the case, however, for a cognition that is imaginarylike, because that remains according to the power of the will and is not preserved by the object. This difference arises from the proper character and nature of each cognition, insofar as nature always does what is better (*Physics* II [198b18]).

The argument introduced as confirmation° [n. 116] also does not go through. For an intuitive cognition in God is a present appearance relative to (*pro*) that now in which the thing that is to be will be. It is not relative to other nows, and for this reason the cognition is true.

121. Thus each of these cognitions should be posited within intellect, although we do not experience intuitive cognition in this life because of

its conjunction with sensory intuition. For although the intellect of a geometer intuits a triangle when he draws one in the dust and proves through intellect something about its angles, still he does not distinguish this by experience, because he at the same time intuits through sense. For, as the Commentator expressly teaches in *De Anima* II [63, 65], the intellect is mixed with the senses and views a sensory object placed in its presence, just as it is mixed with phantasia and views an object of phantasia in the absence of sensible objects. {210}

2. *Intellect Can Cognize God in Each Way*

122. The second proposition is that the intellect can have an imaginary and absentlike cognition of God, and a present and intuitivelike cognition of God, just as it can of other things. This is clear in a number of ways. For if it were incompatible with deity to be conceived in a nonpresent, imaginarylike manner, then this would be repugnant to it either because it is nothing other than pure, subsistent existence, or because it is present in reality everywhere, and so he who cognizes deity cognizes that it is present to himself. But neither of these stands in the way, because pure existence can be cognized imaginarily, in an absent manner. Also, a thing can be known to be present and most intimate° through its penetrating [our minds] in an imaginary manner. One will in this way be certain of this, yet one will not see it as present. Therefore, it is in no way incompatible with deity to be cognized in an imaginarylike manner.

123. Moreover, the essence of God can appear and conform the intellect to itself in just as many ways as can the quiddity of a creature. But the quiddity of a rose (and every created entity) can appear to the intellect both in a present manner and in an absent, imaginarylike manner. Also, the intellect can be conformed to it in both ways. Therefore, so too for the divine essence, it seems.

124. Moreover, pure act and pure actuality can be cognized in an imaginarylike manner. Otherwise it would not be proved in metaphysics that God is pure act. But no other argument is offered by those positing that God can only be intuitively cognized, except that he cannot be cognized unless one understands that he is pure act and that he actually exists. Therefore, there appears to be no argument why the essence of God cannot be cognized in an imaginarylike manner. But it is granted by all that he is intuitively cognized by the blessed. Therefore it is clear that each of these cognitions of God is possible.

3. That Only an Intuitive Cognition of God Is Beatific

125. The third proposition is that a cognition of the distinct and sheer essence of God can be beatific only if it will have been intuitive. This is clear as follows. It is certain that the intellect's beatitude consists in its best operation (according to the Philosopher in *Ethics* I [1098a7–18] and X [1177a11–18]). {211} But an imaginary cognition of the divine essence, however sheer and distinct, is not the loftiest operation of intellect. Instead, an intuitive cognition still remains the best, as was clear above in the first proposition [n. 117]. Therefore, only an intuitive cognition, and in no way an imaginary one, will make the intellect happy.

126. Moreover, a cognition that excites desire rather than quenching it does not have the character of something ultimate. As a consequence it is not beatitude, which is posited as the ultimate end. But an imaginary cognition of God does not quench the desire to see God but rather excites it, as is apparent for anything that is loved. Therefore, as before.

127. Moreover, no cognition of deity beatifies an intellect if it leaves that intellect in darkness and obscurity with respect to deity. But an imaginarylike cognition of deity – however distinctly, sheerly, and imaginatively it is conceived – would leave the intellect in darkness and obscurity. For deity would remain absent to intellect until intellect discerned it as present. Therefore, a cognition of this sort does not beatify intellect.

4. Knowledge of the Articles of Faith

128. The fourth proposition is that if such a cognition is called a light, there is no doubt that such a light can be provided to a wayfarer, nor is there doubt that through it one will demonstratively know the articles of our faith.

129. The first point is easily established. For if an imaginarylike intellection of the proper and distinct essence of God is impossible for a wayfarer, this is so for one of two reasons. First, because it is formally beatific; this is not an obstacle because the opposite has just been proved [nn. 125–27]. Second, because it has a necessary connection to intuitive cognition (as some imagine), insofar as it appears that, for us, imagination presupposes sense and the abstraction of a universal presupposes that a particular has been intuited. Also, God does not cognize things in an imaginarylike way without first having an intuition of himself. And thus it {212} seems to some that abstractive cognition is connected, as if necessarily so, to intuitive cognition. But this is not an obstacle. First, the truth teaches that one

can have an abstractive cognition of things one has had no intuitive cognition of – as appears with the infused wisdom of Solomon, in whom God perhaps infused the species of things that Solomon had never seen. Also, according to some,[21] God could infuse the species of colors into someone born blind, and likewise the angels had the species of things infused before they had intuitively cognized them. Second, whatever the connection is between these two cognitions as regards their generation, nevertheless imaginary cognition is separate from intuitive cognition in existence, as experience teaches. Consequently, they could have been detached through divine power in their generation, so that God provides an abstractive cognition without an intuitive one. Therefore, it is not evident how an imaginary intellection of God's sheer essence is impossible for a wayfarer.

130. It is not difficult to prove the second point either. For every cognition by which one cognizes the cause of why something exists and that it is impossible for it to be otherwise is a luminous cognition and truly produces knowledge, according to the Philosopher in *Posterior Analytics* I [71b9–12]. But an imaginary intellection of God's sheer essence leads evidently to the cause and basis of those truths we believe, and shows clearly that it is impossible for those truths to be otherwise. For deity is the basis of all things believed of God, and consequently is their cause. Therefore, it is possible for a light to be provided to a wayfarer, by which he will know – even *propter quid*[22] – the truths° believed of God: both those regarding what is possible (for example, that God was able to be incarnated, etc.) and those regarding what is actual (for example, that God is actually three and one).

Reply to the Initial Arguments

1. *The First Set of Arguments*

131. Regarding the initial arguments introduced above, it should be said to the first [n. 6] that knowability lies hidden in propositions not on account of the words that are spoken, but rather on account of the

---

[21] Cf. Scotus, *Ordinatio* I.3.1.4 n. 234.
[22] Knowledge *propter quid* is knowledge based on a thing's cause: We understand an event or a fact because we understand what caused it to occur. This is superior to knowledge *quia*, by which we simply know that something is the case without understanding why it is the case.

concepts. And for this reason the articles of faith are not knowable under the concepts a wayfarer possesses of these terms {213} – not by any provided light [except for one] by which the proper concepts of these terms are possessed. But such a light would be nothing other than an imaginarylike cognition of the sort discussed. Nor does it help to say that these propositions are either mediate or immediate. For it should be said that they are immediate under their proper concepts, whereas they are mediate under common and confused concepts. But one cannot reach that which is mediating except through a light leading to the proper concepts from which, as if through mediating premises, these propositions can be demonstrated under their common concepts.

132. To the second [n. 7] it should be said that between the light of glory and the light of faith God can produce the intermediary light of an imaginarylike cognition of deity. But as long as one's concepts of the terms remain confused, he cannot produce that light that is sought, because of the incompatibility touched on earlier [n. 47].

133. To the third [n. 8] it should be said that that demonstrative knowledge, intermediary between faith and vision, can be nothing other than the imaginary cognition discussed in the main reply.

134. To the fourth [n. 9] it should be said that by "necessary arguments," Richard of St. Victor means those that are highly plausible and effective, not those that are absolutely necessary. Anselm means much the same, in *The Incarnation of the Word* [ch. 6], when he says that in his works he has added necessary arguments to what we hold by faith.

135. To the fifth [n. 10] it should be said that God could provide a light by which one would cognize that the truths about God are not impossible relative to propositions taken from creatures. But as regards whether they could be impossible relative to the proper notion of deity, God cannot make this known to someone without providing him with a light by which the notion of deity is cognized. Nor does it work, after refuting every syllogism mistaken in matter and in form, for one to infer that this or that is possible in God. For it can be self-contradictory due to its proper notion, which is unknown to us.

136. To the sixth [n. 11], it should be said that God did not suddenly provide the prophets with a light supplying evidentness. Rather, he supplied an adherence greater than the adherence of faith, on account of the syllogism discussed in the previous question.

137. To the seventh [n. 12], it should be said that a cognition of the premises taken separately is the efficient cause of a cognition of the conclu-

sion. {214} Nevertheless, that cognition has the truth of the conclusion as the object toward which it extends, and it has the truth of the principle as its formal basis (*ratione*) – inasmuch as it is [just] a single cognition pertaining to each truth. Therefore, a cognition of the conclusion cannot be separated by divine power from the truth of the principle. The reply to the eighth [nn. 13–14] is clear for the same reason, because the same holds for principles in relation to their terms.

138. To the last [n. 15], it should be said that when the saints claim to possess demonstrative knowledge and an understanding of the creeds beyond faith, they mean the theological disposition discussed in the previous question.[23]

2. *The Second Set of Arguments*

139. To the arguments introduced second [nn. 16–22], it should be said that their conclusion is true. But those arguments that rely on a distinction between God's essence and existence [nn. 19, 22], and between his essence and presence [nn. 20, 22], so that his essence could be conceived without his existence and presence, they are not framed very effectively. For they seem to suppose that existence and presence could not be cognized in an imaginarylike and abstractive manner.

3. *The Third Set of Arguments*

140. To the arguments introduced in opposition [to the first set of arguments] it should be said that although in proving the impossibility of such a light their conclusions are true, nevertheless their means of argument are not effective.

141. So it should be said to the first [n. 23] that appealing to the apostles and the holy doctors does not prove when a light will have been provided. For the Apostle's claim that we walk *through faith and not through sight* was spoken not in his own voice (*persona*) or the voice of the apostles, but in the voice of the Church. Also, the claim that the holy doctors could not have passed that knowledge on to us in their books is certainly true inasmuch as we lack the light by which to cognize the progression° of their knowledge – though they have passed it on – just as a dullard does not cognize the progression {215} of knowledge in geometry. Or it should

---

[23] Prooemium Q1, esp. nn. 92–95 (ed. Buytaert, pp. 159–60).

be said that although it was possible for such a light to have been provided, it nevertheless was not beneficial for it to be provided to the saints, inasmuch as it would not have made for merit [on their part].

142. To the second [n. 24] it should be said that such a light should not have been provided during baptism, because not all the faithful need it. It should have been provided only to those who are studious and who want to acquire the knowledge of theology, which one cannot acquire without that light.

143. To the third [n. 25], two things should be said. First, such a light will still be possible in the intellect of a wayfarer, even if it excludes faith. For demonstrative knowledge, even if it is supposed to exclude faith, does not suppose [anything] that falls outside this state of life; only intuition does that. Second, it is doubtful that faith could not coincide with such a light. But we should refrain from discussing this issue until elsewhere.

144. To the fourth [n. 26] it should be said that that light is intermediary by participation – not synthesized from the other two lights, but approaching each one. Of such an intermediary it is not true that it exceeds in worth the loftier extreme; this is clear for the rational soul, which is intermediary between the angels and natural forms, and yet does not exceed the angels. Nor even is it always true that a medium synthesized from its extremes exceeds the one that is loftier: for a mule is not loftier than a horse, nor is red a loftier color than white, since white is the measure of colors, as is clear from *Metaphysics* X [ch. 1].

145. To the fifth [n. 27] it should be said that its conclusion is entirely correct: No light can provide an evident cognition of an article of faith without providing a distinct cognition of the terms of those articles. But what it then adds is not true: that only the light of glory can provide such a distinct cognition of God. For there can be a distinct cognition short of the light of glory, even though it would not be visual, but imaginarylike.

146. To the sixth [n. 28] it should be said that it is not absurd for someone having such a disposition to adhere both on the authority of Christ's teaching (and thus through faith) and on account of such a light. For authority and reason can come together on the same point. Or, it should be said that if such a light were provided, the one possessing it would not adhere through faith, and yet he would not on that account be placed outside this state of life. {216}

4. The Fourth Set of Arguments

147. To those that were introduced last against an abstractive or imaginarylike cognition of God, it should be said to the first [n. 29] that an imaginarylike cognition of the essence of deity, however distinct, is not beatific. Only an intuitive cognition is beatific, as was stated in the body of the question [nn. 125–27].

148. To the second [n. 30] it should be said that in God an intuitive cognition is loftier than an imaginary cognition. But it does not follow from this that the actuality of things adds perfection to divine knowledge. For God had an intuitive cognition from eternity, even when things did not exist, as will be stated in the course of this book.

149. To the third [n. 31] it should be said that even when an intuitive and an imaginary cognition concern the same object, they still do not extend toward it in a uniform way, nor is their aspect the same. Consequently it is not true, as that argument concludes, that if one is beatific the other is too.

150. To the fourth [n. 32] it should be said that it is not the relation of presence that beatifies someone intuiting God, but the divine essence as apprehended in the loftiest manner of cognizing, an intuitive manner.

151. To the fifth [n. 33] two things should be said. First, the divine essence and its existence differ conceptually, as will become apparent below.[24] Second, God's existence and actuality *can* be cognized in an imaginarylike way.

152. To the sixth [n. 34] it should be said that an abstractive cognition, as it is taken here, is not that by which a universal is cognized in abstraction from a singular, but is rather as an imaginarylike intellection, which God can provide without an intuitive cognition, as was said in the body of the question [nn. 111, 129]. The reply to the seventh argument [n. 35] is clear for the same reason.

153. To the eighth [n. 36] it should be said that such an imaginary cognition extends to God's sheer essence. As was stated above [n. 112], this would not make it intuitive. To° what is then added about a representation, it should be said that either this imaginary cognition would not occur through an intervening species, but would be a pure act preserved in the mind through divine power, or if it were to occur through a species (not objectively representing [God] but formally determining [the intel-

---

[24] *Scriptum* d. 8 sec. 21 [= Q1], nn. 101–12 (ed. Buytaert pp. 918–22).

lect]) then nothing absurd would be claimed according to those who claim that God will be seen in heaven through a species. {217}

154. To the final argument [n. 37] it should be said that a visuallike and intuitive° cognition within intellect is not material, as was said above [n. 119]. But the phrase 'abstractive cognition' is not very appropriate. Hence it can more fittingly be called *imaginarylike*, as with these others, *visuallike* and *intuitivelike*. For each phrase is carried over from sensory cognition to the intellect.

9

WILLIAM OCKHAM
APPARENT BEING

Introduction

William Ockham (ca. 1288–1347) made his reputation as a brilliant logician and iconoclastic theologian. In 1324, controversy over his views forced him to abandon his scholarly work in England and confront charges of heresy before the pope in Avignon. Rather than receiving an acquittal, Ockham became involved in further controversies, was excommunicated, and spent the last years of his life in exile in Munich, where his interests shifted from logic and metaphysics to politics and ecclesiastics.

Ockham is best known today for his parsimonious ontology, exemplified by his nominalism (or at least antirealism) regarding universals, and expressed by the famous principle of parsimony known as Ockham's razor: Plurality should not be posited without necessity. The selection translated here displays this parsimony at work in Ockham's theory of cognition. The central issue is the nature of mental representation. Ockham quotes at length, verbatim, from the work of his fellow Franciscan Peter Aureol (see Translation 8). Aureol had argued that all cognition, sensory and intellectual, requires that the object itself take form in what Aureol calls "objective being" (*esse obiectivum*). The production of this sort of nonreal being is, for Aureol, precisely what accounts for the experience of being presented with an object (what we now call *conscious experience*). Ockham argues that there's no need to postulate this sort of "diminished being." The act of cognition alone, along with the external object, is entirely sufficient; no intermediary is required. The most problematic cases are those where there is no corresponding external object. Ockham here offers an account of how to explain illusory sensations and universal judgments, cases that Aureol had invoked in support of his own account, and that fourteenth-century authors would take up over and over (see Translation 10).

The occasion for the present dispute is the theological question of how to characterize the second person of the Trinity, described in the Gospel of John as *the Word*, and analyzed in Augustine's *De trinitate* in terms of an analogy to the human mind's formation of a mental word (see Translation 6). The official question addressed here can't be rendered into English without distortion. The Latin asks

> *utrum solus filius sit verbum*

but English requires choosing between definite and indefinite articles, and modern conventions call for capitalizing terms that refer to God. So we have to choose between

> *whether only the Son is the Word*

which was uncontroversial among Christians, and

> *whether only the Son is a word*

which was generally held to be false. Of course, it doesn't take Ockham long to disambiguate these issues. The real interest of the question lies with the underlying problems about mental representation. For further discussion of Ockham's view, see Adams (1987) pp. 73–96; Pasnau (1997), pp. 69–85, 185–89, 247–53, 277–89; Karger (1999).

Apparent Being

Ordinatio I.27.3

Regarding the uncreated Word, I ask whether only the Son is a word.

For the Negative

1. A [mental] word is a conception or intellection, according to the previous question. But it is not the case that only the Son is a conception or intellection. Therefore, etc.

2. It seems that the Son is not the Word, since he is born precisely from the essence of the Father, since otherwise the Son would be of something other than the Father. But the Word is not born precisely from the substance of the Father, according to St. Augustine (*De trinitate* XV.14 [xxiii]), who says that "the Word was born from all the things that are in

the Father." But creatures are in the Father and in the memory of the Father. Therefore, etc.

For the Opposite

There are three who give testimony in heaven: the Father, the Word, and the Holy Spirit [I John 5:7]. Therefore the Father, the Word, and the Holy Spirit are three; therefore the Father is not the Word, and neither is the Holy Spirit. And it is certain that the Son is the Word. Therefore, etc.

[Reply]

Regarding this question, the first thing to be recognized is something granted by everyone, that the Word is engendered. So we should consider

· First, what is engendered in the divine;
· Second, that {229} what is engendered is the Word;
· Third, from what it is engendered (in light of the second argument).

[What Is Engendered]

1. Regarding the first, I say that nothing absolute in the divine is engendered, because (according to St. Augustine, *De trinitate* I [12.xxvi]) there is always a real distinction between what generates and what is engendered. But, within God, nothing absolute is really distinct from anything else. Therefore, etc.

If it be said that the Word is quasi-engendered, or that it proceeds and is engendered conceptually (*secundum rationem*), but not by a real emanation or engendering – I reply to the contrary that what is only conceptually engendered is not engendered in reality from the nature of the thing. Therefore, if something absolute in the divine is only conceptually engendered, then it is not engendered from the nature of the thing, and consequently is not truly engendered, except according to a false mode of understanding.

Moreover, there is always a distinction between what generates and what is engendered. Therefore, when something is engendered conceptually, there is a conceptual distinction between what generates and what is engendered. But it was shown above, in distinction two [qq. 1–3], that nothing absolute in the divine is distinct conceptually from anything else in the divine. Therefore, it is not engendered conceptually.

2. Second, I say that what is engendered is a relational [and not absolute] person. But this cannot be proved through reason; it should be held by faith alone. And that it should be held is clear through many authoritative passages, from both the Bible and the saints. Since they are familiar, I pass over them. {230}

[What Is Engendered Is the Word]

Regarding the second article, it should be held that what is engendered is truly the Word. But different people explain how this is so in different ways.

[A. The View of Peter Aureol]

One modern Doctor says that because in the divine, the Son emanates in perceived and objective being, but in such a way that he truly and really takes on being, so he is called the Word. Accordingly, he proves three propositions:[1]

First is that in every intellection what emanates and proceeds is not something distinct but the very thing itself, cognized in objective being, in virtue of which it serves as the end-term of the intellect's intuition.

Second is that an object is posited and formed and spoken within the mind where it is perceived and where it is the end-term of the cognizer's intuition; this is our mental word.

Third is that in the divine the Son emanates in a similar sort of perceived and objective being, but in such a way that it is truly and really formed and takes on real being.

From these it follows that what is engendered in the divine is truly the Word.

As he himself says, he proves the first proposition elsewhere:[2]

Here it needs to be seen that in an act of intellect the thing cognized is of necessity put into a kind of perceived and apparent intentional being.

---

[1] Peter Aureol, I *Sent.* d. 27 p. 2 a. 2 (ed. Friedman, pp. 429, 439, 443).
[2] Aureol, I *Scriptum* d. 3 sec. 14 n. 31 (ed. Buytaert vol. 2, pp. 696–98).

1. First, the internal or external senses form something no more than an act of intellect does. But the act of an external sense puts things into intentional being, as is clear in many experiences. {231}

First, when someone is carried along the water, the trees on the shore seem to be moving. Therefore this motion, which exists objectively in the eye, cannot be claimed to be the vision itself, since if it were then the vision would be the object of sight and would be seen, and sight would be a reflexive power. Nor can it be claimed that the motion really exists in the tree or the shore, because then they would really be moving. Nor can it be claimed that it exists in the air, because it is attributed to the tree, not to the air. Therefore, it exists only intentionally, not really, in seen being and in judged being.

The second experience occurs with the sudden, circular motion of a stick in the air. For some kind of circle appears to be made in the air by a stick moved in this way. So one asks what that circle is that appears to the one seeing. It can't be something real existing either in the stick (because the stick is straight) or in the air (because a colored and determinate circle cannot be in the air). Nor is it the vision itself, because then the vision would be seen, and further the vision is not in the air where that circle appears. Nor, for the same reasons, can it be anywhere within the eye. So it remains that it is in the air, with intentional being, or in apparent and judged being.

The third experience is of a stick bent in the water.

The fourth is of the doubling of candles apparent when one eye is forced upward. For there are two candles in apparent being even though there is only one candle in real being.

The fifth is of the colors on the neck of a pigeon.

The sixth is of the images seen in a mirror: sometimes beneath it, sometimes on its surface, and sometimes outside in the air between the viewer and the mirror – inasmuch as {232} the image has different locations. (The Perspectivist discusses this in books IV–VI.[3]) But either

- such an image is a real species implanted subjectively in the mirror, which cannot be claimed, as the Perspectivist demonstrates in book IV [1.20]; or
- the image will be claimed to be the true thing itself with real being, and this cannot be, because a face is not really beneath the mirror where the species appears to be; or
- the image will be said to be a vision existing in the eye, or something else existing there, which cannot be, because it appears beneath the mirror, with a different orientation (*situ*), as the Perspectivist proves [V.2.6–7].

What remains, then, is that it is only the appearance of the thing, or the thing with apparent and intentional being, with the result that the thing itself is beneath the mirror in seen, judged, and apparent being.

The seventh experience occurs in someone who sees the sun. For after he averts his glance, various bright spots appear in front of his eyes, which in time fade away, as Augustine says in *De trinitate* XI [ii.4].[4]

---

[3] Alhazen, *De aspectibus*.
[4] For this passage, see Translation 8, n. 82.

The eighth occurs in those who have looked at bright red things, or looked through a lattice. For afterwards, when they look at letters or anything else, these appear to them to be red or latticed. This latticing or redness undoubtedly has only intentional and apparent being.

Generally, anyone who denies that many things have merely intentional {233} and apparent being, and [who holds] that everything that is seen exists externally in its real nature, denies all deception and falls into the error of those who say that everything that appears is so.

Therefore, the external senses put things into intentional being. So likewise does imagination. For my father, imagined by me, is himself put into intentional being: for [the thing I imagine] is not a species, because then my imagination would arrive not at the thing but at the species alone, and it would be a reflexive power, and many other absurdities would follow. And since this is so for the internal and external senses, it follows all the more that the intellect puts things into intentional and apparent being.

It might be said that all these appearances occur in erroneous visions, and accordingly that a true vision does not put things into intentional being, and that only an erroneous and false vision does so.

This reply clearly does not succeed. A true vision, since it is more perfect, should do this all the more. Still, we do not distinguish the image or thing in apparent being and in real being, because in a true vision they occur simultaneously.

2. Moreover,[5] that by which the soul is duplicated, constituted before itself, and put into its own perception as perceived seems to give things objective and intentional being, and perceived and apparent being. But Augustine says in *De trinitate* XIV.vi [8] that "the power of thought is such that not even the mind itself puts itself into its own perception, except when it thinks of itself," etc.

3. Moreover,[6] it is impossible for there to be a formal appearance without something's {234} appearing objectively. For just as by whiteness something is made white, by a representation something is represented, and by a picture something is depicted, so by an appearance something appears. But it is clear that an intellection is nothing other than a kind of formal appearance. For [this is so] just as vision is a kind of appearance established in the eye, so that when things are seen they appear. As the Commentator says in *Metaphysics* IV 24, "there are certain conditions in which we believe the senses to be true, and others in which we believe them to be false: for instance, the condition of things' appearing to sight from afar and up close, in health and sickness, in strength and weakness, while awake and asleep. For the same thing appears large when up close and small from afar, and color appears to be one thing up close and another from afar." From this it is clear, according to him, that vision is nothing other than a kind of appearance.

[5] Aureol, I *Scriptum* d.3 sec. 14 n.32 (ed. Buytaert, vol. 2, pp. 698–99).
[6] Aureol, I *Scriptum* d.3 sec. 14 nn. 55–57 (ed. Buytaert, vol. 2, pp. 712–14).

(Hence phantasia is so-called by the Greeks because of *phanos*, which means *an appearance*.) Consequently, since an intellection is a kind of spiritual vision of things, [it will be] a kind of spiritual appearance as well. So it follows that [through intellection] the things themselves take on apparent being. For it cannot be said that an intellection is an appearance such that nothing appears except for it itself. If that were the case, then the intellection would appear and be cognized, and the intellect would cognize nothing external. Therefore, it is clear *a priori* that every intellection – indeed, every cognition – is that by which things appear and are put into presentive being. {235}

4. Moreover, it is also clear *a priori* that an intellection is fully like (*est simillima*) the thing it is of. Therefore, through this likeness the thing either takes on some being or else it is only denominated. But it cannot be said that it is only denominated, so that being within intellect is nothing other than a kind of denomination, in the way that Caesar when depicted is denominated by the picture. For through this denomination Caesar is not present to the picture, nor made its object, nor made to appear. Therefore, it is necessary to say that through an intellection, insofar as it is fully like the thing, the thing takes on a kind of being, in such a way that this intellectual being is not solely a denomination, but is a kind of intentional, diminished, and apparent being. Accordingly, the Commentator says in *Metaphysics* IX 7, that intelligible things are said to have being not in an unqualified way, but to have being in the soul and in cognition.

5. The same is evident *a posteriori*. For it is clear that the intellect is brought to absolute rose (*rosam simpliciter*), and experiences it as its object objectively. Hence that which is made an object in this way is either

a. a species informing the intellect;
b. an act of intellect;
c. a thing made by intellect;
d. a subsistent thing, beyond intellect; or
e. all externally existing roses, put into intentional and apparent being as if they were one whole rose.

(a) The first (that it is the species of the rose, existing within intellect) cannot be maintained. For since that is made the object of intellect and is discerned by it, either the intellect stops there – which cannot be held because then (i) it would cognize not the external thing but only the species; also, {236} (ii) knowledge would then be of species, and (iii) the proposition *a rose is a flower* would not be true, because the species of a rose is not the species of a flower – or the intuition of intellect does not stop with the species but extends, mediated by the species, to the thing. In that case, we've reached our goal. For the thing itself's existing in the intellect's ultimate intuition in the mode of an appearance is the target of the present inquiry.

(b) Nor can it be held that this apparent rose is the act itself of intellect. For (i) the intellect would first discern its own act and then, mediated by that, discern the object, and consequently would not cognize things directly. Further (ii), this would lead back to the error of the Commentator, that there is a single intellect in everyone: for it is certain that this apparent rose is not and cannot be multiplied, and so it is one in me and in you, and consequently its subject, the possible intellect, would be the same in me and in you, not multiplied.

(c) Nor can it be held that it is some thing made by intellect in real being. For (i) intellection is an immanent operation, from which nothing active follows (as is clear in *Metaphysics* IX [1050a23–b2]). Also (ii), if the intellect's attention stops at that thing, then knowledge would be of these things and not external things, and propositions would not be true because the intellect in conceiving the subject would form one thing and in conceiving the predicate would form another, and so the one thing will not be the other.

(d) Nor can it be said that there is some thing preceding the intellection and possessing some real being. For (i) even if every {237} particular rose were destroyed, absolute rose would still remain. This goes against the Philosopher's remark in the *Categories* [2b5–6] that "if those that are primary are destroyed, it is impossible for any of the others to remain" – speaking of secondary substances. Also, (ii) we would be back to Platonic Ideas. For Plato held that subsisting *human being* is the end-term of the attention of an intellect conceiving of absolute human being. He spoke of these as *human being per se* and *rose per se*, as if they were natural forms subsisting per se, and he called them *ideas*. Also, (iii) predications would be false, as was argued in other cases; also, (iv) neither definitions nor knowledge would be of externally existing things, as the Philosopher argues in *Metaphysics* VII [1039b31–40a2]. So in truth the intellect would know nothing of things that are within us, if the attention of an intellect considering the natures of absolute things had as its end-term something possessing real being.

(e) So we are left with maintaining the last option: that it has only apparent and intentional being. Thus all roses, which are distinct in real being, are held to be one whole rose not in real but in intentional being. In this way, all the difficulties raised are accounted for: for that rose is really the same as all roses, since when it is perceived, all roses are perceived as one, not distinct roses; in this way, too, knowledge is of things, as is predication and definition, and the things are cognized directly. {238}

Therefore, it appears *a priori* and *a posteriori* that a thing cognized by intellect takes on a kind of apparent and intentional being.

[B. Against Aureol's View]

This view seems to me false as regards the conclusion for which the above arguments are advanced. But because I have seen little of what this Doctor says – for if all the time I have had to look at what he says were put together, it would not take up the space of a single natural day – I do not intend to argue much against the one who holds this view. For from ignorance of what he says, I might facilely argue against his words rather than against his meaning. But since his conclusion appears to me false, based on what he says, I will argue against it, regardless of whether these arguments run contrary to his meaning. The arguments that I made in distinction 36 of this book, against one view of cognized being, could also be advanced against this conclusion. I composed that material, and almost everything else in book one, before I had seen the view recited here. Whoever wants to should look for those arguments there and apply them.

For now I argue as follows.

1. I ask of that apparent and intentional being whether it has only objective being, so that it nowhere has subjective being, or whether it somewhere has subjective being. {239}

The first cannot be held, because (i) then a true quality would never be apprehended through the senses, or else two objects would be apprehended in sensation, a real quality and that which has only objective being; also, (ii) nothing is a per se and proper object of sense except for a real sensible quality; also, (iii) such a thing is nothing other than a being of reason, but a being of reason cannot be apprehended per se by the senses.

The second also cannot be held, because (i) that which somewhere has subjective being, when it has subjective being, is truly a real being, not only an intentional one. Therefore if this sort of apparent and intentional being were to have subjective being, it would truly be a real being. Moreover, (ii) if it has subjective being, then it is necessarily a substance or an accident, and so it will necessarily be a real being.

2. Moreover, I ask of that apparent being in which whiteness is constituted when whiteness is seen: Is it or is it not really the same as whiteness?

If it is said that it is really the same, then on the contrary: when things are really the same, they coincide as regards generation and corruption, according to the Philosopher in *Metaphysics* IV [1003b26–30]. Consequently, whenever that apparent being is produced, that whiteness is produced. Likewise, whenever two things are really the same, it is impossible for one of them to exist when the other does not. But this (pointing to whiteness) can exist when this (pointing to the apparent being) does not, because otherwise the apparent being would exist without the vision, just as the whiteness exists without the vision. Therefore, whiteness and that apparent being are not really the same. {240}

If they are not really the same – and certainly neither is part of the other – then they differ totally and with respect to their whole selves. From this I argue as follows: When things differ with respect to their whole selves, whether they are distinct things or one is an absolute thing and the other a being of reason, the absolute thing can (at least through divine power) be apprehended by a power it is the per se object of, without the other's being apprehended. Therefore, whiteness can be apprehended by sight without the apparent being's being apprehended. Consequently, its being sensed does not require such intermediary apparent being, and consequently it is pointless to postulate such being.

3. Moreover, I ask whether or not whiteness itself truly appears to the senses. If not, then it is not seen, which is plainly false. If it appears, and in addition apparent being appears, then there are two apparent and observed things here. From this I argue as follows: Whenever there are two appearances before a single power, by whatever reason one of them is brought into apparent being so is the other. Therefore, if whiteness exists in apparent being that is somehow distinct from the whiteness, then for the same reason that apparent being will itself be brought into a somehow distinct apparent being. Consequently, there will be an infinite regress in such cases, which is plainly absurd.

If it is said that this apparent being appears through itself, without any intermediary, then on the contrary: When one thing is just as much the per se object of a power as another is, if the other can appear to the power without any intermediary between it and the power's act, then for that same reason the per se object could appear to the power without any intermediary between the object and the power's act. Therefore, whiteness {241} could be seen without any apparent being intermediary between whiteness and the vision. Therefore, it is pointless to postulate this sort of intermediary apparent being.

4. Moreover, the immediate end-term of some power's act does not require an intermediary for it to be apprehended by the power. But whiteness is the immediate end-term of an act of seeing. Therefore it does not require this sort of intermediary apparent being.

5. Moreover, when something is naturally apprehended by a power without two items in turn, so that it is apprehended first without one and then without the other, it can by divine power be apprehended without either one of them, with the result that neither of them is apprehended. But the same object — say, whiteness — is apprehended first without true apparent being, and then without false apparent being, as he himself makes quite clear. Therefore, it can be apprehended without any apparent being, and consequently it is pointless to postulate such being.

An argument could be made from the foregoing against the second proposition [p. 222]: for if this sort of apparent being is not in every intellection, then it is clear that such being is not universally our mental word. So with respect to these two propositions I reply in short that the first claim, taken universally, is false.

First, I say that in no intuitive cognition (*notitia*), sensory or intellective, is a thing constituted in any being that is intermediary between the thing and the act of cognizing (*cognoscendi*). I say instead that the thing itself is immediately seen or apprehended, without any intermediary between it and the act. Further, there is no more an intermediary between the thing and the act by which the thing is said to be seen than there is an intermediary between God and a creature {242} by which God is said to be the Creator. Rather, by the very fact that God exists and a creature exists – since a creature could not exist if God did not exist – God is said to be the Creator, and so he is really the Creator without any intermediary. In just the same way, by the very fact that a thing exists and a cognition of this sort exists, the thing is said to be seen or cognized without any intermediary. Nor is there anything else seen there except for the thing itself – just as nothing conceivable (*imaginabile*) is the Creator except for God.

Second, I say that through an abstractive cognition immediately following an intuitive cognition, nothing is made nor does anything take on being beyond the abstractive cognition itself. For the object of an intuitive cognition and of an immediately following abstractive cognition are entirely the same, and under the same aspect.[7] Therefore, just as there is no intermediary between an intuitively cognized object and the intuitive cognition, so there will be no intermediary between an object and an abstractive cognition.

Third, I say that when there is an abstractive cognition by which a universal is held within intellect, one can plausibly maintain either that there is an intermediary or that there is not. If an intermediary is posited, it can plausibly be said (as I've said before)[8] that this intermediary is itself understood, and is nothing other than a kind of *fictum* common to all the singulars. In this case no singular is understood through that intellection. Alternatively, it can be said that it is a certain intellection of the soul,

---

[7] Compare Aureol's account in Translation 8, nn. 102–11.
[8] See *Ordinatio* 2.8, translated in Boehner (1990), pp. 41–43.

possessing subjective being in the soul really distinct from every other object of the soul. It can also be said plausibly that there is no such intermediary, and that the universal {243} is the confused cognition itself, having as its immediate end-term all the singular things to which it is common and universal. (This is in line with how I have recited this view elsewhere.[9] Similarly, whatever I say in support of or against such fictive being I am merely reciting, even if this is not always explicit.)

Fourth, I say that not every [mental] word is an apparent being of this sort. For, as was shown in the previous question, every intellection is a word, but not every intellection is this sort of apparent being. Therefore, etc.

A reply should be made to the arguments for the earlier view. Perhaps out of these replies some points will become clear that go against the meaning of the one who proposes this view. But I am not certain of this, because I have not seen him anywhere else on this subject.

To the first [A1], I say that the act of an external sense does not put things into intentional being – in such a way, that is, that beyond the act of sensing and the external thing there is some intermediary intentional being. Now on account of an act of sensing's being put into real being, the external thing can be denominated as *being sensed*, without anything's being added to it except perhaps, on one view, through predication. But this occurs only through an act of intellect, just as something is added to God from the fact that a creature is put into real being. If this is what the proponent of this view had in mind, I don't disagree with him. But his words suggest the first interpretation.

So I reply to the proof. To the first experience, I say that when someone is carried along the water, there is no motion in his eyes, neither objectively nor subjectively, because there is no motion belonging to {244} the trees themselves. But the proposition

> *The trees are moving*

exists objectively within intellect, and it certainly is true that the intellect can form propositions and assent to them or dissent. This, however, is beside the point.

One might say that the trees seem to be moving not only to intellect

---

[9] E.g., *Expositio in Perihermenias*, prooem. §6, translated in Boehner (1990), pp. 43–45. And see below, p. 237.

but also to the senses, inasmuch as they seem to be moving even to brute animals that have no intellective cognition. To this it should be said that if the proposition

> *The trees seem to the senses to be moving*

is understood in such a way that some motion, real or otherwise, is apprehended by the senses, then it is false. For no motion other than a real one, or one that can be real, is apprehended by the senses, just as no whiteness except for a real one, or one that can be real, is apprehended by the senses. Hence no motion, real or apparent, is constituted by the senses, nor does any motion whatsoever appear to the senses.

If, however, the above proposition is understood in such a way that within sense there is some apprehension (or apprehensions) of different objects in virtue of which the person sensing can elicit operations just like those elicited by someone sensing a body that truly is moving, then the proposition is true. But it does not follow from this that any motion appears. What follows is that within the sense there are apprehensions equivalent, as regards the operations to be elicited, to an appearance or vision through which motion does appear. (Here I speak in the manner of one who claims that motion can be seen.)

I confirm this reply. For this inference:

> *The trees appear to be moving; therefore, some motion appears or has objective being*

no more follows than does this one:

> *The trees appear to be moving {245} in reality; therefore, some real motion appears or has objective being*

since the mode of arguing is just the same. But everyone agrees that the second inference is not valid. Therefore, neither is the first. And so I say that when it is granted that

> *The trees seem to be moving in reality or by a real motion*

it should not be granted that some real motion appears. Grant instead that one has apprehensions equivalent, as regards the operations to be elicited, to apprehensions by which the trees are truly apprehended to be moving. Just the same should be said for

> *The trees seem to be moving*

and so no motion exists intentionally through the senses in seen being or in judged being – no more than it exists in reality – because no motion is seen.

I confirm this reply in a second way. For if some motion is seen there, and it is not a real motion, then it is only a motion with objective being. But such intentional motion is more distinct from real motion than it is from whiteness or blackness. Therefore, through a vision of such intentional motion one would no more judge that there is real motion there than that there is real whiteness or blackness there, which they deny. So I say that no motion is seen there.

Yet because of the motion of the one on the boat, who is moving only with the motion of the boat, he sees those trees from various distances and angles. For this reason, the trees seem to be moving. As a result, these propositions are equivalent:

(i) *The trees, without any intermediary produced or made in any sort of real or intentional being, are seen successively from various {246} distances and angles by an eye moving with the motion of the boat;*

(ii) *The trees seem to the eye to be moving.*

So just as it does not follow from the first proposition that any intentional motion appears, so neither does it follow from the second.

If one says that the trees do not seem to every such eye to be moving, since many viewers judge and know that they are not moving, one should reply that this is because of intellect, which judges that they are not moving. Or, if this occurs in brute animals or in those who lack reason, it is because of an apprehension impeding the action of some natural cause. For the sake of brevity, I refrain from explaining how this could happen.

In the same way, I say to the second experience that no circle appears to the eye. The intellect does sometimes believe this proposition to be true:

A circle is in the air.

But no circle appears to the eye except equivalently – that is, it has an apprehension (or apprehensions) equivalent, as regards the operations to be elicited, to an apprehension (or apprehensions) of a circle. How this could happen would take a long time to set out, but it could to some extent be evident to anyone studious, from what is said in this question.

What the argument infers:

That circle is in the air with intentional being, or in apparent and judged being is unconditionally false, based on what he says, because nothing is conceivable {247} in the air except for what is real. For if it has being in the air, this is either subjective or objective being. If subjective, it is real. If objective, this is impossible, because air is neither cognitive nor volitional. So even if we should postulate this circle, it is not in the air. Nor does it follow:

> *It is judged to be in the air; therefore, it is in the air*

no more than it follows:

> *God is judged to be a body; therefore, God is a body.*

And from this we can derive an argument that goes against his thesis rather than for it. For just as it does not follow from the fact that a circle is judged to exist in the air that a circle exists in the air, really or intentionally, so it does not follow from the fact that a circle is judged to exist that a circle exists, really or intentionally.

In the same way, I say to the third experience that no bend exists due to the sensation, although due to intellect this proposition is believed to be true:

> *The stick is bent.*

Also, there is within the sense an apprehension (or apprehensions) equivalent as regards causing within intellect a state of belief of the sort that a sensation would cause if the stick were out of the water, were apprehended, and were bent.

In the same way, I say to the fourth experience that the sensation (or sensations) there are equivalent, as regards the operations to be elicited either within intellect or within the external or internal powers, to the sensation (or sensations) of two really existing candles. Nor are there two candles there in apparent being [in such a way] that this apparent being mediates between the sensation (or sensations) and the candle itself (or parts of candles). If, however, the claim that there are two candles in apparent being is meant in this {248} way, that there is a judgment there by which two candles are judged to exist, then this can be granted in the cases of intellect and, equally, the senses. But it does not follow from this that anything exists in any way at all other than the candle (and its parts) and the act of cognizing within the [cognitive] power.

To the fifth experience I say that wherever those colors may be, the colors truly have real existence there. As for whether they existed subjectively in the neck of the pigeon or in the nearby air, this is more doubtful and each can plausibly be maintained. This will be discussed in book II, where I will examine the species that are posited *in medio* and in our cognitive powers.[10] One's judgment regarding these colors on the neck of a pigeon is thus the same as for the redness caused on a wall by the course of the sun's rays, and also for other cases that some say involve species.

To the sixth experience I say that the thing itself is seen in the mirror, not its image. And I say that the thing itself is not beneath the mirror, nor is anything seen beneath the mirror, although it can be judged by intellect to be beneath the mirror. But the only conceivable things required for this are the thing cognized by intellect, the mirror and other really existing things, and the judgment itself existing subjectively within the soul, which is not beneath the mirror, neither intentionally nor in reality. In this way, if the sense were to have a judgment distinct from the sensation, it could without intermediary judge that the thing is in the mirror, without any-thing's causing it, intentionally {249} or really, except for that judgment. Still, because the judgment exists, the thing itself would really be judged to be beneath the mirror. Indeed, these propositions are equivalent:

(i)   *That judgment exists within the eye, nothing else having been caused in any sort of being, real or intentional;*

(ii) *The thing is judged to be beneath the mirror.*

One might say that if the thing itself is now judged to be beneath the mirror and before it was not, then it now has judged being, which it did not have before. And, [since] it does not have any real being that it did not have before, it now has intentional being, which it did not have before.

To this and to the like my reply is clear in distinction 36. The fact that a thing is now judged to be beneath the mirror, whereas before it was not, does not result in something's being added to the thing, except perhaps by extrinsic denomination, as a result of that judgment's now being within the [cognitive] power, whereas before it was not. Just as God is now said to be *creating*, whereas before he was not, because a creature now exists

---

[10] See *Reportatio* Bk. III, q. 2. Ockham denies the existence of all such intermediary representational species.

that did not exist before, so I say that the thing itself, without any inter-mediary between it and the vision, appears to be beneath the mirror, but yet is not there.

If someone says that it is there in apparent and judged being, I reply that if you mean some intermediary apparent being is added anew, in virtue of which it is there, then this is false. This is no more the case than that God is now in redeeming being or in glorifying being. If, however, you mean that it appears to be there, I grant this. But {250} it suffices for this that there really is a judgment within the [cognitive] power, just as it suffices for God's glorifying someone that there be glory within that person.

To the seventh experience I say that in such a case true things continue to exist in reality. As for how and where they subjectively exist, this should not be taken up now. And as for why they appear now and not before, the same ought to be said (in one respect) as would be said for why a star appears at night and not by day.

In the same way, I say to the eighth experience that this redness truly exists somewhere. As for the latticing, since it is not a proper object of sight, one's reply ought to follow the same lines as the replies made to the motion of the trees, the circle made by the stick, the stick's being bent, and other similar cases.

To the inference that one who denies such apparent and intentional being denies all deception (*ludificationem*), it should be said that this is not so. For deception occurs in many ways. Sometimes, it occurs through mirrors in nature. For a demon, with his knowledge of the natures of things, can set up various mirrors in various ways, through which far away things will be seen. He can also, in various ways unknown to me, make some parts of a thing be seen while others are not seen, and through this a person can be judged to exist where he does not exist, and so on in other ways. But for all of these, the external thing plus the acts of apprehension within the cognitive powers suffice – without any intermediary of the sort claimed [to have] intentional being.

Nor does it follow from this that those ancients were right who said {251} that all things are as they appear. For something appears to someone to be white which in actual truth is not. But this is not the result of some intermediary between the thing and the appearance. Rather, through the apprehension itself or through the power's act, without any intermediary, a thing appears to be white which is not. This sometimes happens because it is not known whether the whiteness exists subjectively in that thing or in another, although it is believed to be in the one. And so beyond the acts of the powers by which those powers judge, and beyond the things themselves, there is nothing in either real or intentional being.

In reply to the argument, therefore, it is clear that the senses do not form things in any sort of being, no more than they form God in any sort of being. For when an act of sensation occurs within the senses, God can have a new denomination, since God truly caused that act in reality. In just the same way, when that act occurs, a thing is truly seen in reality. And I do not hold that appearances occur differently in erroneous sensations, compared to others [see p. 224]; rather, they ought to be granted in a uniform way. Accordingly, when a sense is deceived (i.e., some deception occurs), a thing is judged to be such as it is not, without any intermediary between the thing and the power's act. So when it is not deceived, the thing is judged as it is, without any such intermediary.

Also, when he says there that

> We do not distinguish the thing in apparent being and in real being, because in a true vision they occur simultaneously

he seems to contradict his entire view. For if in a true vision there is some distinction between the apparent being and the thing, then the vision would no more cause one than the other.

To the second argument [A2], it should be said that all these are {252} metaphorical phrases: *The soul is duplicated, is put before itself, is constituted in perceived being*, etc. And if these phrases are found in any of the saints, they mean nothing else than that in the soul there is a single act of understanding by which, without any intermediary, the soul is truly understood. This is what St. Augustine means. So no being is given to the soul there except an act of understanding – no more than some being is given to God by his now damning someone and his not having done so before.

To the other [A3], it can be granted that by an appearance something appears, that an intellection is an appearance, and that by an intellection something appears. But it does not follow from this that something is *made* by the intellection – just as by creation something is created, and yet the

Creator is not by that creation made in some such being. So just as something is understood by an intellection, so something appears.

To the fourth [A4], granted that "an intellection is fully like the thing," it should be said that the thing takes on no being through this likeness, but that it takes on some denomination now, since the thing is truly understood now and before it was not. Indeed, the thing no more takes on being by being understood than Caesar takes on being by being painted, and it is no more present to intellect through an intellection – speaking properly {253} and according to the word's true force (*de virtute sermonis*) – than Caesar is present to someone through a picture. Still, the thing is made the object of intellect and appears to it, solely by there being an intellection. And that the thing is made an object and appears to intellect is nothing other than that an intellection of the thing exists within intellect.

To the Commentator, I say that an intelligible object's existing within intellect or within a cognition is nothing other than its being understood or cognized.

To the final argument [A5] one can reply in a number of ways, in accord with various views. In one way, one can reply that the division is insufficient. For those who hold the *ficta* view (a view I've often recited) would say that when absolute rose is understood, what is understood is neither (a) a species informing intellect, nor (b) an act of intellect, nor (c) a thing made by intellect, nor (d) a subsistent thing beyond intellect, nor (e) all externally existing roses put into intentional and apparent being as if they were one whole rose. Rather, what is understood is one thing with objective being of the same sort as a particular rose has externally in subjective being. That is neither a species, nor the act, nor a thing made, nor a subsistent thing, nor external roses in any sort of being. Rather, it is one *fictum* in the soul that is not really the same as anything external, and it is common and universal, as I have explained elsewhere.

An alternative reply would come from those who hold that a concept or intention {254} of the soul is really an intellection. For they would say that the [a – e] division is insufficient because by such an intellection one would understand all external roses, but not put into intentional and apparent being as if they were one whole rose. Hence [they would say] that it is not possible, through any sort of causation, for external roses to be one whole rose. Still, these external roses serve as the end-term for an act of understanding, without any intermediary or other end-term.

Alternatively, it can be said that what is understood is some thing made by intellect in real being. And to the first argument to the contrary (c.i), which is not successful, they would say that not *every* intellection produces something. Likewise, even when something made follows from some intellection (as is true, at the least, when a disposition is generated) it still does not follow that something is made *outside* the soul, immediately (although mediated by an act of will, a thing sometimes is made outside). This is what the Philosopher means.

To the second argument to the contrary (c.ii), it should be said (as was said before) that there are two ways in which knowledge is of things: These things are either the parts of the proposition that is known, or they are the things for which the parts of the conclusion supposit.[11]

In the first way, knowledge is not of external things, but of other real things (*aliis rebus*). This would be one view. On another view, knowledge is of beings of reason. Yet I am not asserting this, that knowledge is not of external things. {255} Nor does it follow from this that propositions are not true, because this does not follow:

> The subject is a distinct thing from the predicate; therefore, the proposition is not true.

For a proposition such as

> A human being is an animal

or

> A human being is capable of laughter

does not denote that the subject *is* the predicate, but that they *stand* for the same thing. This is why the proposition is true.

In the second way, knowledge is of external things, because the subject and predicate of a proposition, though not one thing, still supposit for the same thing. And in this way knowledge is of external things: That is, the terms of the proposition that is known supposit for external things.

The other options that he rejects are false, but even so his arguments are not successful. The first argument against the first option (a.i) is not successful, because others don't take it to be absurd that by such an intellection only the species is understood and not the external thing,

---

[11] See *Ordinatio* d. 2 q. 4 (*Op. Theol.* vol. II, pp. 134–38). For Ockham's view that the object of knowledge is a proposition (or conclusion), see Translations 11–12. Roughly, a word *supposits* for a thing when it *refers* to that thing.

though the thing would be understood by another intellection. In this way, those who posit fictive entities (which I have often discussed) would say that when a universal is understood, no external thing is understood. Still, when a singular is understood, whether by intuitive or abstractive cognition, it is the singular that is understood.

The second (a.ii) is also not successful, because it does not consider that knowledge might be only of species, but of ones that supposit for external things – as I say that knowledge is not of external things, since these [things known] are parts of the proposition that is known, but yet the parts supposit for external things. {256}

The third (a.iii) is also not successful, because although only the species would be understood, still the proposition would be true, because the subject and predicate would supposit for external things and for the same things.

The first argument against the second option (b.i) looks to be successful (*habet apparentiam*). The second (b.ii) is not successful, because it does not consider that what is understood, when a rose is understood, cannot be really multiplied, but nevertheless can be multiplied by equivalence, as is the nature of what is predicable of many (as I have explained elsewhere).[12]

Moreover, the first argument against the fourth option (d.i) is not successful, because when the Philosopher says in the *Categories* [2b5–6] that "if those that are primary are destroyed, it is impossible for any of the others to remain," he does not mean that if the individuals are destroyed then no universal predicable of many can exist in the being appropriate to it. Rather, he means that if being is denied of every individual, it will be denied of every universal suppositing personally. This is true, but irrelevant.

The second argument (d.ii) looks to be successful, although it could be blocked. The third argument (d.iii) is not successful, because although the subject and predicate would be really distinct things, it would not follow that predications would be false, unless the subject and predicate were to supposit for themselves and not for the same things. {257} Nor does the fourth work (d.iv), because knowledge is of external things not inasmuch as it concerns the things that are known, but inasmuch as it concerns the things for which the terms of the propositions supposit. Likewise, definitions are of external things not inasmuch as they concern what they are

---

[12] See *Ordinatio* d. 2 q. 8 (*Op. Theol.* vol. II, pp. 274–75), where Ockham illustrates his point with the example of how a single genus is predicated of many different species.

adequately predicated of, but inasmuch as they concern the adequate supposits of what the definitions are predicated of.

Consequently, these arguments that he brings forward all (or almost all) go against his own claim. For I ask whether that which serves as the end-term of an act of understanding, when absolute rose is understood, is or is not external roses. If it is not external roses, then by his own arguments knowledge is not of external things. Also, if that rose is really the same as all roses, as he himself says, then neither definitions nor propositions will be true. Therefore just as the roses themselves are not produced, so neither is that [understood] rose put into such being.

Moreover, he says above [p. 224] that a true vision puts a thing into such apparent being much more than a false vision does. But through a false vision something is made that is not the thing itself that is understood; therefore, [this must occur] through a true vision. Therefore, that apparent thing is not really the particular roses themselves.

Moreover, if that understood rose is not distinct from particular roses but is the particular roses themselves, then there is nothing beyond those particular roses and that intellection. Therefore if those roses now appear on account of an intellection and did not before, then, since this happens only on account of the intellection and the intellection is {258} extrinsic to the particular roses themselves, it will only be an extrinsic denomination when that rose is said to appear, something that he denies.

Moreover, if that rose is the particular roses, and the particular roses have real being, then that rose has real being and not only intentional being.

And if one says that they have intentional being from the fact that they appear, this does not work. For I might just as easily say that from the fact that God creates, God has intentional being, since he has creating being.

Moreover, if that rose is the particular roses themselves, and the particular roses exist even though the appearance does not, then it is not due to the appearance that they are that rose.

Moreover, he says above [p. 226] that it's certain that that apparent rose is not particular and cannot be multiplied. Hence it is one in me and in you. From this I argue: That which is not a particular rose [and] cannot be multiplied is also not really all particular roses. But this is how that rose is, according to you; therefore, it is not the particular roses.

Moreover, it is constantly open to conclude that there is nothing beyond the real things themselves and the cognition itself, although on account of

the cognition a thing could now be denominated otherwise than before –
just as God, on account of a creature's existing, is denominated in a new
way now, compared with before, as he is said to be creating, beatifying,
damning, punishing, etc. {259}

[Reply to the Question]

To the question I say that in the divine only the Son is the Word. This is
clear, because only the Son is engendered, and every word is engendered.
Therefore, only the Son is the Word. This is also clear from St. Augustine,
De trinitate V [xiii.14], who says that the Father is said to be neither the
Word nor the image nor the Son. For the same reason, the Holy Spirit is
not the Word, and consequently only the Son is the Word. Likewise, at
De trinitate XV [xvii.29], "in this Trinity, only the Son is said to be the
Word of God." From these and many other [passages] it is clear that only
the Son is the Word.

But given that only the Son is the Word (in such a way as to be called
the Word only notionally and not essentially), there is a question whether
'Word' implies some relationship to creatures of a sort that neither 'Father'
nor 'Holy Spirit' implies. And in general doctors defend one of three
views:

• that the Word contains its own proper relationship to creatures;
• that it connotes a relationship to creatures;
• that it connotes creatures.[13]

I don't judge the first of these views to be true, because in the divine the
only real relations are paternity, active spiration, filiation, and passive spiration. But none of these is a relation to creatures. Therefore, etc. Nor can
it be said that it contains a relationship of reason, because either a relationship of reason should not be posited, or if it should be then it is not a real
being and consequently does not belong to the essence of a real person.
{260} The second and third views, as they stand, I don't judge to be true,
because 'connote' does not apply to just any thing but only to the sign of
a thing. As a result, the Divine Word no more connotes than does the
Father or Holy Spirit.

---

[13] These views are defended, in turn, by Henry of Ghent (*Summa* 59.5), Thomas Aquinas (*Summa theol.* 1a 34.3), and John Duns Scotus (*Ordinatio* I.27.1–3).

So, as regards this article, I say in brief that the Word which is really the Son in God neither contains nor connotes a relationship, nor does it even connote creatures. Still, the term 'Word' is imposed to signify in such a way that it connotes creatures – due not to the nature of the thing, but to the imposition of the term. This is so because its nominal definition should contain the term 'creatures' in an oblique case, so that its nominal definition is this:

> The Divine Word is the Person engendered from the knowledge that has God and all creatures as its objects.

But the term 'Son' does not have this sort of nominal definition. Its definition, if expressed, ought to be put this way:

> The Son is the Person engendered from the substance of the Father.

In this definition, the term 'creatures' is not included in either the nominative or an oblique case. And for this reason, the term 'Son' does not connote creatures, whereas the term 'Word' does.

One might reply that the Divine Word and the Son are in no way distinct, neither in reality nor conceptually. Therefore, the Son connotes whatever the Divine Word connotes, and vice versa.

Moreover, not only is the Divine Word a Person engendered from the knowledge of the Father that has God and all creatures as {261} its cognitive objects. Equally, the Son of God is truly the Person engendered from the knowledge of God the Father that singly has God and all creatures as its cognitive objects. Therefore, 'Word' connotes creatures no more than 'Son' does.

To the first of these replies, it should be said that in the claim

> The Divine Word and the Son are in no way distinct, neither in reality nor conceptually

if the terms 'Divine Word' and 'Son' supposit personally for what they signify, then it is true. In that case, if these terms are always taken in the same way, then neither the Word nor the Son connotes anything. As a result, the inference made there is not valid, because the consequent implies that the Word or the Son connotes something, which is false (as was said above). If, however, the terms 'Divine Word' and 'Son' supposit for themselves in the above proposition, then the antecedent is false. For when 'Divine Word' and 'Son' are taken in that way, they are not really the same, because these terms are not really the same, and as a result one term connotes something that the other does not.

To the second, it should be said that the Son is the Person engendered from the knowledge of the Father, etc. – just as truly as the Divine Word is. Nevertheless, one proposition predicates a definition expressing {262} the nominal definition, whereas the other does not. As a result, one term connotes something that the other does not.

If one asks why a name for the second Person connotes creatures more than a name for another Person does, I say that just as one name for the second Person in the divine connotes creatures and another does not, because those names have different nominal definitions, so a name connoting creatures could be imposed for each Divine Person. For because the nominal definition of the term 'Word' is this:

> *The Person engendered from the knowledge of the Father that singly has everything, God and creatures, etc.*

it follows that the term 'Word' connotes creatures. In just the same way, if this phrase:

> *The Person engendered from his knowledge that singly has everything, etc.*

were the nominal definition of some° imposed term that was proper to the Father (just as this [definition] is proper to the Word),° then that term that is proper to the Father would connote creatures just as the term 'Word' does. For example,° if this phrase (or one like it in which the term 'creature' is included in an oblique or the nominative case) is the nominal definition for the term 'Speaker,' when taken purely notionally, then the term 'Speaker' will be proper to the Father and will connote creatures. And the same should be said for the Holy Spirit as for the Father. {263}

[To the Principal Arguments]

To the first principal argument [p. 220], it should be said that it's not the case that only the Son is a word. But only the Son is the Divine Word.

One might reply that in the preceding question it was said that every intellection is a word; but not only the Son is a divine intellection; therefore, not only the Son is the Divine Word. To this it should be said that the preceding question said that every intellection of a *created* intellect is a word, because every such intellection is engendered. But divine intellection is not engendered, and so it is not at issue here. And as for whether one ought to grant that God's intellection, which is his essence, is the Word, this is not relevant to the question.

To the second, it should be said that the Divine Word is born precisely from the knowledge of the Father, and so is born precisely from the substance of the Father, as is the Son. For the essence of the Father and the knowledge of the Father are in no way distinct, neither in reality nor conceptually.

As for St. Augustine, when he says that "the Word was born from all the things that are in the Father," it should be said that he does not mean that the Word is born from all the things cognized through the knowledge of the Father. Rather, he means that the Word is born from the knowledge of the Father that singly is of all things cognized by the Father. This is how one should understand all the authoritative passages in which {264} Augustine seems to say that the Word is born from the things that are within the knowledge of the Father. That is: The Word is born from the knowledge of the Father that is singly of all things. This is how he speaks in many different places.

10

WILLIAM CRATHORN
ON THE POSSIBILITY OF INFALLIBLE KNOWLEDGE

Introduction

The Englishman William Crathorn was a Dominican master of theology at Oxford. His only known writings are a collection of questions on the first book of Lombard's *Sentences*, delivered over the academic year 1330–31. Crathorn is by no means the most gifted of theologians working at that time, but he is nevertheless worth reading, because he was willing to take bold and interesting stands on the central philosophical questions of his day. Though sometimes the results seem absurd, at other times they seem prescient.

This is particularly so for the first of Crathorn's questions on the *Sentences*. The ostensible topic is whether we can have knowledge of the faith through our own natural light. This question gets swallowed up, however, by a long series of fourteen conclusions that address general questions regarding cognition (1–7) and knowledge (8–14). The latter group first sets out a series of skeptical arguments showing that the senses do not yield any certain knowledge (8–10), and then offers a most Cartesianlike solution to these arguments (11–13).

The first group of conclusions focuses on the cognitive process, and it is here that Crathorn looks less prescient and more absurd. He defends the traditional theory of species and mental word as internal likenesses of external objects (compare Translation 6), but insists on taking 'likeness' literally, so that in perceiving, and even in thinking, the soul actually takes on the color, temperature, etc., of the things perceived (conclusion 7).

The long first conclusion requires special comment. Here Crathorn makes the obscure claim that that by which we formally cognize is our cognitive power. By this he means to deny that there is any distinction between a cognitive power and its action. So, whereas it is natural to suppose that we are cognizing when we are engaged in a certain sort of action, Crathorn holds that there is no action of cognition, just the cognitive power. (His argument depends on his view that cognition is a

passive process.) This is a strange view, but one that fits quite neatly into
the evolving medieval debate. Thirteenth-century writers such as Thomas
Aquinas had standardly distinguished

> soul – powers – acts – species.

In the early fourteenth century, it became standard (as with Ockham) to
eliminate species and to identify the soul with its powers, leaving only two
elements in cognition:

> soul – acts.

Crathorn accepts the identity of the soul and its powers (see p. 258),
but he holds onto species, instead choosing to eliminate acts. We are left
with

> soul – species.

The view strikes me as nearly indefensible, but it shows if nothing else
how philosophers then, as now, found it hard to resist the easy notoriety
that comes from defending novel views, however implausible.

The length of this question has led me to omit parts of Crathorn's first
conclusion, including a long set of replies to some criticisms attributed to
an unnamed Franciscan (perhaps Walter Chatton). I have also omitted all
of §4 ("the views of others"), where Crathorn explores some of the
implications of that first conclusion.

On Crathorn's career and work, see Tachau (1995) and Pasnau (1998b).
For further discussion of the material translated below, see Pasnau (1997),
pp. 66–67, 89–100, 229–36.

On the Possibility of Infallible Knowledge

Questions on the First Book of Lombard's Sentences Q1

*Is evident knowledge of the articles of faith possible for a wayfarer by the power of
his natural light?*

It seems that it is not, because if an evident cognition of the articles of
faith were possible by the power of one's natural light, then the philosophers would have naturally cognized those articles by an evident cognition.
The consequent is false, therefore so is the antecedent.

On the contrary, a wayfarer who adheres to these articles through faith either does or does not have a sufficient motive for adhering to the articles. If he does, then it seems that he evidently cognizes that the articles are true. If not, then it seems that he believes fictitiously and out of a lightness of mind. Ecclesiasticus 19:4: *He who believes hastily is light of heart*, etc.

For the solution to the question to be seen, five things need to be shown.

- First, certain terms used in the question must be explained.
- Second, a number of distinctions must be drawn.
- Third, some conclusions must be proved, and certain arguments that could be made against those conclusions must be resolved.
- Fourth, the views of others must be presented.
- Fifth, I will reply to the question.

[1. Explanation of Terms]

Concerning the first, we must see what is implied by the term 'wayfarer,' second by 'evident knowledge,' third by 'article of faith,' fourth by 'the power of his natural light.'

1. Ockham says in his first question that "the intellect of a wayfarer is such that it cannot possibly have an intuitive knowledge of deity according to God's ordered power."[1] But that does not seem well said, since for those who are in purgatory an intuitive knowledge of God is not possible according to God's ordered power; nevertheless, they are not wayfarers. So it should be known that here 'wayfarer' is taken {68} metaphorically, in likeness to a living wayfarer. For just as a wayfarer by the work of his journey will merit being rewarded or punished insofar as he will have made his way well or badly, so human beings in this life will merit being rewarded or punished insofar as they have done good works or bad. Hence 'the way,' as far as it pertains to the question, means nothing other than the interaction and life of human beings. For according to Matthew 7:13–14 there are two ways:

Wide is the gate, and broad [is the way] that leads to destruction, and many there are who go in through it. How narrow is the gate, and straight is the way that leads to life, and few there are that enter through it.

---

[1] *Ordinatio* Prologue, Q1 (p. 5).

I say therefore that, dispositionally, a wayfarer is one who does not have an intuitive knowledge of God, in whose power it is to merit or demerit that knowledge. But, actually, a wayfarer is one who lacks such intuitive knowledge of God and freely merits or demerits it. This description excludes the blessed, who intuit God, the just in purgatory, who cannot demerit, and the obstinate damned, who cannot merit.

2. Ockham says,

Evident knowledge is knowledge or cognition of a true complex suited to be sufficiently caused either immediately or mediately by an incomplex knowledge of terms – in such a way, that is, that when an incomplex knowledge of any terms (whether they are the terms of one proposition or of another or of various propositions) in any intellect having such knowledge sufficiently causes or is suited to cause mediately or immediately knowledge of the complex, then that complex is evidently cognized [ibid.].

I argue against this in three ways. [First], not every evident knowledge is knowledge of a complex, etc.; therefore, etc. Therefore, Ockham badly describes evident knowledge in saying that it is knowledge of a complex, etc. The inference is clear, because a description and a definition ought to be said of everything contained under the description and definition. I prove the antecedent: The intuitive knowledge by which God is seen by someone blessed is evident knowledge, and yet is not caused or suited to be caused by the incomplex knowledge of any terms, nor is it the knowledge of any complex. Likewise, the intuitive knowledge of colors naturally possible for us is evident knowledge, and yet it is not the knowledge of any complex, nor is it caused or suited to be caused by any incomplex knowledge of the terms of any proposition.

Second, an incomplex knowledge of the terms of some proposition cannot be the sufficient cause of the knowledge of that same proposition. But he suggests the opposite. I prove the assumption: If the knowledge of some proposition could be sufficiently caused by an incomplex knowledge of the terms of that same proposition, {69} then this would especially be true of propositions known per se. But the knowledge of a proposition known per se (such as *Every whole is greater than its part* and the like) cannot be sufficiently caused by an incomplex knowledge of the terms of that proposition. Therefore, neither can the knowledge of other propositions be sufficiently caused by an incomplex knowledge of those same propositions. I prove the minor: An evident knowledge of the proposition *Every whole* etc. depends on an intuitive knowledge of the things signified by the terms 'whole' and 'part.' For if someone were never to have intuitively cognized any whole or any part, then no matter how often those terms 'whole' and 'part' were set before him, he would never evidently cognize the proposition *Every whole is greater than its part*. But it is obvious – on any way of using the term 'knowledge' – that knowledge of the terms 'whole' and 'part' is one thing, and knowledge of the things signified by those terms is another. Therefore, not every incomplex knowledge of those terms is the sufficient cause of evident knowledge of the proposition *Every whole* etc., much less do the terms of other propositions suffice to cause the evidentness of those propositions.

Moreover, although the terms of that proposition – since they are things of a sort, composed of parts sufficiently cognized by intuitive and abstractive knowledge (both as they are things and as they are signs) – can sufficiently cause the knowledge of the proposition *Every whole* etc., nevertheless an evident knowledge of that proposition is not *always* caused by an intuitive knowledge of those terms. Instead, it is [sometimes] caused by an intuitive knowledge of a house or some other whole, and then knowledge of that proposition depends on the knowledge of such a whole. Therefore, the evident knowledge of that proposition is not always sufficiently caused by an incomplex knowledge of the terms of that proposition.

Third, against Ockham's claim that an evident knowledge of a proposition can be caused mediately or immediately by the terms of another proposition or propositions, I argue as follows: An incomplex knowledge of the terms of a proposition is one thing, and a complex knowledge of a proposition is another. But an incomplex knowledge of the terms of a proposition can cause evident knowledge of another proposition only when mediated by knowledge of the proposition of which those are the terms. Therefore, an incomplex knowledge of the terms of a proposition cannot sufficiently and immediately cause the evident knowledge of another proposition. I prove the minor: It is impossible for an incomplex knowledge of the terms of the proposition *Every whole* etc., to cause sufficiently an evident knowledge of another proposition without having complex knowledge of the proposition *Every whole* etc.

So I hold that evident knowledge is knowledge that is manifest or clear and not obscure. For the term 'evident' implies the denial of obscurity. Hence all knowledge that is not obscure, whether complex or not, whether it is intuitive or abstract, is evident knowledge. Hence the most evident knowledge possible for us, {70} whether in this life or in heaven, is knowledge that is simple and intuitive, and neither abstract nor related to any complex. For evident knowledge of deity, by which the blessed intuit God, is as evident or more evident than any knowledge had by the blessed concerning any complex whatsoever. And the intuitive knowledge by which a wayfarer intuits whiteness is as evident as any knowledge of a proposition able to be caused by such intuitive knowledge.

3. By 'articles of faith' I mean nothing other than the complexes (and noncomplex things signified) that cannot be evidently cognized by any effects occurring in the common and natural course of things, but of which, nevertheless, explicit or implicit knowledge is necessary for a wayfarer in order to attain eternal beatitude. Complexes of this sort are:

> *God is three and one*
>
> *God is incarnate*
>
> *The dead will rise.*

4. By 'the power of a wayfarer's natural light,' I mean a wayfarer's natural cognitive power, not guided by a superinfused or supernatural disposition. Accordingly, the sense of the question is this: *Can a wayfarer, by his natural cognitive power alone, evidently cognize the articles of faith without the infusion of any supernatural disposition or light?*

[2. Distinctions]

1. To make what follows more clear, let me set forth a number of distinctions. The first concerns the term 'cognition' and similar terms. For sometimes 'cognition' supposits in a proposition for the thing by which the cognizer formally cognizes. Sometimes it supposits for that thing that is a likeness of the thing cognized, which likeness is in the cognizer and is immediately cognized. And sometimes 'cognition' supposits for the thing cognized that is outside the cognizer and is cognized mediately – mediated, that is, by its likeness, which it produces in the cognizer, or something that takes its place. Cognition taken in the first way can be called the *formal cognition*, and in the second way the *immediate material cognition*, inasmuch as something is called material not from the matter in which [it exists], but by speaking of the matter as the object, not the subject. Hence such a cognition can be called the immediate material (in the aforesaid way) cognition, or the immediate objective cognition, or the immediate object cognition. Cognition taken in the third way can be called the *mediated material cognition* or the *mediated objective cognition*.

So when someone sees a white wall, his vision {71} taken in the first way is his visual or seeing power. Taken in the second way, it is the likeness of the whiteness that is in the wall, which is generated in the perceiver by the whiteness that is seen. It is called the concept or the word of whiteness, and the generated vision. Taken in the third way, the vision is the whiteness itself of the wall that is seen.

2. The second distinction concerns 'cognitive' and similar terms. For some use that name and similar ones inasmuch as they imply efficient causality, so that something is called cognitive to the extent that it efficiently causes the cognition, just as the heat of fire is said to heat because it efficiently causes the heat that is (or can be) in the thing heated. Others use these terms insofar as they imply material causality, speaking of matter as the subject, so that something is called cognitive to the extent that it is the total or partial effect and the subject of cognition. All these people, or so it seems to me, use these terms badly.

Such terms can be taken in another way insofar as they imply formal causality, so that something is called cognitive to the extent that it is the sort of thing by which someone can formally cognize something and something can be cognized, just as we say that the heat in wood formally heats the wood. And if it were conserved by God apart from every subject, it could truly and properly be said to heat formally, because it could formally heat the wood if it were united to it or created under it. Thus it seems to me that all there is to the concept (*ratione*) of being cognitive is that it is the sort of thing by which some things are formally suited to cognize and some things to be cognized.

3. The third distinction concerns abstract terms. For some abstract terms are absolute, such as 'heat,' 'whiteness,' and the like. Some abstract terms are connotative, and these come in two kinds, since some such terms are imposed to supposit for things by connoting that those things are connected or united with other things, such as 'formal heating' and {72} 'formal illumination.' So when we say

Light is the formal illumination of air

the term 'illumination' taken in this way connotes that light is connected or united with the air itself, and the same should be said of other similar terms. Other abstract connotative terms are imposed so as to supposit for things that are united with others only as with an object° or in another way. These terms do not supposit for those things so as to signify them in a relationship to the subjects or the things with which they are united. Nor do these terms connote by their mode of signifying that those things are united in a subject or connected with other things, even if those things are in a subject and are connected to other things. Instead, these terms supposit for things by signifying and connoting that they are of another such as an object,° an end-term, an effect, or in another such way. This is how the terms 'heating' and 'whitening'° supposit, if taken actively.

Terms of the first kind (absolute abstract terms), even if they are imposed so as to supposit for things that are connected to other things, nevertheless do not by their mode of signifying note or connote that those things are connected to others. And so if such things are not connected to others but are separated from all others, still these terms could truly supposit for them and truly be predicated of subjects suppositing for them. Take, for instance, the term 'whiteness': Even if it signifies a thing united to another, nevertheless if that thing were separate from every other thing, it could still truly be said that that thing is whiteness. And the same should be said of the terms 'heat,' 'sweetness,' and the like.

Terms of the second mode or kind (those that signify things connected to others in such a way that they signify that those things are connected to others) do not supposit for those separate things nor do they hold true of terms suppositing for those things, when they are separated. Hence the term 'illumination,' if taken as suppositing for the thing by which something (air or some other thing) is formally illuminated, does not supposit for that thing or hold true of a term suppositing for it except for as long as [that thing] is united to what is formally illuminated. Thus if the light that is now in the air were separated from the air and from every other thing, then at that time it could not truly be said, speaking formally, that that light is the illumination of something – for the reason already given.

In the case of terms taken in the third way, for them to supposit for the things on which they are imposed, and to hold true of terms suppositing for those things, does not require that those things be in something as in a subject or be united with some other thing. It suffices that those things be either separate or connected and that the other things that {73} are connoted by such terms should be attached in the proper manner to the things for which those terms supposit. Take for instance the term 'heating.' If it is taken to supposit for the thing by which fire actively heats wood, then heating is nothing other than the fire's heat. This fire actively heats by its own heat inhering in it, but formally heats the wood by the heat produced by and inhering in the wood itself. And if, by the power of God, the heat were separated from the fire and were conserved separately, it truly would actively heat the wood attached to it, and then it could truly be said that the separate heat was the active heating of fire. Much the same would hold for the term 'heating' insofar as it supposits for the thing by which something is hot formally, if that thing (that is, the heat) were of such a nature that it could formally heat not only the thing connected to it and indistinct from it in location, but also something distant from it and at a distinct location.

And certainly the thing for which the term 'cognition' supposits is of such a nature, since a cognizer by that cognition formally cognizes not only a thing connected and united to him, but a thing spatially distant from him. I, for instance, when seeing the color of a wall (seeing formally, by means of my vision) see not only something connected to me, but also formally, by means of the same vision, the color of the wall, which is at a spatial distance from me. So if we pretend that my vision, by which I formally see the wall, is a quality superadded to my soul,[2] then if that quality were conserved without any subject, it could still be the formal vision of the color of the wall, just as before, if [the wall's color] were presented to it. Hence even if the term 'vision' were to signify a quality inhering in another, it still would not connote that that quality inheres in something. Nor would it connote that it is *of* something in the sense of being *of* a subject, but rather that it is *of* something, in the sense of being *of* an object. This is clear from the above.

[3. Conclusions]

Having laid out these things, I now set forth some conclusions:

1. Every human cognition taken in the first way [§2.1] is a cognitive or cognizing power.

2. No human cognition taken in the second way is a cognitive power.

3. A cognition taken in the second way is sometimes cognized when there is no cognized thing outside the cognizer of which it is a likeness.

4. Although in this life a human being sees external things only medi-

---

[2] Crathorn's first conclusion, in §3, will argue against this sort of account.

ated by species, nevertheless {74} a human being is naturally able to see an external thing [even] if such a thing does not affect the medium or the perceiver.

5. An object that is seen affects the perceiver.

6. An external object that is seen affects the medium.

7. An external thing seen through the medium of a mirror° affects the mirror.°[3]

8. A visible species is of the same species as the thing seen, of which it is a species.

9. In this life we cannot, through any sensation, have an evident and entirely infallible cognition of the truth of complexes of this sort: *That is a stone; That is bread; That is fire;* nor of others like them.

10. We cannot have an evident and infallible cognition that there is some sensible and sensed quality outside the one sensing.

11. We cannot evidently and infallibly cognize that a sensed quality is within the one sensing.

12. The one sensing can evidently and infallibly cognize that he sees whiteness.

13. Although the one sensing, from the mere fact that he senses, cannot evidently cognize that the form sensed by him was outside him and that a different one was within him, nevertheless he can evidently and infallibly cognize through certain other means of argument (*mediis*) that there was one form sensed by him outside him and another within him, and that complexes of this sort are true: *That is a stone; That is bread;* and the like.

14. Not every complex can be the object of error.

There are other conclusions, more than these here, as will be clear and is clear elsewhere.

[Conclusion 1]

For the first conclusion, I argue first as follows.

1. If a cognition or act of cognizing by which the cognizer cognizes formally were a quality superadded to a cognitive power, then it could by the power of God be put into a stone or into some other noncognitive

---

[3] Crathorn never takes up this conclusion (though see conclusion three, argument four against Crathorn's conclusion [p. 267]). Accordingly, what are here labeled conclusions eight through fourteen are numbered in the text as seven through thirteen. Crathorn also adds a fourteenth conclusion, not mentioned here.

thing. Therefore, when something formally cognizable comes to be close enough to such a quality, a stone having such a quality within itself would cognize that thing. Therefore, by the power of God it is somehow possible for something noncognitive to cognize, which implies a contradiction.

Now if someone says that being the formal perfection of a stone is incompatible with the nature of such a quality, and so such a quality cannot be put into a stone, I reply that this has no force. For the human nature that is in the divine person does not formally perfect that {75} divine person and yet it is united to that person and so exists within it. Therefore, notwithstanding the fact that such a quality could not formally perfect a stone, it could still be united to the stone and exist within it. Consequently the nature of a stone could be denominated by such a quality and its distinctive features.

2. When a thing is such formally because of something else, it can be such because of that thing when the only things posited are those and others necessarily required for its existence. But color is seen, formally, because of that vision or act of seeing. Therefore, if we posit only that color, the vision or act of seeing, and other things necessarily required for the existence of the color and the act of seeing, the color can be seen. But three things suffice for the existence of the color and that quality that is called the vision or act of seeing: the color, the vision, and God,° who conserves the vision and color. Therefore, color can be seen when the visual power does not exist. (I take these propositions in the composite sense always, so that these two will be consistent and jointly possible: Color is seen and there is no visual power.) But whenever something is seen, someone sees. Therefore, without any visual power existing, some-one sees and something is seen, which is impossible.

3. When something is such accidentally, through another, then that other is such essentially and through itself (*per se*). Fire, for example, is hot because of heat, which is a distinct thing from the fire, whereas heat is hot per se, since it is hot because of itself, essentially, and not because of anything else superadded. But if intellection is a quality superadded to the intellective power, then that power is intellective° through another or because of another. Therefore, that other (the intellection) is intellective because of itself, essentially, just as a light illuminates because of itself and whiteness whitens. Therefore, without any contradiction, the intellection can function even if the intellective power has been destroyed – just as, without any contradiction, a light can illuminate even if everything recep-tive of light has been destroyed, and white can whiten. Therefore, these

two could be consistent: A thing intellectively cognizes, and that thing has no intellective power. This is impossible.

[...] {80}

8. If sensory vision – speaking of vision as that by which the perceiver formally sees – were a quality superadded to the visual power, then it would be caused by the visible thing. The consequent is false, therefore so is the antecedent.

Proof that the consequent is false: The thing sensed that causes the vision is either a univocal or an equivocal agent. If it is *univocal*, then the form that is produced, which is called the vision, would be of the same kind (*speciei*) as the quality [that is sensed]. As a result, the vision by which the perceiver formally sees whiteness would itself be whiteness. From this it further follows that a white wall, because of its whiteness, would formally see, if something visible were presented to it. I prove this, because when two qualities are of the same kind, then if one thing is such because of one of those qualities, which it has within itself, then for the same reason the other thing will also be said to be such because of the like quality, if it has that quality within itself.

If it is said that the thing sensed that causes the vision is an *equivocal* agent with respect to the vision, and hence that the vision and the quality sensed are forms distinct in kind, then the vision is either a more or a less perfect form than the quality sensed. If it were *more perfect*, then the effect would be more perfect than its efficient cause. If the vision were a *less perfect* form, then the vision (the form by which the perceiver formally sees) would be a quality less perfect than whiteness and blackness, which does not seem true.

If someone says that the vision is not produced solely by the thing sensed, but by the thing sensed and the visual power, then by the same reasoning I could imagine that *no* [sensory] quality is caused solely by the extrinsic agent, but by its object *and* the receptive power. This contradicts Aristotle, in *De anima* II [426a8–12], and the Commentator, comment 140, where he says:

Just as acting and being acted on are in the thing acted on, not in the agent, so the action of the senses and sensibles is in the one sensing, because the sensibles are the active powers, whereas the senses are active and passive. But that which first senses is solely passive. This fact – that the sensibles are the active powers and the senses passive – is obscured by language, since many sensibles lack names, when considered as active, and the names of many of them are passive in form, of the names of active powers. For this reason, Aristotle said [426a12] that in the case of some senses each term is attributed to the action of the sensible [quality] and the being-acted-on (*passioni*) of the sense – for example, sounding and hearing. For sounding is the action of sound, hearing the being-acted-on of the sense of hearing. In other cases, one of them lacks a name – as in the case of sight, for example. For the being-acted-on of sight has a name, 'seeing' (though it is in the form of an active term), whereas the action of what is sensible, the color, lacks a name. {81}

Based on this comment, it seems that the Commentator's intent was that the visual power is solely passive, with respect to seeing, and that to see is not to produce anything actively. (I invoke the Commentator not because his words move me very much, but because some take his words as the truth.)

So I say that our cognitive power, with respect to our cognition, is not active. For cognition is spoken of either [as a species or] as that by which the cognizer formally cognizes and by which the thing cognized is formally cognized – just as we say that the heat in the wood heats the wood formally, and the wood is formally heated by the heat that is in it. So understood, cognition is nothing other than the cognitive power. And since nothing could cause or efficiently act on itself, it is certain that the cognitive power neither causes nor produces cognition when taken in this way. If, however, cognition is taken for the species of the sensible or cognizable thing, a species that is immediately sensed or cognized and is called the cognition, concept, word, likeness, and image of the sensible thing,° then our natural cognition (so understood) comes effectively, mediately or immediately, from sensible things. And with respect to cognition taken in this way, our cognitive power is not productive, effective, or active, but solely passive (assuming that such a cognition is received in the cognitive power).

Therefore, taking 'cognition' for that by which something is formally cognized, I hold the above conclusion that, in general, every cognition is a cognitive power, and that vision is the visual power, hearing the auditory power, and so on for the others.

[. . .] {83}

So I say in general that cognition is nothing other than the cognitive power, here speaking of cognition as that by which the cognizer formally cognizes, which is cognition in the most proper sense of the term. And because our cognitive powers are not distinct things superadded to our souls (as can be shown sufficiently from the above arguments), I grant that the soul of someone cognizing is cognition, the soul of someone seeing is vision, the soul of someone who hears is hearing, and the soul of someone knowing is knowledge. And I hold that all such similar conclusions are true.

$$[\ldots]\ \{92\}$$

In order to make the aforesaid conclusion more apparent, some arguments should now be set forth that seem to go against it.

First, it is impossible for the same thing to exist and not exist at the same time. But a cognitive power can exist without a cognition existing, and a human soul exists and can exist while it cognizes nothing. Therefore, it is impossible for a human cognitive power to be a cognition, and for a human soul to be a cognition.

Second, it is impossible for something that is not pure actuality, but has some degree of potentiality mixed in, to be its own actuality, because actuality is incompatible with potentiality. But a created cognitive power (*potentia*) is not pure actuality, because this holds only of God. Therefore, it is impossible for a created cognitive power to be its own cognition, because cognition is the *actuality* of a cognitive power.

Third, if cognition were the cognitive power, then since a cognitive power is the essence of the soul, a created cognition would be a subsistent thing. But such a thing can be no more than one, because it would be received in nothing and consequently could not be multiplied. In that case, the intellection of an angel would not be distinct from the intellection of God, which is subsistent intellection, nor from the intellection of another angel, and the same would follow for the intellection of a human being.

Fourth, within the same cognizer, one cognition is more perfect than another, and the same cognition can be intensified and diminished. But the same thing is not more perfect than itself. Also, the cognitive power in a human being and in an angel is not intensified and diminished, since in an angel it is the angel's substance, and in a human being the soul's essence, and these do not take on more and less. Therefore, cognition is not the cognitive power. {93}

Fifth, all of our cognition has its origin in the senses, according to

Posterior Analytics I [81b1–10]; but our cognitive power does not have its origin in the senses; therefore, our cognition is not our cognitive power.

Sixth, by study, through teaching and discovery, a human being acquires cognition. But one does not acquire a cognitive power. Therefore human cognition is not the cognitive power.

Seventh, blessed Augustine says, in *City of God* XI 10,

> A nature° is called simple when it is not the case that there is something for it to have or something it could lose, or that having is° one thing, and what it has is another – in the way that a vase has some liquid, a body has color, air has light or heat, or the soul has wisdom.

But if the soul is not wisdom, it is not knowledge or cognition. In many other places as well, in Augustine and in other doctors, one finds that the soul is not knowledge. But since one reply is enough for all such authorities, there is no need to recite them.

Eighth, if the visual power were vision, it would follow that the blind could see. The consequent is false. I prove the inference: The visual power is the soul itself. But however° blind someone becomes, though that person does not have vision he does not lose his soul; rather, he has the same soul that he had before.

Ninth, Anselm says in *The Incarnation of the Word* that

> those logicians of our time (or rather, logician-heretics) who suppose that universal substances are nothing but a spoken breath, and who claim not to understand color except as a body, nor the wisdom of a human being except as the soul, should be blown straight out of any debate over spiritual questions. [p. 10]

To the first of these it should be said that the major is true: It is impossible for the same thing to exist and not exist at the same time. But the same thing that is now a cognition of something can exist and remain even if it is not a cognition of something, and the same thing that is now not a cognition of something can later be a cognition of something. For heat existing in wood is the formal heating of the wood (that is, {94} it is that which formally heats the wood). Yet if by the power of God the wood were destroyed or moved somewhere else while the heat were preserved in the same place or another place at a distance from the wood, then that same heat (assuming it remains) would not be the heating of anything, but could once again become the heating of wood, if God were to create wood underneath that heat, or if the wood that was preserved were united to the heat in the way it was united to it before. In just the same way, a cognitive power that is not now a cognition of anything becomes the cognition of an object due to the proper linkage of object to power. Also, the power that once was a cognition is made not to be a cognition of that object, due to the object's destruction or withdrawal from the proper linkage to the power. Therefore, the major should be granted.

As for the minor, when it is said that "a cognitive power can exist without a cognition existing," it should be said that this minor must be distinguished, even when taken in the composite sense. For 'cognition' can supposit for something that is now a cognition, and then the sense is that these are consistent: This cognitive power exists, and nothing that's a cognition now exists then. In this sense, the minor is false. For if something is now a cognition, the cognitive power is now a cognition. So to hold that the cognitive power exists at some instant is to hold that, at that same instant, something exists that is now a cognition, even if at that instant it is not a cognition. Similarly, whenever one holds that God exists, one holds that what is now the first cause exists – even though to hold that God exists is not to hold that the first cause exists or that something is the first cause, since God existed before the creation of the world, but he was not a first cause.

In another way, 'cognition' can supposit for something that is or will be a cognition at the same instant or time at which the cognitive power is held to exist. In that case, the sense of the proposition is that these are consistent: A cognitive power exists and no thing exists that is a vision or cognition. In this sense, the minor is true, but from the above major and the minor so understood the above conclusion does not follow, nor does any conclusion similar to it in connotative terms. Similarly, it does not follow: It is impossible for any thing to exist and not exist at the same time; but God can exist while the first cause does not exist (that is, nothing exists that at that time is the first cause); therefore, God is not the first cause. Nor does it follow: This whiteness can exist while nothing exists that at that time is [its] likeness; therefore, this whiteness is not a likeness. Nor does it follow: This whiteness can exist while nothing exists that is the whitening of the bread; therefore, [this] whiteness is not the whitening of the bread.

To the second it should be said that strictly speaking nothing is the actuality of something unless it is distinct from that thing in reality, as its perfection. Less strictly, however, {95} something can be spoken of as its own actuality, for the reason that it is actualized because of itself. Nor does it follow – except in a qualified way – that every thing is simple. For a thing is unconditionally simple that is neither composed of more than one thing nor perfected in reality by something distinct from it.

And when it is said that "cognition is the actuality of a cognitive power," it should be replied that the term 'cognition' sometimes supposits for that by which a cognizer formally cognizes. So understood, cognition is the cognitive power itself. And so cognition taken in this way is not the actuality of a cognitive power – except in the way in which something can be called its own actuality. In another way, the term 'cognition' supposits for the word of the thing cognized, a mental word which is a quality existing subjectively in the mind or in some part of the brain, and which is immediately cognized. This quality is called a cognition not formally but manifestly (*relucenter*) or representatively, because the thing it is a word of manifests itself and is represented in that quality. Taken in this way, cognition is the actuality and perfection of a cognitive power or of some part of the brain, as will be said below [in conclusion two].

Against this one can argue as follows. The quality under discussion exists subjectively in the cognitive power. Therefore, it formally perfects that power and is the cognition and that by which the cognitive power cognizes. Therefore, it is the cognition formally. It should be replied that it is only accidentally true of that quality, considered as a cognition in the above way, that if° a thing is somehow cognized in its word, then that word exists in something subjectively. For if by the power of God it were conserved without any subject and were exposed to that cognitive power, it would then be the medium of cognizing for that power in the same way in which it was before, when it existed in that power subjectively. So the above inference does not hold: This quality is formally the perfection of a power and is a cognition; therefore, it is that by which the cognizer formally cognizes.

To the third it should be said that this argument proceeds from a false and puerile conceit, to the effect that it is not possible for there to be more than one thing of the same species unless they are received in something. Those who embrace this conceit say that such things can be distinguished only by distinguishing their subjects, which is false, because every thing – no matter what it is distinct from – is distinct because of itself. Accordingly, more than one form of the same species can exist in the same thing, in the same respect, as will be clear below when we discuss the intensification of forms [I *Sent.* Q17]. Also, all forms that are now in distinct subjects, even those of the same species, could be conserved by God, without any subject remaining among them, by means of nothing more than the intrinsic distinction that existed before when they were in {96} their subjects. So I marvel at how some men were so blinded as to have said that if God were to separate one whiteness from its subject, he could not separate any more, since that separate whiteness would contain within itself the perfection of every whiteness. For there is no more reason why one whiteness could be separated than that another could, nor does whiteness acquire any perfection by being separated.

So it should be said that if the term 'cognition' supposits for that by which the cognizer formally cognizes, then the cognition is the soul's essence and a subsistent thing. And when it is inferred that therefore there would be only one such thing, because it would be received in nothing, it should be said that the inference is nothing, and has no color at all.[4]

To the fourth it should be said that cognition taken in the above way is neither intensified nor diminished, no more than is the essence of the soul or the substance of an angel. But a human being and an angel can cognize the same thing more and less perfectly, both because they apprehend more of the thing cognized (if it is divisible and composite) and because they conceive within themselves a more perfect likeness or word of the thing cognized. This word or likeness can be intensified and diminished.

To the fifth it should be said that the Philosopher there uses 'cognition' not for that by which the cognizer formally cognizes, but for the intelligible species that are the likenesses and words of the things cognized. These likenesses and words do have their origin in things sensed, as was said above.

To the sixth one should reply in the same way as to the fifth.

To the seventh one should say that the blessed Augustine there uses 'knowledge' for the likenesses of things, not for that by which the knower formally knows. And the same should be said for all the authorities of the doctors that suggest human cognition is a thing distinct from the cognitive power: For by 'cognition' they mean the intelligible species caused by the things that are sensed. Thus blessed Thomas, in *Contra gentiles* I.56 [470], speaking of dispositional knowledge, says that

---

[4] In classical rhetoric, to give color to an argument was to construct it in a way that made it seem more plausible. The point here, then, is that the argument in question is not just false but also utterly unpersuasive.

A disposition is either a certain ability to receive the intelligible species by which one is actually made to have understanding, or it is an ordered collection of species.

But a disposition is not an ability of this sort, because our power is maximally capable when it comes to the cognition of some things – for instance, when it comes to the cognition of first principles and conclusions immediately cognized due to the knowledge (*notitia*) of first principles. So we are left with the second, that the disposition of knowledge is {97} an ordered collection of species or, more properly speaking, the species themselves collected and ordered in the proper way.

To the eighth it should be said that although the blind have the thing itself that would be vision, if the proper linkage of visible thing to perceiver occurred, the blind nevertheless cannot see, because that linkage of visible thing to perceiver does not occur.

[*To the ninth.*] The reply to the authority of Anselm° is clear from the above.

There are° two reasons why people do not accept the above conclusion. First is the mode in which terms like 'intellection,' 'vision,' and 'hearing' signify. For since such terms are relative in their signification, people believe that the things for which they supposit are likewise relative in being. This is false. The second reason for the error is that people believe an operation (in the active sense) is superadded to an active or operative power. And since the terms 'intellection,' 'vision,' 'hearing,' and the like have the same mode of signifying as do terms that supposit for true operations (in the active sense), they believed that the thing for which the° term 'intellection' supposits is a true operation (in the active sense) superadded to the power, and they believed that the power is truly operative and active in its intellection. This is false.

[*Conclusion 2*]

The second conclusion to be proved is that human cognition, taken in the second way – namely, the thing immediately cognized – is not a cognitive power or cognizer. I prove this as follows.

1. It is impossible for numerically one thing to be more than one thing, numerically distinct in species or genus. But a sensible species of whiteness and a species of blackness are more than one thing, specifically distinct, just as whiteness and blackness are. Likewise a species of color and a species

of heat differ in genus. Therefore, it is impossible for some human or other cognitive power to be a sensible species of whiteness, since if a cognitive power were a species of whiteness, it would for the same reason° be a species of blackness and a species of all sorts of heat and colors and a species of all sorts of sensed qualities. Therefore, the human cognitive power is not cognition, taken in the second way, because cognition taken in the second way is either the immediately cognized species of things that are cognizable or else certain conventional (*ad placitum*) signs of those things, as will be clear later [I *Sent.* Q2].

2. Every human cognition taken in the second way is caused by sensible things that are cognized – just as vision [is caused] by a quality that is seen. But no human cognitive power {98} is caused by such sensible things. Therefore, no human cognitive power is a human cognition, taken in the second way. And since that conclusion is obvious, there is no need to introduce additional arguments for it.

[*Conclusion 3*]

The third conclusion is that the aforesaid likeness existing within the cognizer, which is the word and natural likeness of a sensible quality existing outside the cognizer, is sometimes cognized and sensed when the thing of which it is a likeness is not intuitively cognized or sensed. I prove this as follows.

1. At the circular motion of a stick on fire at one end, a circle or circular color is seen when no such circle exists outside the perceiver. Therefore, the circle seen is within the soul or the head of the perceiver.[5]

It will perhaps be said in reply to this that when such a stick on fire at one end is spun around in a circle, no color in the shape of a circle is seen. Rather, it only appears to the one seeing the fire being spun around in a circle that he sees color in the shape of a circle. He sees, however, no such color.

But this is not rightly said, because unless the one seeing that fire spun around in a circle were to see a circular color existing within himself or externally, he would never judge that he sees a circular color. And so it should be said that the color of the part of the stick on fire, existing in

---

[5] This and the following example are taken from Peter Aureol. See Translation 9 (p. 223), where Ockham quotes verbatim from Aureol's discussion of these cases. Compare Crathorn's following analysis with Ockham's very different analysis (pp. 232–33).

one place, causes its likeness within the head of the perceiver, and that the same color of the part of the stick on fire, existing in another place, causes another quality – continuous with the prior quality or likeness – within the head of the perceiver, and that existing in a third place it causes a third likeness continuous with the second, and that existing in turn in this way in a fourth place it causes a fourth likeness. In this way, the color of the part of the spinning stick on fire generates within the head of the perceiver many colors and its many likenesses, from whose continuity to each other results one circular color.

Now each part of that circular color caused by the color of the part of the stick on fire, in every place that part existed during the time that revolution lasted, remains within the head of the perceiver for the whole duration of that time. Since this is the likeness and medium for seeing the color of the part of the stick on fire, it appears to the perceiver that that color exists simultaneously at each place on the revolution. For the first quality created by the color at the beginning of the revolution remains for the entire duration of the revolution and is seen immediately by the one seeing the color. Thus it appears to him for the entire duration of the revolution that that color exists at the same place at which it existed when it created that first quality, which is its likeness – and the same is so for the second, third, fourth, and all the other likenesses. Hence if God were to preserve in your head for a whole year that circular color or another like it while no color existed {99} externally, it would appear to you seeing that circular shape that you were seeing for the whole year a flaming circle and the color of a circular shape existing outside you – when nevertheless there was no such thing.

Therefore, it should be said that when a stick whose end is on fire is moved in the aforesaid way a circular quality is generated in the head of the perceiver. This quality is immediately seen and is the likeness of a circle on fire, but it is not a circle on fire. Hence the perceiver in the aforesaid case sees no circle on fire, but only the likeness of one. And the same should be said of a falling raindrop, which appears to be of a length that it cannot be.[6]

2. I argue as follows: Someone seeing the neck of a pigeon can see distinct colors and judge that the pigeon's neck is various colors, if the neck is presented to him from various directions. But in this case the perceiver does not see those different colors existing outside him on the

---

[6] This example comes from Avicenna, *Liber de anima* I 5 (p. 88), quoted in note 78 to Translation 1.

pigeon's neck, but only the colors' likenesses existing within his own head. Therefore, the likenesses of colors are sometimes seen when the external colors of which they are likenesses are not seen.

3. Someone seeing a thing through the medium of a broken mirror or several different mirrors will see as many images and likenesses of that thing as there are mirrors or parts of the broken mirror. But there are not that many images of the same thing outside the perceiver. Therefore, sometimes a number of things are seen that exist within the perceiver and to which there is not a corresponding number outside the perceiver.

4. If there were a moving hoop painted in many different kinds of colors, then someone seeing the moving hoop will see a mixed color and it will appear to the perceiver that the hoop is just one color. The reason for this is that the quality caused within the head of the perceiver by the color of one part remains within that part until the quality and likeness of a second, a third, and a fourth part of the hoop are caused within that same part of the head. So from the likenesses of distinct colors caused within the same head, one mixed quality results which is immediately seen. It is by means of that quality that one sees such a moving body painted in many kinds of colors, and as a result it appears that this moving body has a similar color, and that it is just one color. Hence the perceiver in this case sees one color that is not outside him but is its likeness remaining within him. {100}

5. Many experienced this year, when the eclipse of the sun occurred (namely, on the 17th Kalends of August, on the vigil of blessed Alexius),[7] that those who looked at the sun and then turned to look at green grass saw the color scarlet, and it appeared to them that the grass had that same color. The same appeared with the clouds. But it is certain that neither the clouds nor the grass had such a color, nor was such a color outside the perceiver. Therefore, that color seen was within the perceiver. I say, therefore, that the species of sensible qualities that are outside the perceiver are frequently seen when the quality of which they are species is not seen (or when the qualities of which they are species are not seen).

Against this conclusion it can be argued as follows. [*First*], if a species generated by a sensible quality could remain and be seen in the absence of a sensible quality for one length of time, so for the same reason for another, and just as it could be seen for a short time, so for a long time. In this

---

[7] I.e., July 16th, 1330.

way, a human being could for a day or a year naturally see and hear without any external visible or audible thing being presented to him. But we don't experience this.

Second, if someone sees a stick with its end on fire being spun around in a circle and judges that he is seeing a flaming circle because in his brain there is such a circular form, which is the likeness of the flaming circle, then for the same reason if he were to judge that he sees a flaming circle of a certain quantity, a circular form of equal quantity would have to exist within his head. This is not possible, because such a flaming body could be moved circularly in such a way that it would appear to the perceiver that he sees a flaming circle whose diameter is greater than the diameter of his head. And then it would follow that in the perceiver's head there would be a circular quantity some of whose parts would be spread out beyond any of the parts of his head, since its diameter would be greater than his head's diameter.

Third, a sensible species is caused by the sensible or sensed quality of which it is a likeness. Therefore, if someone seeing the neck of a pigeon from different directions were to see different kinds of sensible species, then those sensible species would have to be caused by various different kinds of colors existing on the pigeon's neck. Therefore, such colors exist on the pigeon's neck in reality, not just in appearance.

Fourth, contrary to what was said in the third argument about a broken mirror, a mirror is somehow the cause of vision when taken in the second way (that is, the cause of a visible species), and a mirror is somehow the cause of the multiplication {101} of the visible or seen species existing within the perceiver. But there is no way to account for how a mirror would be the cause of vision taken in this second way unless the object presented to the mirror first affects the mirror by causing within it its likeness, and then by means of this likeness, the informed mirror causes within the perceiver a likeness of the thing presented. Therefore, an image of the thing presented to the mirror really exists within the mirror.

Fifth, everything that is seen is either light or color. But the fourth argument assumes that the hoop painted in many different kinds of colors is seen. Therefore, the painted hoop moving in this way is light or color. But the consequent is false. Therefore, that fourth argument assumes something false.

Sixth, someone seeing the moving hoop sees either some color of the hoop or none. If he sees no color of the hoop, then he does not see the hoop, because a body is seen only if its color is seen. If he sees some color that is on the hoop, and he doesn't see one of the four different kinds of colors that are on the hoop, then he sees some other color. But the only one he would see is the one by which it appears to him that the hoop is colored. Therefore, that intermediary color is not only in the perceiver, but on the hoop that is seen.

Seventh, if a human being could see without seeing some color outside of himself of which it is a likeness, then that vision would be either intuitive and intuiting or abstractive and abstracting. If intuitive, then it follows that something could be seen and nevertheless not exist or be present to the cognitive power itself – which does not seem true. Nor can it be called abstractive, since every sensory vision seems to be intuitive or intuiting.

To the first it should be said that some things receive a quality well and retain it badly. This is clear in the case of corporeal things. For air receives heat easily and retains it badly, and so if the thing that heats it is absent or removed, [the air] for a while retains the heat, but not for very long. So it does not follow that what a thing retains for a short time, it retains always or for a long time. Thus although a sensible species received in the eye of the perceiver could naturally remain and be seen for a short time in the absence of the sensible quality by which it was impressed on the eye, it does not follow that it could remain always or for a long time. And so the inference should be denied.

To the second it should be said that for the perceiver to judge that he sees some color, or for it to appear to him that he sees some color located outside him, it is required that a likeness of such a color be within him. But for it to appear to him that he sees a color of such a quantity it is not required that there be within him a likeness or a species of the color of equal quantity. The reason for this is that someone seeing some color sees the species and {102} the color under the same angle. So the color outside the perceiver and the color's species within the perceiver appear to him to be of the same quantity. For it is a principle in the theory of perspective that things will appear equal to a perceiver that are seen under equal angles. Therefore, the same reason holds for things seen under the very same angle, such as the color outside the perceiver and the color's species within him. But a sensible species that remains in the perceiver after the quantity sensed before is removed is seen under the same angle under which that quantity sensed before was seen. For this reason, then, it appears to the perceiver that that quantity, which is a species and likeness of the quantity° sensed before, has just the quantity that the quantity sensed before appeared to have. And so for it to appear to the perceiver that he sees a flaming circle of such a quantity, there need not be within him a likeness of equal quantity. For the circular shape in the head of the perceiver is seen under the same angle as is the quantity that appears to be seen (if it really were seen).

To the third it should be said that such feathers on a pigeon have of themselves, in their different parts, various different kinds of colors. These colors, depending on differences in position, affect the eye° in various ways and cause likenesses of various colors. For some of the colors of the various parts act more strongly from one direction and more weakly from another. So as a result of the different actions of the colors that are in those feathers at different positions, various and distinct intermediate colors are caused within the perceiver, via light, and are immediately seen. As a result, it appears that the external things present have similar colors.[8]

[Conclusion 4]

The fourth principal conclusion is that although a human being in this life sees color only through a species, nevertheless a human being could naturally see a color (e.g., the whiteness in a wall or something else of that sort) even if such an object (e.g., the whiteness in a wall) did not naturally affect the medium or the eye of the perceiver.° That is, a human being could see whiteness without a species, assuming there is no impediment in the eyes or elsewhere. Proof:

1. When an external thing (one that is outside the perceiver) is seen by the perceiver mediated by its species, the vision of the species and of that of which it is a species are numerically the same thing. For example, when someone sees whiteness mediated by a species, he sees in the same vision the species immediately and the whiteness mediately, since the species mediates. But if the whiteness were corrupted or removed while the already seen species of whiteness were preserved within the perceiver and presented to the visual power as before, then that species would still be seen. So, as is clear from the third conclusion, a human being often sees such {103} a species without seeing any other thing outside him of which

---

[8] There is no reply to the other arguments.

that is a species or likeness. Therefore, for the same reason, if the species were corrupted or finished or removed, still the whiteness could be seen and would be seen.

This argument and inference holds due to the following premise: When two things are seen in numerically one vision and each is seen naturally, then for whatever reason one could be seen without a medium, so too could the other. But the species and the whiteness of which it is a species are naturally seen in a single vision. Therefore, if the species could be seen without the whiteness, then for the same reason it could be said that the whiteness is seen without the species. At the least, there is no contradiction in saying this.

2. For whiteness to be seen, the species of an external whiteness does not necessarily cooperate as either an efficient cause, a material cause, a formal cause, or a final cause. Therefore, etc. (This is defended in the *reportatio*.)°

3. Although a visible color affects the surrounding air, nevertheless it does not seem true that it affects the air for an unlimited distance – otherwise one small amount of whiteness would affect an infinite amount of air. Therefore, let a be the terminus of change: that part of the air beyond which the visible color does not affect the air. In this part let there be an animal seeing the aforesaid color. And suppose that God creates another animal of more acute sight or having a more perfect visual power so that it exceeds in perfection by two or three times the visual power of the animal that, existing at a, sees the aforesaid color. Let that created animal be b. Therefore b, located beyond a, either can or cannot see the color that is seen by the animal existing at a. If it is said that it can, then animal b sees a color of which it has no species within itself, since the assumption is that the color seen does not affect the air beyond a. But we are supposing that animal b is *beyond a;* therefore, the color seen causes no likeness or species in animal b. (I assume in this argument that the color seen is not moved toward a, but remains unaffected. For if the color were to approach a, it could affect the air beyond a.)

If it is said that created animal b, located beyond a, cannot see that color, then on the contrary: Created animal b is more perfect in sight or visual power than is the animal that exists at a and sees the aforesaid color. Therefore, animal b can see the same color at a greater {104} distance. Therefore, although it is located beyond a, it will still see the same color.

This is why we say of the lynx that there were many walls between it and the flesh that it saw.[9] But it does not seem true that the color of the flesh it saw would have made an impression on all those walls by impressing its likeness on each and every part of each wall. Therefore, it seems that that beast sees the color of the flesh without receiving in itself any species of that color. So I say that if an illuminated external color is presented to the visual power at the proper distance, without any action in the medium or the perceiver, it could be seen while no other thing is seen or received in the perceiver. And the same should be understood of other sensible things.

Against this conclusion it is argued as follows. *First*, if a human being could see an external color without an intermediary visible species, then it would have been pointless for the author of nature to order that the external color affect the medium and the perceiver. For what can be done through fewer things, etc. Therefore, sensible species would be superfluous.[10]

Second, if this conclusion were true, then something could be made in a vacuum and be seen, which is contrary to the Philosopher in II *De anima*, comment 74 [419a10–21], where he refutes Democritus's assertion that something could be seen in a vacuum.

Third, if this conclusion were true, then someone not seeing could see without any change occurring on the part of the one seeing, but only on the part of the cognized object. This does not seem true.

Fourth, something indivisible could then be seen, since for something to be seen nothing more is required – per se, essentially, and intrinsically – than a visual power and the object's being directly presented to the power at a certain distance. This can occur with something indivisible.

Fifth, the visual power would then not be passive, which is contrary to the Philosopher in *De anima* II [418a1–6]) and to the Commentator, in comment 52.[11]

To the first it should be said that sensible species, caused in the perceiver by sensible things, are not superfluous, even though sensible qualities can actually be sensed without them. For sensory animals need not only to

---

[9] The lynx was traditionally thought to have exceptional eyesight.

[10] William Ockham accepted every step of this argument and so concluded that sensible species and species in medio are superfluous and should not be posited to exist. See *Reportatio* II.12–13 and III.2.

[11] See Conclusion 1 arg. 8 (pp. 256–57).

sense in actuality things that have been naturally presented to them in the past, but they need to be naturally able {105} to cognize or imagine absent things and to remember and recall sensible things once they are gone. This could happen only through the reception of such species.

To the second it should be said that a luminous body or light could be seen in a vacuum. Color too, if it were to have light adjoined to it, could be seen, even if it were separated from the visual power solely by a vacuum. But the Philosopher does not sufficiently disprove Democritus. For he assumes in his argument that a thing could be sensed only through the impression of species on the medium and on the perceiver. This is not true, because although it is so in fact, nevertheless it could be otherwise, as was said above.

The Philosopher assumes something else that is not true: That light is necessary for color to be seen only with respect to the medium, because color cannot affect a medium that is not illuminated. This assumption does not seem true. For however much the medium is illuminated, color is seen only if light is united to the color itself. Hence for color to be seen, light is necessary with respect to the object. This seems clear from the experience of things that are seen only at night when the medium is not illuminated – as with a rotten oak, the bones of certain fish, and certain worms. Therefore, because the Philosopher in this passage assumes many things that are neither known per se, nor demonstrated, nor appear true, there is no need to adhere to what he says there.

To the third it should be said that the argument's conclusion is true, because for a [visual] power that is not seeing to be made seeing it would suffice in the imagined case that a change occur on the part of the object alone.

To the fourth it should be said that more is required than the argument admits. For it is required that an object thus presented to the power be visible to such a power, which is not true of the indivisible with respect to our visual power. Nevertheless I believe that God could create a visual power that would distinctly see something indivisible, if it were presented to it at just the right distance. But that is uncertain, and it is likewise uncertain whether or not some such thing has been produced by God. {106}

To the fifth it should be said that in such a case the power would passively receive nothing from that object. Nevertheless it would be passive, because it could be affected by that object at another time, or by another object.

[Conclusion 5]

The fifth conclusion is that the object seen affects the perceiver. Proof:

1. Frequently, after someone has seen an external object, when the object is removed, it appears to the perceiver that he still sees the external thing seen before. Therefore, he sees something similar, which is in him and which was not there before he saw the object. But nothing can reasonably be assigned as the efficient cause of the thing that is seen except for the external thing seen before. Therefore, the external thing seen before really affects the perceiver.

2. Anyone can experience within himself that an excessive sensible object harms the perceiver, which would not happen if the external sensible quality were not impressing something on the perceiver.

Also, this conclusion matches the intent of the Philosopher and the Commentator, in *De anima* II [417a14–21], and of blessed Augustine in *De trinitate* XII [XI.ii.5, iv.7], where he says that these cooperate in something's being sensed: someone sensing, an external thing sensed, a species impressed on the sense from the thing sensed, and a combining will.

Against this conclusion it is argued as follows. *First*, according to the Philosopher and the Commentator, in *De anima* II [424a8–10], comment 104, if sight were to have actual color, it would not receive colors. But the likeness of a color seems to be a color. Therefore, if the likeness of the color seen were in the eye, that eye would not receive the likenesses of other colors, and so a human being, after having seen one color through one eye, could not through that same eye receive the likeness of another color. But there is no more reason why one external color impresses its likeness on the eye of the perceiver than that another does. Therefore, since not every color can make an impression, it follows that none can do so.

Second, mover and moved coincide spatially, but the color seen does not coincide spatially with the perceiver, but is at a spatial distance from him. Therefore, it does not move the eye of the perceiver. {107}

Third, someone can see a great portion of the sky all at the same time. Therefore, if the likeness of the thing were in the eye of the perceiver, each part of that likeness would correspond to each part of the thing seen. But that such a likeness could be placed in an eye so small does not seem reasonable.

To the first it should be said that as long as such a likeness remains in some part of the eye, the perceiver can through that same part see only that likeness and the thing of which it is a likeness. Nevertheless the eye, with respect to that same part, can be perfected by further likenesses. This is clear from the fact that the eye, with respect to the same part, can be affected more and less perfectly as regards the same object at different times. Therefore, the form impressed on the eye at one time is more perfect than the form impressed on it at another time. And since those two forms were of the same species, it is necessary that the more perfect form contain in itself more of the same character than the imperfect form contains, as will be clear when we consider the intensification of forms [I *Sent.* Q17].

Also, the same part of the eye, informed by the likeness of whiteness, can, while that remains, be perfected by the likeness of another color. Then from those likenesses an intermediate likeness would result, which would be directly seen (as is clear from the third conclusion proved above). But the claim of the Philosopher, which for some is a great principle, is not true. For air that is actually illuminated can be illuminated, and something actually hot can be heated, and something wet made wet, and something colored made colored. If his claim is to have any truth, it should be understood in this way: If a sense were to have in itself some color, it would not receive in itself other colors so as through such a reception to see other colors distinctly. Or in this way: If a sense were to have in itself some color to the ultimate degree of perfection, it could not receive other colors.

To the second it should be said that the first mover and first moved coincide – that is, they touch one other. But the thing first moved or affected by a color seen is not the eye of the perceiver, but the mediating air, as the Philosopher says in *De anima* II [419a9–21] and *Physics* VII [245a2–8]. {108}

To the third it should be said that the various parts of that likeness that is in the eye do not correspond to every part of the external thing that is seen. Otherwise there would be as many parts in the likeness as there are in the thing seen, however great, which is false. This will be clear when we ask whether the continuum is infinitely divisible [I *Sent.* Q3 concl. 6].

[*Conclusion 6*]

The sixth conclusion is that the external object affects the medium between the perceiver and the object, and does not immediately affect the perceiver. I prove this by a single line of argument: If an external color were to affect the perceiver without affecting the medium, then for any given distance that visible color could affect someone capable of seeing. The consequent is false, therefore so is the antecedent.

Against this conclusion and rationale it is argued,[12] *first*, that the sun causes light in lower parts of the air without illuminating every higher part. Therefore, if the illuminating sun is at a distance from every lower part of the illuminated air, it is clear that not every alterant is immediately adjoined in space with the thing altered. Rather, some alterant can be at a spatial distance from something else, via many intermediaries, and can immediately alter it.

Second, the part of the air in this building that is directly exposed to the illuminating sun is more intensely illuminated than is the [resultant] sunbeam. Therefore, let *a* be one part of the intense light or sunbeam directed into the middle of the building. Light *a* is caused immediately by either the sun or some light near *a*. If the first, then the desired conclusion follows – namely, that something is immediately altered by the alterant, the sun, and nevertheless is at a spatial distance from it (its being that part of the air where *a* is). If the second, namely that light *a* is caused by light near *a*, then let that causing light be *b*. That light *b* is uniformly related to the part of the air where *a* is, and to other parts of the air that are not directly exposed to the sun. For just as the part of air where *a* is is directly exposed to that light *b* on one side, so another part of the air is directly exposed to *b* on another side. Now we can suppose that parts other than the part that is informed° by light *a* are disposed to receive light just as much as is that part where *a* is, given that they are at an equal distance from *b* and are uniformly exposed to it. It then follows that light *b* would not cause a more intense light in one such part than in another, but would at every place equally illuminate parts at an equal distance from it and equally disposed to receive light. It is plain to the senses that this is false.
{109}

---

[12] Many of the following arguments are drawn from William Ockham, *Reportatio* Bk. III d.2 and *Ordinatio* d.37.

Third, if two candles with different positions are exposed to one hole in a wall or a table, they will cause rays extending from a distinct part of the hole toward separate and opposite locations. Therefore, those rays of light are caused not by the light existing in the hole, but immediately by those candles. For this reason, if the candles were removed and the light in question were preserved in the hole, those distinct rays would not be caused.

Fourth, a magnet attracts iron from which it is spatially distant. Therefore, the proximate mover and moved do not always spatially coincide.

Fifth, in the case of a stone put in motion by being thrown, there seems to be no mover but the first, the one who throws the stone, who is spatially distant from that stone.

Sixth, Avicenna says that the proposition

> *Mover and moved coincide*

was taken by the Peripatetics not as necessary, but merely as plausible (*probabilis*). For it can happen that something at a great spatial distance moves something else. Indeed, as he says, this can happen through will and imagination alone, so that someone willing the death of someone and intently imagining it can, solely by imagining, bring about his death and kill him. He himself says this about fascination: For in this way it can happen that the eye of the fascinator drives a camel into a pit.[13]

Seventh, according to the Philosopher in *De caelo et mundo* I [270a12–b4], celestial bodies are unalterable. But corruptible things like us and the things around us are somehow affected by the higher celestial bodies. Therefore, the higher celestial bodies affect the elements and things generated by the elements without affecting the lower celestial bodies. Therefore, something moving and altering naturally affects and alters something from which it is distant, without affecting the medium.

Eighth, if an object that is sensed were to affect the medium, then contrary forms would coexist in the same part of the medium. For let it be posited that one wall of a house is white and another black, and each affects the entire medium. Therefore, in each part of the medium there is a species of whiteness and of blackness. But just as whiteness and blackness are contrary forms, so (as it seems) the species of whiteness and blackness

---

[13] Avicenna, *Liber de anima* IV.4 (pp. 64–65).

are contraries. {110} Therefore, in the same part of the medium there are distinct contrary forms, which seems impossible.

Ninth, if in each part of the medium there are species of whiteness and blackness (which one has to assume if [the colors] are present, since each will affect the entire medium), it would follow that a human being would at one time no more see whiteness than blackness, nor would a species of whiteness be more impressed on him than a species of blackness. This is false and contrary to experience. I prove the inference, because the alteration of the perceiver is brought about through the alteration of the medium. Therefore, since each part of the medium is really altered, affected, and informed by a species of whiteness and a species of blackness,° through such a medium (or such a part of the medium) a species of whiteness would no more be impressed on the perceiver (or someone capable of seeing) than would a species of blackness.

Tenth, if a color were to affect the medium, then so would each part of the color. The inference is clear. From this it follows that in each part of the medium there is a species of the whole and of a part, and so the whole is equal to a part. These results seem paradoxical (*insolubilia*).

To the first, one should say that the sun illuminates every lower part of the air only if it first (in natural or temporal order) illuminates with some amount of light the higher parts and those more immediate to it. For not every light is visible to us. Hence sometimes, even in the lower parts of the air, light exists in some minimal amount and is not to our power visible.

Others reply to this argument by distinguishing between immediate causes: One cause is immediate in location whereas another is immediate not in that way but in some other way they don't explain. Perhaps it could be said that this is immediacy in effect. But this reply has no force. It also does not accord with the Philosopher's intent, because he intends mover and moved to coincide spatially so that nothing intervenes locally between what moves and what is proximately moved. For as is stated in *De generatione* I [322b25–26], what acts and what is acted on must touch one another. Moreover, if the mover did not have to be immediately adjoined in location with what is moved, then (as was said above [concl. 4]) the mover could immediately move and alter something at a spatial distance from it without altering the medium. This is [in fact] false, and so one should reply as above.

To the second, one should say that light *a* – that is, that part of the sunbeam that comes into the middle of the building – is not immediately caused by the sun. And if light *a* is meant to be some light divisible along all dimensions, then it is also not {111} immediately caused in its whole self by some one light in between *a* and the sun. For if so then that light would immediately cause a light spatially distant from itself, since some part of *a* is spatially distant from every light between *a* and the sun. So we ought to imagine that the last part of the luminous sunbeam (namely, the part most distant from the sun, a part that is indivisible in depth) is caused by the part totally and immediately next to it, and this part too is indivisible in depth. That second part is caused by a third, similar part, up to the first part of the sunbeam, which is in the hole or window where the sunbeam begins. But that first part of the sunbeam is not entirely caused by another part of the light in the air directly between it and the sun. For if so then the effect would exceed its total and immediate cause, since the first part of the sunbeam is a more intense light° than that part of the light that is immediately adjoined in the direction of the sun. Rather, that first part of the sunbeam is caused partially by sidelong lights adjoined to parts of the body exposed to the sun, parts that are continuous or contiguous with the hole in which the sunbeam begins.

Consider as well that the parts of the air contiguous with the parts of the body exposed to the sun are more intensely illuminated than other parts of the air that are at a distance from the body exposed to the sun. How this happens° can be understood as follows. If we suppose that all the parts of the air in between the earth's surface and the sun are equally disposed to receive light, then the first part of the air toward the sun is illuminated by the sun to some degree, and this illuminated part illuminates the next nearest part to an equal or lesser degree, and that one a third, and so on descending to the final part of the air, which is adjoined to the earth's surface or to the parts of a body in between the earth and the sun and exposed to the sun. The light of that last part is not so imperfect as not to be suited to cause something like it. But since the parts of the opaque body to which it is contiguous or near are not receptive of light or else receive it with difficulty, this light is conserved in the same part of the diaphanous medium on which it is first impressed. (For according to Albert, commenting on *De anima* II [tract. 3 ch. 7], a limited diaphanous medium conserves the light impressed on it better than one that is unlimited.) Likewise, [this light] is impressed on that same part of the air (the part contiguous to the part of the body {112} exposed to the sun in that light), due mediately to the sun and immediately to the light near the air. From this [new impression] and° the light that had already been impressed and conserved, a light results in this same part of the air that is more intense than was the light first impressed on the same part of that air. But such a light, caused in that part of the air in the way explained above, affects the air toward the sun to a greater or lesser distance, according to whether the first light was of a greater or lesser strength.

It should also be known that every active and alterative power acting on the parts of a nearby passive thing acts more strongly on those parts that are directly exposed to it than on those parts that are exposed to it sideways. Also, the first form impressed by the first acting form on the part that is immediately and directly exposed to it affects that part more strongly than it affects the part that is obliquely and sideways exposed to it and to the first acting form.

Therefore, it should be said in reply to the form of this second argument that light *a* is not caused immediately by the sun. Rather, it is caused – either totally or partially – by a light immediately adjoined to it, a light that lies in between light *a* and the sun. It can also happen that some part of *a* is caused immediately by some light immediately adjoined to it on the side where the sunbeam ends. As is clear from the above, this can happen if that sunbeam is partially caused by the light's reflexive action, due to an obstacle or body exposed to the sun.

The argument claims that some parts of the air are (i) equally disposed [to receive light], compared with the part where light *a* is, and (ii) are just as close to that light that is between *a* and the sun and that immediately causes *a* (either totally or partially), and (iii) are just as directly exposed to it in its own location as *a* is. This clearly holds for the parts of the air on each side. Therefore, light *b* (posited as an immediate cause of *a*, either totally or partially) would equally illuminate these parts and the part where *a* is. To this claim, it should be replied that the conclusion doesn't follow, and that the reason has been explained above. For, by nature, an alterative form (or another similarly productive form) acting on a passive part exposed to it at the same place where it itself is exposed to its productive cause, acts more strongly on this part than on parts exposed to it sideways – unless something else impedes its action.

To the third, it should be said that those rays extending toward different locations from a distinct part of the hole are caused by the candles, mediated by distinct lights within the hole that are caused by the candles. These lights more strongly affect the parts of the air that are directly exposed to them and to the candles than they affect other parts of the air located differently.

To the fourth, it should be said that a magnet affects the medium before it affects the iron, even though the form impressed on the intermediary air is not as perfect as the form impressed on the magnet. {113}

To the fifth, it should be said that a thrown stone, when it is thrown or separated from the thrower, is moved by a form that was impressed on it by the thrower when that° stone was contiguous either to the thrower or to something else through which such a form was impressed on it. Or, it should be said that it is moved by *part* of that form. I say the latter because the entire form caused in the thrown stone does not remain for the entire movement of the throw, but diminishes and finally ceases entirely. At that point the stone ceases to move (assuming its motion is forced), unless perhaps it continues a bit more through the movement of parts of the air continuous with the stone.

To the sixth, it should be said that Avicenna was of the view that mover and moved need not coincide, wanting with this to preserve and maintain the view that separate intelligences could move human souls apart from moving intervening bodies. He offered fascination as the cause of this. But in this matter Avicenna's view shouldn't be upheld, not because he contradicted Aristotle, but because he contradicted the truth. And his claim that the eye of the fascinator drives a camel into a pit can be denied, because a camel's fall can occur for other reasons. Even if this is not granted, it still need not be the case, based on what he says, that the proximate mover and moved do not coincide.

To the seventh, it should be said that the last thing altered, and everything in between that is altered or alters, does not have to be altered by an alteration of the same species. The sun, for example, in heating the parts of the lower air does not heat the parts of the higher air, but illuminates them. Hence the alteration of the lower and the alteration of the higher are of two different species. And if it is said that the Philosopher says in *De caelo et mundo* I [270a12–b4] that celestial bodies are unalterable, it should be replied that he doesn't prove this. But if his claim has to come out true, it has to be understood to apply not to all alteration, but to alteration that leads as an intermediary toward corruption. For, as is commonly asserted, the body of the moon is illuminated by the sun.

To the eighth, it should be said that in the case posited it is necessary to grant that there are contrary forms in each part of the medium: For just as whiteness and blackness are contraries, so too are their species, which are in each part of the medium. So just as in the case of a mixed color that results from whiteness and blackness there really is whiteness and blackness, since such a mixed color is nothing other than whiteness and blackness (assuming {114} every part of it is colored), so it should be said that in each part of the air there is really a species of whiteness and, in that same part, a species of blackness.

On the contrary, every part in which there is whiteness is white, and every part in which there is blackness is black. But according to these claims whiteness and blackness exist in the same part of the colored thing. Therefore, the same part of a colored body is white and black. The consequent is false, therefore so is that from which it follows.

To this one should reply that we name the things sensed just as we sense them. We distinctly sense an intermediate and mixed color, but not the parts composing it (the whiteness and blackness or other colors from which the intermediate color is composed). Consequently, we impose one name to supposit distinctly for the intermediate color, but we do not impose names to supposit distinctly and separately for the parts of the intermediate color, as long as they are its parts. But distinct names that supposit distinctly are imposed on things that are not parts of any intermediate color and are distinct in location, not united to one another. For example, as long as the whiteness of a wall is distinct from blackness and redness and other colors, and is not part of another color, we use the term 'whiteness' to supposit for that quality and that thing in which there is whiteness. But if blackness or redness were added to that whiteness so that from the whiteness and the added color an intermediate color resulted on the wall, someone seeing the wall would not use the term 'whiteness' to supposit for that wall, but would describe it differently, by saying "that wall is green and scarlet," or would impose some other name on it. The reason has been stated above.

So to the form of the argument, I reply by granting the major and denying the minor. For although in a thing colored by a mixed and intermediate color there is really that color that was whiteness, nevertheless because that quality is part of an intermediate color it is not called white-ness, nor is the thing in which there is such an essence called white. It is instead given some other name, as the things just said make clear. In much the same way, although a species of whiteness in part of the air is of the same species as the whiteness, nevertheless because that species is part of a mixed form coinciding with another species of a contrary form, that part

should be called neither white nor black nor, further, whiteness or blackness. It ought instead to be given some other name that supposits distinctly
for that intermediate form or for whatever has that form.

It could also be said {115} that a thing colored by an intermediate color
composed of whiteness and blackness is white and black, insofar as that
proposition has a conjunctive predicate and is not a copulative proposition.[14] For an intermediate color composed of whiteness and blackness is
neither whiteness nor blackness, since the whole is not its part, but it is
whiteness and blackness and nothing else. Accordingly, this proposition is
true:

> *This color is whiteness and blackness*

insofar as it has a conjunctive predicate and is not a copulative proposition.
Likewise, a thing with that sort of intermediate color could be said to be
white and black. Still, this would be false:

> *This thing is white; this thing is black.*

Much the same could be said of a part of the air that is informed at the
same time by a species of whiteness and of blackness.

To the ninth, it should be said that in the same part of the medium from
where a species of whiteness is impressed on the perceiver, there is also a
species of the blackness that lies above or behind the head of the perceiver,
unseen. Still, a species of blackness is not impressed on the perceiver
through such a species of blackness. The reason for this is that a species
impressed on that part by the blackness naturally affects parts more distant
from the blackness and the perceiver than is that part where the species in
question lies. These parts are directly exposed to the perceiver, the blackness, *and* that part where the species in question lies, and they thus lie
beyond the part informed by that species. The species does not reverse
course (*reagit*) and affect the parts of the medium continuous with the
perceiver that lie between him and the part informed by the species. And
so a species of blackness is not impressed on the perceiver through the
species in question.

On the contrary, let us grant that this blackness, posited as unseen, first
naturally affects the part of the air contiguous with it, and this affects a
second part contiguous or continuous with it, and the second a third, and
so on up to the last part of the air, which is contiguous with the white

---

[14] See Ockham, *Summa logicae* II. 37 (p. 194; *Op. Phil.* I, p. 355).

wall.° In this way, none of those species of blackness reverses course and affects parts of the air in the direction of the blackness. Nevertheless, assuming the white and black walls° are not very far from each other, it seems that once the air has been affected in the above way from the blackness all the way to the whiteness, the species of blackness at the far end of the air adjacent to the whiteness will be multiplied. As a result, it seems that an intense species of blackness will be generated in that part of the air, which will naturally reverse course and affect parts of the air in the direction of the blackness, toward the perceiver. In this way, as it seems, a species of blackness will be impressed on the perceiver, and not just (as was said above) a species of whiteness. {116}

To this one should reply by allowing that at the far end of the air contiguous with the whiteness that is seen there may be a form of blackness that is more intense than the form of a second part in the direction of the blackness. Nevertheless it will not be so intense as to be able to illuminate all the parts of the air between itself and the perceiver. And suppose a species of blackness at the far end of the air adjacent to the whiteness is so intense as to be able to affect all the air between itself and the perceiver and to some extent affect the perceiver himself so that the species of blackness is to some small degree received in the perceiver. Still, the whiteness directly exposed or presented to the perceiver affects him more strongly. As a result, he receives a species of whiteness to such a degree, so far exceeding the species of blackness received to such a degree in the same part of the perceiver, that he does not distinctly intuit the species of blackness.

All the same, I say that through the power of God and otherwise, a species of color not so perfectly presented to the perceiver *could* so exist at the far point of the air continuous with the whiteness directly presented to the perceiver, and *could* so completely affect° that perceiver, that neither the whiteness nor any species of whiteness would be seen, but only the species of this other color located to the side of the perceiver. Also, this whiteness and such a color positioned next to the perceiver (or the species of that color, which would be next to the whiteness) can affect the perceiver in such a proportion that neither the whiteness or a species of the whiteness, nor another color or a species of that color would be distinctly seen. Instead, a single intermediate species would be distinctly seen, which would have a single mixed color resulting from the species of those two colors.

To the tenth, it should be said that the terms 'whole' and 'part' are equivocal. For [in one way,] something is called a whole essentially, and likewise a part. In another way, something is called a whole dimensively, or according to dimension. Likewise, something's being equal to another can be understood in two ways: either according to essence and perfection, or according to dimension. So I say that by taking the terms 'whole' and 'part' insofar as they supposit for an essential whole and an essential part, and by taking equality in the second way, a part can be equal to its whole and the whole to a part. For example, the matter of a log is equal to the whole log, not according to essence or perfection, but according to dimension: for the matter has the same size as the whole log composed of matter and form. (Likewise a form, if it is an extended form, is as long as the whole composite.) If, however, 'whole' and 'part' are taken dimensively, then although the whole is not equal to a part according to dimension, nevertheless it is possible for the whole to be equal to a part in the divided sense. In this way, it is possible for the whole taken dimensively to be equal to its part — that is, to that which is now its part according to dimension, although once this occurs it is not its part according to dimension, but only according to essence. For example, let a be a two-foot-long log divided {117} into halves b and c. Then b is one foot long, given that a is two feet long. By the power of God it could have happened that b was in c in such a way that b and c were in the same initial place (that is, the two halves of a). If this were to occur then the whole log a would be only a foot long. But half of a (that is, b or c) was of such a size when a was two feet long. Still, once this occurs, b (that is, half of a) is not a part of a according to dimension, but only according to essence.

From these claims it is clear that one thing can be part of another according to essence alone or according to essence and dimension. But it is not possible for one thing to be part of another according to dimension unless it is part of it according to essence. Accordingly, these two claims aren't compatible: that one thing is part of another according to dimension and equal to it according to either dimension or essence. For if it is part of something according to dimension, it is part of that same thing according to essence. These two claims are compatible, however: that° one thing is part of another essentially and equal to it dimensively. For although it is a part according to essence, it is not a part according to dimension. I say, therefore, that in each part of the medium and consequently in the same part of the medium there is a species of the whole and a species of part of that whole. And I grant that a species of part of the whole is equal dimensively to a species of that whole, but it is not equal according to essence. And the reason for this is that the species of part is part of the species of the whole essentially, but not dimensively.

[*Conclusion 7*]

Another conclusion is that the quality that is a [mental] word and natural likeness of the cognized thing existing outside the soul is of the same species as the thing of which it is a likeness. I prove this as follows:

1. It is impossible for one quality to be the likeness of another from which it differs in species. But the quality that is a word of the whiteness existing outside the soul is its likeness. Therefore, that quality does not differ in species from the whiteness of which it is a likeness. The minor premise everyone grants; the major is clear to the senses in the case of such sensible qualities. For the whiteness of a stone is not the likeness of redness or vice versa. Likewise, cold is not the natural likeness of heat, but the natural unlikeness or naturally unlike.

2. The means possible for us in this life for proving that one thing does not differ in species from another is that one thing is the natural likeness of another. For if someone seeing two whitenesses could not by means of vision conceive that one is the likeness of the other, he would never by means of vision conceive that they were of one species or that they don't differ in species. Rather, as a result of cognizing by means of vision that one is a natural likeness of the other, he cognizes that {118} they are all of the same species.° Therefore, since everyone grants that that quality that is a word of the whiteness outside the soul is its natural likeness, they consequently have to say that that quality and the whiteness existing outside the soul, of which it is a likeness, are of the same species.

3. The whiteness seen that generates its likeness in the visual power is either a univocal or equivocal agent. Not equivocal, because in an equivocal action the effect is not made to be like the agent. But a visible species is naturally like the whiteness that causes it. Therefore, the whiteness seen that causes a visible species in the visual power or the perceiver is a univocal agent. But every univocal agent, according to everyone, generates something like itself in species. Therefore, the generating whiteness and the generated visible species are of the same species.

4. Everything visible is either light or color. But a species generated in the visual power is visible. Therefore, it is either light or color. Everyone grants the major. They cannot deny the minor, because they say that that quality is a visible species. Therefore, say the color green generates its

species in the visual power. That visible species is either a light or a color. It cannot be said that it is a light (insofar as 'light' signifies a quality distinct from colors), because light taken in this way is not a natural likeness of the color green. Therefore, it is a color, but not of a different species from the color green, since (i) it does not seem true that the color green generates a color distinct in species in the visual power; also, (ii) a color differing in species is not a natural likeness of the color green, whereas the species that is generated is a natural likeness. Therefore, if it is a color, it does not differ in species from the generating color.

5. If someone attentively looks at the color green or red and suddenly turns toward the dark, he will still see the color. But the color that is then seen is not the color existing outside the perceiver. Therefore, that color is generated within the perceiver by the color that was seen before and that exists outside the soul. Therefore, it seems that the visible species generated in the perceiver does not differ in species from that thing by which it is generated. Rather, they are forms of the same species, and the same should be said of audible species and sounds, and also of all intelligible species and the things by which they are generated° in the one intellectively cognizing.

6. The Philosopher and the Commentator, in *De anima* II [424a7–9; comment 119], say that if sight were actually to have some color, it would not receive color. Through these words they suggest well enough that they think sight receives colors. But it is clear {119} that sight does not receive numerically the same colors that remain subjectively in the colors that are at a distance in place and location from the perceiver. Therefore, what the Philosopher and Commentator are calling colors are forms received in sight, generated by colors existing outside the senses. But those forms are called visible species. Therefore, a visible species existing in the perceiver is a color. Therefore, since no form can be a natural likeness [of something] from which it is distinct in species, it is clear from the above that a quality that is a word and likeness of some thing is of the same species as that thing.

Against this conclusion it can be argued as follows: [*First*], it is impossible for two forms to be of the same species, one of which is material, the other immaterial. But a color existing outside the soul is a material form, whereas its likeness in the cognizer is immaterial. Therefore, those two forms cannot be of the same species.

Second, if the aforesaid likeness of color were a true color, then a soul intellectively cognizing color would be truly colored, and one intellectively cognizing heat would be truly hot, which is false.

Third, it is impossible for two forms of the same species to exist in the same subject simultaneously. But two likenesses existing outside the soul could exist simultaneously in the perceiver, one received through one eye, the other through the other eye. Therefore, if the visual power is the soul's very essence, as many assert, it follows that two forms of the same species would exist simultaneously in the same subject. But that those two likenesses are of the same species is clear from the fact that each of them is of the same species as the color existing outside the soul. Therefore, each is of the same species as the other.

Fourth, if the soul seeing a color were truly colored (which one has to grant if the likeness of color existing within it is a true color), then the color seen by the soul and existing outside it would color the soul itself. The consequent is false; therefore, so is the antecedent. The falseness of the consequent is clear, since it is impossible for an agent to be less perfect than the thing it acts on. But a color existing outside the soul is less perfect than the soul; therefore, it cannot act on the soul.

Fifth, the Philosopher says in *De anima* III [431b29] that "it is not the stone that is in the soul, but the species of the stone." Therefore, the species of the stone existing in the soul is not a stone and consequently neither is it of the same species as the stone outside the soul. {120}

Sixth, if the likeness of a thing intellectively cognized were of the same species as the thing itself, then an angel intuitively seeing the substance of a stone would have in itself the nature of a stone, which is false.

Seventh, if the word of the thing intellectively cognized were of the same species as the thing itself, then the blessed forming the word of God would form something that would be of the same species as God creator of all. All of these are false, absurd, and impossible.

In reply to the first of these it should be said that a form can be called immaterial in three ways. In one way because it is an indivisible form, not composed of extended corporeal parts, and conversely a form can be called material that is composed of such parts. In a second way, a form can be called immaterial because it exists in an immaterial subject, and conversely that form is called material that perfects a material subject. In the third way a form is called immaterial because it is a form naturally separate from matter, as is an angelic form. And conversely a form is called material that is naturally the perfection of a material and corruptible subject.

In the first way an immaterial form can be of the same species as a material form – just as an indivisible nonextended whiteness is of the same species as a divisible extended whiteness. In the second way as well an immaterial form can be of the same species as a material form. This is why I grant that the color that is in a stone and the likeness of color in the soul seeing the stone are of the same species. When a form is taken to be immaterial in the third way, it is not of the same species as a material form – if we are speaking of a substantial form. But if we are speaking of an accidental form, then I do not see that it is illogical to say that a form naturally separate from corporeal matter is of the same species as the form that naturally perfects corporeal matter. Thus when an angel intuits a color, for as long as the vision remains, the species of color that exists in the angelic mind naturally and separate from all corporeal matter is of the same species as the color that the angel intuits (assuming that in the angelic mind there is such a species of the thing being cognized).

To the second it should be said that the argument's conclusion is true. A soul seeing and intellectively cognizing color is truly colored, not by any color existing outside the soul but by its likeness, which is a true color. And the same should be said of a soul's *intellectual* cognition, whenever a natural word of that color is formed within it. {121}

To the third it should be said that it is not absurd for two forms of the same species to exist within the same subject when those forms are not distinct in location. And although a visible species existing within the visual power is partially received through the two eyes, that form is nevertheless one in location, although in essence and power it is more than one. Also, forms of the same species that are distinct in location can exist in the same subject if the subject can exist in two places at once. Hence if the human soul exists essentially in each part of the body, it would be the subject of multiple forms of the same species, distinct in position or location.

To the fourth it should be said that it is impossible for an agent or efficient cause to be less perfect than its per se effect. Hence color outside the soul is no less perfect than color existing within the soul. Nevertheless an agent or efficient cause can be less perfect than the subject receiving its effect, absolutely speaking, although relatively speaking the agent is always more perfect than the patient – that is, with respect to such an effect – since the patient is of itself less perfect at receiving the form that it has from the agent. The agent, however, if univocal, has an actual form of the same species; or, if it's an equivocal agent, it has a more perfect form. Therefore, I grant that color really causes color within the soul. It is nevertheless consistent with this that the soul is absolutely more perfect than the color acting on it. For the soul has color only if it comes from that color.

If someone says that a spiritual nature such as the soul cannot be acted on by a corporeal and material nature such as the color outside the soul, it should be replied that a corporeal nature cannot act on that soul by corrupting or destroying it, but can act by impressing some form.

To the fifth it should be said that the Philosopher calls a species of a stone the likeness of an accidental property of the stone – e.g., of color or heat or some other accident – but not a likeness of the stone's substance, since no such thing is in the human soul in this life.

To the sixth it should be said that if an angel were to intuit the substance of a stone through the stone's likeness, it would have to be granted that the stone's true nature exists in the angel intuiting the stone. If someone then says that a true substance cannot be of the same species as some accident or quality inhering {122} in a subject, it can be replied that a likeness of the stone's substance existing in an angel intuiting the stone is neither an accident nor a quality inhering in the angel, but a true substance existing simultaneously with the angel and within the angel and depending on it, just as the fire in a flaming iron is neither an accident nor a quality inhering in the iron, but a true substance depending on the iron. Alternatively, it could be said that the angel intuits the stone's substance without any likeness mediating, something I do not take to be impossible. For if God were to suspend the action of color so that it could not act on our visual power, still we could see color if it were presented to our visual power without obstacle. For that by which the perceiver formally sees, or by which color is formally seen, is not the likeness of color existing within the visual power, but rather the visual power itself.[15] And so even if every likeness of a color were removed from a visual power, the power could still produce a vision of that color – just as the power, by a likeness, is a vision of a likeness of the color.

To the seventh it should be said that it is impossible for some blessed creature to form a word of God that is God's natural likeness. Not even God could form such a likeness in the mind of the blessed. Hence God is

---

[15] See conclusions four and one, respectively, for a defense of these last two sentences. This same argument will reappear in conclusion 10.

seen without any mediating likeness, just as our Doctor St. Thomas teaches.[16]

[Conclusion 8]

Another conclusion to be proved is that in this life we will not be able, on the basis of any sensory cognition, to have a natural, evident, and altogether infallible cognition of complexes of this sort: *That is a stone; That is bread; That is water; That is fire;* and so on for others. Proof:

1. An infidel can have every natural cognition of sensible things that a Christian can have, regarding the existence of bread. But an infidel having the natural cognition possible for him of bread, if he were seeing the consecrated host, would judge that there was true bread there and yet would be deceived. Therefore, an infidel cannot naturally have an altogether infallible cognition of the existence of any bread whatsoever, because he cannot naturally cognize whether it is consecrated or not. Therefore, neither can the Christian.

2. Let someone secretly consecrate the host when no one is looking, and then present it to some great Christian philosopher. It's evident that that Christian could in no way naturally cognize that there is bread under or within those accidents. Therefore, for the same reason he will also not be able to know (*scire*) or cognize naturally that the {123} substance of bread lies under any similar accidents. For he has to be in doubt, regarding any bread, whether or not it's consecrated – unless he were to have information from some source other than cognizing its accidents.

3. God could annihilate the nature of any given corporeal substance, and preserve its accidents in the same form and shape that they had before. Therefore, a wayfarer cannot through the existence of accidents infallibly cognize that any corporeal substance exists. But a wayfarer has a natural cognition of a corporeal substance's existence only through the cognition of accidents. For a substance is not in this life cognized through its own species.

[Conclusion 9]

The ninth conclusion is that a wayfarer cannot on the basis of sensory cognition have a certain and altogether infallible cognition of the existence

[16] *Summa theologiae* 1a 12.2.

of any accident whatsoever outside the soul. And I understand this conclusion in such a way that a wayfarer in this life cannot evidently and infallibly cognize complexes of this sort:

> *Some whiteness, some color, some odor, or some sound is or was outside the perceiver*

and so on for others. I prove this conclusion as follows.

1. Someone seeing whiteness sees at the same time, indistinctly, both whiteness and a species of whiteness, and he cannot by the mere fact of his seeing distinguish between whiteness and the species of whiteness. Therefore, even if he sees a whiteness that is outside him, he cannot be made certain on the basis of that vision (i.e., by the mere fact that he sees it) that it is outside him. The inference is clear, because if from the fact that he sees a whiteness that is outside the soul he could conclude with certainty and infallibly that that whiteness is outside of him, he could for the same reason and with the same certitude and infallibility conclude that it is not within him. And consequently he would be distinguishing it from that whiteness within him that is called the species of whiteness.

The reasons why someone seeing whiteness cannot by the fact that he sees it distinguish between the whiteness and its species are (i) the likeness of the species of whiteness to the whiteness. Further (ii), the location of the species of whiteness is not perceived by the perceiver in virtue of his seeing the species, nor can the location even of the whiteness existing outside the soul be cognized evidently by the cognizer or perceiver. Now it is generally true that whiteness outside the soul (if it is seen) and the species of whiteness always appear to the perceiver to be in the same location, assuming that the outside whiteness is directly exposed to the perceiver. But when two exactly alike things are or appear to be in the same location, the perceiver cannot in virtue of seeing them distinguish between those things. For if there were two stones like and equal to each other in all respects and they were through the power of God placed in the same location and were seen by someone, the perceiver could not in virtue of seeing them distinguish between those stones, or conclude with certainty or infallibly that there are two stones there or that he sees two stones. And the same would have to be said if the stones were distinct in location and place and it were to appear to the perceiver that they were in the same place. Therefore, the truth of the antecedent is clear, as is the reason for its truth. {124}

2. Someone intensely looking at the color green who suddenly turns

toward the dark will judge that he sees a color existing outside himself. He is nevertheless deceived, because he sees only the species of the color, which still for a brief moment remains in the anterior chamber of the brain of the one who saw° the outside color. Therefore, the perceiver cannot in virtue of his vision have an evident and altogether infallible cognition that the color he sees is a color outside him.

3. Those who are deluded judge that they see many colors existing outside themselves and yet they are deceived. Therefore, a perceiver cannot from his vision infallibly judge that a color is or is seen that exists outside him.

4. God could preserve a species generated by a color and, while the perceiver is unaware, annihilate the thing° seen before and existing outside. But if he were to do this then the perceiver would judge that he sees some color seen before and that it exists,° and yet he would err in that judgment. Therefore, the perceiver cannot in virtue of his vision infallibly judge that some color is seen that exists outside himself.

5. Without any whiteness existing or present to someone capable of seeing it, God could create a species of whiteness in that person's brain, in the part first receptive of a visible species, without his being aware of the fact. He would then judge that he sees whiteness existing outside himself, exposed and presented to him, and yet there would be no such thing. Therefore, seeing a color is not a sufficient reason for concluding that the color exists outside the perceiver.

6. Someone seeing a color existing outside himself can, while such a vision goes on, judge that he sees no such color. Therefore, on the basis of such a vision one cannot have an infallible and evident vision of the existence of color. The inference is clear by itself. The antecedent is clear from the story in Acts 12: 6–11, where it is read that Peter, after being struck and awakened by an angel while in prison, put on his sandals. Passing through a street, he passed through an iron gate which was opened for him. Yet he did not believe that those things happened in actual truth, but only in an imaginary vision. Therefore, Peter at that time saw many colors – of his sandals, his clothing, the buildings, walls, stones, the body assumed by the angel, the iron gate – and yet he judged that he had not seen such colors. This would not have happened to him if from the vision alone of such colors he could have had a certain and infallible judgment that he had seen them. {125}

So I maintain that a wayfarer cannot, on the basis of seeing some color existing outside himself, have a certain and infallible judgment that such a color exists or is seen by him.

[Conclusion 10]

The tenth conclusion is that someone seeing a color cannot in virtue of his vision have an infallible and certain knowledge that there is some species of color or some color in his soul. I prove this as follows.

1. These claims are consistent: that someone sees a color existing outside himself and that no species of color is in the perceiver's soul, visual power, or head. Therefore, from the vision of a color existing outside a perceiver, it cannot evidently and infallibly be concluded that a species of the color is in the perceiver or in his visual power. The inference is obvious. I prove the antecedent, because by the power of God it could happen that a color is exposed without obstacle to someone able to see, that the exposed color does not affect the visual power it is exposed to, and that nevertheless such a color is seen. This is clear from the fourth conclusion proved above, since that by which a color is formally seen is the visual power itself and not (as some say) a species of the color. And so if a color were exposed to someone able to see, such a color would be seen by him if he were to will to open his eyes and turn toward that color. But that color would in no respect affect his visual power.

2. When someone sees a color mediated by a species, he cannot on the basis of seeing the color distinguish between the color and the species. Therefore, such a perceiver, from the fact that his power is a vision, cannot infallibly cognize that a species of color exists within his visual power.

3. Many seeing color are unaware whether or not they see by means of a species. This wouldn't be the case if vision were a sufficient cause for proving that some species of color exists within the perceiver.

[Conclusion 11]

The eleventh conclusion is that someone seeing whiteness can have an evident and altogether infallible knowledge of complexes of this sort:

> I see whiteness
> Whiteness is something
> That which I see is something
> I hear a sound

A sound is heard by me
The sound that is heard by me is something in real nature
The sound heard by me is a true thing.

And the same should be said about every sensation. I prove this as follows.

1. If a perceiver could not on the basis of his seeing have an evident and infallible knowledge of complexes of the sort just mentioned, it would follow that no complex could be cognized by a wayfarer evidently and infallibly, and {126} consequently he would not have an infallible and evident knowledge of complexes of this sort:

Every whole is greater than its part.

And thus all cognition and human knowledge (*scientia*) would perish, which is absurd to say.

2. Anyone can experience within himself that, from the very fact that he sees, he assents without any doubt to complexes of this sort:

I see
Something is seen by me
What is seen by me is something

assuming that he understands what is signified by such complexes. Therefore, someone can evidently cognize such complexes, solely from the fact that he sees. The same should be said of someone seeing whiteness and the corresponding complexes, and something similar should be said for any sensation. This way of speaking does not destroy evident and infallible cognition of first principles nor, as a result, all human knowledge (*scientia*). For since whiteness is an extended thing having part after part, someone seeing whiteness (whether this whiteness is a thing seen outside the perceiver or a species of whiteness existing in his head) can from the very fact that he sees such a thing evidently and altogether infallibly cognize this complex

This whole is greater than its part

and

This part of that whole is less than its whole.

And with respect to other things that have been sensed he can evidently cognize similar complexes and thus evidently conclude that every whole is greater than its part and the part less than its whole.

3. Unless that cognition were true, a human being could in no way become certain that he sees something or that he intellectively cognizes something – neither by divine power nor in any other way. I prove this as follows. Suppose that a human being seeing whiteness could not by that very fact evidently cognize that he sees whiteness, but yet by the power of God is made to cognize evidently that he sees whiteness. This is unintelligible. For it would [then] be possible for something to be cognized by the perceiver that was not cognized before [God's intervention]. Let this be *a*. Then the one seeing and cognizing *a* either can or cannot on this basis alone evidently cognize that he sees or cognizes *a*. If it is said that he cannot, then neither on the basis of his seeing *a* can he evidently cognize that he sees whiteness. If it is said that can, then for that same reason if he were to see whiteness he could on that basis alone evidently cognize that he sees whiteness.

[*Conclusion 12*]

The twelfth conclusion is that although a wayfarer on the sole basis of sensory cognition cannot have evident and altogether infallible cognition that such sensed qualities are outside him, nevertheless on the basis of a sensory cognition and this complex known per se,

> *God or the first cause does nothing groundlessly and supernaturally so as to lead human beings into error*

he can evidently conclude that such {127} sensed things exist. For a conservation of species so general that a human being through his whole life would see nothing but such qualities existing within himself would be astonishing and pointless, and would produce many errors. Everyone of sane mind judges that such an action is incompatible with divine goodness.

So the above arguments rightly conclude that, solely on the basis of a sensory cognition of such sensible qualities, someone who senses such things cannot evidently conclude that they exist in real nature. But these arguments do not prove that, using sensory cognition plus the above complex and similar ones, a perceiver still cannot evidently conclude that such sensed things exist. I will say more on this subject later, in discussing the existence of the body of Christ in the sacrament of the altar.[17]

---

[17] This discussion does not seem to appear in Crathorn's *Sentences* Commentary.

[*Conclusion 13*]

The next conclusion, the thirteenth, is that not every complex or sign of any complex can be the object of error. Proof:° A human being either does or does not assent to principles of this sort:

> It is impossible for the same thing to be and not to be at the same time;
> Every whole is greater than its part;
> It is impossible for contradictory claims to be true at the same time.

If he assents, then it is clear that such complexes are not the objects of error. If he does not assent to such principles, this can happen in three ways.

- First, because he assents neither to such principles, nor to their opposites, nor to any other principles – as when a human being is asleep, or when he is awake but does not assent to any complex. In this way, not assenting to some complex does not imply that such a complex is the object of error.
- In another way, it can be said that he does not assent to such complexes because he assents neither to them nor to their opposites but to certain other ones. In this case such complexes are not the object of error.
- In a third way, someone is able not to assent to the aforesaid complexes while assenting to their opposites. Not even in this way are such complexes the object of error; instead, their objects are.[18]

So if someone does not assent to this complex

> Every whole is greater than its part

in the first, second, or third way, that complex is not the object of error. But its object would be (taken in either a contrary or a contradictory way), if the person were not to assent (or were to dissent) in the third way.

Against this conclusion I argue as follows. Someone could be so disposed as to judge that this complex,

> It is impossible for contradictory claims to be true at the same time

is false. Therefore the object of such an erroneous judgment – a complex – can be the object of error, and consequently every complex can be.

It should be replied that someone can be disposed in such a way that he

---

[18] See Translations 11 and 12 for discussion of this issue.

On the Possibility of Infallible Knowledge

would judge that° complex to be false, and the same should be said for any other complex. But it {128} does not follow from this that that complex is the object of error, but that this whole is,

> This complex: 'It is impossible for contradictory claims to be true at the same time.'

For it is one thing to judge that every whole is greater than its part, and another to judge that this complex, *Every whole*, etc., is true. Hence someone can judge the first without judging the second. Likewise, it is one thing to judge that not every whole (or no whole) is greater than its part, and another to judge that this complex, *Every whole is greater than its part*, is false. Someone can judge the first without judging the second. The same should be said of that complex:

> It is impossible for contradictory claims to be true at the same time.

For someone who judges that contradictories cannot be true at the same time does not necessarily judge at that time that this complex is true. Likewise, someone who judges that contradictories *can* be true at the same time does not necessarily° then judge that this [particular] complex is true and its opposite not false. I grant, therefore, that someone can be so disposed that he will judge that this complex is false:

> It is impossible for contradictory claims to be true at the same time.

And the same should be said for other complexes. Yet the object° of the judgment is this whole:

> This complex, 'It is impossible for contradictory claims to be true at the same time,' is false.

[Its object] is not this:

> It is impossible for contradictory claims to be true at the same time.

And the same should be said for other complexes.

[Conclusion 14]

The fourteenth conclusion is this, that there is no complex but that a human being can be disposed so that he would assent to it. Hence it is possible that a human being will believe that no whole is greater than its part and that contradictory claims are true at the same time, and that he is nothing or that he is dead, and so on for others. I prove this as follows.

1. Many who seek to solve paradoxes (*insolubilia*) say that the same complex is true and false, and consequently that its contradictory is true and false. Therefore, for such people, contradictory claims will be true at the same time.

2. It is a principle of mathematics that things equal to one and the same thing are equal to each other.[19] Yet some deny this principle in the case of infinite amounts.

3. The Philosopher in *Metaphysics* IV argues against those who deny first principles, something he would not have done unless they could be denied.

4. *Ethics* VII [1151a15–17] holds that, in practical matters, malice corrupts principles, and yet first practical principles are as certain in practical matters as speculative principles are in speculative matters. Thus it is said in the same work [1148b22–24] that some enjoy {129} eating raw human flesh, and some invite one another to communal banquets where they eat their own children.

5. I once heard someone who thought himself ingenious and nevertheless denied this principle: All right angles are equal.

Against this conclusion it is argued as follows. [*First*], there is not an infinite regress of evident propositions; therefore, one has to reach some proposition compared to which no other is more evident; therefore, one necessarily assents to that one. The final inference is clear, because if one were not to assent to that, it would be on account of something more evident.

Second, Augustine says in *De trinitate* XV [xii.21] that no one can doubt complexes of this sort: *I know that I live; I wish to be happy.*

Third, *Metaphysics* IV [1005b25–26]: With the mouth, perhaps, but with the mind no one denies first principles.

Fourth, *Metaphysics* II [993b5]: First principles are like the door to a house.

Fifth, if someone doubts some proposition like this one

> *I exist*

it follows that he exists, because this follows:

> *I doubt that I exist; therefore, I exist.*

---

[19] This is the first axiom of Euclid's *Elements of Geometry*.

For anyone who does not exist does not doubt. Therefore, no one can doubt this proposition:

> *I exist.*

To these five it should be replied that they do indeed prove that someone with a sound head who uses reason would not doubt the above claims. Nevertheless if a human being has been or is accustomed to assent to the testimony of others, such a person could doubt the above, and could on account of the testimony of others believe or assent to their opposites.

[4. The Views of Others]

[. . .] {149}

[5. Reply to the Question]

I reply to the question asked principally and say that a wayfarer, by the power of his natural light, can evidently cognize that there are three persons in the divinity, that God is incarnate, and all the articles of the faith. I prove this as follows.

Whoever can evidently cognize several premises, can evidently cognize that a complex necessarily following from those premises is true {150} – assuming he evidently cognizes that such a complex does necessarily follow from the premises. But a wayfarer, by the power of his natural light, with no supernatural light infused in him, can evidently cognize that this complex is true:

> *God produces no supernatural effect so as to verify a lie or induce a multitude of human beings into error.*

For this would be incompatible with his goodness. The following complex is also naturally and evidently cognizable by us:

> *This man preaches that there are three divine persons, that God is incarnate, and so on.*

Also, this° complex is similarly° cognizable by us:

> *This man preaching such things invokes God for their verification*

and this complex:

> At the invocation of this man preaching such things a leper is cleansed and a dead man revived – effects which could not be brought about through the action of a natural agent according to the common course of nature.

But from these complexes it would be evidently established to a wayfarer that such complexes preached by such a man are true. Therefore, a wayfarer could in his natural light alone evidently cognize that such complexes are true.

And so those who were converted to the faith when they saw the works of Christ and the Apostles seem to have formed this sort of syllogism:

> It is impossible that the highest perfection performs such supernatural acts in order to verify the lies of one in subversion of a whole multitude; but we clearly cognize that at the invocation of these men the blind are illuminated, lepers are cleansed, and the dead are revived; therefore, the things these men preach are true.

This conclusion seems to match the intent of our Doctor, in the second half of the second part [of the *Summa theologiae*], question one on faith, article four, in reply to the second argument, where he says that

Things belonging to faith can be considered in two ways: In one way, specifically, and [in this way] they cannot be seen and believed; in another way, generally – that is, under the common aspect of believing or the believable. And in this way they are seen by one who believes. For he would not believe unless he sees that they ought to be believed – due either to evidence from signs, or to something of this sort.

Therefore, I take it from this Doctor that someone can see through "evidence from signs" that "things belonging to faith" are true and "to be believed." (And by 'seeing' he means evident cognition, as is clear in the body of the same article.)

Nor can anyone imagine that {151} the only way a wayfarer is able to establish that such effects were brought about is if some supernatural light is infused in him. For it is clear that a wayfarer could evidently cognize, without any supernatural light, that the sun is not moving from east to west today (when the sun remains all day in the east).[20] And the same should be said of other supernatural effects. Even though they are supernatural, it does not follow from this that cognizing such an effect lies beyond human nature – just as the [stationary] sun is a supernatural effect,

---

[20] See Joshua 10:12–14.

and yet it is not supernatural to see the sun. Therefore, I say that from the cognition of supernatural effects along with this complex,

> *God does nothing supernaturally and groundlessly, so as to lead human beings into error*

a wayfarer can evidently cognize that everything pertaining to the faith is true.

To the [initial] argument for the opposite, it should be said that the philosophers could not have naturally cognized those things belonging to the faith, because they did not have those things preached to them, nor did they see such supernatural effects as did the Apostles and the other faithful. By cognizing these in the way described above, the Apostles and the faithful evidently cognized the truths we must believe.

11

ROBERT HOLCOT
CAN GOD KNOW MORE THAN HE KNOWS?

Introduction

The English theologian Robert Holcot (d.1349) lectured at Oxford in the early 1330s. Like Thomas Aquinas, he was a member of the Dominican order, but Holcot is by no means a Thomist. Though his work borrows eclectically from many different sources, Holcot always remained a critical and independent thinker.

The peculiar sounding topic of this quodlibetal question (debated circa 1333) was in fact a standard item of debate among fourteenth-century theologians. The issue is not God's perfection as an epistemic agent; all parties to the debate took for granted that God is omniscient. Given this, one might suppose that Holcot's question must be answered in the negative. How could an omniscient God know more than he knows? But what if, tomorrow, there are simply more things to be known? Then wouldn't God know more than he knows today?

The entire dispute circles around the difficult philosophical problem of what the objects of knowledge are. Article I considers the following alternatives:

· William Ockham's view that the object of knowledge is a mental construct or *complex*;
· Walter Chatton's view that the object of knowledge is the thing signified by the mental construct.

Holcot roughly agrees with Ockham, but extends Ockham's view to anything that has a truth value (linguistic utterances, etc.). Then, in Article II, Holcot takes up the question of God's knowledge. Here it emerges that Holcot takes the objects of knowledge to be individual tokenings of propositions: a particular written sentence, for example, or a particular thought. (He uses the term *propositio* to refer to these sorts of sentence tokens. Unfortunately, he doesn't consider Wodeham's view, described in Translation 12, that the objects of knowledge are abstract sentence types.) Holcot's conclusion is that God can know more than he knows, and that in fact God regularly knows more and less as the number of extant propositions (i.e., sentence tokens) waxes and wanes.

Though Holcot is little studied today, he was for several centuries after his death a well known figure, and his writings (particularly his Biblical commentaries) circulated widely. It was his clarity of thought and verbal wit that made him famous in the later Middle Ages, and these qualities are apparent in this selection.

For further reading on this subject, see Moody (1964), Nuchelmans (1973), and CHLMP IV.10, "The Semantics of Propositions." For further information on Holcot, see Tachau (1995), Pasnau (1998c).

Can God Know More than He Knows?

(*Quodlibet* I.6)

He cannot, it is argued, because God's knowledge cannot be increased. Therefore, etc.

To the contrary: He can know what he does not know; and there are things that are false which he does not know, because they are not true, which he can know when they become true. Therefore, etc.

Two articles need to be set out in addressing this question:

I. What is it that is said to be known, believed, doubted, or assumed (*opinatum*)?
II. We will see to the truth of the question.

I.

Regarding the first, there is uncertainty over what should be said to be known as an object. One view, Ockham's, is that only the [mental] complex is known.[1] Another view, Chatton's, is that the object of an act of

---

[1] See, e.g., William Ockham, *Ordinatio* prologue Q1 (*Op. Theol.* vol. I, pp. 16–21).

knowing or believing is not the complex but the thing signified by the complex.[2] Thus the act of believing

>   *God is three and one*

has God himself for an object, and the act of knowing {4}

>   *Man is an animal*

has man for an object. Further, an act of knowing through a demonstration has for its object not the conclusion of the demonstration but the thing signified by the conclusion.

[*1. Against Chatton's View*]

Against this latter view it is argued as follows. Only what is true is known, but the thing signified by the conclusion is not true. Therefore, etc.

Likewise, only that is the object of an act of knowing that is truly known through the act of knowing. But the external thing is not truly known through the act of knowing. Therefore, the external thing is not the object of the act of knowing.

Moreover, one can frame many true propositions that precisely signify no thing, such as this true proposition,

>   *Man is not a chimaera*

and likewise this one,

>   *Man is not a donkey.*

For by whatever reason a man would be the object of this act of knowing this negative proposition, by the same reason a donkey would be the object, because this complex signifies equally a donkey and a man. Therefore.

Moreover, if the truth were the thing itself signified by the parts of a proposition, then external things would be contradictories. For the same reason, the thing would be its own contradictory, because every thing signified by

>   *Socrates exists*

is signified by

[2] Walter Chatton, *Sent.* prol. q.1 a.1.

Socrates does not exist.

Consequently, if one is true then the other is in reality true.

Moreover, that is known or believed that once was in doubt. But this is a complex. Therefore, etc.

[2. *A Modified Version of Ockham's View*]

It is said that just as the first thing cognized is the likeness or species of the thing (speaking of an incomplex cognition along the lines of Augustine and {5} Saint Thomas), so the first thing cognized by a complex cognition (an act of knowing, believing, or assuming) is the complex itself. And just as the incomplex cognition is nothing other than the species itself or some concept, so the complex cognition is many ordered species or many ordered cognitions. Thus that claim of the Philosopher, that knowledge is the same as the thing known,[3] can be verified by taking 'knowledge' for the act of knowing: For this complex (or the composite, somehow, of [incomplex] cognitions) is an act of knowing when it is evident to the intellect on account of other evident propositions that things are just as this complex denotes them to be. And so the conclusion of a demonstration is both the act of knowing and the thing known.

Now when I know this claim, formed by me,

A triangle has three [etc.]

then equivalently I know (or am truly said to know) another proposition formed by you, because that one is equivalent in its signification to this one. God, however, by knowing his essence, knows all true things. And if we suppose that there once was no such complex, he would then have known no less about triangles than he knows now, although he would not have known as *many* truths about triangles as he knows now. So God knew that God exists when 'God exists' was not true – that is, when the proposition

God exists

was not true. For when this proposition did not exist, then 'God exists' was not true.

On the contrary. The divine essence represents things to the divine

---

[3] *De anima* III 7, 431a1.

intellect just as a complex represents things to us, and with greater certainty than there is in our cognition, even when we have a perfect intuitive grasp {6} of the thing or things signified by that complex. It must, therefore, be granted that the divine essence is true. But then it becomes unclear how the divine essence sometimes represents things as is denoted by the proposition

> *Socrates exists*

and sometimes as is denoted by the proposition

> *Socrates does not exist.*

If this did not occur, then one would have° to concede that the divine essence would sometimes represent things in the way that a false proposition does. Then the divine intellect could be deceived, and the divine essence would sometimes be true, sometimes false – a result which is false.

To this I say that the divine essence is one cognition by which everything cognizable is cognized just as it is. So before anything was created, God was one cognition by which he knew that things are just as propositions about the future (if there were any) would have designated them to be.° And I grant that the first thing cognized or known by God is God himself. So if there were no propositions in the world, and there were other things, then God would know about these things only through himself and through the things, just as he knows now; but in that case he would not know as many true things. For I say that in one true thing [his essence], he knows all the true things that there are. And I grant that the divine essence is true, because God's cognition is always true. Without changing, it represents things sometimes as one of two contradictories represents them to be, and sometimes as the other does, solely as a result of a change in things. And so God is never deceived in cognizing. {7}

So I therefore maintain in this present article that the object known, believed, or assumed is the complex and not the thing signified. For it is not ordinarily appropriate among philosophers to say

> *I know stone*
> *I know wood*

but rather

> *I know that stone is hard*
> *I know that wood is soft*

and so forth. Likewise, it is not ordinarily appropriate among Catholic theologians to say

> *I believe God*

but rather

> *I believe that God exists*
> *I believe that God is three and one*

and so forth. And I mean all these claims with respect to our own knowledge. Yet I say that the complex is not the only thing that is true, because God is true and is one true cognition equivalent and prior to every true complex. So by knowing himself he knows everything that is true, and he knows whatever is denoted by all the propositions that would be true if they were to exist, in whatever mode or time they were to exist. Also, I do not say that *all* things are true (speaking strictly about what is true) but only a thing equivalent in signification to some formed complex° – and perhaps only the divine essence is of this sort naturally. But any thing that is under human control can be established at will to have an equivalent signification,° if human beings will to use it so. So in fact we see that a single circle of a certain material signifies as much as does this whole° proposition written on a tavern wall,

> *In this cellar there is wine.*[4]

So one could grant that° this circle is true, because matters are as it denotes them to be. {8}

II.

As for the second article,

1. I will recite one way of responding;
2. I will argue against this;
3. I will say what seems to me most plausible.

---

[4] It was customary for wine cellars to hang outside their door the metal hoop from a barrel of wine.

[1. One Way of Responding]

As for the first, we should note that William's view on this question, in distinction 39 of book I,[5] is that 'to know' is taken in two ways. In one way it is taken broadly, so as to be the same as 'to cognize,' and in this way it concerns the complex, the incomplex, and all things whatsoever. In another way it is taken strictly, and in this way it is the same as 'to cognize something true.' In this way nothing is known except what is true. In the first way God can know neither more than he knows nor anything that he does not know, because there is nothing he can acquire knowledge of for the first time. But if we take 'to know' in the second way, then (a) God can know something that he does not know, but yet (b) he cannot know more than he knows. William proves each of these.

He proves (a) as follows: Something can be true that is now not true, such as this,

> *I am in Rome.*

This is now false and can be true, but that which is false and can be true *can* be known by God and is *not* now known by God. Therefore, something can be known by God that is not now known by God, and consequently God can know something that he does not now know. Of course, this is so not because of a change on the part of God, but because of a change in creatures, because something is true that once was not true.

He proves (b) as follows: Everything that is true is known by God, and there is always an equal number of things that are true. Therefore, there are always equally many things known by God. That there are always equally many things that are true is proved as follows: It is impossible for more things to be true at one time {9} than at another, because one part of a contradiction is always true, though not always one and the same part. Therefore, there are always equally many things that are true, and not less or more at one time than another. These are the claims made by William.

[2. Against this Last Response]

Against this last conclusion I argue in the following way: I prove that on his view it ought to be entirely granted (i) that God can know more than

[5] Ockham, *Ordinatio* I.39 (*Op. Theol.* vol. IV, pp. 588–90). Translated by Adams and Kretzmann, pp. 92–95.

he knows; (ii) that on his premises God can know less than he knows; (iii) that this is possible:

Nothing is known by God.

I prove (i). Letting everything that now exists remain the same, one proposition can be made true that never has been true or equivalent to any of these truths. Then I argue as follows: This is now true for the first time, and therefore it is now known by God for the first time, and all the other things that were true are still true and known by God. Therefore, more things are known by God now than was so immediately before this.

Moreover, supposing that God grasps (*manuteneat*) everything that is now true, still I can write one proposition equivalently thirteen times, intending that God grasp these.° So then he does grasp° more truths now than before; therefore, God knows more truths now than he knew before. Therefore, etc.

I prove (ii) – that God can know less, etc. – as follows: By whatever reason he can grasp one [proposition] that before he did not, etc., by that same reason he can destroy one, etc.

It can be said that the inference is not valid, because infinitely many things were previously known by God. {10} On the contrary, we are supposing that there are only finitely many *propositions*. Also,° referring to all things that are true, it is clear that God knows all those things, and plain that, without producing any more, God can annihilate one of them. Then there will be less that is true and consequently less known by God.

In the same way, (iii) is clear (viz., that it is possible on his [Ockham's] premises that God knows nothing). For it is possible for nothing to be true. And certainly, if only complexes are true, and nothing is a complex except for a creature or creatures, then it is possible for nothing to be true, just as it is possible for there to be no creatures.

Moreover, against the proof of (b) – viz., that God cannot know more or less than he knows, because there are always equally many things true, because it is always the case, of necessity, that one part of a contradiction is true, etc. – it is clearly false that there are always equally many things true and equally many things false, and that therefore there are always equally many propositions. For after many books have been written or after many people have been thinking and talking, many propositions exist that did not exist before.

Moreover, it is possible for a thousand true propositions to contradict one false proposition. Say I order this to be written in a thousand places:

Socrates runs

and so it is in actual fact. Say I likewise order this to be written in just one
place alone:

Socrates does not run

which is false. Then the thousand true propositions contradict this one.
Suppose, then, that {11} Socrates sits down, while the truth of all other°
propositions remains unchanged. It necessarily follows that God knows less
than he knew – by 999 propositions – because for those 1000 that he once
knew, he now knows only one *de novo*, namely

Socrates does not run

because no other is true *de novo*, by hypothesis. So if we posit that God
knows only 2000 propositions, he would now know only 1001, because a
thousand propositions became false when Socrates sat down, and none
became true except for this one,°

Socrates does not run.

Moreover, if one part of a contradiction is always true, then consider this
contradiction,

Something is true; nothing is true.

If one part of this has always been true, then one part was true when God
alone existed. But, clearly, this was never true:

Nothing is true

because if it were true, then there was something true. Therefore God
alone existed and no creature existed, and if this proposition was true,

Something is° true

then this proposition was true when it itself° did not exist, which is
impossible.

Moreover, each of these is false:

> *One part of a contradiction is always false.*
> *There are always equally many true things, so that there are not sometimes less*
> *and sometimes more.*

This is so on the supposition of these two propositions that belong to this
Doctor [Ockham]:

Everything true is a being.
Only a complex is true, whether it is a concept, something written, or a vocal utterance.

So in this article he seems to contradict himself in many places. For in his ever so {12} usefully compiled *Summa logicae* (part two, chapter two, at the end, where he speaks of necessary propositions),[6] Ockham himself says

One should know that a proposition is said to be necessary not because it always was true or always will be true, but because it is true and cannot be false. For example, the spoken proposition 'God exists' is necessary, and yet it is not always true, because when it does not exist, it is neither true nor false. But it is necessary because if it exists then it is true and cannot be false.

Here he says clearly that the proposition 'God exists' was not always true; and it is certain that its opposite was never true. Therefore, there was a time at which neither part of the contradiction

God exists; God does not exist

was true, and this is true because at some time neither of these propositions existed. Therefore, I hold that it is possible for God to know more than he knows, and that this too is possible:

God knows more than he knew.

To the contrary. If this is possible:

God knows nothing[o]

then it can be true, because opposite follows from opposite. (For if it cannot be true, then it is impossible.)[7]

One can reply by denying the first inference, because there are many possible propositions that can never be true, such as these:

---

[6] Ockham, *Summa logicae* pt. II ch. 9 (*Op. Phil.* vol. I, p. 275). Translated by Freddoso, p. 111.

[7] That is, the opposite of the antecedent follows from the opposite of the consequent. So, given the consequence supplied parenthetically, it follows that if it is possible, then it can be true.
   The force of this objection rests on the implicit point that it never could be true that

   God knows nothing.

For if this proposition were true, then God would have to know it, because God knows all true propositions. But God cannot know this proposition, because his knowing it would obviously make it false, and there can of course be no knowledge of what is false. Therefore, the proposition cannot be true. Therefore, given the stated premise of the objection, it cannot be possible that God knows nothing. (Recall that Holcot's aim at present is to establish that on Ockham's premises it is possible that God knows nothing.)

No proposition exists {13}
No sign exists
Nothing is true
God causes nothing
God conserves nothing.

So a proposition is said to be possible not because it can be true, but because things can be just as it denotes them to be. But it is clear that none of these propositions can be true. Take the proposition

No proposition exists.

If this proposition is true, then it exists, and if it exists, then some proposition exists, and if some proposition exists, then this is true

Some proposition exists.

[An analogous contradiction] can be deduced in the same way for the other propositions given as examples above.

[3. *What Seems Most Plausible*]

I hold a different view in this article: [First,] that God can know something that he does not know, and can know both more than he knows and less than he knows. Still, he is equivalent° to every proposition that would be true if it existed. So if God were to know only himself, he would be just as *wise* as he is now. Second, it must be said that, whenever I want to, I can make God not know many things that he knows, and know many things that he does not know. For if I say or think many true things, or put down in a book many true things, then it is certain that God knows all those things. Suppose then that I burn my book and fall asleep. All these truths will perish, and if they cease to exist, they cease to be true, and consequently they cease to be known by God. Likewise, whoever writes a true proposition makes {14} God know what he did not know before, because everything true is known by God, and this is now true for the first time, so it is now known by God for the first time.

It might be said that this proposition was already known by God, because God already knew another proposition equivalent to it, and so he knew it. Likewise, [it might be said], God already knew things to be in all just as this proposition denotes them to be; therefore, etc. I reply that neither of these inferences is valid.° For suppose that I know in Latin that

A triangle has three, etc.

Then° I know that things are just as it denotes them to be, etc. So I order that a proposition precisely corresponding to this one be written on a wall in Greek. I know nothing of Greek. With regard to that proposition in Greek, then, it is plain that it is true, and I know that things are in fact just as it denotes them to be. Still, it is certain that I do not know this to be true, for I do not know whether or not those characters have *any* significance. And so this inference is not valid:

> *I know that things are in fact just as this proposition denotes them to be; therefore, I know that this proposition is true.*

For the opposite of the consequent is consistent with the antecedent. Indeed these are at once consistent:

> *I know that things are just as this proposition denotes them to be, and yet I am in doubt as to whether or not this proposition is true.* {15}

It is likewise clear from these [remarks] that logical rules (*regulae de virtute sermonis*) of the following sort do not hold:

> *Some proposition is true; therefore, its contradictory is false*
> *The antecedent is true; therefore, the consequent is true*
> *The inference is valid; therefore, the opposite of the antecedent follows from the opposite of the consequent*
> *The premises are true and the syllogistic form is valid; therefore, the conclusion is true*
> *The consequent is false; therefore, so is the antecedent.*

This is likewise contingent, not necessary:

> *Only the true is opposed to the false*

and so are many such rules. It is possible, for example, that some proposition be true and have no contradictory. For it is possible that there is no proposition except for this one,

> *You are running*

and then it does not follow

> *This is true; therefore, its contradictory is false*

because its contradictory does not exist.° In the same way it is possible for an inference to be valid, and for the opposite of the consequent not to exist. Likewise, it is possible for the premises to be written and yet for the conclusion to exist nowhere,° and so on for the others. It is clear, then, that these rules and others like them should be understood to presuppose

the existence of those propositions that they mention. So if some proposition is true, then its contradictory is false *if it has some contradictory*, and
the other rules have to be glossed likewise.

Now there are some who say that a proposition {16} can be true whether
or not it exists, because a proposition is true when things are as it denotes
them to be, or as it would denote them to be if it were to exist. Hence
they say that a necessary proposition is always true.

But this view is not true, because what is nothing signifies nothing, and
consequently signifies neither truly nor falsely.° Moreover, according to
Metaphysics VI [1027b25–27], "true and false exist in the soul; good and
bad in external things." Here the Philosopher takes 'to exist in' in one of
two ways:

• in reality, subjectively. This is how he speaks in *De anima* III [431b30],
  where he says that "not the stone but the species of the stone exists in
  the soul."
• objectively. This is to say that what is true exists in the soul because the
  soul cognizes what is true as its cognitive object.

If he takes 'to exist in' in the first way, then the true is a true thing or
things, because it is a true quality or qualities informing the soul. In this
way, what does not exist cannot be true. If he takes 'to exist in' in the
second way, objectively, then there is no difference between good and bad,
true and false, because good and bad exist objectively in the soul just as
truly as true and false do.

So the Philosopher means to say that what is true is a statement or else
an intellection° existing subjectively in the intellect, when things are in all
just as it denotes them to be. And this is what he says, {17} in *De
interpretatione* I [16a7–9], speaking of the likenesses of things (variously
called concepts, species, images, or idols, and also intellects, intentions,
mental words, cognitions, intellections, and passions of the soul): Such
things are the same among all (that is, equivalent in signifying or in
representing) because the things too are the same among all, because such
likenesses are caused by the things and signify naturally, not by convention,
the things they are likenesses of. They are caused either entirely by the
soul itself (according to the Platonists) or entirely by the object (according
to the Stoics[8]) or by both the soul and the object (according to the
Peripatetics).

---

[8] See Boethius, *Consolation of Philosophy*, Bk. V met. 4.

These likenesses exist in the soul subjectively. But when the intellect uses the likeness for the thing, then the intellect is said to understand or to apprehend simply the thing itself that the likeness is of (or that it would be of if there were such a thing). Not that the simple apprehension or incomplex intellection is some further new thing distinct from the intellect and the species. Rather, that species is called the simple apprehension, or else 'apprehension' is an abstract term that holds true for no thing or things, but yet serves in {18} speech to express the things that it signifies either more briefly° or else differently from° how other terms would signify.

When the intellect uses different species suppositing for a single thing, or uses the same species twice, placing in between either the concept that corresponds to the spoken word 'is' or else some other verbal concept, then it is said to compose. But when it adds to such a verbal concept or copula° the syncategorematic concept corresponding to the term 'not,' then it is said to divide. And this composition or division is nothing other than the intellect's causing in an ordered way such concepts within itself (or else its using ones already caused). Truth and falsity come with this composition and division. Thus Aristotle says (as cited [16a9–11]), "just as sometimes an intellection is in the soul without being true or false, whereas sometimes one of these necessarily applies, so too with utterances. For truth and falsity° pertain to composition and° division."

From these [remarks] it is clear that every mental proposition is composed of at least two things – for example, when it is said

> *This exists*°

which is one of the simplest of propositions. It is also clear that everything true or known by a human being is a complex that has been formed,° {19} not the thing signified by the complex. And it should be granted that the proposition doubted is the act of doubting, the proposition known is the act of knowing, the proposition assumed (*opinata*) is the act of assuming, the proposition in which one errs is the act of erring. So in order to verify and uphold° all that we are claiming about cognition, two kinds of things suffice: the soul and its concepts. A concept is sometimes a species, when it is representative of an external thing, and sometimes it is not. Of the latter sort are the concepts of the copula° and of verbs, syncategorematic concepts, and concepts that connote something concrete or abstract that can be verified of no thing or things by means of the copula 'is,' although they import and signify things, and function° in speech by being added to other words. These are concepts such as *likeness, union, composi-tion, division*, and many such others. These are not presently in question.

It should also be known that this thing that is the species of the stone is not always an act of understanding, nor is it at once a disposition, just as it is not always a part of a proposition nor is it always used by intellect. This thing [the species] is an act of understanding when the soul uses it for the thing understood.° And if the same thing [the species] becomes hard to change, then it becomes a disposition (*habitus*) of that soul. That is, it [the species] is then called a disposition – this term 'disposition' holds true only of a thing that is hard to change. Similarly, a knowable proposition is not always known, because a knowable proposition is sometimes doubted.° But the term 'knowledge' is one term suppositing {20} for a number of signs ordered to signify what is true or false, and at the same time as this it connotes or imports that it is certain to intellect that things are in fact just as it denotes them to be. And the term 'doubt' supposits sometimes for the same proposition, and at the same time it imports or connotes that the intellect was not certain whether or not things are in fact just as it denotes them to be. And so when the same proposition is at first doubted and later known, then the same thing will be knowledge which was doubt.

Alternatively, it can be said that these terms – 'knowledge,' 'doubt,' 'assumption,' 'intellection,' 'operation of intellect,' 'composition,' 'divi-sion,' 'formation,' 'apprehension,' 'assent,' and many other such terms – are certain abstract [terms] not verifiable of any pronoun demonstrating a thing or things, because along with all the things that they import, they connote the equivalent of one or more complexes. 'Knowledge,' for instance, imports certain qualities ordered in the soul, and also that the intellect is certain° that things are just as these qualities so ordered denote them to be. So, for example, suppose that I know that Socrates is in this house. I say that this noun 'knowledge' is verified not of qualities ordered in the soul (as of its significate precisely) nor of these qualities plus Socrates and the house. For even if all these things exist I could err with regard to this proposition {21}

> Socrates is in this house

solely because of Socrates's or the house's moving, without the destruction of anything that was there. So just as many° verbs are appropriately verified of no thing or things (there is no thing that is *to run*, and no things that are *to write*, nor any thing that is *to build*, nor any thing that is *to move*), so it seems that we should say the same for nouns importing being (*esse*) –

for example, 'operation,' 'consideration,' 'building,' 'doubt,' 'run,' 'motion,' 'cognition,' 'intellection,' and others of this sort. No more needs to be said of these for now.

I hold, therefore, in light of the foregoing, that God can know a proposition that he does not know, and second that he can know more or less than he knows, as was shown above.

To the reply to the contrary. When it is supposed that God's knowledge cannot be increased or diminished, I grant this, because his knowledge is his essence. Nevertheless, that knowledge knows sometimes more and sometimes less, inasmuch as sometimes there are more true things and consequently more knowable things, and sometimes there are fewer. In the same way,° his power cannot be increased or diminished, and yet sometimes he can do more, sometimes less.

12

ADAM WODEHAM
THE OBJECTS OF KNOWLEDGE

Introduction

With Adam Wodeham (c. 1298–1358) we arrive at the zenith of subtlety and complexity in later medieval philosophy. An English Franciscan, Wodeham was deeply influenced by his predecessors in the Order, particularly Scotus, Ockham, Aureol, and Walter Chatton, all of whose views come in for criticism in the present selection. The lectures from which this selection is drawn (his *Lectura secunda*, or second lecture on Lombard's *Sentences*) appear to date from around 1330. What we have is a single manuscript containing a *reportatio* of those lectures: that is, an official classroom transcript never edited by Wodeham. This at least partly accounts for the obscurity of some sections.

Wodeham was a contemporary of Robert Holcot, and the present selection, like Translation 11, concerns the things we have knowledge about. Initially, the question is whether the immediate object of knowledge is things or mental signs. Wodeham has little sympathy for the first answer, despite its immediate plausibility (§6 n.2). He also thinks it won't do to identify the objects of knowledge with signs (§§4–7). These latter sections of the question are immensely complex, and it is not always clear how the Latin should be construed, or whether it even is construable, as it stands. Keep in mind that by 'signs,' Wodeham means mental signs, and that he assumes from the start that these mental signs will be sentencelike "complexes" or "propositions." (Holcot used this same terminology in Translation 11.) To say that knowledge concerns signs or a complex is to say that it concerns a sentence in the language of thought.

The most basic problem with this view is that such mental "propositions" are concrete, individual tokens of thought. Whereas Holcot simply embraced the consequences of this position, Wodeham attempts a novel solution: He introduces abstract sentence-types to serve as objects of knowledge and belief (§§8–9). These are what we would now call a proposition or state of affairs. Wodeham himself introduces no technical terminology, though he does remark that it "is something signifiable by the complex" (§8), which would lead Gregory of Rimini, a decade later, to defend similar entities under the phrase *complexe significabile*. As for their ontological status, Wodeham treats all such questions as misconceived. To someone who asks what man-being-an-animal (*hominem esse animal*) is, his only answer is to offer another such sentence-type, such as rational-animal-being-a-sensible-animate-substance.

With these resources in hand, Wodeham turns in the second article to a rather different issue: In knowing some proposition, must one's knowledge somehow extend to the evidence on which that knowledge is based? As always in medieval discussions, the paradigm is demonstrative knowledge, and so the question focuses on whether knowledge concerns only the conclusion, or the conclusion and the premises. Wodeham proposes a subtle and complex compromise, based on a distinction between kinds of knowledge (§14). This debate, though directly relevant to contemporary debates in epistemology, has to my knowledge never been studied by scholars of medieval philosophy.

Though largely forgotten now, Wodeham was once included among scholasticism's greatest theologians. Deserved or not, it seems unlikely that his reputation will ever recover. For unless the fashions and priorities of modern scholarship dramatically change course, it does not appear that philosophers (let alone theologians) will ever take the time to enter into the daunting complexity of his thought. For better or worse, and despite the heroic efforts of a few scholars, Wodeham may always remain largely a closed book to us.

For the broader medieval context of debates over the objects of knowledge, see CHLMP IV.10, "The semantics of propositions." The Introduction to Wood's edition of the *Lectura secunda* provides a useful overview of Wodeham's life and work. On Wodeham as a source for Gregory of Rimini, see Gál (1977).

The Objects of Knowledge

(*Lectura secunda* dist. 1 Q1)

Does the Act of Knowledge Have as Its Immediate Object Things or Signs?

[*§1. Initial Arguments*]

According to Augustine, in *De doctrina christiana* I [ii.2] (as cited by Lombard in the first distinction [of the *Sentences*]), "All teaching concerns either things or signs." Having asked in the prologue about the acts that precede the act of knowledge, we should ask now about the act of knowledge itself, which is an act of judgment, something we have just now considered [Prol., Q6]. And in accordance with the text cited, I ask first whether the act of knowledge has as its immediate object things or signs – that is, a complex in the mind or the things signified by the complex.

1. It seems that its immediate object is things. Consider a proposition by means of which an assent is caused (or else the incomplex cognition out of which the proposition is composed). According to the previous question, doubt two [§18], whatever the proposition signifies or represents, that is what the assent signifies or represents. But the proposition immediately signifies the thing itself. Therefore.

The minor is clear: If it were denied, there would be an infinite regress, because no sign immediately signifies itself. And so further: The immediate object of assent is what the assent immediately signifies. But such is the thing, as I have just proved. Therefore.

2. If this were not the case, then no knowledge would be real. For no knowledge is unreal because it is not, in itself, a true thing – for that is impossible. Rather, [knowledge is unreal] because its objects are not true external things but only signs of things in the mind. This is clear in the case of logic: Its objects are genera and species, which are not the external things themselves but the signs of external things. Therefore, if all knowledge were to have only the signs of things as its objects, then no knowledge would be any more real than logic. {181}

On the contrary.

1. Understanding (*intellectus*) and knowledge are distinguished in that understanding is a dispositional grasp (*habitus*) of principles, whereas knowledge concerns conclusions. See *Ethics* VI [1140b31–41a8] and the

frequent remarks of both the Philosopher and the Bishop of Lincoln in the *Posterior analytics*.[1]

2. The true and the false are found not in things but in the mind (see *Metaphysics* VI, part 8 [1027b25–27]). But the object of an act of knowledge is true. – Otherwise, it would not be a veridical sign or a veridical act (that is, it would not say or signify what is true). But an act of mind signifies only that which is its object. Therefore, the object of an act of knowledge is something true. – Therefore the object of an act of knowledge is found not in external things but in the mind.

There are two things to investigate here.

• First, is the immediate object of an act of knowledge the thing signified by the complex or the complex itself?
• Second, if it is the complex, is it one or many? And if it is the thing, is it things signified by one complex or things signified by many complexes?

(Each article assumes, on the basis of the previous question [§18], that the act itself is one and simple in its being.)

[Article One]

[§2. *Arguments for Things as Objects of Knowledge*][2]

Concerning the first question it might reasonably seem to someone that an external thing is the object of an act of knowledge and of any assent that can be caused immediately by a proposition signifying an external thing, whether that assent is an act of knowledge, understanding, opinion, or belief. In the same way, [it might seem to another] that the object of assent is the thing itself in the mind and the complex signifying that thing, which is the means of causing the assent. So I will set out arguments first for the one side and then for the other.

It seems that it can be proved in many ways [that the object is an external thing]. {182}

---

[1] E.g., II 19, 99b15–100b17; Robert Grosseteste, II 6 (pp. 403–8).
[2] The following seven arguments closely follow those of Walter Chatton. See *Sent.* prol., q.1 a.1. Within the text, I supply the line numbers as given in J. Wey (ed.).

1. If the soul were to form a demonstration without any other prior cognition, an act of knowledge will still be caused. But if it were to form a demonstration without any other prior cognition, no act of assent to that complex will be caused. Therefore, the assent will concern the thing signified by the complex.

The first premise is evident, because an act of knowledge requires only that the soul produce a demonstration (since a demonstration is a syllogism that produces knowledge,[3] and knowledge is the effect of a demonstration). Therefore, leaving everything else aside, to posit a demonstration is to posit an act of knowledge [Wey, 106–19]. The same also seems to hold for an act of belief, because what seems to suffice for that act is the will's command and the complex *God is three and one*, if the soul forms it. Consequently, leaving aside every other prior cognition and positing these things, the act will be caused.

The minor is evident, because the soul assents only to what has been cognized. Therefore, if that complex does not signify [itself], then the soul will not assent to it [Wey, 120–27]. Therefore, if that demonstration or an article of faith is posited, and neither the article nor the demonstration nor its conclusion is cognized, then the assent that is caused has as its object neither the article of faith nor the conclusion of the demonstration.

2. The cognition of a proposition no more suffices to cause assent to the proposition itself than that proposition, composed of cognitions of an external thing, suffices to cause assent to that thing – given that the thing is as evidently and perfectly cognized by the cognitions that compose the proposition as the proposition itself is by the cognition through which it is cognized. Therefore, if assent to the proposition is caused in the one case, then assent to the thing signified by the proposition is caused in the other case. But assent to the proposition is caused by a cognition of the proposition. If not, then no one would assent to any complex truth, which is false, because with regard to syllogisms and propositions there can be demonstration, knowledge, opinion, and the like. Therefore, it follows that assent to a thing will be caused by a proposition composed of cognitions of that thing [Wey, 324–36].

3. Some of the articles of the faith had a different character in the Old Law and the New: Then they were propositions about the future (such as *God will be incarnate*); now they are about the present or the past. These complexes have a different character, since one was true then whereas the

---

[3] Cf. Aristotle, *Post. An.* I 2, 71b17–18.

other was false. So if the act of belief corresponding to these propositions were to have such a complex as its object, then that act of belief would have had a different character now and then. As a result, since both belief and faith concern the same object, faith (acquired and even infused) would have a different character [then] and now [Wey, 363–76]. {183}

4. A disposition (*habitus*) causes a cognition of the thing it is a disposition of, and so likewise does a species. Likewise, acts of knowledge and imagination cause cognitions concerning their objects. Therefore, to a much greater extent, a proposition composed of a thing represents the external thing more perfectly than a disposition or species does [Wey, 338–52].

5. The proposition in the mind and the external thing it signifies are distinct. Therefore, they can be cognized by different cognitions, and consequently the soul assents with two different assents to the thing signified and to the proposition. Consequently, its assent to the thing itself does not have the proposition as its object [Wey, 359–61].

6. Assent to a proposition presupposes assent to the thing signified by the proposition. For one first assents that a thing is in reality as the proposition denotes it to be, and then assents that the proposition is true. Therefore, an assent caused by a proposition signifying some thing has as its object not that proposition but the thing signified by the proposition.

Confirmation: By natural order, knowledge of the soul's acts (e.g., in logic) presupposes knowledge of the things signified [by those acts]. For one acquires no knowledge of the nature of demonstration without the experience of a demonstration. But experiencing a demonstration and forming it causes the assent and the act of knowledge that it is naturally suited to cause. Consequently, knowledge and assent concerning a complex in the mind presuppose assent to the thing signified by that complex [Wey, 291–303].

7. It is not apparent how the premises of a demonstration would cause an act of assent to the conclusion, because they no more signify or represent the conclusion than the conclusion signifies or represents them. But they cause a cognition concerning only what they represent, or else concerning themselves. Therefore, the act of knowledge that they cause concerns not the conclusion but the thing signified [by the conclusion] [Wey, 305–22].

These are the fundamental arguments that persuade some to say that every theological truth signifying God (or composed of proper cognitions° of God) is capable of causing in its own way an act of assent – for example, an act of belief – whose object is God himself. More generally, they say that a complex truth is never the object of the assent that it causes in us.

[§3. *Arguments for the Complex as the Object of Knowledge*]

Some arguments should now be introduced that can establish the opposite position.

1. It appears that no one believes or assents to nothing. But frequently that which is signified by a complex causing assent to belief is absolutely (*pure*) nothing, as is the assent that can be caused by this complex, *the soul of the Antichrist will exist.* {184}

2. One does not assent and believe less when the complex *the devil is the devil* is formed than when the complex *God is three and one* is formed. Therefore, if assent is not to the complex but only to the thing signified by the complex, then one assents and believes as firmly in the devil as in God – even assents more firmly and more clearly, because more evidently.

3. It follows not only that one believes in and assents to the devil, but that at the same time one dissents from and disbelieves in God. Proof: I ask, what is it that one dissents from and disbelieves in, once the complex *God is not God* is formed? For one experiences the dissent's being caused in oneself. If that which one dissents from and disbelieves in is God himself, then I have my conclusion. If that which one dissents from and disbelieves in is not God but the complex, then I have my main conclusion. For the complex that causes assent is no less the object of such an assent than the complex that causes dissent is the object of dissent. Therefore, etc.

4. That is not all that follows. It also follows that at one and the same time one assents to and dissents from the same thing. For as I assumed yesterday [Prol. Q6 §20], and as the Philosopher and the Commentator make clear, in the last comment on *Metaphysics* VI [8], contradictory propositions can exist at the same time in the soul. So let these two propositions exist at the same time in one's soul:

> God is God
>
> God is not God.

Forming the one will cause assent; forming the other will cause dissent. And if one's assent is not to the complexes themselves – which would be our main conclusion – then it is to exactly the same thing, namely, to

God. And this is confirmed, because even according to him,[4] contradictories signify altogether the same thing. Otherwise, as he says, they would not be contradictories.

5. This view contends that God is either the total object or only the partial object of the assent caused by a proposition composed from proper cognitions of God. If partial, then the complex that caused the assent would not be excluded from being its object at the same time. If total, then [I argue] to the contrary that forming the complex would be superfluous once there was a simple evident apprehension, because an evident grasp of the total object of assent is suited, as it seems, to cause an assent with respect to that object. Also, what is neither the total object of some proposition nor the proposition is not the total object of the assent. But no simple thing (which is precisely what God is) is the total object of some proposition, and certainly it is not the proposition. Therefore, etc. That it is not the total object of a proposition, I prove. For a present proposition signifies or consignifies something further than what its subject signifies {185} no less than does a past or future proposition with the same predicate and subject. But insofar as these [propositions] signify or consignify something further – namely, an actual or possible time – each one of the three propositions could be true while the others with the same subject and predicate were false.

6. *To be*, which is the mark of composition, signifies either something or nothing. If it signifies and consignifies nothing, then there is no reason for it to appear in speech. If it signifies something, it signifies no more one thing than another, because it is indifferently related to all entities and can connect (*copulare*) anything with anything. And whether it signifies connection or composition on the part of a thing, or unity and identity between the terms (*extrema*) or the things signified by the terms of the proposition, it will always be the case that the proposition signifies some thing or things not signified by the subject or the predicate. And then as before: The total object° of assent is either the complex itself – and then we have our conclusion – or the total of what the complex signifies. Consequently,° the habit [of faith] would have a different character in the Old and the New Law as a result of its being caused by a complex of a different character, just as it would as a result of its having a complex of a different character as its object [see §2 n.3].

[In reply] it is said that an assent of a different character would be caused

[4] Chatton, *Reportatio* I, d.2, q.1.

if the predicate or the subject were to have a different character, because a more evident grasp [of the terms] causes a more evident assent. This would not occur, however, if only the copula were to change.

On the contrary: When the copula changes its species, the predicate changes its species, because the force of the verb plays a part in the predicate (*tenet se a parte praedicati res verbi*). Indeed, changing the copula causes dissent in one case and assent in another.

7. That that assent has a different character, etc., establishes nothing. Proof: No two acts differing only numerically with respect to numerically the same object are so related that one is the faith and the other heresy. But to believe that the son of God will be incarnated is heresy, whereas to believe that he has been incarnated is the true faith. Therefore, these acts do not differ only numerically.

8. No proposition would be known per se unless a proposition were the object of assent.

Seven against seven.[5]

[*§4A. The Complex Is Not the Total Object of Knowledge*]

In reply to this article, first, it does not seem to me that the complex is the total object of an act of knowledge.

1. If it were, then to know {186} would not be to cognize the cause of a thing, both that it is its cause and that it is impossible for it to be otherwise.[6] The inference is plain, because the complex is not the cause of a thing, and because to cognize the complex alone would not be to cognize that it is its cause and that it is impossible for it to be otherwise.

2. Also, experience shows that one's assent frequently encompasses the thing's being so in reality. Take, for example, the assent that you are sitting there. It is as if the assent extends (*fertur*) not to the complex but completely directly to the thing's being so in reality.

3. Also, as was proved in the previous question [§20], an assent is not just the proposition itself. (And if it were, we would have our conclusion, because the proposition is not a distinct apprehension of itself.) Nor is it blind approval on the part of the mind, because then no assent would be a cognition or be evident, except by extrinsic denomination. Therefore,

---

[5] There were seven arguments in §2, but here there seem to be eight. Indeed, the last argument is explicitly labeled the eighth (*octavo*). But perhaps the scribe gets this wrong: Perhaps it should be counted as the seventh, and the seventh should be counted not as an independent argument but as a preemptive reply to the argument in §2 n.3. Then we would have "seven against seven."

[6] Cf. Aristotle, *Posterior Analytics* I 2, 71b9–12.

an assent is an apprehension either of those things that are apprehended by prior apprehensions, as I held there [§18], or of both those things and the complex, at the same time. Thus an assent does not solely concern the complex.

[§4B. *In Defense of the Rejected View*]

The view that I have just rejected could be defended on two interpretations, each of which would hold that it is solely the complex that is the object of the act of assent.

The first would hold that the subject or predicate is that which is understood, whether it be a thing or a mental construct (*fictum*). And then one would have to say next, as I mentioned in the previous question [§6], that the assent has the thing itself as its immediate partial object, but has the whole complex of which the thing is a part as its total object.

The second would hold that the thoughts (*intentiones*) themselves are the subject and predicate, and not that which is understood, whether that be a thing or a concept mentally constructed (*fictus*) or formed. On this interpretation, the assent would immediately encompass solely that complex, in such a way as not to encompass the thing.

Ockham, as I said in the previous question [§6], follows the first approach, in the first book of his *Sentences* commentary [prol. Q1]. And here I add that Scotus follows the same approach: For in the penultimate question of his commentary on *Metaphysics* VI [Q3 n.37] he holds that truth or falsity is always in the proposition formally {187}, because the proposition always corresponds or fails to correspond to the external thing (that is, to the thing signified, whether internal or external). But truth or falsity is not always in that act of composing as an object, because that correspondence is not always apprehended.

Scotus raises an objection against this [ibid., n.38], "because it seems that at once when first principles are apprehended they are cognized to be true." He replies that "on account of the evident relationship between the terms, the intellect that composes them at once perceives that the act of composition corresponds to the reality (*entitati*) of the terms being composed." And "therefore, it could be said that there is another act there, a reflexive one, but one that is not perceived because it is simultaneous. In other cases, such as conclusions, these acts differ in time."[7]

---

[7] A marginal note at this point in the manuscript remarks that "this solves almost all the arguments of Chatton." Indeed, Wodeham himself will make use of this strategy several times below (§6, §10 n.1).

But Scotus raises an objection [ibid., n.39]: "How will the first act concerning first principles be reflexive?" He replies: "It is not the first act, the composition, [that is reflexive,] but the second, the assent, and it could be said to judge that which can be judged."

Here Brother Scotus plainly indicates that those terms that the intellect composes are the entities that are signified and not the thoughts (*intentiones*) of those entities: For he holds that an act of composition is true on account of its correspondence to the reality of the things being composed. And this is certainly not on account of its correspondence to simple acts, because that would be consistent with the proposition's being false.

Also, in his commentary on *Perihermenias* I, Q2 [n.9], he holds the same view – namely, that the external thing is the term of the proposition, though not insofar as it is external. He plainly says there that the composition is not of species or likenesses but of things, "not as they exist but as they are understood." (In the same way, we understand that which is signified by a word, "but yet this whole composite, the thing-as-understood, is not signified, because it is a being only *per accidens*" [ibid., n.8].) So he says there next [n.9] that "there is said to be truth and falsity in the intellect's composition and division, because this composition is caused by the intellect." (Supply *in reality*, with regard to the nature of the composition, but *intentionally*, with regard to the terms.) "And it exists in the intellect as what is cognized exists in the cognizer, not as an accident exists in a subject." {188} (Gloss this exactly opposite to the first gloss.[8]) "And so I grant that the parts of the composition exist in the simple intellect as what is cognized exists in the cognizer. And in this way the things in the intellect are not just species." – Therefore, it is clear that according to Scotus the object of assent is a complex, and a complex of this sort.

Here I should mention that someone holding that this sort of complex is the immediate object of assent can imagine the complex in one of two ways:

(a) One can imagine that there are three acts in the intellect: two absolute and one comparative. As was mentioned in the previous question [§5], the mark of mental composition is not the apprehension of the terms, although we use the absolute apprehensions of the terms as instruments in making comparisons.

(b) Alternatively, one could coherently enough imagine that although

---

[8] Perhaps Wodeham means that the first phrase should be read *intentionally*, the second *in reality* (reversing the order of the previous parenthetical remark).

simple absolute apprehensions are naturally presupposed, still the comparative act that naturally presupposes them is formally a kind of apprehension of those same terms. On this view, if God were to annihilate those absolute apprehensions and conserve the comparative act (which in itself is in fact a kind of absolute entity), we would thereby have the whole proposition. And so it could be said that any proposition in the world is in itself a simple act, as regards its being, although not as regards its signifying – just as is claimed for an act of assent [see Prol. Q6 §18].

Whichever option is maintained, it should be said on this view that the process is as follows:

(i) The thing is apprehended by a simple act of understanding (*simplici intelligentia*).

(ii) A composition evident in the third degree is formed.[9]

(iii) That composition or complex is apprehended by a simple act of apprehension.

(iv) One assents to the complex, in such a way that although the assent is a kind of apprehension (not the one by which it is caused, of course), still it is not an apprehension that things are as the proposition signifies. (For that the evident proposition suffices.) Instead, the assent concerns only the complex itself. By this, one apprehends its correspondence to what is apprehended through it (that is, through the proposition [=ii]) and through the simple cognition [=iii] that mediates between the conceived proposition and the assent.[10]

And so as to the experience alleged for the contrary view – namely, that when I assent I experience myself being drawn to things being so in reality [§4A n.2] – this will occur not through the act of assent [=iv], but through the act of evidently apprehending things being so. This act is the composition itself [=ii]. {189}

[§5. *Arguments against the View of Scotus and Ockham*]

1. Against the view just set out, I am persuaded by the fact that no assent would be evident by intrinsic denomination [see §4A n.3].

---

[9] A proposition evident in the third degree cannot fail to signify correctly and is designed to compel the intellect, assuming God's general influence (see Prol. Q6 §13).

[10] This passage is obscure, but seems to go as follows: The assent formed at stage (iv) apprehends the conformity between how things are and how they are signified by the proposition formed at stage (ii). This assent is caused by the simple apprehension formed at stage (iii), which is an apprehension of the stage (ii) proposition, and thereby acts as a bridge between stages (ii) and (iv).

Keep in mind that Wodeham is constructing this account on behalf of his opponents, Scotus and Ockham. Its obscurity is no embarrassment to Wodeham.

2. Nor would knowledge be to cognize the cause of a thing, both that it is, etc. For on this view, if God were to annihilate a proposition, then even though I might have a noncomplex apprehension of a thing, insofar as assent takes the place of the absolute simple cognition that was in its way a part of the proposition on that view, I would still not apprehend its being so or not so.[11]

3. I am persuaded, third, by the fact that a simple cognition never suffices to cause assent except when a complex is formed from it. For otherwise, if a simple apprehension did suffice to cause assent, then a proposition would not be posited as an entity (*ut quid*). Now a simple understanding may be an act of cognizing a proposition as its object, just as much as a house or paleness is also an object. As a result, if a complex were first formed from that simple understanding, such as

> *This proposition corresponds to reality*

and [if] the assent has as its object the total object of the complex apprehension by means of which it is caused (for why one part more than another?) then, through the assent, one immediately apprehends that things are so in reality.

4. Also, it is impossible to apprehend that a proposition corresponds to a thing without apprehending that the thing is so in reality. For to apprehend that something corresponds is to apprehend it relationally, and this does not occur without an apprehension of the relatum. In this case, the relatum is *being so*. But even when the proposition itself does not exist, one can apprehend through the assent that it corresponds, according to this reply. And then its being so is apprehended not through the proposition, because we are supposing that God preserves the assent without any proposition. Therefore, it is apprehended through the assent.

5. Also, for the same reason that that second proposition could cause an assent that the first corresponds to the external thing, so the first proposition – since it is equally evident – could cause assent that things are so in reality.

[§6. Conclusions 1–3]

1. Therefore, I grant, as before [§4A], that the complex is not the adequate object of assent.

---

[11] Compare §4A n.1. Perhaps the idea here is that one might satisfy the Aristotelian definition of knowledge, in virtue of one's simple apprehension, and yet be unable to grasp the proposition, because God has destroyed that.

2. Second, I say that the adequate object of assent is not God himself, nor {190} any simple thing (*res*). Five of the arguments stated above against Chatton's position persuade me of this conclusion, beginning with the second and continuing [§3 nn.2–6].

3. The third conclusion (as it seems to me) is that the complex is not the partial object of an act of assent necessitated (given God's general influence) by such a complex.[12]

3.1 For everything that is a partial or total object of an act of assent is by nature previously comprehended. For as the first disputant assumes [§2 n.1] – rightly in this case – "the soul assents only to what has been cognized." But I do not want to say with him that the soul assents to whatever has been previously cognized, because then it would assent to the devil when assenting that

> The devil is the devil.

Rather, I want to say that (i) nothing is the object of an act of assent – either total or partial – without being previously cognized by a distinct cognition that is solely an apprehension, not an assent. But (ii) the complex necessitating° the assent is not° cognized prior to the assent. Therefore, etc.

i. Proof of the major: Otherwise there would be no need to posit that either a proposition or a simple apprehension is a necessary prerequisite for the assent. As a result, the assent could be the first apprehension of that which is partially assented to – i.e., [the assent itself] would be the partial object of the assent. [This is absurd.]

ii.1. I prove the minor: An assent necessitated by a complex is necessary unless God impedes it, provided the necessitating complex exists; other-wise [that complex] would not necessitate. But the intellect is necessitated to no reflexive and solely apprehensive act in such a way as to be unable to avoid it by the will's command – even if there is a direct act. The act which would apprehend the complex would clearly be reflexive, however, and it is not naturally necessary, [even] if the direct act exists.

I prove the minor (that the intellect is necessitated to no reflexive act): Either that act would be (a) an assent or an act of judgment, and [this is irrelevant because] the only thing under discussion now is a cognition *prior*

---

[12] The ensuing arguments for this conclusion are extremely difficult to follow, and the correct translation is sometimes unclear, perhaps because of faults with the original Latin text. Wodeham's basic claim seems to be that while some complexes (propositions) do necessitate assent, in that one can't form the proposition without assenting, nevertheless in such a case it is not the proposition itself that one assents to.

to the assent, by which the partial object of the assent would be cognized. Or (b) it would be a proposition, and a proposition by nature presupposes a simple act. Or (c) it would be a simple [act], and then I do not see by what reasoning one direct act could necessitate the intellect (be it willing or not) to a simple reflexive cognition without *every* direct act doing so, by the same reasoning. If that were the case, then there would be an infinite number [of acts] at once. For this reason I held elsewhere that no [direct act necessitates a simple reflexive cognition].

ii.2. Also, that prior [reflexive] cognition would be either (a) a simple act or (b) a complex or compounding act. Not the first, because no simple apprehension produces assent unless a complex is previously formed from it. Otherwise, it would produce infinitely many assents at once, because it could successively produce infinitely many by means of infinitely many complexes. And without its being a part of the complex there is no more reason for it to produce one of these than another.

Neither is it (b) a complex act, because for whatever reason it would be suited to cause assent, so for the same reason would the first [act] composed of direct acts, {191} since it is just as much evident without this [complex reflexive act] as that is without a posterior [act]. And if that [complex reflexive act] does also require a posterior [act], then there will be an infinite regress, with every act of assent presupposing infinitely many propositions. This is false. But once this act is formed then, provided the prior direct proposition was evident (in the way frequently explained earlier [Prol. Q6 §13]), it necessitates another assent – namely, the assent that the first complex sign corresponded to what it signifies. Two things follow from this: First, that what is signified by this reflexive proposition is that the direct proposition corresponds to what it signifies. The second thing that follows is that there will be an infinite regress in complexes, if these [reflexive acts] are posited. For by whatever reason a first complex necessitates assent to a second complex, it necessitates assent to a third, if the first and second are evident complexes in the way explained earlier. Therefore,° [no such complex reflexive act should be posited].

3.2. Also, for my principal thesis: As that other one argued [§2 n.1], a demonstration is a syllogism producing knowledge. And I add that not [only is this the case], but also any principle known per se is a proposition producing the assent that is called *understanding*.

But you would very easily reply that to say it would cause a naturally prior apprehension of itself and together with that apprehension concur in causing an act of knowledge is not to deny but to affirm that it is a syllogism producing knowledge. The definition of the syllogism from *Prior analytics* I [24b18–20] confirms this reply: "A syllogism is a [discourse] in which, certain things being posited and granted, something else necessarily follows" – that is, assent to the conclusion or to the thing signified by it or to both. Aristotle does not say just "certain things being posited" but "posited *and granted*." But something is apprehended before it is mentally granted; therefore. Therefore, this is likewise the case for a demonstration in which, certain things being posited, etc. But that act of granting is neither the demonstration nor part of the demonstration. And without that act of granting – that is, an assent – the assent corresponding to the conclusion will not be caused.

Now I suppose that I can very well believe in this way that [the assent], though naturally prior, would necessitate another assent. Therefore, a demonstration does not cause knowledge in this way without there being another concurrent cause apart from God and the soul. And so that argument [3.2], though it is attractive, is easily evaded.

But for me, as far as my conclusion is concerned, the previous argument [3.1] suffices in reduction against this evasion. For although the assents corresponding to the major and the minor and to the evidentness of the syllogism are presupposed by the assent corresponding to the conclusion, still no simple apprehension of any part of the whole demonstration [is required]. [For] however much from the impact of its force (*activitatis*) {192} a principle known per se or the whole demonstration would at once cause an apprehension of itself, either unperceived (as Scotus imagines above [§4B] in the case of first principles) or else perceived, still, if by divine omnipotence we set this apprehension aside and retain the demonstration with its force, then, provided the premises are assented to, it does not seem that it will fail to be sufficiently evident to necessitate intellectual assent, if the intellect is ever necessitated. And yet [this assent] will not concern the complex, given that no complex is then conceived; therefore. Therefore, the complex is not part of the aforesaid assent which it necessitates.

[§7. *Conclusions 4–6*]

4. The fourth conclusion is that the complex certainly is the partial object of some reflexive assent – but one that it does not necessitate. For example, it is the partial object of the assent in which one assents that that complex is true or corresponds to the thing signified's standing so, and the like. For

whatever is apprehended through a complex necessitating some assent is the partial object of that assent, as is clear from the preceding. But it is the *initial* proposition that is apprehended through a complex necessitating the assent in which one assents that the proposition is true. Therefore.

5. The fifth conclusion is that no proposition is the total object of any possible assent. For any possible assent corresponds in object with some complex by means of which it is caused, so that the total object of this complex is the object of assent. But no proposition is the total object of any proposition. Therefore, neither is it the total object of any assent.

I prove the minor: For such a proposition would necessarily be composed from an incomplex cognition of the terms of a proposition; but no proposition is equivalent to its subject in its significance, as long as its subject is a simple apprehension, because no such apprehension complexly signifies that something is or is not [so]; therefore.

6. The sixth conclusion is that the immediate object of an act of assent is the total object of the complex necessitating the assent, speaking of an assent that is unconditionally evident.[13] Or, speaking generally, its immediate total object is the total object or total significate of the proposition immediately corresponding to it, co-causing that assent and necessarily presupposed by it – or it is the total of the objects of many such propositions.

I prove this. First, because its object is either (1) a proposition or (2) the thing signified by the subject of the proposition, when it is composed solely of proper cognitions of the thing, {193} or (3) both together, or (4) the total significate of the proposition or propositions (since this remains in doubt until the second article[14]). But none of the first three; therefore the fourth. The major is clear, because nothing else can be assigned. The minor is clear from the preceding conclusions.

Also, of all the other things that could be posited as its total and sole object, it seems that the *correspondence* of the complex to its total significate would be the object. But this is false, because then if by divine omnipotence the assent caused by the complex remained in the absence of that proposition, the assent would be false, since now there would be no

---

[13] In the case, that is, of an assent evident in the third degree, where the complex necessitates the assent (see note 9).

[14] The second article asks whether an assent has for its total object only the conclusion of an argument or else the whole argument, conclusion and premises.

correspondence, its foundation having been removed. The consequent is false.[15]

Also, if we suppose that the total object of the assent is the total significate of the complex necessitating the assent, all the absurdities adduced in the arguments previously posited for both sides are avoided. Therefore.

[§8. *Doubts and Replies*]

1. But contrary to this reply. First, what is it that you are calling the total object of the proposition?

2. Also, whatever you will have posited as its total object, it is either something or nothing. If nothing, then nothing is the object of an act of assent, which is certainly false. If something, then either God or a creature. And whether it is this one or that one, it is nevertheless a substance or an accident. And every such thing can be signified by the subject of some proposition.

3. Also, whatever can be the total object of a proposition can be the object of assent or dissent, as you hold. But a simple thing is such [as to be the total object of a proposition]. Therefore. Proof of the minor: For it seems that any thing at all, however simple, can be signified complexly and incomplexly. Therefore, there need not be a difference in the significate but only in the mode of signifying.

4. Also, the principal arguments of the article are against you, on either side [§§2–3].

[*Reply to the First Doubt*]

In reply to the first of these we should say that the total object of a proposition is its significate. Its significate is either being-so-as-the-proposition-denotes or not-being-so. For example, the object of *God is God* is God-being-God and the significate of *Man is pale* or *Paleness inheres in man* is man-being-pale or paleness-inhering-in-man. These are not propositions, because {194} if no proposition existed in the natural realm, God would nonetheless be God, and man would be pale or paleness would

---

[15] That is, it is false that the assent would be false. An assent formed in such naturally impossible circumstances would still be true. Compare the similar argument in §5 n.2.

inhere in man. And just as I have said for affirmatives, so I say for negatives. The object of *Man is not a donkey* is man-not-being-a-donkey. And man-not-being-a-donkey is not a proposition, except when understood materially or simply (namely, for the sign). For if there were no proposition, man would still not be a donkey. And that man is not a donkey no more depends on a proposition than does a man or a donkey.

From this I argue for my thesis: Being-so-in-reality or not-being-so does not depend on an act of the soul or on any sign. And every such thing can be signified, and not by any incomplex mental act (that is, not by a simple understanding); therefore, by a composite or divided sign (that is, by means of an affirmative or negative proposition).

You will say that the same question still remains. For what is God-being-God-in-reality or man-being-an-animal-in-reality? Either it is complex or incomplex. You deny it is complex.[16] If incomplex, it is either a substance or an accident. And in the first example no substance is to be granted except God, nor any substance but man in the second example. And thus the first view holds [§2], that God himself is the subject of the first proposition and of the corresponding assent, and man the subject of the second.

I say that God-being-God is the-first-entity-being-God or infinite-entity-being-God or pure-act-being-God (or the converse). In the same way, man-being-an-animal-in-reality is rational-animal-being-an-animal-in-reality and man-being-a-sensible-animate-substance-in-reality. Or, to give a complete analysis, man-being-an-animal is rational-animal-being-a-sensible-animate-substance.

And when you ask: Is man-being-an-animal complex or incomplex?, I say that for each of these a distinction must be drawn – as in any statement where one term is a second intention and the other a first intention. For instance, *Man is a species* needs distinguishing, but not *Man is an animal* or *A species is predicated of many numerically different individuals*.[17] Therefore, a distinction must be drawn regarding these [propositions], because man-being-an-animal can supposit for and be taken for the dictum of a proposition,[18] and in this sense it is indeed complex or incomplex. Or it can be

---

16 That is, Wodeham has denied that it is a proposition, in the first paragraph of the reply to this first doubt.

17 *Man is a species* needs distinguishing, because it is true only when 'man' is taken to refer to the species *mankind* (second intention) rather than to an individual (first intention).

18 The dictum of a proposition refers to a way of expressing a sentence in Latin, by putting the verb

taken for that which is signified by such a dictum, in which case it is neither complex nor incomplex, but is something signifiable by the complex – for example, by the complex *Man is an animal*. {195}

[§9. *Reply to the Second Doubt*]

In reply to the second [doubt] we should say that man-being-an-animal is not a thing (*aliquid*) or a substance, but is instead man-being-something and man-being-a-substance-or-accident. And this agrees with Aristotle, who says in the *Categories* [1b25–27] that of incomplex things, "each signifies substance or quantity or quality," etc. He does not say that *each and every* thing signifies substance or quantity, etc. For one sign signifies adequately not substance but something-being-a-substance and so forth, whereas another sign signifies something-not-being-a-substance and so forth. Also, elsewhere in the *Categories* [4b8–10]: "because the thing exists or does not exist, the statement [is said to be] true or false." He does not say "because the thing or nonthing." Again, in the chapter of the *Categories* that begins "Things are said to be opposed," he says [12b12–15]: "For just as an affirmation is opposed to a negation (*he sits*, for example, to *he does not sit*) so too for the thing underlying each (that is, *sitting* versus *not sitting*)."

You will say: man-being-an-animal is either something or nothing. I say that neither should be maintained, and that it is not something but rather man-being-something, as was said. So I ask you: Is a people a man or not a man? One should maintain neither, and say that it is not a man but men.

You will say: If it is not nothing, it is something. So I argue in the other case: If a people is not a nonman, it is a man. [We should deny] each inference.

You will say: So what is it? The correct reply is that it is a-rational-animal-being-a-sensible-animate-substance. More properly, man-being-an-animal is not a what (*quid*) but rather being-a-what. And so the question is inept, just as it would be an incongruous and quibbling question to ask "What is *Man is an animal*?" For man is an animal in reality, leaving aside every proposition. And it should not be maintained that *Man is an animal* is a substance or an accident, or that it is something or nothing, because

in the infinitive and the subject in the accusative. The example here is *hominem esse animal* (man-being-an-animal).

none of these replies would be intelligible or say anything (*aliquid dictu*). Such questions presuppose something not true. And when the interrogative question is posed "What follows (*accidit*)?" it would be more proper to reply "Many things" rather than "Only one," etc.

Further, in reply to the main argument [§8 n.2]: I do not deny that man-being-an-animal is signifiable by the subject of some proposition, since otherwise in denying the claim I would be granting the claim. But it is not signified by the subject of a proposition {196} necessitating an assent in which we agree precisely that man is an animal, nor [even] by the subject of a proposition signifying precisely that man is an animal. For it is signifiable by the subject of this proposition:

> That man is an animal is true,

and is also signifiable by

> It is true that a man is a sensible animate substance.

But the first and second need to be distinguished according to the third mode of equivocation, whereas the third does not.[19]

[Reply to the Third Doubt]

In reply to the third doubt, I deny the minor. In reply to the proof, it is true that any thing is signifiable either complexly or incomplexly. But I say that it is not signifiable by a complex sign adequate to it, because the mark of any composition[20] (and every sign equivalent in its mode of signifying) co-signifies at least a present, past, or future time, which is not co-signified in this way by any sign signifying only incomplexly (any mental sign, though not any vocal sign).

You will say: Leaving aside every conceivable thing, and positing only God, God is God. Therefore, God-being-God is nothing but God. And so there are those (namely, Chatton and [John of] Reading in his *Quodlibet* q.5, in treating and proving his third conclusion) who grant that God is the significate of that mental proposition, though not the vocal one.

I reply: Leaving aside every time and positing an angel, the angel is

---

[19] That is, equivocation based on differences in supposition. See Ockham, *Summa logicae* III-4, ch. 4. It's not clear what three items are intended here.

[20] The mark (*nota*) of a composition is the copula: to be (*esse*). See §3 n.6.

created or conserved, and yet the angel is not angel-being-created-or-conserved, nor is the angel angel-existing because then angel-not-existing would openly include a contradiction, and yet provided only that we posit an angel, an angel exists. I say, therefore, that it is one thing to ask

What is that which, when it is posited, God is God or an angel exists?

and another to ask

What is God-being-God or angel-existing?

To the first we should reply that it is God or an angel. To the second we should reply not in this way but through another dictum, composed from a description of the prior dictum.[21]

Moreover, although God is that which, when it is posited, by that very fact God is God, and an angel is that which, when it is posited, an angel exists, still God is not God-being-[God], and an angel is not angel-existing. For God is no more God-being-God than an angel is {197} angel-existing or angel-existing-and-God-existing. But just because we posit the existence of an angel and so° an angel exists, it does not follow that an angel is angel-existing or angel-and-God-existing, because then for the same reason an angel would be angel-having-existed and angel-going-to-exist. For we need not posit any thing else in order that an angel has existed or is going to exist. And since whatever things are the same to the same thing are themselves the same,[22] angel-existing would be angel-having-existed and angel-going-to-exist. The consequent is false.

Moreover, if an angel and angel-existing were the same, then to understand one would be the same as to understand the other. But to understand angel-not-existing° is to understand an angel. Therefore, to understand angel-not-existing would be to understand angel-existing. [This is absurd.]

Also, just as God is that which when it alone is posited God is God, so God is that which when it alone is posited an angel does not exist. Therefore, God would be angel-not-existing.

Also, this is not valid: Socrates is that which when he alone is posited, every man would be Socrates; therefore, Socrates is man-being-Socrates. Many similar examples show that just because when God alone is posited, God is God, it does not follow that God is God-being-God.

---

[21] For an instance of this strategy, see the penultimate paragraph of §8.
[22] See Euclid, *Elements of Geometry*, axiom 1.

[§10. Reply to the Fourth Doubt]

The replies for the first side [§2] do not go against my conclusion, in that they neither prove nor disprove my view. Instead, they prove only that the object of assent is not the complex by means of which the assent is caused. And this is granted.

To the first for the other side [§3 n.1]: Prima facie it seems no more absurd, even in this case, to posit one object of assent than to posit an object of a different intention. But still, according to the above [§9], the total object of that assent is neither something nor nothing, neither an entity nor a nonentity, neither a man nor a nonman. It is rather angel-going-to-exist or something-going-to-exist. The second argument and those following [§3 nn.2–8; see §6 n.2] support my view.

You will say on the contrary: Given at least that the devil is a partial object of assent, it follows that you partially assent to the devil. I say this does not follow, as is clear in this example: God is the partial object of the hatred with which I supremely hate God's not existing, and yet I neither partially nor totally hate God. {198}

1. If, however, someone wants to hold that the complex is the partial or total object of the act of assent, then he would reply to the first argument [of §2] as Scotus does [§4B]: Once the demonstration is formed, before someone assents to the conclusion, he perceives the apprehension itself before he assents. Every assent, then, is a reflexive act. And it should be denied that the demonstration would cause the assent, even setting aside every other cognition prior to assent.

2. To the second, one should say that a proposition suffices to cause assent neither to the proposition nor to the thing until it itself is apprehended. But I say that in each case the proposition (assuming it is unconditionally evident on the basis of its terms) together with the apprehension of that proposition does suffice to cause assent to such a proposition. Yet it does not follow from this that it would equally or even nearly suffice to cause an assent to the thing, because the thing is not suited to be an object of assent directly, but only an object of apprehension, just as sound is not the object of vision.

3. To the third, I grant that their act of belief, and also their acquired habit of faith, had in some sense a different character. But it does not follow that therefore their *infused* faith had a different character. For ac-

cording to those [who hold this view] it has the same character with regard to all articles of belief. This is not the case for acquired faith.

4. To the fourth: If it were valid, it would show that the soul could cause an infinite series of specifically distinct acts with respect to numerically the same object, without any other [object]. So the inference is invalid.

5. To the fifth: The inference is invalid, and the reason has been stated [n.2].

6. To the sixth, I grant that we assent that a thing is so in reality before we assent that the proposition is true. For, according to those [who hold this view], to assent that a thing is so in reality is just to assent to a proposition signifying this, although the proposition signifying it is not the proposition signifying that the proposition exists. So the argument is irrelevant.

To the confirmation, one should give the same reply as to the first argument [n.1] and at the same time add that the logical assent concerning a demonstration does not have as its total object the demonstration, but a proposition having the demonstration as its subject or predicate.

7. To the seventh, I grant that premises do not cause assent to the conclusion, just as they do not represent it − as you assume. But the premises, together solely with the apprehension of the conclusion, plus the assent to the premises, surely are sufficient for this. {199}

[Article Two]

[§11. *Outline*]

The second article asks whether an act of knowledge has as its object (i) things being as is signified by one proposition alone (namely, the conclusion), or (ii) things being as is signified by it and the premises all at once, joined syllogistically. In terms of the other view (which holds that the complex is the object of assent), this is to ask whether the assent, which is the act of knowledge, has for its total object (i) the conclusion alone or (ii) also the premises, all at once − that is, the whole demonstration.

First, I will state some of the more effective arguments suggesting that its object is things being as is signified by all the propositions required to make it evident. Second, I will state some arguments that could establish

that its object is only things being as the concluding proposition signifies.
Third, a choice must be made about which I believe to be true.

[*§12. That Knowledge Concerns the Whole Demonstration*]

1. One could argue first as follows. That an assent caused by a demonstration (that is, an act of knowledge), has as its object (i) things being as the
conclusion signifies, and in addition (ii) things being as the premises signify
– this is no less true than that an assent caused by some principle has as its
object (i) things being as that principle signifies and in addition (ii) whatever is signified by the incomplex cognitions from which the principle is
composed. For the act of knowing the premises is just as much required –
with equal necessity – as assenting to what a principle signifies requires a
cognition of its terms (or of what the terms signify). But an evident assent
corresponding to some principle has for its partial objects the objects of
the simple apprehensions from which the principle is composed.
Therefore. {200}

A proof of the minor: It is impossible to apprehend one thing relatively
to another without apprehending both what is being compared and also
what it is being compared to. But to apprehend this to be this (or to
apprehend that this is this), is to apprehend *this* relatively, in comparison to
that. Therefore, anyone who apprehends or assents that things are as a
principle signifies, apprehends this to be this. And this is to apprehend the
objects of the simple apprehensions from which the principle is composed.
Therefore.

A further proof of the same minor:° Either an assent corresponding to
the principle apprehends the terms (and then I have my conclusion) or it
does not. [Suppose it does not.] On the contrary,[23] God cannot take an act
directed at some object and split off the basis (*ratio*) by which it is formally
directed at that object. For instance, if one sees a wall through its color as
the formal basis, then it is impossible for the apprehension of the color to
be split off while one continues to see the wall. The same goes for
choosing the means to an end and intending the end. But the formal basis
by which the intellect is directed at the connection between the terms is
the terms themselves cognized in their immediate propositions. For we
cognize principles insofar as we cognize their terms (*Posterior Analytics* I

---

[23] The bulk of what follows in this paragraph comes verbatim from Peter Aureol, as translated in
    Chapter 8, nn.44–45.

[72b23–25]). Therefore, principles are cognized through their terms – that is, things being as the principles and conclusions signify; that is, things being as these signify through their principles; ultimately, things being as the principles signify. Here one might say that cognizing the terms is the efficient cause of cognizing the principle, and that cognizing the premises effectively causes a cognition of the conclusion, leading to an assent that is always uniform (that is, that things are as the conclusion signifies). An objection in the first article [§6 n.3.2] was understood in this way.

On the contrary: Although that reply is true for a cognition by which the terms are cognized separately, and likewise for a cognition by which the principles are cognized separately, it is nevertheless also the case that the cognition that signifies the connection between the terms of the principle (that is, that things are as the principle signifies) is also a cognition of the terms. For it is a contradiction to assent that a is b without apprehending both a and b. But there is no contradiction in there being an assent and its being conserved without any simple cognitions causing an assent at the same time as the proposition. Therefore the assent that a is b is to apprehend a and b.

The minor is clear, because God can conserve and be the cause of any absolute thing that is really and totally distinct from another absolute thing, without the other's existence. But that assent is something absolute, distinct {201} from the simple cognitions and from the proposition. (This must be your view: For otherwise you would not posit that they effectively cause that assent.) Therefore. Proof: That [major premise is a] commonly accepted theological dictum. Also, nothing absolute depends on another more than an accident depends on a subject. But in the Eucharist, God makes an accident without a subject. Therefore.

2. God can do whatever does not contain a contradiction. This is clear through the article on omnipotence[24] and *because no word will be impossible for him* [Luke 1:37]. But it is not a contradiction for any absolute thing that is really and totally distinct from another to have existence without that other (unless the other is God, since it would be a contradiction for something to exist without God).

Proof of the minor: It does not seem contradictory for something to exist without all the other things on which it does not necessarily depend causally in some way. But this is the case for every absolute thing with

---

[24] That is, through the first sentence of the Apostles' Creed, "I believe in God the Father omnipotent."

respect to another absolute and totally distinct thing (except with respect to God).

As a [second] proof [of this minor] there is another commonly accepted theological principle, that God can supply all extrinsic causality. Therefore, he can maintain any absolute effect in the absence of any other absolute thing. He can also make form without matter, just as much as accident without subject, and conversely he can equally make matter without its form: both because matter is more independent from form than vice versa, since it is naturally found without form but not vice versa; and because for three days he made his [Christ's] body exist without its soul. Therefore, God can make an assent that corresponds to a principle without the principle and an apprehension of the terms. But he cannot make a person assent that this is this without apprehending this and this. Therefore, the assent is the apprehension of each. And the same argument holds for an act of knowledge with respect to its premises. Therefore.

3. Anyone who clearly cognizes and knows some connection (that is, a match or identity of the thing signified by the predicate with the thing signified by the subject, or vice versa) cognizes that this connection is necessary, and that it is impossible for it to be otherwise. But this occurs only through apprehending the terms, because the connection derives its necessity, both in reality and as it is cognized, from the nature of the terms. For the necessity of a relation stems from the nature or condition of its end-terms. Therefore one cannot evidently cognize that a is necessarily b without cognizing a and b. Therefore.[25]

4. Things being as the conclusion signifies depends on their being as the premises signify. This is so for their existence, and, therefore, for their cognized existence, because {202} (according to *Metaphysics* II [993b30–31]) each and every thing is related to being as it is related to truth and knowability.

5. The end and the means to the end are related to goodness and appetite just as principles and their conclusion are related to truth (that is, to cognizability) and intellect, as is clear from *Physics* II [200a15–30]. But the means to an end, considered as such, have the goodness that makes

---

[25] One might take the arguments I've labeled nn.2–3 as further arguments for the minor premise in n.1, rather than as new arguments for the same conclusion reached in n.1. The Latin suggests the latter, but isn't entirely clear.

This third argument closely follows an argument in Aureol, translated earlier in Chapter 8, n.46. The following eight arguments (nn.4–11) are inspired by, and in places taken verbatim from, elsewhere in Aureol's *Sentences* commentary: Bk. I prooem. sec. 4 art. 1 nn.42–47.

them desirable to a morally good appetite (not only extrinsic but also intrinsic goodness) only on account of the end or in comparison to that end. Therefore, conclusions have an evidently cognizable truth only through acts [of intellect] apprehending them (that is, the things signified by them) in comparison to their principles. But to apprehend in this way is to apprehend the principles themselves (that is, the things signified by the principles). Therefore.

6. An intellect apprehending that things are just as a proposition signifies knows evidently that this is so either from the nature of the terms as they are joined, or from the weight of its own nature. If the first then the conclusion would be [its own] principle. The second is not true, because it knows the principle only if necessitated to assent by something else – for instance, a cognition of the terms and their being joined. Therefore, when the intellect evidently cognizes a conclusion in the way in question, it must always be fixed on things being just as the principles signify. Otherwise, the evidentness that things are as the conclusion signifies would be lost.

7. It is impossible to cognize evidently solely through the intellect's being drawn simply to the conclusion. Therefore, whenever a thing is evidently cognized with the utmost intrinsic evidentness, this will be by apprehending and cognizing it in comparison to its premises (that is, to the things signified by those premises). And thus we have our conclusion, that {203} an act will count as knowledge only by apprehending the conclusion in relation to its principle, not by simply stopping at the conclusion.

8. The sign of someone who knows is being able to teach as well.[26] But someone who knows simply the conclusion alone, not in comparison to its principles, cannot teach that conclusion. Therefore. Thus one commonly asks of someone who cognizes that things are as the conclusion designates: Whence does he know that this is so? This suggests that to know just is to cognize the cause of why things are. As *Posterior Analytics* I [71b9–12] says, we are held to know a thing when we cognize its cause: that it is so, and that it cannot be otherwise.

9. Here is a proof that the intellect is drawn to the principles and the conclusion by the same simple intention. For it is no more the case that the truth of a conclusion is evidently cognizable without an apprehension of the things signified by the principles (or without any relation to the

---

[26] Cf. Aristotle, *Metaphysics* I 1, 981b7.

principles) than that a bitter medicine designed to bring health is desirable in its own right, without health's being desired. But one is not drawn to the bitter medicine, or at least one need not be drawn to it when one is. Likewise, then, from the other side, there is desire only to the extent that it is joined with health. Therefore.

10. Knowing, for the intellect, is what choosing is, for the will (according to *Physics* II [200a15–16]). But a simple act of choice encompasses the means to the end, for the sake of the end, and can encompass both. Therefore, knowing also encompasses each truth at the same time, principle and conclusion.

11. The act by which one cognizes that this is because of this, or that this is the cause that this is, covers both at the same time. But the act of knowing is of this sort, by definition [see n.8]. Therefore.

12. It was established earlier [§4A n.3] that every evident assent is an apprehension of all the things cognized through the complex and incomplex apprehensions that necessitate the assent. But knowing is an evident assent. Therefore.

13. To know is a single act such that, when it informs the soul, putting everything else aside, it is a contradiction for the soul not to know. But there is no such act except one that encompasses the things signified by both the conclusion and the premises. For otherwise it would not be evident to the soul that things are as the conclusion signifies. Therefore, etc. {204}

[§13. *That Knowledge Concerns Only the Conclusion*]

1. For the opposite side I argue first as follows: The dispositional cognition of a principle suffices for knowledge of a conclusion (that is, that things are as the conclusion signifies). Therefore, the cognition involved in an act of knowledge is not the actual cognition that things are as the principles signify.

I prove the premise: for otherwise it would be impossible to cognize the thirtieth conclusion of Book I of [Euclid's] *Geometry* without actually cognizing that things are as all the preceding conclusions signify. (The posterior of these conclusions always presupposes those that precede it.) But this would be impossible, as experience shows. Indeed, this would certainly detract from the various branches of knowledge, the conclusions of which presuppose (as the Bishop of Lincoln says[27]) that the posterior

---

[27] Robert Grosseteste, *Commentarius in Posteriorum analyticorum libros* I.2 (pp. 101–2).

conclusions are evidently known. Therefore, it seems that what suffices for the actual knowledge of any conclusion is to cognize solely that conclusion, but with a dispositional cognition of the principles, through which the conclusion could be analyzed into its principles and derived from them.

2. Someone can assent that things are as the conclusion signifies, on account of evidently assenting that things are as the principles signify, without that assent's extending (*feratur*) to the principles. Indeed, someone can do this no less firmly than someone can, on account of loving an end, induce the love of some means to that end, without through that love loving the end. But one can do this. For someone is not drawn by love to an end without apprehending the end. But we experience {205} that often, after someone's love has caused in him the love of his neighbor, he wants to do many things for his neighbor and benevolently initiates many acts on that person's behalf, without thinking about God and, therefore, not actually loving God. Therefore.

3. One experiences that after some conclusion to which one assents has been established through many different arguments (*a priori* and *a posteriori*, through experience and through its cause, through various experiences and various causes) one assents more than before, and more firmly, but without at the same time thinking that things are as all those arguments signify. Therefore, one's assent is firmer than before, extending only to that conclusion. For an assent caused by the evidence of one syllogism is intensified by another. This could not be if they were not of the same species, and they would not be of the same species if each one extended to an object of a different species. But they would extend to objects of different species if they were to encompass things being as is signified by the principle from which they derive their conclusion. Therefore.

4. There is no contradiction in causes of different species being able to cause effects of the same species. Therefore, there is no apparent contradiction that would prevent syllogistic evidence *or* other evidence suited to cause knowledge from causing knowledge of the same species. The assumption is clear, because we experience that both the sun and fire cause the same kind of heat, and the same holds in many other cases.

5. God and nature do nothing that is pointless, according to the Philosopher.[28] But it would be pointless to apprehend evidently through the principles themselves, formally, that things are as the principles signify and

---

[28] See, e.g., *De caelo* I 4, 271a33. The argument that follows is obscure, and the Latin is dubious. Perhaps Wodeham is thinking of a case like those in the previous two paragraphs, where the same conclusion is grasped via two different arguments.

at the same time to apprehend again through another act that things are as those [principles] signify. Yet this would follow since, according to the claim in question, syllogistic evidence necessitates such an assent and causes it. But nothing is the active efficient cause of something, except while it exists. Therefore.

6. We never find ourselves assenting except on the basis of some prior apprehension. But often, when we have once had demonstrative evidence that things are so and then later we form the conclusion alone, we immediately assent that things are as the conclusion° signifies. This assent has no temporally prior apprehension that things are as the principles signify. Therefore, it does not extend to things being as the principles signify. For to say that without any prior apprehension one initiates an act of assenting that things are so is equivalent to saying that one initiates an act of assenting that things are so or so without the person's apprehending that they are so or so. And this is as much as to say that I now begin to initiate an act of assenting that things are as the principles signify without my now apprehending that things are as they signify. {206}

[§14. Wodeham's View]

It now remains to establish what ought to be said in this article. First, I make a distinction regarding the act of knowledge, which can be taken in one way for an evident judgment such that, when it is posited in the soul with everything really distinct set aside, it is a contradiction for the soul not to assent evidently that things are as the conclusion signifies. In another way it can be taken for every act by which the soul assents firmly and without hesitation that things are as the conclusion signifies, and in such a way that that assent either is evident or has an evident act attached to it regarding that same conclusion.

I likewise make a distinction regarding knowing. Knowing can be taken either for an act that is simple in being, or for many acts at once such that, were they posited all at once in the soul, the soul would be certain that things are as the conclusion signifies, even if there is no one act through which it has certain evidentness.

1. With these distinctions in mind, my first conclusion is that an act of knowledge spoken of in the first way never has as its object solely and totally that things are as the conclusion signifies. Almost all the first set of arguments [§12] yield this conclusion, although the fourth is not evident to me. And those concerning the desirable and choiceworthy [nn.5,9,10]

are sound when consistently understood in this sense: that the act of initiation (given which, when posited in the soul, it would be a contradiction for the soul not to initiate the act virtuously) encompasses the end – assuming there is such [an end].

2. Second conclusion. Some acts of knowledge evident in this [first] way are solely direct acts, and hence do not encompass any act of the soul. An evident act necessitated by demonstrative evidence is of this sort: No part of it signifies any act of the soul, but only external things. For every demonstration composed of evident premises in the way repeatedly explained is naturally suited, when one assents to the corresponding principles, to necessitate the intellect to an act of knowledge evident in such a way that, if it were posited in the soul with everything else set aside, it would be evident to the soul that things are as the conclusion signifies. But every assent naturally suited to be necessitated by such a demonstration without any further reflexive apprehension is a direct act. Therefore.

3. Third conclusion. Some assents by which one evidently assents that things are as the conclusion signifies are reflexive acts. For every assent {207} evident in this way has for its total object all the things apprehended through the apprehended evidence that necessitates and is required for such an assent. But some such things are reflexive acts – that is, acts that have an act of the soul for their object. Therefore.

The minor is proved, because those premises concluding that things are as the direct conclusion signifies are evident in the following way: It is necessarily the case that, if I have evidently assented that things are so, then I am necessitated to assent that things are so, by demonstrative evidence or at least by evidence necessitating an assent that things are so. So, necessarily, a triangle has three, etc. That assent, if it is to be an evident act of knowledge in the first way, necessarily encompasses the things signified by the premises of that syllogism [see n.1]. So it will be a reflexive act. Therefore, etc.

Also, one who assents that things are so might argue still more evidently: It is necessarily the case that I have the knowledge, habitually, to show how a thing is so, through propositions known per se, analyzing [the conclusion] into them. But a triangle's having three is of this sort. Therefore.

4. The fourth conclusion is that some acts of knowledge taken in the second way extend solely to the conclusion. For if I have in advance an assent caused by this demonstrative syllogism:

Every *a* is *b*;
Every *c* is *a*;
Therefore,
Every *c* is *b*

I can immediately argue as follows: Every *c* is *b*, because every *a* is *b* and every *c* is *a*. Likewise it follows: This is this, because that is that. Therefore, this is this. And I will firmly assent to the conclusion through an absolute act, if I want to, because I hold that the first such absolute act lies under my control just as an act of believing does. Thus the evidentness will not come from that act formally, but the firmness° of its adherence will, whereas its being evident comes from the premises, or from an act of knowledge that is evident in the first way. Therefore, it will not be evident through any intrinsic evidentness but through extrinsic denomination, because with other things set aside, although the firmness of its adherence would remain, it would do so without being evident.

5. The fifth conclusion is that the evidence by which the geometer evidently assents to the thirtieth conclusion without apprehending that things are as the prior conclusions signify [§13 n.1] is not solely a direct assent but a reflexive one, having an act of the soul as its object – having as its object, for instance, the memory° that by beginning from things known per se he has deduced in turn every conclusion up to the one to which he now assents. This would be in effect to argue as follows: Nothing follows syllogistically, directly or indirectly, from principles known per se except for what is true. But a triangle's having three etc. is of this sort. Therefore. The major is evident logically and the minor experientially, to memory; therefore, the conclusion holds. And it further follows: A triangle's having three is true; therefore, a triangle [has three], etc. – these {208} are convertible.

Other conclusions could be advanced, and objections against them resolved, but for now I omit them.

To the arguments on each side it is clear that the first set [§12] goes through and many of them reach true conclusions regarding the act of knowledge taken in the first way. Some on the opposite side [§13] also reach true conclusions. Which ones do, and how they do, is clear by comparing them to the conclusions just stated.

With respect to the principal arguments of the question [§1], I grant the first in this sense: that an act of knowledge has as its object things being in reality as the conclusion signifies. Its object is not just the thing signified by the subject of the conclusion.

To the second, I grant that real knowledge has as its object things being so in reality, not just the signs of things.

To the first on the other side, the authorities were calling "knowledge of the conclusion" the knowledge that things are as the conclusion signifies. And the same holds true for understanding a principle.

To the second, being as the conclusion signifies is true by extrinsic denomination, through an act of the soul. But the conclusion is what is true, formally speaking, even though the conclusion is not being in reality as it signifies.

TEXTUAL EMENDATIONS

Each reference is keyed to the page number and closest word in this translation. In brackets I supply the page and line numbers of the Latin text. In general I note only emendations that make a substantive difference to the translation. Except where noted, I have relied on the editors' textual apparatus rather than consulting the manuscripts themselves.

2. Anonymous, Questions on *De anima* I–II

Giele (1971) reconstructs the text on the basis of a single erratic manuscript, and makes many plausible suggestions for revision. Problematic passages remain, however.

40, three: *tertio* for *secundo* [25.16]
45, intellect: omit *unde intellectus nobis copulatur, non quia intellectus, sed quia intellecta* [39.80–81]
49, constitution: *constitutionem* for *consituationem* [55.8–9]
51, Why: *quare* (ms) for *quoniam* [58.3]
52, can: *potest* for *postest* [59.60]
53, proved: *probabatur* for *probababur* [60.74]
67, another: *altero* for *alterius* [77.13]
70, passive: *passivae* for *passiva* [86.20]
71, that: *quod* for *nam quod* (ms), *nam* (Giele) [86.37]
75, then: *tunc* (ms) for *ita* [91.31]

3. Bonaventure, Christ Our Own Teacher

Q: Bonaventure, *Opera Omnia* (Quaracchi, 1882), vol.V, pp. 567–74.
M: Madec (1990)   R: Russo (1982)

This sermon has survived in two manuscripts, only one of which was known to Q. Though R contains a number of mistakes, it generally contains the most coherent text, based on both manuscripts. M, though carefully edited, relies heavily on the recently discovered manuscript.

80, word: *verbo* (Q, M) for *verba* [100.4]
80, inspired: add *inspirati* (Q, M) [102.31]
82, it: add *et quoniam ipsius* (M) [106.82]
84, Platonic: *Platonicam* (Q, M) for *Platonica* [110.140]

84, eyes: *oculus* (M, mss, *De trin.*) for *oculis* (Q, R) [110.144]

85, Father: *Patre* (Q, M) for *Padre* [114.177]

87, grounding: *fundantes* (Q, M) for *fundates* [118.230]

87, also: *etiam* (M) for *enim* [118.235]

88, doctors: add *doctor maximus* (M) [122.277]

90, So: *ergo* (Q) for *enim* (R), *etiam* (M) [126.340]

90, questioning: *quaerebant* (Q, M) for *quaerabant* [126.343]

90, us: *nos* (Q, M) for *non* [126.351]

91, foreknowledge: *veritatem et praescientiam* (M, mss) for *virtutem et praesentiam* (Q, R, Vulgate) [128.364]

91, ignorant: *indoctas* (M, mss) for *doctas* (Q, R, Vulgate) [128.363]

91, right: *decet* (Q, M) for *debet* [128.369]

91, right: *decet* (Q, M) for *debet* [128.370]

92, foolishness: add *de nostra imbecillitate* (M) [132.407]

92, Amen: *dignetur qui vivit et regnat cum Deo Patre et Spiritu sancto in saecula saeculorum. Amen* (M, drawing on the conclusion of another sermon) for *etc.* (mss) [132.410]

6. Peter John Olivi, The Mental Word

135, 1280s: my edition of this text concludes that it was composed "sometime during the 1280s" (p. 122 n.2). But in reaching that conclusion I confused the dating of Olivi's question commentary on the *Sentences*, completed by 1283, with a distinct *Sentences* commentary from the late 1280s. The correct conclusion is that the *Lecture on John* was written between 1280 and 1283.

147, when: omit *si* (with ms) [144.307]

7. William Alnwick, Intelligible Being

V: Vat. Lat. 1012
A: Assisii 166
L: Ledoux (1937)

155, soul: add *quia praecedit esse in anima* (A) [3.18]

156, unity: *unitate* for *entitate* (AVL) [5.2] – cf. II.D.1 [18.26, 19.20]

157, comparative: *comparativum* for *comparativi* (AVL) [5.24] – cf. I.B.1 [3.11], etc.

157, equally: omit *convenit tam universali quam singulari, ideo esse intelligibile* [*intentionale* L] (with V) [6.18–19]

157, intentional: *intentionale* for *intelligibile* (AVL) [6.20]

158, Otherwise: *aliter* for *similiter* (VL), *alter* (A) [8.4–5] – cf. II.D.3 [25.7]

159, either: *aut* for *ut* (VL), *vera* (A) [9.14]

160, represented: omit *cognitum* (with A) [9.30]

160, intelligible: *intelligibile* for *inteiligibile* (L) [10.6]

160, IV: *IV* (A) for *IX* (VL) [10.24]

161, being: add *esse* (A) [11.1]

161, something: *alicuius* for *alicui* (AVL) [11.1]

161, which: *quod* (AV) for *quae* (L) [11.30]

162, cognition: add *in repraesentante et illud terminat cognitionem quod* (for *quae* [V]) *habet esse obiectivum* (V) [11.31]

163, representing: *repraesentanti* for *repraesentati* (L) [13.14]

165, stone: *lapidis* for *lapidem* (AVL) [16.4]

165, or: *aut* for *et* (AVL) [16.6] – cf. [16.14]

168, modified: *determinatur* (V) for *diminuitur* (AL) [19.29]

171, represented: omit *esse* (with A) [22.20]

172, represented: *ipsa [res] sic repraesentata* for *ipsa sic repraesentatum* (AL) [23.21]

173, distinct: *distincto* for *distincta* (AVL) [24.33]

175, account: . . . *formaliter, ita quod esse cognitum distinguatur in eis et sic ista formalis ratio qua distinguuntur, sicut dicimus.* . . . Unintelligible as written [26.25–26]

176, stone: omit *etiam* (with A) [27.30]

8. Peter Aureol, Intuition, Abstraction, and Demonstrative Knowledge

(B) Buytaert (1956)

(V) Vatican Borghese 329

B transcribed V but introduced a number of errors. I have compared the transcription against a photocopy of the manuscript.

180, cognized: *cognoscatur* (V) for *cognoscantur* (B) [178.25]

180, even: add *et* (V) [178.40]

186, relation: *respectum* (V) for *respectu* (B) [184.27]

188, God: omit *de* (with V) [186.38]

188, of: *huiusmodi* (V) for *habitus* (B) [186.41]

189, similar: *similibus* (V) for *similibis* (B) [187.81]

190, desired: *appetitur* for *appetit* (V), *apprehenditur* (B) [188.112]

194, voluntary: *voluntariae* (V) for *voluntarie* (B) [192.61]

198, relative: *aliquid* (V) for *aliud* (B) [196.76]

199, designation: *denominatio* (V) for *demonstratio* (B) [197.4]

204, as: *et* (V) for *est* (B) [202.174]

204, regarding: *de hac* (V) for *ad hac* (B) [202.185]

204, only: *tantum* (or *non . . . nisi*) for *non* (V, B) [202.197] – cf. n.98

205, as: *quod* (V) for *quid* (B) [204.17]

205, cognition: *cognitio* (B) for *cognito* (V) [204.17] – unnoted in apparatus

207, positing: *positive* (V) for *positivae* (B) [205.64]

207, whatever: *quovis* (V) for *quamvis* (B) [206.91]

208, evident: *extetit* for *extitit* (V, B) [206.11]

210, confirmation: *confirmatione* (V) for *conformitate* (B) [209.75]

211, intimate: *intimissimum* (V) for *intuitissimum* (B) [210.11]

213, truths: *veritates* (V) for *veritatum* (B emends) [212.38]

215, progression: *processum* (V) for *processus* (B) [214.11]

217, To: add *ad* [216.30]
218, intuitive: *intuitiva* (V) for *untiitiva* (B) [217.37–38]

9. William Ockham, Apparent Being

243, some: *alicuius* (mss) for *istius* [262.15]
243, Word: *Verbi* for *Patri* [262.16]
243, example: *ut* (ms) for *et* [262.18]

10. William Crathorn, On the Possibility of Infallible Knowledge

A: Erfurt, Wissenschaftliche Bibliothek, Ampl. Q. 395a
B: Basel, Universitätsbibliothek, B. V. 30
W: Wien, Österreichische Nationalbibliothek, lat. 5460
H: Hoffmann (1988)

I have compared these emendations against W, an abridged and perplexing manuscript only partly collated by H.

251, object: *obiecto* for *subiecto* (ABWH) [72.5]
252, object: *obiecti* (B) for *subiecti* (AWH) [72.10]
252, 'whitening': *albefactio* for *albedo* (ABWH) [72.11]
254, mirror: *speculo* (A) for *specie* (H) [74.4]
254, mirror: *speculum* (A) for *speciem* (H) [74.4]
255, God: *deus* (BW) for *actus* (AH) [75.11]
255, intellective: *intelligens* (W?) for *intelligibilis* (H) [75.20]
257, thing: omit *vel cognitio* [81.14]
259, nature: *natura* (Aug) for *nulla res* (AH), *nulla* (B) [93.8]
259, is: *sit* (Aug) for *sic* (ABH) [93.9]
259, however: *quantumcumque* (A) for *quantumcumque vel quandocumque* (BH) [93.18] – *vel* in B indicates a doubtful reading; cf. [111.19, 118.1]
261, if: *si* (A) for *scilicet* (BH) [95.20]
263, Anselm: *Anselmi* for *Augustini* (ABH) [97.6]
263, are: omit *enim* (with B) [97.7]
263, the: *hoc* for *noc* (H) [97.15]
264, reason: *ratione* (B) for *res* (AH) [97.25]
269, quantity: *quantitatis* for *qualitatis* (H) [102.8]
269, eye: *oculum* (AB) for *obiectum* (WH) [102.16]
269, perceiver: add *nec oculum videntis* (ABW) [102.25–26]
270, *reportatio*: add *Illud habetur in reportatione* (A) [103.12]
275, informed: *informatur* for *informantur* (H) [108.28]
277, blackness: add *et specie nigredinis* (om. HW) [110.9]
278, light: *lumen* (A) for *lumine* (BH) [111.12]

278, happens: *Quomodo hoc fiat* (A) for *Quomodo de hoc sit vel fiat* (BH) [111.19] – cf. [93.18, 118.1]

279, and: add *et* (B) [112.1]

280, that: *ille* (W) for *illis* (H) [113.3]

283, wall: *parieti* (ABW) for *parti* (H) [115.24]

283, walls: *paries* (AW) for *partes* (BH) [115.26]

283, affect: *immutare* (B) for *immutaret* (AHW) [116.14]

284, that: *quod* for *quo* (H) [117.15]

285, species: *quod omnes sunt eiusdem speciei* (A) for *quod omnes sunt eiusdem speciei vel quod illae sunt speciei eiusdem* (BH) [118.1] – cf. [93.18, 111.19]

286, generated: add *sed quod sint formae eiusdem speciei; et idem est dicendum de specie audibili et sono et de omni specie intelligibili et re illa, a [qua] generatur* (B) [118.29]

292, saw: *vidit* for *videt* (HW) [124.4]

292, thing: *rem* (W) for *speciem* (ABH) [124.11]

292, exists: *aliquem colorem videre prius visum et ipsum exsistere* (A) for *se videre albedinem prius visam et ipsam exsistere* (BH) [124.12]

296, Proof: *Probatur* (A) for *Ratio* (B), *Probatur: Ratio* (H!) [127.13]

297, that: *illud* for *id* (H) [127.34]

297, necessarily: omit *oppositum* (ABH) [128.12]

297, object: *obiectum* for *oppositum* (ABH) [128.16]

299, this: *illud* (W) for *id* (H) [150.8]

299, similarly: *similiter* (B) for *simpliciter* (AH) [150.8]

11. Robert Holcot, Can God Know More than He Knows?

P: Cambridge, Pembroke College ms. 236
R: British Museum, Royal 10.C.VI
B: Oxford, Balliol College ms. 246
C: Courtenay (1971)

On the basis of two new manuscripts (P, B), C reedited the work of Moody (1964), but introduced many errors.

306, have: *oporteret* (P) for *oportet* [6.63]

306, be: *sic esse sicut per propositiones de futuro fuisset designatum* (P) for *sic esse sicut per propositiones de futuro formatae futurum designassent* (C), *sic esse sicut propositiones de futuro formatae futurum designassent* (R) [6.69–70]

307, complex: omit *vel* (with P) [7.95] – cf. [5.47, 5.49]

307, signification: omit *verum* (with P) [7.97]

307, whole: *tota* (P) for *faciet* [7.99]

307, that: *posset concedi quod* (P) for *hoc posset concedi* [7.100–101]

309, these: *possum scribere unam propositionem aequivalenter terdecies; volo quod illas manuteneat Deus* (R) for *possum scribere unam propositionem aequivalentem uni de eidem, 'Volo quod illam manuteneat Deus'* [9.140–42] – cf. [10.167–68]

309, grasp: *manutenet* (P) for *manuteneat* [9.142]

309, Also: *item* (P) for *nam* [10.148]

310, other: *alterarum* for *illarum* (RC), *istarum* (P) [10.171]

310, one: omit *quae prius fuit* (with P) [11.178–79]

310, is: *est* for *fuit* (PR) [11.186]

310, itself: *ipsamet* (R) for *ipsa creatura* [11.187]

311, nothing: add *nihil* (R) and omit *etc.* (with BR) [12.208]

312, equivalent: omit *aliquid est* (with PR) [13.223–24]

312, valid: omit *Deus scivit prius sic esse totaliter sicut per eam denotatur, ergo scivit hanc esse veram vel ergo scivit hanc, quod est idem* (with P) [14.239–41]

313, Then: *tunc* (PB) for *nunc* [14.242]

313, exist: omit *falsa* (with PR) [15.265]

313, nowhere: *Nusquam* (PR) for *numquam* [15.267]

314, falsely: omit *aliquid* (with PR) [16.278]

314, intellection: *intellectio* (PB) for *intentio* [16.292]

315, briefly: *quas significat brevius* (BR) for *brevius quas significat* (C) [18.313]

315, from: *quam* (PB) for *quod* [18.314]

315, copula: *copulae* (P) for *temporali* (C) [18.319]

315, falsity: *falsitasque* (P, *De int.*) for *vel falsitas* [18.327]

315, and: *et* (P, *De int.*) for *vel* [18.327]

315, exists: *hoc* (P) for *homo* [18.329]

315, formed: *formatum* (PR) for *significatum* [18.331] – cf. [5.47, 5.49, 7.95]

315, uphold: *et salvanda* (PR) for *vel falsificanda* (!) [19.336]

315, copula: *conceptus copulae* (BP) for *copulae conceptus* [19.339]

315, function: *important et significent res, et deserviant* (BP) for *important, significent, et designent* [19.342]

316, understood: *intellecta* (R) for *et intelligit* [19.350]

316, doubted: *dubitata* (B) for *dubitatio* [19.354]

316, certain: omit *et* (with BP) [20.370] – cf. [20.356–57, 20.359]

316, many: *multa* (BP) for *infinita* [21.378]

317, way: *sicut* (PR) for *et sic* [21.392]

12. Adam Wodeham, The Objects of Knowledge

Wodeham's Lectura secunda *is known to exist in only one, often faulty manuscript. From this, Gál (1977) produced an admirably coherent text, and Wood's critical edition made many more improvements. Even so, many problematic passages remain.*

323, cognitions: *propriis cognitionibus Dei* for *propriis [conceptibus significantibus] cognitionem Dei* [183.70] – cf. [184.29–30]

325, object: *totale obiectum assensus* for *[causa] totalis assensus* [185.50]

325, Consequently: omit *si* (supplied by Wood within brackets) [185.51]

331, necessitating: *necessitans* for *necessitat* [190.17] – cf. [192.6–7]

331, not: *non* (ms) for *ut* [190.18]

332, Therefore: omit *etiam principium aliquod per se notum est propositio evidens, faciens assensum, qui vocatur intelligere* [191.53–54] – cf. [191.56–57]

339, so: Retaining *et ideo* (excluded by Wood) [197.64]

339, angel–not–existing: Retaining *non* (excluded by Wood) [197.70]

342, minor: *minor* for *maior* [200.21]

348, conclusion: *per conclusionem* for *per principia* [205.50]

350, firmness: *firmitas* for *firmiter* (ms), *ex firmitate* (Wood) [207.56]

350, memory: *memoriam* for *querimoniam* [207.63]

BIBLIOGRAPHY

The bibliography is divided into three sections:

1. Primary literature cited in the texts;
2. Secondary literature cited in the texts;
3. A comprehensive list of English translations of later medieval texts on mind and knowledge, listed in rough chronological order, with annotations.

1. Primary Literature

Adelard of Bath, *Quaestiones naturales*, ed. M. Müller. *Beiträge zur Geschichte der Philosophie des Mittelalters* 31,2 (Münster, 1934).

Albertus Magnus, *De anima*. Opera Omnia VII, 1 (Monasterii, 1968).

Alexander of Aphrodisias, *De intellectu et intellecto*, in G. Théry (ed.) *Autour du décret de 1210* (Kain: Le Saulchoir, 1926).

Alexander of Hales, *Glossa in quatuor libros Sententiarum* (Quaracchi: Collegium S. Bonaventurae, 1951–57).

Alfred of Sareshel, *De motu cordis*, ed. C. Baeumker. *Beiträge zur Geschichte der Philosophie des Mittelalters* 23,1 (Münster, 1923).

In libros Meteorologicorum. Durham Cath. C. III. 15.

Algazel, *Metaphysics. A Medieval Translation*, ed. J. T. Muckle (Toronto: Pontifical Institute of Mediaeval Studies, 1933).

Alhazen, *De aspectibus*, in F. Risner (ed.) *Opticae thesaurus Alhazeni Arabis libri septem* (Basel, 1572; repr. New York, 1972).

Ali ibn al-ʿAbbâs, *Liber regalis dispositionis (Pantegni)*, in *Opera omnia Ysaac* (Lugduni 1515), vol. 2.

Anselm of Canterbury, *Opera omnia*. Ed. F. S. Schmidt (Stuttgart: F. Frommann, 1968).

Augustine, *Confessiones*. Edited, with commentary, by James J. O'Donnell (Oxford: Clarendon, 1992).

De diversis quaestionibus octoginta tribus. Corpus Christianorum, Series Latina 44A (Turnhout: Brepols, 1975).

De trinitate libri XV. Corpus Christianorum, Series Latina 50 (Turnhout: Brepols, 1968).

Sermones. Patrologiae Cursus Completus, Series Latina, vol. 39, ed. J. P. Migne (Paris, 1844–55).

Sancti Aureli Augustini Opera (Vindobonae: Tempsky, 1887).

Averroes, *Commentarium magnum de anima*, ed. F. S. Crawford (Cambridge, MA: Mediaeval Academy of America, 1953).

De sompno et vigilia, in A. L. Shields and H. Blumberg (eds.) *Compendia librorum Aristotelis qui Parva Naturalia vocantur* (Cambridge, MA: Mediaeval Academy of America, 1949).

Commentaria in libros XIIII Metaphysicorum, in Aristotle, *Omnia quae extant opera* (Venice apud Iuntas, 1552).

Avicebron, *Fons vitae*, ed. C. Baeumker. *Beiträge zur Geschichte der Philosophie des Mittelalters* 1, 2–4 (Münster, 1892–95).

Avicenna, *De congelatis*. Paris B.N. lat. 6325.

Liber de anima seu Sextus de naturalibus, ed. S. Van Riet (Leiden: E. J. Brill, 1968, 1972)

Liber de philosophia prima sive Scientia divina [=*Metaphysics*], ed. S. van Riet (Leiden: E. J. Brill, 1977–83).

Sufficientia (Venice, 1508).

Boethius, *Contra Eutychen (De duabus naturis)* in H. F. Stewart and E. K. Rand (eds.) *The Theological Tractates and The Consolation of Philosophy* (Cambridge, MA: Harvard University Press, 1918).

Philosophiae consolatio, ed. L. Bieler. *Corpus Christianorum*, Series Latina, 94 (Turnhout: Brepols, 1957).

Costa Ben Luca, *De differentia animae et spiritus*, ed. C. G. Barach (Innsbruck, 1878; repr. Frankfurt a.M., 1968).

Dominicus Gundissalinus, *De anima*, ed. J. T. Muckle. *Mediaeval Studies* 2 (1940) 23–103.

De divisione philosophiae, ed. L. Baur. *Beiträge zur Geschichte der Philosophie des Mittelalters* 4, 2–3 (Münster, 1903).

Godfrey of Fontaines, *Le huitième Quodlibet de Godfroid de Fontaines*. Ed. J. Hoffmans (Louvain: Institut supérieur de philosophie de l'Université, 1924).

Henry of Ghent, *Henrici de Gandavo Opera Omnia* (Leiden: Brill, 1979–).

Quodlibeta (Paris, 1518; repr. Louvain, 1961).

Summa quaestionum ordinariarum. Paris, 1520; repr. St. Bonaventure, 1953).

Hervaeus Natalis, *Quodlibeta* (Venice, 1513; repr. New York, 1966).

Hilary of Poitiers, *The Trinity*. Tr. S. McKenna (New York: Fathers of the Church, 1954).

Historia Alexandri Magni: The Greek Alexander Romance, tr. R. Stoneman (London: Penguin, 1991)

Isaac Israeli, *Liber de definitionibus*, ed. J. T. Muckle. *Archives D'Histoire Doctrinale et Littéraire du Moyen Age* 11 (1937–38) 299–340.

Isidore of Seville, *Etymologiae*, ed. W. M. Lindsay (Oxford, 1911).

Jerome, *Epistolae. Corpus Scriptorum Ecclesiasticorum Latinorum* vol. 54 (Vienna, 1866).

Johannes Blund, *Tractatus de anima*. Ed. D. A. Callus and R. W. Hunt (London: British Academy, 1970).

John Chrysostom, *Homiliae in Joannem. Opera Omnia*, vol. 8 pt. 1, ed. Montfaucon (Paris, 1835).

John Damascene, *De fide orthodoxa*. Ed. E. M. Buytaert (St. Bonaventure, NY: Franciscan Institute, 1955).

John Duns Scotus, *Ordinatio*. In C. Balic et al. (eds.) *Opera omnia* (Vatican: Scotistic Commission, 1950–).

God and Creatures. The Quodlibetal Questions. Tr. Felix Alluntis and Allan Wolter (Washington: Catholic University of America Press, 1975).

Liber sex principiorum, ed. L. Minio-Paluello. *Aristoteles Latinus* I.7 (Bruges-Paris: Desclée de Brouwer, 1966).

Nemesius, *De natura hominis*, ed. G. Verbeke and J. R. Moncho (Leiden: E. J. Brill, 1975).

Origen, *Commentaire sur Saint Jean. Sources Chrétiennes* vol. 120, ed. C. Blanc (Paris, 1966).

Peter Aureol, I *Sent*. d.27 a.2, edited in Russell Friedman, "*In principio erat Verbum*: The Incorporation of Philosophical Psychology into Trinitarian Theology, 1250–1325," Ph.D. dissertation, University of Iowa (1997).

Peter John Olivi, *Quaestiones in secundum librum Sententiarum*, ed. B. Jansen (Rome: Quaracchi, 1926).

Peter Lombard, *Sententiae in IV libris distinctae* (Quaracchi: Collegium S. Bonaventurae, 1971–81).

Philip the Chancellor, *Summa de bono*, in O. Lottin (ed.) *Psychologie et morale aux XIIe et XIIIe siècles*, vol.2 (Louvain, 1948).

Priscian, *Institutio Grammatica* ed. M. Hertz in H. Keil, *Grammatici Latini*, vol. 2 (Leipzig, 1855).

Robert Grosseteste, *De artibus liberalibus*, in L. Baur (ed.) *Die philosophischen Werke des Robert Grosseteste. Beiträge zur Geschichte der Philosophie des Mittelalters* 9 (Münster, 1912).

Commentarius in Posteriorum analyticorum libros. Ed. P. Rossi (Firenze: L. S. Olschki, 1981).

Summa fratris Alexandri (Summa theologica) (Quaracchi: Collegium S. Bonaventurae, 1924–48).

Themistius, *On Aristotle's* On the Soul, tr. R. B. Todd (Ithaca: Cornell University Press, 1996).

Thomas Aquinas, *Quaestiones disputatae*. Ed. R. M. Spiazzi (Rome: Marietti, 1953).

S. Thomae Aquinatis Doctoris Angelici Opera Omnia (Rome: Commissio Leonina, 1882–).

Summa theologiae. Ed. P. Caramello (Rome: Marietti, 1950–53).

Vincent of Beauvais, *Speculum naturale* in *Speculum Quadruplex*, vol. 1 (Duaci, 1624).

Walter Chatton, *Reportatio et Lectura super Sententias*, ed. J. C. Wey (Toronto: Pontifical Institute of Mediaeval Studies, 1989).

William Ockham, *Ockham's Theory of Propositions* [*Summa logicae* Part II]. Tr. A. Freddoso (Notre Dame: University of Notre Dame Press, 1980).

Opera Philosophica et Theologica (St. Bonaventure: Franciscan Institute, 1967–89).

Predestination, God's Foreknowledge, and Future Contingents, second edition. Tr. M. Adams and N. Kretzmann (Indianapolis: Hackett, 1983).

2. Secondary Literature

Marilyn McCord Adams (1987). *William Ockham* (Notre Dame: University of Notre Dame Press).

Dales, Richard (1995). *The Problem of the Rational Soul in the Thirteenth Century* (Leiden: E. J. Brill).

Ebbesen, Sten (1998). "The Paris arts faculty: Siger of Brabant, Boethius of Dacia, Radulphus Brito," in J. Marenbon (ed.) *Medieval Philosophy (Routledge History of Philosophy, vol. III)* (London: Routledge).

Gál, Gedeon (1977). "Adam of Wodeham's Question on the *Complexe Significabile*," *Franciscan Studies* 37: 66–102.

Giele, Maurice (1960). "La date d'un commentaire médiéval anonyme et inédit sur le Traité de l'âme d'Aristote," *Revue Philosophique de Louvain* 58: 529–56.

Karger, Elizabeth (1999). "Ockham's Misunderstood Theory of Intuitive and Abstractive

Cognition," in P. V. Spade (ed.) *The Cambridge Companion to Ockham* (New York: Cambridge University Press), pp. 204–26.

Madec, Goulven (1990). *Le Christ Maître. Édition, traduction et commentaire du sermon universitaire "Unus est magister noster Christus"* (Paris: Vrin).

Marrone, Steven (1985). *Truth and Scientific Knowledge in the Thought of Henry of Ghent* (Cambridge, MA: Medieval Academy of America).

Maurer, Armand (1961). "Henry of Harclay's Questions on the Divine Ideas," *Mediaeval Studies* 23: 163–93.

Moody, Ernest (1964). "A Quodlibetal Question of Robert Holkot, O.P., on the Problem of the Objects of Knowledge and of Belief," *Speculum* 39: 53–74.

Nuchelmans, Gabriel (1973). *Theories of the Proposition: Ancient and Medieval Conceptions of the Bearers of Truth and Falsity* (Amsterdam: North-Holland).

Pasnau, Robert (1995). "Henry of Ghent and the Twilight of Divine Illumination," *Review of Metaphysics* 49: 49–75.

  (1997). *Theories of Cognition in the Later Middle Ages.* (New York: Cambridge University Press).

  (1998a). "Aureol, Peter," in E. Craig (ed.) *Routledge Encyclopedia of Philosophy* (London: Routledge).

  (1998b). "Crathorn, William," in E. Craig (ed.) *Routledge Encyclopedia of Philosophy* (London: Routledge).

  (1998c). "Holcot, Robert," in E. Craig (ed.) *Routledge Encyclopedia of Philosophy* (London: Routledge).

  (1999a). "Divine Illumination," *Stanford Encyclopedia of Philosophy* (http://plato.stanford.edu/entries/illumination).

  (1999b). "Peter John Olivi," *Stanford Encyclopedia of Philosophy* (http://plato.stanford.edu/entries/olivi).

Perler, Dominik (1994). "What Am I Thinking About? John Duns Scotus and Peter Aureol on Intentional Objects," *Vivarium* 32: 72–89.

Spade, Paul Vincent (ed.) (1999). *The Cambridge Companion to Ockham* (Cambridge: Cambridge University Press).

Tachau, Katherine (1988). *Vision and Certitude in the Age of Ockham: Optics, Epistemology and the Foundations of Semantics, 1250–1345* (Leiden: Brill).

  (1995). "Introduction," in P. A. Streveler & K. H. Tachau (eds.) *Seeing the Future Clearly: Questions on Future Contingents by Robert Holcot* (Toronto: Pontifical Institute).

van Steenberghen, Fernand (1980). *Thomas Aquinas and Radical Aristotelianism* (Washington, DC: Catholic University of America Press).

Wippel, John (1995). *Mediaeval Reactions to the Encounter Between Faith and Reason* (Milwaukee: Marquette University Press).

Yokoyama, T. (1967). "Zwei Quaestiones des Jacobus de Aesculo über das Esse Obiectivum," in L. Scheffczyk et al. (eds.) *Wahrheit und Verkuendigung*, vol. I, (München), pp. 31–74.

3. English Translations (in chronological order)

Alhazen, *The Optics of Ibn al-Haytham. Books I-III: On Direct Vision.* Translated, with commentary, by A. I. Sabra (London: Warburg Institute, 1989).

Dating from the second quarter of the eleventh century, this belongs in the front rank of masterpieces from the history of science. It contains substantive discussions of the nature of perception and illusion. Ernst Gombrich once wrote that Alhazen "taught the medieval West the distinction between sense, knowledge, and inference." Though Alhazen has been badly neglected by historians of philosophy, Sabra's masterful translation and commentary may bring him the attention he deserves.

Averroes, *Long Commentary on the* De anima, translated by Richard C. Taylor (New Haven: Yale University Press, forthcoming).
Written around 1190 and translated from Arabic into Latin some thirty years later, this work became astonishingly influential during the later thirteenth century. Averroes quickly became known simply as the Commentator.

Robert Grosseteste, *Commentary on Aristotle's* Posterior Analytics. Translated by Scott Mac-Donald (New Haven: Yale University Press, forthcoming).
The first and most influential scholastic commentary on the Posterior Analytics, written in the late 1220s. A key text for understanding the medieval Aristotelian notion of scientia as knowledge produced through a demonstrative syllogism.

William of Auvergne, *Treatise on the Soul*. Translated by Roland Teske (Milwaukee: Marquette University Press, forthcoming).
The most important and original work on the soul from the first half of the thirteenth century.

Robert Kilwardby, *On Time and Imagination*. Translated by Alexander Broadie (Oxford: Oxford University Press for the British Academy, 1993).
Contains a translation of De spiritu fantastico, *an interesting treatise from the middle of the thirteenth century on the workings of sense and imagination. Most notable is Kilwardby's account of sensation in Question 3: He argues that sensible qualities make a physical impression on the sensory organs, and that the immaterial sensory soul then perceives those impressions.*

Bonaventure, *Disputed Questions on the Knowledge of Christ*. Translated by Zachary Hayes (St. Bonaventure: Franciscan Institute Press, 1992).
Question 4, "Whether that which is known by us with certitude is known in the eternal reasons themselves," provides a more technical and detailed treatment of the issues discussed in Translation 3. Debated in 1254.

Albert the Great, *On the Intellect and the Intelligible*. Translated by Richard McKeon in *Selections from Medieval Philosophers. I: Augustine to Albert the Great* (New York: Scribner's, 1929), 326–75.
A useful treatise, divided into three parts: (1) The nature of intellect; (2) What is intelligible; (3) The relationship between intellect and what is intelligible.

Thomas Aquinas, *Treatise on Human Nature (Summa theologiae I.75–89)*. Translated, with commentary, by Robert Pasnau (Indianapolis: Hackett, forthcoming).
Aquinas offers the richest and most influential treatment of soul and cognition from the Middle Ages, and this is his best known and most accessible treatment of these issues. Completed in 1268.

Summa contra gentiles. Book Two: Creation. Translated by James Anderson. (Notre Dame: University of Notre Dame Press, 1975; repr. of 1956 edn.).
Composed around 1262. Chapters 46–101 contain what is in some ways Aquinas's most exciting discussion of soul and mind. Here one can watch him first working out the views that he would polish in his writings from the late 1260s.

Questions on the Soul. Translated by James Robb (Milwaukee: Marquette University Press, 1984).
This is Aquinas's most detailed study of the relationship between soul and body. Composed in 1266–1267, it develops at greater length material that would be summarized in the Treatise on Human Nature.

A Commentary on Aristotle's De anima. Translated by Robert Pasnau (New Haven: Yale University Press, 1999).
Contains Aquinas's most detailed discussion of sensation, as well as valuable material on soul and intellect. Composed in 1268.

On the Unity of the Intellect Against the Averroists. Translated by Beatrice Zedler (Milwaukee: Marquette University Press, 1968).
Aquinas's reply to the Averroistic theories of the intellect; see Translation 2 of this volume.

Commentary on the Posterior Analytics of Aristotle. Translated by F. R. Larcher (Albany, NY: Magi Books, 1970).
Though very much a commentary rather than an original work of philosophy, this work sheds valuable light on Aquinas's own thinking about scientia. It should be read in conjunction with Scott MacDonald's "Theory of Knowledge" in Kretzmann and Stump (eds.) The Cambridge Companion to Aquinas *(Cambridge: Cambridge University Press 1993), 160–95.*

Siger of Brabant, *On the Intellective Soul,* ch. 7. Translated by J. A. Arnold and J. F. Wippel in Wippel and A. Wolter (eds.) *Medieval Philosophy. From St. Augustine to Nicholas of Cusa* (New York: Free Press, 1969), 360–65.
Here Siger reconsiders the radical Averroism of his earliest writings, and seems to modify his view under the influence of Aquinas's criticism.

Matthew of Aquasparta, *Ten Disputed Questions on Knowledge.* Translated by Richard McKeon in *Selections from Medieval Philosophers. II: Roger Bacon to William Ockham* (New York: Scribner's, 1930), 240–302.
Translates the first two questions from Matthew's Quaestiones disputatae de cognitione, *debated in 1278–79. These questions articulate a post-Aquinian defense of the Franciscan-Augustinian theory of cognition set out by Bonaventure. The second question defends at length the theory of divine illumination.*

John Duns Scotus, *Questions on the Metaphysics of Aristotle.* Translated by Girard Etzkorn and Allan Wolter (St. Bonaventure, NY: Franciscan Institute, 1997), in two volumes.
The questions on Books I–II are rich in epistemology, especially I.4, which considers Henry of Ghent's antiskeptical arguments from Translation 4.

Philosophical Writings. Translated by Allan Wolter (Indianapolis: Hackett, 1987; repr. of 1962 edn.).
Contains important selections from Scotus's Sentences Commentary on intellectual cognition (Ordinatio I.3.1.4) and the human soul's immateriality (Opus oxoniense IV.43.2). The first of these consists largely in a reply to Henry of Ghent's theory of divine illumination (Translation 5).

God and Creatures. The Quodlibetal Questions. Translated by Felix Alluntis and Allan Wolter (Washington, D.C.: Catholic University of America Press, 1975).
Written near the end of Scotus's career (c. 1306), these contain extremely difficult but worthwhile discussions of mind and cognition, particularly questions 6–7, 13–15.

Anonymous, *Beatitude and the Agent Intellect.* Translated by John Wippel in Wippel and A. Wolter (eds.) *Medieval Philosophy. From St. Augustine to Nicholas of Cusa* (New York: Free Press, 1969), 423–44.
Composed sometime between 1308 and 1323, this short treatise provides an interesting catalogue of ancient and medieval views on the nature of agent intellect. In the end it defends the view of "Brother Thomas."

William Ockham, *Philosophical Writings.* Translated by Philotheus Boehner; revised by Stephen Brown (Indianapolis: Hackett, 1990; orig. pub. in 1957).
Various excerpts on knowledge and cognition.

   Whether a Higher Angel Knows Through Fewer Species than a Lower? Translated by James Walsh in A. Hyman and J. Walsh (eds.) *Philosophy in the Middle Ages*, 2nd ed. (Indianapolis: Hackett, 1973), 670–79.
Translates extended excerpts from Reportatio II.13 (c. 1318), where Ockham discusses intuitive and abstractive cognition, and explains why he thinks intelligible species are superfluous.

   Quodlibetal Questions. Translated by Alfred Freddoso and Francis Kelley (New Haven: Yale University Press, 1991).
These questions, composed from 1322–1324, range over almost every aspect of Ockham's philosophy, including important discussions of intellect, soul, knowledge, and cognition.

Nicholas of Autrecourt, *Correspondence with Master Giles and Bernard of Arezzo.* Edited and translated by L. M. de Rijk (Leiden: Brill, 1994).
In these extremely interesting letters dating from the 1330s, Nicholas articulates the skeptical view that knowledge is limited to what can be derived from the principle of noncontradiction.

INDEX